"The work of Borghesi is a wonderful contribution to understanding the thinking and person of Pope Francis and to receiving and implementing his magisterium at a time of change in the Church and the world. It is my sincere hope that bishops, priests, seminary professors, lay theologians, and leaders will profit greatly from this text as they carry out the important work of the New Evangelization."

—Archbishop Christophe Pierre
Apostolic Nuncio to the United States

"Massimo Borghesi has provided an indispensable resource for all who want to understand why Pope Francis thinks the way he does. Both erudite and scholarly, *The Mind of Pope Francis* reveals the intellectual and cultural formation of Jorge Mario Bergoglio, with the added benefit of recently recorded and highly reflective interviews with the subject himself. Beautifully translated, this is a vital addition to the anthology of books on this most captivating and consequential religious leader."

—Kerry Alys Robinson
Global Ambassador, Leadership Roundtable

"Massimo Borghesi's book is the first real intellectual biography of Jorge Mario Bergoglio and it builds a bridge between the different universes of today's global Catholicism: different generations of Catholics; different areas of the world; different theological, philosophical, and socio-political backgrounds. This book is an invaluable contribution for the comprehension of this pontificate and potentially a game-changer for the reception of Pope Francis, especially in the English-speaking world."

—Massimo Faggioli
Professor of Historical Theology, Villanova University

"Pope Francis' predecessor was an internationally renowned theologian. Perhaps because of that, many have dismissed the Argentinian pope as lacking in intellectual 'heft.' Massimo Borghesi's fascinating and informative study of the intellectual influences on Pope Francis has exploded that canard, demonstrating the intellectual breadth, subtlety and perspicacity of Francis' thought. Borghesi helps us see that behind Pope Francis' famous 'evangelical simplicity' lies 'a rich and original thought process,' one informed by such thinkers as Amelia Podetti, Alberto Methol Ferre, and Romano Guardini. Thanks to Borghesi we can better appreciate the subtle and creative mind of this 'simple' pope."

—Richard Gaillardetz
Joseph Professor of Catholic Systematic Theology, Boston College

"In *The Mind of Pope Francis*, Massimo Borghesi reveals that Francis's remarkable simplicity and openness as pope is no accident. An indispensable study of how Jorge Bergoglio became the strikingly original thinker and believer who has renewed the Church in his ministry as Pope Francis."

—Mollie Wilson O'Reilly
Editor at Large, *Commonweal*

"Far from being just a set of ideas and influences, what Professor Borghesi's magnificent study shows is a way of thinking, one that navigates and reconciles this world's polarities and dialectic tensions in a compellingly original way. If ever a mind reflected the Incarnation, it is Jorge Mario Bergoglio's; and no one is better equipped to take us on a tour of that mind than Borghesi in this masterful translation. There is no more important or illuminating book on Pope Francis. We will never see him the same way again."

—Austen Ivereigh
Author, *The Great Reformer: Francis and the making of a radical pope*

"Any Catholic thinker, priest, or seminarian who wants to grasp the intricacies of the intellectual formation of Pope Francis has to read this book. Even the best biographies have up to now been unable to recount the true influence of Gaston Fessard, Amelia Podetti, and Alberto Methol Ferré. This book was hard to put down. The interplay of the modern dialectic and classical analogy under the rubric of Jesuit polarity is itself worthy of a small monograph. The record is now corrected. Friends and foes can learn for the first time the multiple and diverse strands of Latin American, Ignatian, and European thought that the inquisitive Bergoglio brought from the Southern Cone of his native hemisphere to the chair of St. Peter."

—Peter Casarella
University of Notre Dame

"If Massimo Borghesi's book, *The Mind of Pope Francis*, had been published earlier in the pontificate it could have helped prevent the surprisingly easy adoption of a superficial narrative depicting the new pope as an intellectual lightweight set on undoing much of what his predecessors had accomplished.

"Those who have tried to understand Pope Francis by acknowledging that he is Catholic, he is a Jesuit, and he is Latin American will find in Borghesi's book a detailed description of how those three currents come together in Pope Francis, in his writings, and in his ministry. *The Mind of Pope Francis* is an important and unique contribution to the books that have been written about him."

—Cindy Wooden
Chief of Rome Bureau, Catholic News Service

The Mind of Pope Francis

Jorge Mario Bergoglio's Intellectual Journey

by Massimo Borghesi

foreword by Guzmán Carriquiry Lecour

translated by Barry Hudock

LITURGICAL PRESS
ACADEMIC

Collegeville, Minnesota
www.litpress.org

Originally published as *Jorge Mario Bergoglio: Una biografia intellettuale*
© 2017
Editoriale Jaca Book SpA, Milano
All rights reserved

1   2   3   4   5   6   7   8   9

Library of Congress Control Number: 2018941003

ISBN 978-0-8146-8790-1   ISBN 978-0-8146-8791-8 (e-book)

In memory of Alberto Methol Ferré (1929–2009)

Contents

Foreword

by Guzmán Carriquiry Lecour
Vice President, The Pontifical Commission for Latin America

Since Pope Francis was elected in March of 2013, a massive number of books and articles have been published in a variety of languages. Some have been biographical, while others have recounted the pastoral work of the bishop Jorge Mario Bergoglio in Buenos Aires. There are many texts on his reform of the church or of the Roman Curia in particular, on his option for the poor, his style of communication, or his leadership in the current international context. This abundance of publications is a sign of a time full of surprises and of the widespread empathy and interest aroused by the witness and the intense activity of the Holy Father. It undoubtedly demonstrates the curiosity of a vast audience of readers, which transcends the ecclesiastical sphere and embraces people very far from the Church of Rome. Conversations about "Pope Francis" are being carried on among ordinary people as well as the elites of the world.

Among all of these, Massimo Borghesi's *The Mind of Pope Francis: Jorge Mario Bergoglio's Intellectual Journey* stands out. It is, in fact, a very important study that examines an essential and neglected aspect of the current pope: *the genesis and development of his thought*. In this book, the author takes an original approach with respect to all the other literature on Francis. Demonstrating an extraordinary capacity for research, the text offers a systematic analysis of the cultural background and the intellectual influences that have contributed to forming the personality and the mind of Jorge Mario Bergoglio. It is an indispensable contribution to a better understanding of the complex personality of Pope Francis, in which his pastoral, mystical, and intellectual experiences come together.

The scarcity of resources relating to his intellectual background is due, in the first place, to Francis himself, who does not like to show off his talents and qualities in this regard and certainly would not like to be labeled an "intellectual." Bergoglio, as we know, considers abstract intellectualisms, always at risk of being taken up in ideological currents, to be walls that close off and distract from the relationship between God and God's people. Moreover, in every homily, catechesis, or address, he avoids theological observations that are not short, clear, and communicated in a simple way. He always prefers a "grammar of simplicity"—which is never simplistic—in his direct and authentic way of expressing himself, in order to address everyone and to reach the hearts of all those who are listening, at whatever their level of Christian development and education. So his language includes colorful expressions and images that are like "snapshots" of everyday reality. Pope Francis speaks simply because he *wants* to!

It is no coincidence that the pope describes the power of communication as a "power of proximity," full of tenderness and compassion, proper to the pastor guided by the realism of the incarnation. Jesus, too, thanked the Father for having "hidden these things from the great and the wise" and having "revealed them to the little ones" (Matt 11:25). And Pascal, in his *Pensées*, said of Jesus, "He said great things so simply that he seems not to have thought about them, and yet so clearly that it is obvious what he thought about them. Such clarity together with such simplicity is wonderful." For Pope Francis this is the essential method of approach to the men and women of our time, especially to those who are far from the church and do not possess a Christian formation. We must, he insists, focus on the essential, "on what is most beautiful, most grand, most appealing and at the same time most necessary. The message is simplified, while losing none of its depth and truth, and thus becomes all the more forceful and convincing" (*Evangelii Gaudium*, n. 35). This is the "little way" of faith today. Francis's *simplicitas* represents, as Massimo Borghesi explains, a point of arrival, and "behind it lies a rich and original thought process." This complexity can escape those who, accustomed to the literary, aesthetic, and theological flavor of the texts and the addresses of Pope Benedict, the greatest living theologian, are now confronted with a more "direct" language, aimed at the multitudes of common people rather than the intellectually prepared few.

Along with the confusion of some who are unfamiliar with this pope's style of communication, one must also note the diffidence of some ecclesiastical and intellectual environments toward a "Latin American," "Argentine," "populist" pope, considered to fall short of European cultural parameters. These critics have missed the pope's universal embrace and his simple, evangelical appeals. They remain closed up in an old Europe, where the embers of the great fire of the fine tradition still burn, but which today generates nothing—no children (we are in the middle of demographic winter) and no new intellectual currents, movements, or political visions that open the way to a destiny of hope. They are like those "doctors of the Law" who wondered if anything good could come from Nazareth, from a "carpenter's son." In this case Nazareth indicates the southern end of the world. With respect to this framework, the value of Professor Borghesi's book is to situate Bergoglio within a rich intellectual tradition that finds its roots in Argentina and its fruitfulness in close dialogue, which it knows how to conduct, with the most fruitful currents of European Catholicism. The stereotype of the "Argentine" pope certainly bears its own truth. However, as this book demonstrates, it falls short. Bergoglio is Argentinian and, at the same time, in the sources of his formation and in his reading, he is deeply European. As his polar dialectic indicates, particularly in the intellectual connections with Romano Guardini, he himself is a "bridge" between two continents. Hence the usefulness of this book by Massimo Borghesi, which offers a picture of extraordinary richness, showing the different cultural and intellectual strands that intertwined in the personality of the future pope and that constitute the illuminating substratum of his magisterium and of his pastoral action.

The reader will thus have the opportunity to understand the true genesis of the thought of Jorge Mario Bergoglio, which until now has remained concealed from his various interpreters. It is a dialectic, "polar" conception of reality that the young student of philosophy and theology of the Colegio San Miguel developed thanks to the renewal of the Ignatian vision carried out by his professor, Miguel Ángel Fiorito, and by the interpretations of the Spiritual Exercises offered by Jesuit intellectuals like Gaston Fessard and Karl-Heinz Crumbach. Here is rooted his discovery of Jesuit mysticism and his appreciation for the figure of Peter Faber, through Michel de Certeau. The dialectical vision proved invaluable when Bergoglio, as a young provincial of the Argentine Jesuits in the fiery 1970s, developed a synthetic vision of the Society of Jesus, of the church, and of society, in order diligently to avoid the contradictions embraced by the followers of the military dictatorship and pro-Marxist revolutionaries. It is the same dialectical vision that led him to encounter Amelia Podetti, the most perceptive Argentine philosopher of the 1970s, and Alberto Methol Ferré, the most important Latin-American Catholic intellectual of the second half of the twentieth century. Bergoglio's thought, as Borghesi clearly shows, owes much to a tradition of Jesuit thought. It is a tradition that, starting from Johann Adam Möhler, understands the church as *coincidentia oppositorum*, a vision that we find in the work of Erich Przywara, Henri de Lubac, and Gaston Fessard. This orientation explains why Bergoglio chose the "polar opposition" of Romano Guardini as the subject of his doctoral thesis in 1986.

In this way, Borghesi traces a thread in the thought of Bergoglio the presence of which has been missed by many scholars. This also explains, to a large extent, the accusations of those who, hostile to the direction of his pontificate, have not hesitated to accuse Francis of inadequate theological or philosophical expertise. The merit of Borghesi's volume is to locate Bergoglio's intellectual vision within the historical, ecclesial, and political context of Argentina in the 1970s and '80s. We can thus understand his particular position on "Peronism" and his critique of political theology from an exquisitely Augustinian horizon. It also illuminates his sympathy for the "theology of the people," the current of liberation theology developed by the Rio de la Plata school, in which the preferential option for the poor, embraced in the 1979 Puebla document of the Latin American church, united with a firm opposition to Marxism. This school—which included Lucio Gera, Rafael Tello, Justino O'Farrell, Juan Carlos Scannone, and Carlos Galli as protagonists—left its mark in the Puebla and Aparecida (2007) documents. It also prompted the rediscovery of popular religiosity, a theme very dear to Bergoglio, who is not therefore less attentive to the important place of the "encounter" to Christian witness within the secular horizon of the great metropolises. We also see in his more recent thought the development of the category of beauty and its unity with the good and the true. It is a development that owes much to his reading of the great theologian Hans Urs von Balthasar.

Pope Francis has emphasized "open" discussion, with the wind at its stern, open to the ever greater, always elusive Mystery. For this reason, it is fitting that Massimo Borghesi's volume certainly does not pretend to close the discussion so much as open the way to further investigation concerning the intellectual biography of Jorge Mario Bergoglio/Pope Francis. The two large, recently published volumes of Lucio Gera's pastoral and theological writings, for example, offer new material from a key source for further investigation. The thought of Lucio Gera, the father and teacher of a generation of Argentine priests who was buried in the Buenos Aires cathedral at the behest of Archbishop Bergoglio, was profoundly echoed in the most recent General Conferences of the Latin American episcopate. And in any complete account of the intellectual background of Bergoglio—who was professor of philosophy, theology, and literature—his literary passion deserves a place. He succeeded in better understanding the reality of his people by moving from the native, gauchesque poetry like the *Martín Fierro* to the metaphysical, but very different, contemporaries such as Jorge Luis Borges and Leopoldo Marechal. He read Alessandro Manzoni's *I promessi sposi* several times, with all its implications of popular religiosity, and he loved Dostoevsky's reading of the intertwining of the human soul between sin, guilt, punishment, forgiveness, and redemption. He also appreciated the paradoxes of Chesterton, and it is not by chance that he described the mystery of the incarnation in the thought of the fathers of the church as "paradox of paradoxes." He was a reader of León Bloy, this irascible, "politically incorrect" convert, who would have enjoyed seeing himself mentioned in the first homily by Pope Francis: "Anyone who does not pray to the Lord, prays to the devil." Bloy was important for the conversion of Charles Péguy, whose pages the pope loves to peruse in the short time his busy schedule of commitments allows him to pick up one of the books in the pile that accumulates on his desk at the Domus Sanctae Marthae. Francis even quoted Bernanos's *Diary of a Country Priest* in an address to priests during the Jubilee Year of Mercy. Familiarity with such work does not constitute a minor aspect of anyone's intellectual biography. As Hans Urs von Balthasar wrote, referring to the great French literature of the first half of the twentieth century, "It could be that among the great Catholic writers there was a greater, more original intellectual life, expansive and able to flourish in the fresh air, than among our modern theologians, short of breath and content with little" (*Bernanos: An Ecclesial Existence* [1956]).

If intellectual formation and priestly and pastoral experience are related, in the biography of Jorge Mario Bergoglio they are both marked by the mystical experience and prayerful discernment that accompanies his days. In the company of the saints—von Balthasar will always say—there is a "theological existence," inasmuch as their life displays, in an existential form, a living doctrine, given by the Holy Spirit for the good of the whole church. Every pastoral action and every theological reflection begins "on their knees," as Pope Francis has often repeated. His intellectual biography, then, is undoubtedly inseparable from the ways along which Providence has led him toward his evangelical radicalism, in encounter with the Lord, for the good of the whole church in the current historical moment.

Introduction

On the evening of February 28, 2013, a white helicopter lifted off from Vatican City and flew over the city of Rome, accompanied by the sound of church bells throughout the capital. It bore Benedict XVI, who had just become the first pope of the modern era to resign from his ministry. The greatest theologian of our time had inherited a difficult legacy, that of John Paul II and a church marked by problems and scandals that had twisted and stained its image in the eyes of the world. His determination to resolve and repair them had proven insufficient in the face of his failing strength.

In Benedict's place came the Argentine Cardinal Jorge Mario Bergoglio, "from the other side of the world." Ratzinger's mild sweetness was replaced by Francis's impetuous sweetness, with his simple and direct way of expressing himself and of touching people's hearts. It was a witness that was persuasive enough to change—in the arc of just a few years after his March 13, 2013, inauguration—the face of the church, whose heavy legacy was no longer such an indictment against itself. The global success of the figure of Francis has not drowned out, as in the years of John Paul II, the progressive voice of churches. It supports the humble faith of the peoples, of the simple, of those who are invisible on the stage of history.

Yet this encounter between the papacy and popular reality has not received the applause and appreciation of everyone. As Agostino Giovagnoli writes:

> [Francis's] popularity, however, does not extend everywhere and in all environments and, above all, the novelty it brings is not always accepted and understood. This is the case for most European leaders

and, in particular, for the intellectuals and scholars of the old continent. In Europe, in fact, the world of culture seems, at the very least, uncertain about him. There have been few visits by Pope Francis to great cultural institutions, and meetings with academics have been rare. He does not offer scholarly lectures like those Benedict XVI presented at the University of Regensburg or the Collège des Bernardins in Paris. And there have been few opportunities in which he has talked explicitly about works of culture, scientific research, or intellectual problems. But all of this is not enough to explain the distance between Francis and the world of European culture.[1]

Actually, Giovagnoli observes, it is not true that Francis is uninterested in culture, and in European culture in particular. "From his writings, in fact, emerges a more complex and elaborate body of thought than might at first seem apparent. Contrary to what is sometimes thought, the more one studies his documents, his addresses, or his homilies, the more one sees that Francis knows the world of intellectuals and has a solid set of beliefs on the role of culture in contemporary society."[2] This complexity of Bergoglio's thought has not yet received, with a few exceptions, the attention it deserves.[3] On the contrary, critics, would-be theologians who deduce the pope's vision from newspaper articles, abound.

Two objections are repeated with disarming monotony. First, Francis is a populist, an Argentine "Peronist" who lacks the ability to understand the subtle distinctions of liberal, modern Europe. Second, Bergoglio lacks the theological and philosophical preparation to handle the Petrine office. The two criticisms blend in the presumption, expressed all over Europe and North America, that whatever comes from Latin America is not up to Western standards. This point of view is expressed well, for example, by Angelo Panebianco:

1. Agostino Giovagnoli, "Francesco sfida gli intellettuali," *Avvenire*, November 3, 2015, https://www.avvenire.it/agora/pagine/intellettuali-.
2. Ibid.
3. Cf. Victor Manuel Fernández with Paolo Rodari, *The Francis Project: Where He Wants to Take the Church*, trans. Sean O'Neill (New York: Paulist Press, 2016); Alberto Cozzi, Roberto Repole, and Giannino Piana, *Papa Francesco: Quale teologia?* (Assisi: Cittadella Editrice, 2016).

It is inevitable—since each of us are children of our own histories—
that this pope, like all those who preceded him, will carry with him,
along with his faith and his reading of the Gospel, also the experiences, ideas, and feelings that make up the tradition of his land. These
traditions do not necessarily coincide with ours. It is plausible that
in a country of mature capitalism, which Italy, despite everything,
certainly is, there will be many, even among Catholics, who will
disagree with Bergoglio on the topics of labor and profit or who do
not believe that contemporary wars are the result of greedy capitalists
pursuing their wealth. And it is also plausible that many will realize
that the pope's economic views derive from a certain interpretation
of the Scriptures but also, perhaps, from a strong anticapitalist tradition rooted in his country of origin. In Italy, we have excellent
scholars of Latin America in general and of Argentina and its history
in particular. Perhaps they should begin to explore the cultural ties
between this pope and that tradition.[4]

Francis's limitation is his origin, his being Argentine; Panebianco
is far from alone in this judgment. He echoes, in a less moderate
tone, Loris Zanatta, according to whom Bergoglio is "the child of
a Catholicism suffused with visceral antiliberalism, erected, through
Peronism, to guide the Catholic crusade against Protestant liberalism, the *ethos* of which is understood to be a colonial shadow on
Catholic identity of Latin America."[5] We hear the same criticism
from the liberal philosopher Marcello Pera, known for the book he
coauthored in 2004 with Joseph Ratzinger, in which he called for
a new "civil religion" and, in the context of the war in Iraq, the

4. Angelo Panebianco, "L'equilibrio che cerca la Chiesa," *Corriere della Sera*,
August 21, 2015.

5. Loris Zanatta, "Un papa peronista?," *il Mulino* 2 (2016), 240. Zanatta's
article gave rise to a critical discussion with the Vatican affairs journalist Riccardo Cristiano: Riccardo Cristiano, "'Bergoglio peronista': per *il Mulino* è
un peccato l'empatia umana," *Reset*, June 22, 2016; Loris Zanatta, "Le mie
critiche a Bergoglio e ai guasti del peronismo," *Reset*, June 27, 2016; Riccardo
Cristiano, "Così l'empatia di Francesco ha riportato la Chiesa nella storia,"
Reset, June 29, 2016. Cristiano is the author of *Bergoglio, sfida globale: Il
Papa delle periferie tra famiglia, giustizia sociale e modernità* (Rome: Castelvecchi, 2015).

return of Europe to a warlike spirit rather than pacifism.[6] According to Pera, "Both John Paul II and Benedict XVI gave their missions a strong Western grounding. They steadfastly addressed their message to Europe and there was an obvious Western perspective, with our continent seen as the cradle of Western values. Francis, on the other hand, has a purely South American view."[7] Francis's approach to the subject of immigration, says Pera, makes clear that he "detests the West, aspires to destroy it, and does everything to achieve this. . . . The pope displays every South American prejudice toward North America, toward the market, liberties, capitalism."[8] According to Pera, "His vision is South American, one of Peronist justice that has nothing to do with the Western tradition of political liberties and its Christian matrix."[9]

Panebianco, Zanatta, and Pera each express, in imperious tones, the distance with which the secular, *liberal* world views Bergoglio. The Westernist, capitalist, liberalist ideology sees in the Argentine pope a skepticism about the singular way of thinking that has dominated the era of globalization. The pontiff is an adversary and must be treated as such.

To these critics one can add the Catholic conservatives of theocon orientation, similar in mentality to so much of United States Catholicism. They reinforce the opposition between the West and South America that is typical of the liberal, secular right.[10] The simplifica-

6. Joseph Ratzinger–Pope Benedict XVI and Marcello Pera, *Without Roots: The West, Relativism, Christianity, Islam*, trans. Michael F. Moore (New York: Basic Books, 2006).

7. "Il Papa sta secolarizzando la chiesa," interview with Marcello Pera, *Il Foglio*, November 22, 2016.

8. "Bergoglio vuole fare politica, il Vangelo non c'entra nulla," interview with Marcello Pera, *Il Mattino*, July 9, 2017.

9. Ibid.

10. Cf. Sandro Magister, "Da Perón a Bergoglio: Col popolo contro la globalizzazione," August 12, 2015, http://chiesa.espresso.repubblica.it/articolo/1351113.html; Magister, "Quando Bergoglio era peronista: E lo è ancora," August 26, 2015, http://chiesa.espresso.repubblica.it/articolo/1351119.html; Magister, "'Il popolo, categoria mistica': La visione politica del papa sudamericano," April 20, 2016, http://chiesa.espresso.repubblica.it/articolo/1351278.html. In 2013, Magister's approach was very different: "Bergoglio, rivoluzionario a modo suo," May 16, 2013, http://chiesa.espresso.repubblica.it/articolo/1350519.html.

tions of terms—populism, Peronism—that ignores their historical contexts, in fact, follows a logic of delegitimization, a refusal to tolerate any criticism of the dominant model of globalization. What is surprising among these critics is the absence of any documentation or support of their assertions, as if the present Pontiff lacks any cultural background or ecclesial experience worthy of exploration.[11]

Massimo Franco aptly writes that "when Bergoglio is depicted as a kind of South American Don Camillo, an obfuscation takes place; the former Archbishop of Buenos Aires cannot be described with European or, worse, Italian categories. But he is not a country curate like Giovanni Guareschi's fictional character, but an urban priest, indeed, of a megacity. And his simple language comes from a profound knowledge of the territory and its inhabitants, and from a long reflection upon—even at a lexical, in-the-field level—his priestly identity."[12] Bergoglio's language, in other words, is "simple" because he *wants* it to be simple. It is simplicity that is rooted in long reflection and in evangelical simplicity, not in any limitation of expression. Behind it lies a rich and original thought process, derived from the Jesuit school and nourished not only by Argentine teachers but also, and above all, by European ones. When young Bergoglio was a student of philosophy and theology at Colegio

---

11. Andrea Riccardi correctly observes, "When one studies the thought and personality of Francis, the simplifying myths of a populist or sentimental pope disappear. It is captured by studying his background and his thought. Jorge Mario Bergoglio has developed, over the years, an articulate reflection on the crucial issues of the life of the church and its location in contemporary society. He followed with particular attention the changes of the last two decades with the undeniable affirmation of globalization and its consequences on economic and social life. He has given great consideration to the place and the mission of the church today in a transformed, pluralist world, marked by huge cities. He did this by having as his point of reference the Second Vatican Council and the postconciliar years, those of Paul VI and John Paul II. The "laboratory" of this reflection of Pope Francis was Argentina, with its difficulties and contradictions, connected as it was—if only from a religious point of view—to Latin America" (Andrea Riccardi, *La sorpresa di papa Francesco: Crisi e futuro della Chiesa* [Milan: Mondadori, 2013], viii–ix).

12. Massimo Franco, *Imperi paralleli: Vaticano e Stati Uniti: due secoli di alleanza e conflitto* (Milan: Mondadori–Corriere della Sera, 2015), 262. Cf. Franco, *Il Vaticano secondo Francesco* (Milan: Mondadori, 2015).

Máximo in San Miguel, his standard references were the Jesuit intellectuals of the French sphere: Henri de Lubac, Gaston Fessard, Michel de Certeau. Some were representatives of the Lyon school. These are his teachers. They are "European" teachers. They are the same teachers who guided, in part, the thinking of the person who would become both his friend and intellectual point of reference, the Uruguayan Alberto Methol Ferré, the most brilliant Latin American Catholic intellectual in the second half of the twentieth century, editor of *Vispera* and *Nexo*, journals that Bergoglio read assiduously.

European and Argentine teachers: a complex mix that demands to be investigated by anyone who cares to move beyond the simplifications that find fertile ground in ignorance of facts. As Rodrigo Guerra López observes:

The absence of study in Europe of Latin American philosophers and theologians is widespread. I sometimes get the impression that some European (and North American) academics consider Latin American thinking a kind of inferior or secondary exercise, as opposed to the real work being carried out in countries like Germany, France, and even Italy. This would be nothing more than an anecdotal observation if it were not, in my opinion, such an important factor in understanding what is happening with regard to Francis. . . . When John Paul II was elected pope, a special effort was necessary to understand his teaching in the context of his intellectual and pastoral background. For many, it was necessary to study the history of Christians in Poland and the various philosophical traditions at the roots of Wojtyła's thinking, and to master his arduous philosophy in order to understand in depth the true meaning and scope of, for example, his *Redemptor Hominis*, *Laborem Excercens*, or what would eventually be known as the "theology of the body." Scholars like Rocco Buttiglione, Maxim Serretti, Tadeusz Styczen, Angelo Scola, and others did incredible work of exploration and explanation that continues to bear fruit today. In my opinion, a similar effort must be made in the case of Jorge Mario Bergoglio, SJ. How many misunderstandings might be avoided if we were to get a better understanding of our pope's intellectual and pastoral biography! In the major academic institutions dedicated to the dissemination and deeper understanding of the pontifical magisterium, professors and students have scarcely begun to undertake a serious and systematic study of the writings of Jorge Bergoglio and his most beloved authors, such as Lucio Gera, Juan Carlos Scannone, or Alberto Methol Ferré, not to mention a profound study of the theology of the people or the magisterium of the Latin American episcopate.[13]

Guerra López's demand is entirely justified. English and Italian readers can turn to, among other works, *The Great Reformer: Francis and the Making of a Radical Pope,* an excellent biography of Bergoglio by Austen Ivereigh, who reconstructs with precision the formation, intellectual and otherwise, of the future pope.[14] It is an essential text for understanding Bergoglio's "political" positions, so often misunderstood by his critics. As Ivereigh writes:

> Francis's radicalism is not to be confused with a progressive teaching or ideology. It is radical because it is missionary, and mystical. Francis is instinctively and viscerally opposed to "parties" in the Church: he roots the papacy in the traditional Catholicism of God's holy faithful people, above all the poor. He will not compromise on the hot-button issues that divide the Church from the secular West—a gap liberals would like to close by modernizing doctrine. Yet he is also, just as obviously, not a pope for the Catholic right: he will not use the

---

13. Rodrigo Guerra López, "Aprender los unos de los otros," August 18, 2016, http://chiesa.espresso.repubblica.it/articolo/1351355.html. On Argentine philosophy, cf. Diego F. Pró, *Historia del pensamiento filosofico argentine* (Mendoza: Facultad de Filosofía y Letras, Universidad Nacional de Cuyo, Instituto de Filosofía, 1973); Alberto Caturelli, *Historia de la filosofía en la Argentina 1600–2000* (Buenos Aires: Ciudad Argentina–Universidad del Salvador, 2001). On Argentine theology, cf. Carlos María Galli, "Investigando la teología en nuestra Argentina," *Teología* 110 (2013), 163–188.

14. Austen Ivereigh, *The Great Reformer: Francis and the Making of a Radical Pope* (New York: Henry Holt, 2014). For a bibliography of biographies of Jorge Mario Bergoglio, cf. Walter Kasper, *Papst Franziskus—Revolution der Zärtlichkeit und der Liebe. Theologische Wurzeln und pastorale Perspektiven* (Stuttgart: Kardinal Walter Kasper Stiftung, 2015). The bibliography appears on pp. 14–15, n. 12, of the Italian edition, *Papa Francesco: La rivoluzione della tenerezza e dell'amore* (Brescia: Queriniana, 2015). An essential biographical synthesis is provided in Alberto Melloni, "Papa Francesco," in Alberto Melloni, ed., *Il conclave di Papa Francesco* (Rome: Istituto della Enciclopedia Italiana, 2013), 63–95.

papacy to fight political and cultural battles he believes should be fought at the diocesan level, but to attract and teach; nor does he feel the need endlessly to repeat what is already well known, but wants to stress what has been obscured—God's loving-kindness and forgiving mercy. And where Catholic conservatives would like him to speak more about morality than social issues, Francis is happy to do quite the opposite, to rescue Catholicism as a "seamless garment."[15]

Ivereigh's judgment is important in part because it helps us overcome the misconception about a supposed opposition between Francis and Benedict XVI that is promoted especially by conservatives. In fact, the reality is a difference in style and emphases, not in content. Theologian Massimo Faggioli comments:

If the long Wojtyła-Ratzinger pontificate was characterized by the teaching of the Church on moral and social issues, with a strong emphasis on "anthropology" linked to the idea of "natural law," Pope Francis appears to be motivated by a more historical and cultural vision, in line with the Latin American theology he comes from, and by a more spiritual than theological vision for the ministry of the Roman pontificate. The pontificate of Benedict XVI, "the theologian pope" (in the sense of academic theologian), may be an exception in the history of modern Catholicism.

The shift of emphasis with Bergoglio, from the theological to the spiritual papacy, has some unknowns for the future structure of Catholicism. But presenting an alternative to Ratzinger does not make Bergoglio a progressive or a liberal (just as Ratzinger was not a reactionary). Bergoglio is a "social Catholic" with a subtle and complex vision of "modernity."[16]

This "social" Catholicism, in vogue in the postconciliar years and then forgotten in the age of globalization, conflicts with a certain Catholic approach that is committed to the value of unborn life but not to other social values. That approach criticizes what it considered to be Francis's theological progressivism (which does not really exist), starting from its distrust of a pope it sees as overly critical

15. Ivereigh, *The Great Reformer*, 386.
16. Massimo Faggioli, *Pope Francis: Tradition in Transition* (New York: Paulist Press, 2015), 77–78.

of the values of the market. In fact, the pope's criticism is of a society that excludes, takes away opportunities for work, creates new divisions, and does not want to allow a political party for Catholics or face the opposition of the church. As Massimo Franco writes:

> Francis is the man of reconciliation in South America's divisive and at times tragic stories. The global equivalent of the reforms he has undertaken within the Vatican, which have met with both controversy and opposition, is the destruction and removal of all the ideological debris and waste left behind after the Cold War. In Latin America, this means tearing down the last "Berlin Wall," that is, the "Havana Wall," as well as other, less visible walls, hidden in the secret archives and in the collective memory of those peoples. It means consigning to the past the civil wars fought in the name of Marxism and capitalism, with the Catholic Church and its bishops in the role of victim, and sometimes of accomplice. Many were shocked by the gift offered to Francis by Bolivian President Evo Morales: a crucifix with the sickle and hammer, crafted by Father Luís Espinal, who was killed in the 1980s for his work defending the poor and democracy. Failing to notice Francis's perplexed expression at the moment, some wanted to see in the gift an embrace by Francis of an already dead liberation theology of the most Marxist form. In reality, with that gesture, Morales was acknowledging in the pope a kind of leadership never before attributed to the Church, and he was doing so with a gesture of subordination and submission that would have been unthinkable a decade ago.[17]

Franco notes that "Francis has destroyed the revolutionary myths of Communism by offering his powerful support to popular movements and giving them a different expression: peaceful, inclusive, but no less critical of what he has called the 'technocratic paradigm' to which he has called for resistance."[18] This is the same paradigm criticized by Romano Guardini, whose work is dear to Bergoglio, and by Augusto Del Noce, an author of reference for Methol Ferré. It is a model that excludes people who are "useless," who are "refuse," the unproductive, the unemployed, the poor, the elderly, those born inferior and those not yet born, the gravely ill, the weak in

---

17. Franco, *Imperi paralleli*, 263.
18. Ibid., 264.

general. The way out is a way of reconciliation, between the weak and the protected, which creates concord and therefore social and political peace. *Bergoglio's entire system of thought is one of reconciliation*—not an irenic, optimistic, naively progressivist thinking, but rather a dramatic thinking, marked by a tension, that, having matured during the course of his Ignatian studies in the 1960s, finds its first formulation in the 1970s, in the tragic context of an Argentina divided between a right-wing military and left-wing revolutionaries. It is a contrast that marks both the church and the Society of Jesus. From here grows his idea of a "polar," "antinomian" dialectic that constitutes the golden thread of Bergoglio's thought, his original, conceptual core.

Bergoglio fought for a synthesis of the oppositions that lacerated the historical reality—not a "meet in the middle" synthesis, nor a mere "centrist" solution, but a theoretical/practical/religious attempt to propose an antinomian unity, an agonic solution achieved by way of the contrast. It is, therefore, a dialectical view in which reconciliation is not entrusted, as in Hegel, to philosophical speculation, but to the Mystery that acts in history. The model was constructed by Gaston Fessard, in his foundational work *La dialectique des "Exercices spirituels" de saint Ignace de Loyola*, first published in 1956. Subsequently, while living in Germany in 1986, Bergoglio had the opportunity to compare this perspective with the system of polar opposition elaborated by Romano Guardini in his 1925 book *Der Gegensatz: Versuche zu einer Philosophie des Lebendig-Konkreten*. From that point, Guardini, whose philosophical thought was the subject of Bergoglio's doctoral work, became a key author of reference for Bergoglio, one who accompanied him in his efforts to think through social and ecclesial antinomies and their solutions. Bergoglio's thought, which in many respects is similar to that of Methol Ferré, is structured as *a symphony of opposites*. It is a philosophy that is situated firmly in the flow of Catholic tradition, understood as a *coincidentia oppositorum*, as expressed in the work of Johann Adam Möhler, Erich Przywara, Romano Guardini, and Henri de Lubac. Bergoglio said while still a cardinal:

> "Harmony," I said. This is the right word. In the church harmony is created by the Holy Spirit. One of the first fathers of the church wrote

that the Holy Spirit "*ipse harmonia est.*" The Spirit is harmony itself. He alone is author of, at the same time, plurality and unity. Only the Spirit can inspire diversity, plurality, and multiplicity, and at the same time create unity. Because when we try to create diversity, we end up creating schisms, and when we want to achieve unity, we make uniformity, homogeneity.[19]

He has repeated the same perspective as pope:

In other words, the same Spirit creates *diversity and unity*, and in this way forms a new, diverse and unified people: the *universal* Church. First, in a way both creative and unexpected, he generates diversity, for in every age he causes new and varied charisms to blossom. Then he brings about unity: he joins together, gathers and restores harmony: "By his presence and his activity, the Spirit draws into unity spirits that are distinct and separate among themselves" (Cyril of Alexandria, *Commentary on the Gospel of John*, XI, 11). He does so in a way that effects true union, according to God's will, a union that is not uniformity, but *unity in difference.*

For this to happen, we need to avoid *two* recurrent *temptations.* The first temptation seeks *diversity without unity.* This happens when we want to separate, when we take sides and form parties, when we adopt rigid and airtight positions, when we become locked into our own ideas and ways of doing things, perhaps even thinking that we are better than others, or always in the right, when we become so-called "guardians of the truth." When this happens, we choose the part over the whole, belonging to this or that group before belonging to the Church. We become avid supporters for one side, rather than brothers and sisters in the one Spirit. We become Christians of the "right" or the "left," before being on the side of Jesus, unbending guardians of the past or the avant-garde of the future before being humble and grateful children of the Church. The result is diversity without unity. The opposite temptation is that of seeking *unity without diversity.* Here, unity becomes uniformity, where everyone has to do everything together and in the same way, always thinking alike. Unity ends up being homogeneity and no longer freedom. But, as

---

19. Gianni Valente, *Francesco, un papa dalla fine del mondo* (Milan: EMI, 2013), 35.

Saint Paul says, "where the Spirit of the Lord is, there is freedom" (2 Cor 3:17).[20]

In this complex relationship between unity and diversity lies the nucleus of Bergoglio's "Catholic" thought. Here, its three polar pairs (fullness/limit, idea/reality, globalization/localization) take shape with four principles: time is superior to space; unity is superior to conflict; realities are superior to ideas; the whole is superior to the part. On this foundation rests his classical doctrine of the unity of the transcendentals of Being (beautiful/good/true) in close contact with the theological reflection of Hans Urs von Balthasar. It is fundamental doctrine because it represents the key to the relationship between Mercy and Truth in the contemporary world. If, as Balthasar affirms, *only love is credible*, then the cosmological-theological way of the medievals and the anthropological way of the moderns must, in this era of relativism and nihilism, give way to Mercy as the "manifestation" of Truth.[21] It is the evangelical way, the *kerygmatic* path that is at the center of this pontificate, along which Christianity can return, today, to the dynamic of its own beginning. But it is a point strongly rejected by the conservatives, who insist, with the modernists, on holding Mercy and Truth in opposition.

As is clear, a careful analysis of the roots and the development of the thought of Jorge Mario Bergoglio reveals for the European scholar a vision of extraordinary wealth. It is nourished by various sources, linked to each other by a profound logic. As Diego Fares writes:

The reference to Guardini, with his phenomenological capacity to "see" the "living figures" in which the parts contribute to the function of the whole, and the whole to the function of the parts, seems

20. Pope Francis, "Homily on the Solemnity of Pentecost," June 4, 2017: https://w2.vatican.va/content/francesco/en/homilies/2017/documents/papa -francesco_20170604_omelia-pentecoste.html.

21. Hans Urs von Balthasar, *Love Alone Is Credible*, trans. David C. Schindler (San Francisco: Ignatius Press, 2004); orig. *Glaubhaft ist nur Liebe* (Einsiedeln: Johannes Verlag, 1963).

to give consistency to what Pope Francis tells us. . . . Remember too Erich Przywara, with his thinking on God as the one who is always greater and the Spirit as the one who puts everything in motion and creates harmony in diversity; and Hans Urs von Balthasar, with his ordering of the transcendentals, which places the Beautiful and the Good (always dramatic) before Logic; with his way of opening every finite, philosophical truth to Christ (to push all truths towards Christ) and his art of clarifying transposition (which brings unity in multiplicity; which translates the one Word into many, always with a look of creative and merciful love).[22]

We stand before a vision made up of cultural exchanges between Europe and Latin America, an interweaving of ideas from which emerges with strength the Catholic *communio*. Bergoglio is, in his apparent simplicity, a complex figure. He himself is, in his personality, a *complexio oppositorum*. This man, who is criticized as a pontiff for being too concerned about worldly matters, is a "mystic." The depths of his thought and of his very soul are nourished by the *Exercises* of St. Ignatius, by the mystical thread within the Society of Jesus, which so insistently unites contemplation with action. As Fr. Antonio Spadaro has written: "The key to understanding his thought and his action can be sought and found in the Ignatian spiritual tradition. His Latin American experience is incorporated into this spirituality and must be read in its light if one is to avoid interpreting Francis by falling into stereotypes. His own episcopal ministry, his style of acting and thinking are shaped by the Ignatian *vision*, by the antinomian tension to be always and everywhere *contemplativus in actione*."[23] Peter Faber—the companion of Ignatius, the tireless traveler in a Europe divided by wars of religion, the sweet and gentle proclaimer of the Gospel and of the peace of Christ—is his model. A "mystical" thinker is an open thinker, who

22. Diego Fares, *Papa Francesco è come un bambù: Alle radici della cultura dell'incontro* (Milan: Àncora–La Civiltà Cattolica, 2014), 37 (cf. also, on the same page, n. 38).

23. Antonio Spadaro, introduction to Jorge Mario Bergoglio–Pope Francis, *Nel cuore di ogni padre: Alle radici della mia spiritualità* (Milan: Rizzoli, 2016), x. Orig., *Meditaciones para religiosos* (Buenos Aires: Ediciones Diego de Torres, 1982).

does not close the spirals. As Francis has said, "The mystical dimension of discernment never defines its edges and does not complete the thought. The Jesuit must be a person whose thought is incomplete, in the sense of open-ended thinking."[24] For this reason, Bergoglio's antinomian dialectic is, unlike Hegel's, an "open" dialectic, because its syntheses are always temporary, so they must always be sustained and restored, and because reconciliation is the work of God, not primarily of humans. This explains his criticism of a "self-referential" church, closed in on its own "immanence," marked by the double temptation of Pelagianism and gnosticism. The Christian is "decentered"; the point of balance between opposites is outside of herself.

This book represents a first attempt to outline the thought of Jorge Mario Bergoglio. It benefits from four audio recordings of exceptional importance that the Holy Father very graciously sent me in response to a list of questions that I had sent to him. These recordings are dated January 3 and January 29, 2017, and two of March 13, 2017 (the latter date being the fourth anniversary of his pontificate). Much of their content is reflected in the text of this book and is cited each time. The recordings were accompanied by two communications by the pontiff's secretary, on February 7 and March 12, 2017, bearing two texts useful to our work. The pope, with his answers, emphasized the essential points of his formation that would have been otherwise difficult to understand. He clarified, in particular, the genesis of his thinking in the 1960s, starting with his reading of interpretations of the *Exercises* of Ignatius of Loyola.

---

24. Pope Francis with Antonio Spadaro, *My Door Is Always Open: A Conversation on Faith, Hope, and the Church in a Time of Change*, trans. Shaun Whiteside (London: Bloomsbury, 2013), 24. An earlier translation of this interview, prepared by a group of translators, was published as Antonio Spadaro, "A Big Heart Open to God: An Interview with Pope Francis," *America* 209, no. 8 (September 30, 2013), available at https://www.americamagazine.org /faith/2013/09/30/big-heart-open-god-interview-pope-francis. The quotations of the interview in this book will come from *My Door Is Always Open*.

These interpretations centered on the dialectic tension between grace and freedom that lies at the heart of the Ignatian perspective. From here a line of thought took shape that then led him to the encounter with Romano Guardini's polar dialectic. Among the many new insights that emerged from the pope's audio recordings that deserve to be noted are the decisive influence exercised upon him by Gaston Fessard and by the "theology of *as if*," the importance of the French Jesuit journal *Christus*, the mine of ideas and readings, the acknowledgment of debts in his thinking to Amelia Podetti and Alberto Methol Ferré, the direction of his doctoral thesis on Guardini, the importance of von Balthasar's essay on Irenaeus for his anti-gnostic sense, and so on. For all these clarifications and for the time that he has given me, I can only be deeply grateful to the Holy Father, to whom I express my profound thanks.

I would also like to thank Professor Guzmán Carriquiry Lecour, vice president of the Pontifical Commission for Latin America. His support and advice as a disciple and friend of Methol Ferré, who is the protagonist of many Latin American intellectual exchanges described in the book, have been of great help and comfort. Thanks are also due to Dr. Alver Metalli, who is responsible for the blog *Terre d'America* and the former editor of the magazines *Incontri: Testimonianze dall'America Latina* and *30 Giorni*, which were for me the "bridge" to Methol Ferré and other protagonists of Latin American Catholicism. Without him, I might never have encountered the extraordinary intellectual stature of Methol. I would also like to thank Dr. Marcos Methol Sastre, director of the "Archivio de Alberto Methol Ferré en el Centro de Documentación y Estudios de Iberoamerica (CEDEI) de la Universidad de Montevideo (Uruguay)," particularly for two previously unpublished 1982 letters from Augusto Del Noce to Methol, now published here for the first time. Similarly, I thank Prof. Enzo Randone, president of the Fondazione Centro Studi Augusto del Noce in Savigliano for providing two previously unpublished letters of Methol Ferré to the Noce, 1980–1981, published in this volume. A thank-you to Prof. Roberto Graziotto, who translated the essay by Karl-Heinz Crumbach, "Ein ignatianisches Wort als Frage an unseren Glauben," and to Dr. Serena Meattini for valuable bibliographic guidance. Particular thanks to my wife, Carmen, who shared with me, patiently, this project and the time involved in it. With her I thank our children, Daniela, Luisa, and Alessandro, who have put up with my hard work.

A Horizon Marked
by Profound Contrasts

At the Origins of a System of Thought:
Gaston Fessard and the Theology of "As If"

When the twenty-one-year-old Jorge Mario Bergoglio entered the novitiate of the Society of Jesus on March 11, 1958, the course of studies that lay ahead of him and the set of teachers who would be leading it did not shine with a particularly brilliant light. The manualist tradition, characterized by a neoclassical approach, was weighed down by formulas far removed from real life. Pope Francis's lapidary judgment of this approach, expressed in his 2013 interview with Father Spadaro, is eloquent: "We must not confuse the genius of Thomas Aquinas with that of decadent Thomist commentaries. Unfortunately, I studied philosophy from textbooks that came from decadent Thomism."[1]

It would be a mistake to understand Francis's comment as criticism of the thought of Thomas Aquinas. In a preface he prepared for Enrique Ciro Bianchi's book on Rafael Tello (a theologian of Argentine popular devotion), Bergoglio wrote that he was impressed by how much Tello's thinking owed to Thomas: "In an era that has set aside the *Summa theologica*, when anyone who dares to teach based on the *Summa* is considered an antediluvian beast, [Tello]

---

1. Pope Francis with Antonio Spadaro, *My Door Is Always Open: A Conversation on Faith, Hope, and the Church in a Time of Change*, trans. Shaun Whiteside (London: Bloomsbury, 2013), 120.

kept the *Summa* as a consistent reference of his thought. He understood more than anyone else the depth and originality of St. Thomas Aquinas."[2] In fact, a Thomistic character is one of the constants of Bergoglio's thinking; this is where his gnoseological-metaphysical *realism* and his appreciation of the *tangible* world find their source.

Young Jorge's studies included two years of novitiate, a year of juniorate while studying the humanities, three years of philosophy, three years of teaching, three years of theology, and one year of tertianship: thirteen years in all, from 1958 to 1971. His philosophical and theological studies took place at the Colegio Máximo de San José, in the city of San Miguel in the Buenos Aires province. A thorough record of his teachers during that time no longer exists. Austen Ivereigh has observed that "most of [Bergoglio's] professors were old, foreign, and unprepared for . . . engagement with the contemporary world."[3] The instruction he received repeated the worn-out formulas of a school of thought preserved from a different age. "When does a formulated thought cease to be valid?" Francis said to Fr. Spadaro. "When it loses sight of the human, or even when it is afraid of the human or deluded about itself. The depiction of the deceived thought is like Odysseus's encounter with the song of the Siren, or like Tannhäuser in an orgy surrounded by satyrs and bacchantes, or like Parsifal, in the second act of Wagner's opera, in the palace of Klingsor. The thinking of the Church must recover genius and a better understanding of how human beings understand themselves today, in order to develop and deepen the Church's teaching."[4]

Not everything, however, was worth discarding. In his theological studies at Colegio Máximo, between 1967 and 1970, Bergoglio was influenced by the renewal of the Ignatian vision that had been set in motion by his philosophy professor, Father Miguel Ángel Fiorito. One of Argentina's leading authorities on Ignatian spirituality, Fiorito

---

2. Jorge Mario Bergoglio, preface to Enrique Ciro Bianchi, *Introduzione alla teologia del popolo: Profilo spiritual e teologico di Rafael Tello* (Bologna: EMI, 2015), 21; orig. *Pobres en este mundo, ricos en la fe (Sant 2,5): La fe de los pobres de América Latina según Rafael Tello* (Buenos Aires: Agape libros, 2012).

3. Austen Ivereigh, *The Great Reformer: Francis and the Making of a Radical Pope* (New York: Henry Holt, 2014), 76.

4. Pope Francis with Spadaro, *My Door Is Always Open*, 120.

had successfully promoted a restoration of the original method of doing Saint Ignatius's *Spiritual Exercises* as an individually guided retreat. A group of students—several of whom would one day lead the Argentine province in various capacities—formed around Fiorito and helped him produce a new periodical on spirituality.[5] "The Fiorito group took seriously the idea of *ressourcement*, a renewal that involved a return to the 'primitive charism' of the first Jesuits and adapting it to modern times. This was very different from another version of renewal that involved rejecting that heritage as passé and uncritically embracing contemporary ideas."[6]

This different understanding of Ignatius and the contemporary value of his *Exercises* marked the difference between Bergoglio and, on one side, his elders in the order, who were immovable in their formulaic repetition of Jesuit tradition and, on the other, the "moderns," influenced by new sociological perspectives coming out of the United States and Europe, who dismissed the spirituality of the Jesuits' foundational texts as archaic and outdated. For the young Bergoglio, true reform of the church could not happen through an uncritical modernization, but through a thoughtful recovery of the teaching and the witness of Ignatius that took account of new circumstances and contexts.[7] What guided him to a way of thinking that was both Catholic and open, understanding the value of the past, was the Second Vatican Council.

Like many who made up the new generation of Catholics in Argentina, Bergoglio was an assiduous reader of *Criterio*, a journal published in Buenos Aires under the editorship of Father Jorge Mejía, which gave voice to new currents of thought coming out of France.[8] Among those who wrote for the journal were two young

5. Ivereigh, *The Great Reformer*, 92.

6. Ibid., 93.

7. On the distinctive Ignatian formation of Bergoglio, see Antonio Spadaro, preface to Jorge Mario Bergoglio–Pope Francis, *Nel cuore di ogni padre: Alle radici della mia spiritualità* (Milan: Rizzoli, 2016), v–xxx. Orig., *Meditaciones para religiosos* (Buenos Aires: Ediciones Diego de Torres, 1982).

8. Jorge M. Mejía (1923–2014) was editor of *Criterio*, together with Gustavo J. Franceschi, from 1957 to 1978. From 1978 to 1990, he was the journal's sole editor. He was created a cardinal by Pope John Paul II in 2001.

seminary professors who would later become cardinals: Eduardo Pironio, who would serve as a close collaborator of Popes Paul VI and John Paul II, and Antonio Quarracino, who would one day persuade John Paul II to make Bergoglio a cardinal. Its editorial board and authors included Jorge Luis Borges, Homero Manzi, Francisco Luis Bernárdez, Baldomero Fernández Moreno, Leonardo Castellani, Ernesto Palacio, Manuel Gálvez, Ignacio B. Anzoátegui, Julio Irazusta, Julio Meinvielle, Basilio Uribe, and José Luis Romero. The journal also published the work of important writers such as G. K. Chesterton, Hans Urs von Balthasar, Gerardo Diego, Eduardo Frei Montalva, Jean Guitton, Jacques Maritain, Julián Marías, and Gabriela Mistral.

Another periodical also served as a rich mine of ideas for young Bergoglio. This was the triannual Jesuit journal *Christus*, edited in France, starting in 1954, by Fr. Maurice Giuliani.[9] In one of the audio recordings prepared by Pope Francis for the author, he recalls

> reading the journal *Christus* under the direction of Father Giuliani. There were so many articles in the early days—the journal's approach changed later—but in those early days, those of Fr. Giuliani, there were so many articles that inspired me. I believe that in the history of Catholic spirituality and especially of postconciliar spirituality, we cannot forget the work done by *Christus*, a magazine desired by Fr. Arrupe and the center of spirituality he founded and placed under the guidance of Father Luis Gonzalez, who contributed so greatly to the renewal of the Society. Here, allow me a digression. When Fr. Arrupe was elected, the Company was at such a point of uniformity that discernment was reduced to choosing between good and evil but not between good and better. For me, the greatest symbol of this reduction to uniformity was the Society's *Epitome*, under the guidance of Fr. Dóchowski. When it was brought to the Abbot Primate of the Benedictines, he said: "With this he killed the Society. He took away its mobility." Because everything was foreseen, the sources of the Society, of its rules.

---

9. Maurice Giuliani was editor of *Christus* from 1954 to 1962. Later, he served as editor of Études from 1965 to 1972 and as regional assistant of the Society of Jesus in France and advisor to Father General Pedro Arrupe.

The legal structure of the Society has three sources. [First,] the Formula of the Institute, which one cannot touch because Ignatius's insights are there. Second, the Constitutions, which must be applied according to place-time-person and which therefore have a ductility capable of being updated and inculturated. Third, the rules are to help accomplish a task, but they have no universal and permanent value. The only one that really matters is the Formula of the Institute. In the *Epitome* everything was together, mixed. Any differences were globalized spherically, removing any tension, for example, the tension in the Constitutions between place-time-people. Fr. Arrupe took Fr. Jansen and reorganized government in the years after the war. When he was elected, Fr. Arrupe used many tools, but above all these two: the Center of Spirituality and the journal *Christus*, in order to rediscover this tension that allows the Society to grow. I lived this, and I have it inside me. Perhaps these things come from there.[10]

This is an important window into the "laboratory" of the young Bergoglio's thought. The articles published in *Christus* helped the Society broaden its horizon and overcome the immobility imposed on it by the *Epitome*, which Francis also mentions in his interview with Fr. Spadaro: "There have been periods in the Society in which Jesuits have lived in an environment of closed and rigid thought, more instructive-ascetic than mystical: this distortion of Jesuit life gave birth to the *Epitome Instituti*."[11]

Through *Christus*, Bergoglio was able to become familiar with the work of a French Jesuit who would later achieve great prominence: Michel de Certeau. His studies of Jesuit mysticism and in particular of Peter Faber—whom we will consider at greater length below—became very important to Bergoglio. They offered a deeper understanding of authentic Ignatian spirituality and provided important breathing room for Miguel Ángel Fiorito's efforts related to the *Exercises*. It is clear that Bergoglio's formation took place within the intellectual world of the Society. His teachers—not those who lectured in the classes he attended, but those whose work formed his way of thinking—are the intellectuals, philosophers, and theologians of the Jesuit order. Among them, one author would

10. Pope Francis, audio recording of January 29, 2017.
11. Pope Francis with Spadaro, *My Door Is Always Open*, 24.

have particular influence on him: the French philosopher-theologian Gaston Fessard.

In 1956, Fessard published the first volume of *La Dialectique des 'Exercices Spirituels' de Saint Ignace de Loyola*,[12] an important reference point in the thinking of Alberto Methol Ferré (whom we will consider at length below). It would become a major force in Bergoglio's intellectual formation.

"Perhaps the first contact [with Fessard] was between 1962 and 1964," Pope Francis said.[13] From Fessard, Bergoglio received a model of dialectical thought that would soon take a central place in his thinking—an antinomian, deeply Catholic way of thinking rooted in the synthesis of opposites. Strangely, Bergoglio has rarely made explicit reference to it, but it is clear that he has drawn fruitfully from this system of thought through the decades, in his efforts to address the most pressing problems of the Society of Jesus, the church, and the Argentine political reality of his time. Francis said, "The—in quotes—'Hegelian' writer—but he is not Hegelian, though it may seem like he is—who had a big influence on me was Gaston Fessard. I've read *La Dialectique des 'Exercices Spirituels' de Saint Ignace de Loyola*, and other things by him, several times. That work gave me so many elements that later became mixed in [to my thinking]."[14]

This is an acknowledgment of great importance. Bergoglio here points to Fessard as the key thinker in his intellectual formation. A Jesuit of the Lyons school and close friend of Henri de Lubac, Fessard identified deeply with Hegel and dialectics, an unusual direction in Catholic thought of the 1930s and '40s. Between 1926 and 1929, he translated and commented on the *Vorrede* of the *Phenomenology of the Spirit*, which he intended to publish, with the support of Jean Wahl, in the *Revue philosophique*. This never happened, but it did not prevent Fessard from adopting the Hegelian perspective in an original and creative way, reformulating it for contemporary times. This explains his deep friendship with Alexandre Kojève, the brilliant interpreter of Hegel's *Phenomenology*, who, in the 1930s, from

12. Gaston Fessard, *La Dialectique des 'Exercices Spirituels' de Saint Ignace de Loyola,* vol. I (Paris: Aubier, 1956).

13. Pope Francis, audio recording of January 29, 2017.

14. Pope Francis, audio recording of January 3, 2017.

his chair at the École Pratique des Hautes Études in Paris, was among the most revered of the philosophical intelligentia of his day.[15] Fessard's discussions with Kojève and study of Hegel resulted not only in the volume on the *Exercises* of St. Ignatius but also his development of the threefold dialectics (servant/master, man/woman, Jew/pagan) in *De l'actualité historique*,[16] which we will consider below. This latter text, which Augusto Del Noce considered "a model of philosophical-theological analysis of the present reality and criticism from within it, truly unsurpassable,"[17] offers a

15. Cf. Gaston Fessard, "Deux interprétes de la 'Phénoménologie' de Hegel, J. Hyppolite et A. Kojève," *Études*, December 1947, 368–373. Republished in Fessard, *Hegel, le christianisme et l'histoire* (Paris: PUF, 1990), 275–279. On the friendship between Fessard and Kojève, cf. Marco Filoni, *Il filosofo della Domenica: La vita e il pensiero di Alexandre Kojève* (Turin: Bollati Boringhieri, 2008), 199–203. The recollection of Stanley Rosen is interesting: "But the most important discovery at Royaumont by far was for me the remarkable personage of Father Gaston Fessard, SJ. Fessard is not only important in himself; he was one of Kojève's closest friends, perhaps his closest friend in Paris. . . . Fessard was also famous in France for the pamphlets he had written against the Nazis during the Second World War under the pseudonym Monsieur X. Of his religious and theological disputes I will mention only his long polemic against the worker-priest movement. He was in no sense a Marxist but at the same time was regarded by Kojève as potentially the greatest authority on Marx in France. . . . Fessard is the highest instance in my experience of someone who combined the virtues of the priest and the philosopher. I had been educated to believe that such a combination is in principle impossible. Fessard taught me otherwise by his personal example. In lucidity and quickness of intellect, the ability to take in at once views alien to his own beliefs, and in that peculiar combination of profundity and childlike simplicity that marks thinkers of the first rank, Fessard surpassed everyone I saw in Paris with the single exception of Kojève. One could say that Fessard accepted Christ, whereas Kojève accepted only himself. But both men exerted every sinew of their spiritual being to give a *logos* of their faith" (Stanley Rosen, *Metaphysics in Ordinary Language* [South Bend: St Augustine's Press, 2010]). For Augusto Del Noce, Fessard was "the finest French interpreter and critic of Marxism" (Augusto Del Noce, *Il problema dell'ateismo* [Bologna: Il Mulino, 1964 (3rd ed. 1970)], 561–562, n. 16).

16. Gaston Fessard, *De l'actualité historique, I: À la recherche d'une méthode* (Paris: Desclée de Brouwer, 1960).

17. Del Noce, *Il problema dell'ateismo*, 128, n. 89.

historical method marked by a "resolution of antinomies" that Del Noce adapts in his own work, *Il problema dell'ateismo*.[18]

But the similarities between Fessard and Hegel, and the fact that they both make use of the dialectical method, should not deceive us. As Pope Francis observes, Fessard was not "Hegelian," even if he might seem so to an inexperienced eye. In fact, the source of Fessard's dialectical thinking is upstream of Hegel and precedes his encounter with Hegel. As Giao Nguyen-Hong notes, Fr. Fessard's "fundamental inspiration" is Maurice Blondel, the Catholic philosopher of *L'Action*: "It is primarily under the influence of Blondel that he studied the *Spiritual Exercises*."[19] This is confirmed by Peter Henrici, who reports that "Father Fessard had personally confirmed to me a few years earlier regarding his *Dialectique des 'Exercices Spirituels' de Saint Ignace*: 'Most fundamentally, it was Blondel's work that inspired me and not Hegel's.' "[20] Fessard himself admitted, "The *Phenomenologie de l'Esprit* . . . from the first moment seduced me by its resemblance in design to Maurice Blondel's *L'Action*."[21] Fessard, like his confrere de Lubac, was a Blondelian—in fact, one among several Jesuit Blondelians of the school of Lyons—not a Hegelian.[22] As Henrici writes, "The Blondelian inspiration is clear in the very structure of Fr. Fessard's dialectic, which

18. Ibid., 293, n. 1.

19. Giao Nguyen-Hong, *Le Verbe dans l'histoire: La philosophie de l'historicité chez G. Fessard*, preface by Jean Ladriere (Paris: Beauchesne, 1974), 62.

20. Peter Henrici, "La descendance blondélienne parmi les jésuites français," in Emmanuel Gabellieri and P. Cointet, eds., *Maurice Blondel et la philosophie française* (Paris: Parole et Silence, 2007), 317.

21. Fessard, *La Dialectique des 'Exercices Spirituels' de Saint Ignace de Loyola*, I, 6.

22. Cf. Michel Castro, "Henri Bouillard lecteur de Saint Thomas, et 'l'affaire de Fourvière,' " *Théophilyon: Revue des Facultés de Théologie et de Philosophie de l'Université Catholique de Lyon* 1 (2005), 111–143. On the influence of Blondel on Henri de Lubac, cf. Antonio Russo, *Henri de Lubac: teologia e dogma nella storia: L'influsso di Blondel* (Rome: Studium, 1990) (on the influence of Blondel on Fessard, cf. pp. 102–104); Giovanni Moretto, *Destino dell'uomo e Corpo mistico: Blondel, de Lubac e il Concilio Vaticano II* (Brescia: Morcelliana, 1994); Gianfranco Coffele, *Apologetica e teologia fondamentale: Da Blondel a de Lubac* (Rome: Studium, 2004).

explores the before and after of Ignatian discernment; this corresponds to the Blondelian option."[23] And so Bergoglio's dialectical model has, by way of Fessard, Blondelian roots, though Bergoglio will bring to it an original approach. This is an important key to understanding the genesis of Bergoglio's thought, *which owes much to the Blondelism of Fessard and de Lubac.*[24]

The question that remains is its source. At whose instigation did the young Bergoglio take an interest in Fessard's book? It was most certainly not easy reading for a young student. The answer, in all probability, is his philosophy professor, Miguel Ángel Fiorito. In a 2015 article, Juan Carlos Scannone was the first, and so far the only one, to suggest a convergence of Fressard and Fiorito behind Bergoglio's inspiration: "The similarity between Gaston Fessard's interpretation of the *Exercises* and that of the Argentine Jesuit Miguel Ángel Fiorito—acknowledged, at least orally, by both—is known; on the other hand, also known is Bergoglio's veneration of Fiorito, who was known throughout the Argentine Jesuit Province as 'the master' for his understanding of Ignatian spirituality."[25]

Scannone's intuition is correct, but he misses the central place that Fessard holds in Bergoglio's intellectual journey, suggesting instead that Blondel, Fessard's teacher, occupies that place, because of a set of similarities between the two.[26] In reality, Blondel's influence on Bergoglio is second-hand. Fessard, with his dialectical

---

23. Henrici, "La descendance blondélienne parmi les jésuites français," 317.

24. Cf. Étienne Fouilloux, *Une Église en quête de liberté: La pensée catholique française entre modernism et Vatican ii (1914–1962)* (Paris: Desclée de Brouwer, 2006), in particular "Des Jésuites blondéliens" (174–181).

25. Juan Carlos Scannone, "La filosofia dell'azione di Blondel e l'agire di papa Francesco," *La Civiltà Cattolica* 3969 (2015): 216. Scannone, dean of the School of Philosophy at the Universidad del Salvador (Buenos Aires/San Miguel) and vice president of the Società Argentina di Teologia, was Bergoglio's professor of Greek and of literature when he was a seminarian. His doctoral thesis in philosophy was *Sein und Inkarnation: Zum ontologischen Hintergrund der Frühschriften Maurice Blondels* ("Being and Incarnation: The Theological Foundations of Maurice Blondel's Early Writings") (Freiburg-Munich: Alber, 1968).

26. Scannone, "La filosofia dell'azione di Blondel e l'agire di papa Francesco," 216–233. "The philosophy of the former [Blondel] illuminates the theological depth of the pastoral action of the latter [Bergoglio], and this demonstrates the human, Christian value of Blondelian thought in practice" (233).

method, is the true inspirer, and it is Fiorito who introduces Fessard to Bergoglio. This is clear in a footnote Bergoglio includes in a 1981 article, citing two articles by Fiorito: "La opción personal de S. Ignacio" from 1956 and "Teoría y práctica de G. Fessard" from 1957.[27] The latter article was on a commentary on the so-called epitaph of Saint Ignatius: "Not to be confined to what is greater, but to be concerned with what is smaller: this is divine."[28] Explaining its meaning, Bergoglio wrote, "We could translate it this way: without turning away from that which is higher, we must bend down to pick up what is apparently small in the service of God; or, while remaining attentive to what is farther away, we must worry about what is closer. It is applied to religious discipline . . . *and is useful for characterizing Ignatian spirituality dialectically (in the sense adopted by Fessard)*."[29] This Ignatian motto, analyzed by Fessard in *La Dialectique des 'Exercices spirituels' de Saint Ignace de Loyola*, became, for Bergoglio, the expression of the polar tension that animates the spirituality of Saint Ignatius.[30] His understanding of this was guided by Fiorito, whose 1957 article, "Teoría y práctica de G. Fessard," offers an interpretation in the light of Fessard's dialectic model:

> The (so-called) epitaph of St. Ignatius contains two complementary sentences. . . . The first sentence (*non coerceri a maximo, contineri tamen a minimo, divinum est*) highlights a fundamental characteristic of Ignatian spirituality . . . because it expresses dialectically—that is, by the opposition of contraries—the fundamental dynamism of the holy soul of Ignatius, who points always to the highest ideal, God, but is at the same time attentive to the smallest details of the divine plan. . . . The second sentence (*coelum, animo, Roma corpori: illi . . . aliquid summo maius attribuit; huic . . . modum posuit*

27. Miguel Ángel Fiorito, "La opción personal de S. Ignacio," *Ciencia y Fe* 12 (1956); "Teoría y práctica de G. Fessard," *Ciencia y Fe* 13 (1957). The two articles are cited in Jorge Mario Bergoglio, "Farsi custodi dell'eredità" (June 1981), in Bergoglio-Francis, *Nel cuore di ogni padre*, 282, n. 4.

28. Fiorito, "La opción personal de S. Ignacio," 43–44.

29. Bergoglio-Francis, *Nel cuore di ogni padre*, 282, n. 4. Emphasis mine.

30. Cf. Fessard, *La Dialectique des 'Exercices spirituels' de Saint Ignace de Loyola*, I, 210ff.

mediumque virtutis) features a juxtaposition of the whole world, which Ignatius wanted to permeate with his work, and the city of Rome, where he wished his body to be laid to rest. And so the characteristic of his spirituality that this second sentence highlights is the *romanità* of the Ignatian spirit; and it is not manifested through a dialectical opposition, but through the composition of elements which, we maintain, are the love of God, which in Saint Ignatius knows no limits, and its discretion which limits not his love, but its realization within the Church. . . . The epitaph therefore manifests, in two essential sentences, the Ignatian *magis* and its particular application. And at the same time it points to the ideal of love without limits that is God, and the concrete way of particular application in love, which is the Church of Rome.[31]

Bergoglio constantly recalled the Ignatian maxim, which he read in both Fessard and Fiorito. Later, as pope, he would say:

I was always struck by a saying that describes the vision of Ignatius: *non coerceri a maximo, sed contineri a minimo divinum est* ["not to be limited by the greatest and yet to be contained in the tiniest— this is divine"]. I thought a lot about this phrase in connection with the issue of different roles in the government of the church, about becoming the superior of somebody else: it is important not to be restricted by a larger space, and it is important to be able to stay in restricted spaces. This virtue of the large and small is magnanimity. Thanks to magnanimity, we can always look at the horizon from the position where we are. That means being able to do the little things of every day with a big heart open to God and to others. That means being able to appreciate the small things inside large horizons, those of the Kingdom of God.[32]

31. Fiorito, "Teoría y práctica de G. Fessard," 350–351.
32. Pope Francis with Spadaro, *My Door Is Always Open*, 21. On the Ignatian "epitaph," cf. Jorge Mario Bergoglio, "Condurre nelle grandi e nelle piccole circostanze," *Boletín de Espiritualidad* 73, October 1981. In a "Letter on Inculturation to the Whole Society" of May 14, 1978, Father General Pedro Arrupe recalls the Ignatian maxim: "The ignatian spirit was once summed up in this sentence: '*Non cohiberi a maximo, contineri tamen a minimo, divinum est.*' In our context, this maxim challenges us to hold on to the concrete and the particular, even to the last cultural detail, but without renouncing the

The dialectic of the large and the small, this tension that characterizes the faith and spirituality of Ignatius, becomes a firm point in Bergoglio's thinking. In fact, through Fiorito the "dialectic" of Fessard's Ignatian *Spiritual Exercises* became, for the young student, a reference point. This perspective opened him to further reading that became determinative in his formation. Fiorito and Fessard attuned Bergoglio to "polarity," *the opposition of contraries* that guides the Ignatian soul. From this intuition, the rest flows.

"In Ignatian spirituality," the pope said, "there is always this bipolar tension. I remember that a little book, written in German, that I read around 1968 helped me: *Über die Theologie des 'als ob'* ['On the Theology of "as if"']. It was about the tension of the 'as if' (*als ob*). For example, in the contemplation described in the *Exercises*, St. Ignatius tells the practitioner to imagine the gospel scene *as if* one were present. The author offers a beautiful reflection on the theology contained here. The title is *On the Theology of 'as if.'* Gaston Fessard also helped me a lot."[33]

In the pope's memory, the book *On the Theology of "as if"* is connected to the dialectical thinking of Fessard. He remembers having read it in the late 1960s, after reading Fessard's first volume of *La Dialectique des 'Exercices Spirituels' de Saint Ignace de Loyola.* Acknowledging the difficulty of identifying the name of the author of the former, the pontiff went on to recall still another work

---

breadth and universality of those human values which no culture, nor the totality of them all, can assimilate and incarnate in [a] perfect and exhaustive way" (Pedro Arrupe, "Letter on Inculturation to the Whole Society," in Arrupe, *Other Apostolates Today*, Selected Letters and Addresses, vol. 3, ed. Jerome Aixala, SJ [St. Louis: Institute of Jesuit Sources, 1981], 171–181 at 176). The maxim was also studied by Hugo Rahner, "Die Grabschrift des Loyola," *Stimmen der Zeit*, February 1947, 321–339.

33. Pope Francis, audio recording of January 29, 2017. Unfortunately I am not able to identify the author or the book to which the pope refers. The only title that comes close to it is the essay by B. Wald, "Theologie des 'als ob': Das Dilemma nichtrealistischer Selbstdeutungen des christlichen Glaubens," afterword to J. Pieper, *Werke*, vol. 7: *Religionsphilosophische Schriften* (Hamburg: Felix Meiner Verlag, 2000), 627–633. But this is an "afterword," not a book, and it was published too recently. It cannot be the "little book" to which Pope Francis refers.

that was important for him during his years of formation, a 1969 article by the Jesuit Karl-Heinz Crumbach entitled "Ein ignatianisches Wort als Frage an unseren Glauben" ["A word of Ignatius as a question to our faith"].[34] In the audio recording of March 13, Pope Francis said, "This text [*Über die Theologie des 'als ob'*], together with that of Crumbach, was important for my thinking, because it helped me to rethink this tension present in the *Exercises* and that St. Ignatius uses continually. This way of thinking has grown unconsciously. I did not realize it until the moment when I could explain this thinking on bipolar tensions."[35]

We can therefore say that *the first seed of thinking on "dialectical polarity,"* which is the core of the thought of Jorge Mario Bergoglio, *was planted during the course of the 1960s.* Chronologically, his reading of the book on the theology of "as if" precedes that of the Crumbach article: "I'm sure I read it first, because in '69 I was ordained a priest and I read this [text] in the years when I was studying philosophy or in the first year of theology. But it is true that the argument is the same. . . . But the starting point was before '69."[36]

These memories of the pope are important. They allow us to locate *the origins of his thought* and the important place in it of an interpretation, offered by two Jesuit authors, of Ignatius's *Spiritual Exercises.* Through the category of "as if," this interpretation made clear to Bergoglio the polar tension that undergirds all Ignatian theology. It is clear that the pope is not referring to the book *Die Philosophie des Als Ob,* published in 1911 by the neo-Kantian philosopher Hans Vaihinger;[37] the insight gained by Bergoglio from the work he remembers was not related to the value of knowledge, whether it was true or illusory (Vaihinger's subject), but rather to *the fundamental dialectic between the grace of God and the freedom of the human person.* Crumbach's article was a commentary on a

---

34. Communication of the secretary of Pope Francis, March 12, 2017.

35. Pope Francis, audio recording of March 13, 2017, 15:57.

36. Ibid., 12:12.

37. Hans Vaihinger, *Die Philosophie des Als Ob: System der theoretischen, praktischen und religiösen Fiktionen der Menschheit auf Grund eines idealistischen Positivismus: Mit einem Anhang über Kant und Nietzsche* (Berlin: Reuther & Reichard, 1911).

particular maxim published by an eighteenth-century Jesuit. Crumbach wrote:

> The Hungarian Jesuit Gabriel Hevenesi published, in 1705, a collection of Ignatian sayings for each day of the year, the *Scintillae Ignatianae*. One of the most profound maxims of this collection, translated literally, is: "Trust in God as though your success in what you do depends on you and not on God; but work as if your efforts mean nothing, but God alone does everything." Trust in God and human efforts are closely related. Precisely the greatest trust in God's action is intimately connected to the experience of fatigue on the part of the human person; when this is at its greatest, it becomes unshakable trust and knowledge "that you do nothing and that God does everything." Already by virtue of its terse construction, the sentence is stretched to the point of tearing. Such a sentence tempts one to smooth over the tension in one's mind, molding it into a more "bearable" form. The circuitous history of this maxim includes many versions that attempt precisely this flattening. Most commonly, it becomes: "Trust in God as if you can do nothing and God does everything; but work as though the success of things undertaken depends on you and not on God."[38]

This is a misleading reading, Crumbach argues, which removes all of the "tension" that Hevenesi's maxim holds in play. He continues, "G. Fessard's interpretation is very different. In his book on the dialectic of the Ignatian *Exercises,* he returns with precise analysis to the sources from which Hevenesi had formed his formula and shows that even in the 'crossed' and 'wrapped' form, it corresponds in the best way to the Ignatian sources, or still better that in its intensity it concentrates in itself the *Exercises* in their entirety. H[ugo] Rahner agrees with this judgment and adds only the observation that Hevenesi himself in 1714 had flattened his formula."[39]

Crumbach, who shares the understanding of the Hevenesi maxim offered by Fessard in the first volume of *La Dialectique des 'Exer-*

38. Karl-Heinz Crumbach, "Ein ignatianisches Wort als Frage an unseren Glauben," *Geist und Leben* 42 (1969): 321.

39. Ibid., 321–322. Cf. Hugo Rahner, *Ignatius von Loyola als Mensch und Theologe* (Freiburg: Herder, 1964).

cises spirituels' de Saint Ignace de Loyola, does not concern himself with the historical-philological question. "Here we are interested only in the affirmation that it is precisely the most 'difficult' version of the formula that corresponds best to Ignatius's theology and to his inner struggle and that asks us a question that is capable of putting into motion our spiritual efforts."[40] The "most difficult" version is the one that maintains the tension rather than dissolves it into a dualism of two separate levels, two parallel lines that never meet. This latter model calls for

> trust as if everything depended on God, and work as if everything depended on oneself. Both, however, are found side by side in a sort of "dual-level theology" of "coordinated interaction" of God and the person. Trust in God is sufficient in itself and wants, in a first addition, to perfect itself in absolute trust. And human action is also left completely in its own sphere, understood independently, "as if everything depended on oneself." The subordinate and the principal propositions catapult each other into a boundless dimension and are lost in an infinite measure of faith and trust on the one hand and human action on the other. The absolute self-affirmation of both faith and human action oscillates in the air without any connection. Absolute faith on one side, radical human activity on the other; the encounter with God on one side, the sphere of human possibilities on the other; Sundays on one side, weekdays on the other. Both sentences remain without claim, because they catapult the person beyond his experience. The problem is solved and silently abandoned: trust in God and human freedom are found of two different orders, as though living in two different nations that have cut off all diplomatic contacts. If the first sentence ("trust as if everything depended on God") solemnly proclaims the primacy of a faith that has no need for human work to make it effective, in the second the freedom of the person ("work as if everything depends on you") claims a total autonomy that is no longer connected to its origins in faith. No one can deny that this parallel, disconnected understanding of "nature and grace" conditions, even today, not only theology, but also, in a secret and barely noticed way, the mentality and practice of many Christians.[41]

---

40. Crumbach, "Ein ignatianisches Wort als Frage an unseren Glauben," 322.
41. Ibid., 322–323.

The "flattened" formula results in a "dualism" between grace and nature that relieves the tension between them. "Precisely here we can see the immeasurable value of the first formula: the relationship between grace and freedom, between divine and human action, retains its vitality only as a question and not as a 'perfect' formula. This question must be lived. The judgment of the historians is important, that the sources support only the first formula as representative of 'one of the most profound characteristics of the Ignatian theology of grace.'"[42] *The relationship between grace and freedom, between divine and human action, retains its vitality only as a question and not as a "perfect" formula*: this is a conviction that will be at the center of Bergoglio's thought. His criticism of "doctrinalism," abstract dogmatism, and the petrifaction of revelation originates here—from the idea that faith, before being an answer, is a *question*, an opening of one's heart to a Presence of grace. *This question must be lived*; it must become experience, evidence of a real relationship between the human person and God on the stage of history.

Crumbach continues: "Faith cannot live when it becomes closed in on itself. . . . Faith refers to another, beyond oneself. Only in this way can it survive. Only in this way can it also become true, can it be verified. Faith becomes true in expectations that concern reality. In the 'as if everything depended on you,' the expectations of faith must penetrate into the reality of life, and they must 'point out their meaning in ways of living.' Faith must take responsibility for a world in which understandable behavior is only possible in practice."[43]

Faith cannot live closed in upon itself, but only by opening itself up. Bergoglio, as pope, will say that the church lives when it comes out of its "self-referentiality." But the idea is already present in this 1969 essay that he read so attentively. The escape from the sphere of immanence is not, however, merely a human work. Crumbach writes:

Faith, then, means this: Do you think everything depends on you? If it were so, then faith could be reduced to a sort of working therapy,

42. Ibid., 323.
43. Ibid.

which, disconnected from faith, would be sufficient in itself. If we look more carefully at the maxim, it becomes clear that we must consider the "as if." The "as if" is revealed as the design of faith itself. Faith projects a relationship with the world, "as if" everything depended on me. Here we recognize the form of the hypothesis. A hypothesis must leave open its verification because it can be partly true and partly false. By implicating itself in the adventure of its verification, it makes possible the anticipation of new experiences. Faith is not here beside or beyond our experiences, it does not conclude itself, but it makes possible for the human person an experience and opens within us a space in which we can become authentic. Faith keeps us constantly open for new experiences and decisively insists that we never stop searching or trying. Only in this way can we remain open to the surprising and mysterious experience of God. By virtue of my faith, my will is called to do what is extreme, "as if everything depended on me and not on God." The hypothesis, however, implies *a priori* that the success of things depends "in part" on God. It is an urgent warning not to overestimate in my actions my own real possibilities, which always remain "finite." At the same time, one cannot calculate the "part" of God and "part" of the person in the success of things. The relationship between the work of God and the action of the person is not a petrified formula, extraneous to my actions; rather, it comes to light through history, with which faith is involved. We cannot say, "Up to *this point* human effort is necessary and then God must intervene." Rather, one must commit to the extreme of one's possibilities and only in this way can one encounter God's own action. In this lies the truth of the hypothesis, which frees me from the illusion of believing that I can throw myself completely, with trust, into the arms of God without first doing all that is possible for me to do to change the world. But one point remains: faith leaves open in the "as if" the future of God's omnipotence, not rejecting it from the sphere of our experience. Involving ourselves in our own human possibilities can reveal itself ultimately as being involved in the surprising possibilities of divine work, being involved in the very future of the world. One thing is clear: faith requires an involvement with the problems of our world and our extreme effort to resolve them without thereby loosening the dependence of our action on faith in the power of divine grace.[44]

44. Ibid., 324–325.

This clarifies the intimate dialectic at the heart of Gabriel Hevenesi's formula: "Trust in God as though your success in what you do depends on you and not on God; but work as if your efforts mean nothing, but God alone does everything." Stated in this way, the formula does not betray Ignatius; on the contrary, it illustrates his profound spiritual tension.

> The inestimable value of this Ignatian formula consists in the fact that it offers an interpretation of our experience, but also that it provokes a restlessness that allows us to question the experience itself. Faith in God requires effort and struggle to overcome all needs, so that they are fulfilled in their own dynamics in the absolute trust that encounters the Lord of the world and thus the "law" with which it began. Both G. Fessard and H. Rahner see in this maxim a short summary of the *Exercises* and of Ignatian spirituality. One can think here of the tension between the "foundation" and the "contemplation to attain the love of God" in the *Exercises*. Even the "foundation" invites us, starting from faith, to make use of our natural abilities to reach the maximum for the glory of God. The "contemplation to attain love" invites all human activities to the *Suscipe*, the prayer of absolute trust in God, acknowledging that not I "but God will do everything." In this tension one finds the "more" that dominates the rhythm of the *Exercises*. The "more" is revealed for our question "as a fundamental word" of the person grasped by the "ever greater" God, of a man who continually allows God to demand too much from him in accepting the cross of daily efforts. The maxim reveals that the Ignatian spirit, which Hevenesi has formulated in a singular way, can apply to the Christian as the "*magis*," as "the very axiom of one's life revealed by Christ," which can give him impetus and direction.[45]

The interpretation of the *Exercises* of St. Ignatius offered by Karl-Heinz Crumbach and the author of *Über die Theologie des "als ob"* is, then, at the foundation of Bergoglio's thought. To this should be added, as interpreters of reference, Gaston Fessard and Hugo Rahner.[46] The Ignatian dialectic keeps firmly in place the two ends of the

---

45. Ibid., 328.

46. The interpretation of the *Spiritual Exercises* of Saint Ignatius is a theme that occupied many Jesuit intellectuals of the twentieth century. Cf. Michael Schneider, *Unterscheidung der Geister: Die ignatianischen Exerzitien in der*

chain: the action of the person and the grace of God. It unites them in a way that Henri de Lubac identified as *paradox*: "Trust in God as though the success of things depends on you and not on God; work, however, as though you did nothing, but God alone did everything." Christian thought is based on a paradox, on a *dialectical tension* by which acting *as if* everything depended on the person implies, at the same time, acting *as if* the person does nothing and God does everything. It is, clearly, a "mystical" dialectic in which the two poles, God and humanity, interact in the form of the Mystery that simultaneously unites and distinguishes grace and freedom.

Christian life is *tension*, a drama. It is a continuous question to God and, at the same time, an indefatigable commitment to the world. It is cross and resurrection. From here comes the idea of a *tensioned* thought, as Bergoglio would say, not ideological, not crystallized in abstract formulas, but tense, always, to grasp the "magis" of God, the opening of God within the immanence of the world.[47]

Juan Domingo Perón and the Church

During the 1960s, in the period in which the young Bergoglio was studying philosophy and theology, he was assimilating an original system of thought that would slowly settle in him until it became a true intellectual structure. In addition to the authors noted above, two other masters—one Jesuit and one Dominican—also began exerting their influence, particularly with regard to ecclesiology: Henri de Lubac and Yves Congar.

Bergoglio's debt to Congar came by way of his book *True and False Reform in the Church*,[48] first published in 1950. In it, Congar argued that

---

Deutung von E. Przywara, K. Rahner und G. Fessard, Innsbrucker Theologische Studien 11 (Innsbruck-Vienna: Tyrolia, 1983).

47. On God the "always greater" in Ignatius's *Exercises*, the essential study is Erich Przywara, *Deus semper major: Theologie der Exerzitien* (Freiburg: Herder, 1938).

48. Yves Congar, *True and False Reform in the Church*, trans. Paul Philibert (Collegeville, MN: Liturgical Press, 2010); orig. *Vraie et fausse réforme dans l'Eglise* (Paris: Éditions du Cerf, 1950).

true reform was always rooted in pastoral concern for ordinary faithful people: it was oriented to, and shaped by, the periphery, not the center. In other words, it valued tradition—the Catholic constants such as eucharistic worship, a teaching magisterium, devotion to the saints, and so on—which were valued by the ordinary faithful, rather than the avant-garde elites. True reform sought to make the Church more true to itself and was on guard against attempts to align it with contemporary secular movements. . . . True reform attacked the spiritual worldliness that stopped the Church from looking like and acting like Christ. This, in Bergoglio's reading, was the early Jesuit story—a reform that had revitalized the Church by restoring its poverty, holiness, missionary focus, obedience to the pope, and unity.[49]

With these ideas as a starting point, Bergoglio found himself skeptical of the reforms that took hold in the Argentine church of the 1970s. In reaction to a clergy and an episcopate allied with political power and the military junta, this reform took the form of a radical break with the past and the advent of a "new" church led by "enlightened" elites who were disconnected from the faith and devotion of the people. Bergoglio desired a different reform, a return to the origins that differed both from the modernists and from an official church that was deeply compromised by its relationship with the Argentine military government that had risen to power after Perón was exiled in 1955. "Like the bishops in bed with the anti-Peronist military, defending the myth of the Catholic nation, distant from the poor, the church had become, in its structures, disincarnate, absent from the contemporary world, responding primarily to itself."[50] From 1955 to 1976, the life of the country was marked by deep political instability. What was called the *Revolución Libertadora* took advantage of a growing fissure between the church and President Perón to call for a rejection of the Peronist reforms. Perón, who was not an ideologue but essentially a politician, had come to power with his electoral victory of 1946. His merit, initially, was to dismantle the wall that Argentine liberalism had erected against the church.

49. Ivereigh, *The Great Reformer*, 93–94.
50. Ibid., 74–75.

Perón explicitly identified his government's doctrine with the social teaching of the Church—he spoke of humanizing capital and dignifying labor—and recruited Catholic Action leaders to put forward proposals on issues they had long campaigned for, such as the family wage and regulation of child labor, that quickly became law. . . . But the relationship broke because the Church refused to be bought. In the negotiations over a new constitution, Perón rejected the Holy See's call to remove the *patronato*, the colonial-era right of the state to control the Church in a variety of ways, which the 1853 Constitution had continued to uphold. The Vatican, recently emerged from the fascist era in Europe, was sensitive to the dangers of supposedly Catholic states seeking to use the Church as an instrument of social control. And it knew that long after the Peronist government had gone, another, more hostile government could use that power seriously to inhibit the Church's mission. For his part, Perón was not about to renounce his constitutional power to appoint politically loyal bishops; it was the logical corollary of Peronism as the political embodiment of the Catholic nation.[51]

The rupture was fatal for the political future of Argentina, although Perón later reconciled with the church. "From the 1950s to the 1970s Argentina was paralyzed by a political paradox that is hard for foreigners to grasp: the antiliberals (the nationalists, the Peronists) were popular and came to power by winning elections, while the liberals—the democrats, the pluralists—used dictatorship to keep the Peronists out of power."[52] This means that the period of Bergoglio's theological-philosophical formation in the Society of Jesus and, subsequently, his time as Provincial of the Society for Argentina, coincides with a tragic period in the nation's history. It was a period of struggle, marked by a civil war of unparalleled violence. *It is impossible to understand the thought of Jorge Mario Bergoglio outside the context of the conflict that marked this time and place.*

51. Ibid., 27–28. On the relationship between the "first" Perón and the church, cf. Lila Caimari, *Perón y la Iglesia Católica: Religión, estado y sociedad en la Argentina, 1943–1955* (Buenos Aires: Ariel, 1995).

52. Ivereigh, *The Great Reformer*, 30.

His "dialectical" thought, which had initially developed through careful reflection on the tension between grace and freedom that stands at the center of St. Ignatius's *Exercises*, took on the characteristics of a "polar" philosophy aimed at unifying the hard contrasts of history. Like the thought of Hegel or Romano Guardini, Bergoglio's too is marked by the conflict of his time, struggling for reconciliation.

In Argentina, the decade of violence began in 1969, the year Bergoglio became a priest at the age of thirty-three, when the army killed dozens of students and workers during a massive protest demonstration in Cordoba. On the wave of the Castro revolution in Cuba, the Trotskyite *Ejército Revolucionario del Pueblo* (ERP) and the *Movimiento Peronista Montonero* (MPM) began a guerrilla movement that carried out over eight hundred murders and 1,748 kidnappings, as well as countless attacks in the heart of the city between 1969 and 1979. Perón's return and his electoral victory in October 1973 brought a brief pause to the violence. But soon, in May 1974, the Montoneros resumed the armed struggle. Perón died in July and was succeeded by his wife Isabelita, who, unable to cope with the situation, decreed a state of siege supported by death squads that initiated the *guerra sucia*, the "dirty war." At the beginning of 1975, the so-called Triple A was responsible for four hundred fifty murders and two thousand "disappearances." In March 1976, the army took control of the country and held it until 1983. The repression reached unprecedented levels of violence. Between 1969 and 1983, the military, state security forces, and right-wing death squads killed 8,368 people, almost half of whom were civilians, not guerrillas. Argentina was divided between those who, while opposing the army, feared the revolutionary wave of the Montoneros, and those who sided with the revolutionary cause out of hatred of military repression. The church did not escape this dramatic dialectic and also ended up divided by the extreme positions.

This was the context in which Bergoglio became Provincial of the Jesuits. In his opinion, "Christianity in Argentina had been taken hostage by violent ideologies. His generation had succumbed to the temptations of the revolutionary messianism of the guerrillas or the anti-communist crusade of the men in khaki, and the result was diabolic: the Body of Christ had been split along temporal lines."[53] This meant, for Bergoglio, a sharp rejection not only of the military government and its methods but also of guerrilla violence. The latter enjoyed the theological support of certain exponents of liberation theology, who rightly emphasized the crucial questions of poverty and social justice, but did it in the context of an uncritical acceptance of the Marxist methodology.[54] The foundational work on this was provided by the 1971 book, *Liberation Theology*, by the Peruvian theologian Gustavo Gutiérrez.[55] The book theologically consecrated the division that marked the Latin American church in the late 1960s. Gutiérrez wrote:

> The Latin American Church is sharply *divided* with regard to the process of liberation. Living in a capitalist society in which one class confronts another, the Church, in the measure that its presence increases, cannot escape—nor try to ignore any longer—the profound division among its members. Active participation in the liberation process is far from being a uniform position of the Latin American Christian community. The majority of the Church continues to be linked in many different ways to the established order. And what is worse, among Latin American Christians there are not only different political options within a framework of free interplay of ideas; the polarization of these options and the extreme seriousness of the situation have even placed some Christians among the oppressed and persecuted and others among the oppressors and persecutors, some among the tortured and others among the torturers or those who condone torture. This gives rise to a serious and radical confrontation between Christians who suffer from injustice and exploitation and those who benefit from the established order.[56]

53. Ibid., 142. On Bergoglio's efforts on behalf of victims of the military repression, cf. Nello Scavo, *Bergoglio's List: How a Young Francis Defied a Dictatorship and Saved Dozens of Lives*, trans. Bret Thoman (Charlotte: Saint Benedict Press, 2014).

54. Cf. Juan Carlos Scannone, "La teología de la liberación: Caracterización, corrientes, etapas," *Stromata* 38 (1982): 3–40.

55. Gustavo Gutiérrez, *A Theology of Liberation: History, Politics and Salvation*, trans. Caridad Inda and John Eagleson (Maryknoll: Orbis, 1973); orig. *Teología de la liberación* (Lima: CEP, 1971).

56. Ibid., 137.

The political-social division was reflected in the division of the church. Eucharistic communion was threatened. Gutiérrez wrote, "Because of the options which, with the qualifications we have indicated, the Christian community is making, it is faced ever more clearly with the dilemma now confronting the whole continent: to be for or against the system, or more subtly, to be for reform or revolution. Many Christians have resolutely decided for the difficult path which leads to the latter."[57]

Gutiérrez's revolutionary option led him to reject *desarrolism*, the quest for economic development through industrialization that had guided Latin American policy during the 1960s. He also rejected reform as a political method. The option for class struggle calls for confrontation, not the peaceful resolution of conflict. Fascinated by the movements of Fidel Castro and Che Guevara—who are cited often in the text—and by the symbolic figure of the guerrilla priest Camillo Torres, Gutiérrez justified "counterviolence," revolutionary violence in response to that perpetrated by the state. Following the Marxist theory, liberation theology identified liberation primarily as liberation from structures, the only path that could lead to Latin American socialism and the birth of "the new man." This resulted in a confusion of theological and political aims that became typical of liberation theology. Gutiérrez, along with German political theologians of the same period Johann Baptist Metz and Jürgen Moltmann, understood the path of liberation as a process of "salvation," the progressive realization of the kingdom.[58] In this way, the critique of the theological dualism between the natural and the supernatural became, for Gutiérrez, a political-religious messianism in which the socialist goal becomes the implementation of the kingdom of God.

Gutiérrez would in later years correct this thinking, as is evident in his new introduction to the revised (1988) edition of his book. Criticizing the primacy of praxis that he had previously developed, he wrote, "The ultimate norms of judgment [in theology] come from the revealed truth that we accept by faith and not from praxis

---

57. Ibid., 138.

58. On the political theologies of Metz and Moltmann, cf. Massimo Borghesi, *Critica della teologia politica: Da Agostino a Peterson: la fine dell'era costantiniana* (Genoa-Milan: Marietti, 2013), 203–245.

itself."[59] He acknowledged that the circle that joins orthopraxis and orthodoxy does not allow one to speak, in Marxist terms, of the primacy of praxis, nor does it allow the problem of poverty to be framed only in socioeconomic terms. This self-criticism by Gutiérrez, whose more developed liberation theology retains the preferential option for the poor and the critique of injustices, was the result of a more serene political and theological climate. But it is clear that the ideas he offered in his original edition, transferred to Argentina in the 1970s, served to legitimize a violent response to the violence carried out by the state and its dictatorship. In this way, Bergoglio observed, the church was "taken hostage" by the opposing extremisms. A Christianity divided between "order" and "revolt," between clericalism and messianism, was no longer able to witness to the world a message of peace and fraternity. The church had failed.

Young Bergoglio's criticism of the two opposing forces that tore apart Argentine political and ecclesial life of the 1970s does not mean that he felt equally distant from all political realities. As Ivereigh writes, he, like many Catholics, certainly "always had a natural affinity with the cultural and political tradition represented by Peronism."[60] Bergoglio "was part of a generation of young Catholics who were increasingly angered by the veto exercised by the army over Peronism, which prevented it taking part in elections and in countless other, often petty, ways sought to humiliate its supporters."[61] In fact, Peronism represented the largest democratic movement in Argentina, the only one attentive to the needs and the social rights of the less prosperous segment of the population.[62]

But Bergoglio's general acceptance of Peronism did not mean he shared its radical, populist-messianic goals. This was the perspective

---

59. Gustavo Gutiérrez, *A Theology of Liberation: History, Politics, and Salvation*, trans. Caridad Inda and John Eagleson, rev. ed. (Maryknoll: Orbis 1973, 1988), xxxiv.

60. Ivereigh, *The Great Reformer*, 30.

61. Ibid., 71.

62. Cf. Daniel James, *Resistance and Integration: Peronism and the Argentine Working Class, 1946–1976* (Cambridge: Cambridge University Press, 1988).

of the Movement of Priests for the Third World (*Movimiento de Sacerdotes para el Tercer Mundo*, or MSTM), which, in the early 1970s, included about 10 percent of priests in Argentina. Most famous among them was Father Carlos Mugica, whose adherence to Peronism was motivated by a desire to bridge the divide between the church and the working class, which grew from the workers' disgust at the official church's anti-Peronist stance. In this total adhesion, "Mugica and the Third-World priests had a messianic view of Peronism as a force of popular liberation, while seeing politics through a socialist prism. For the MSTM, the people were Peronist, and therefore the church, in order to be with the people, should be, too. Yet the political agenda was more Castro's than Perón's."[63] (Mugica was killed in 1974, probably by the "Triple A.")

This was certainly not Bergoglio's perspective, nor was it his *theological-political* understanding of Peronism. In *Between Heaven and Earth*, the book he coauthored with Rabbi Abraham Skorka, Bergoglio recalled:

> Initially, the Church remained associated with the Perón regime, and even obtained things, such as religious education; whether that is good or bad is something else. After Evita died [1952], the distancing began. Perhaps the hierarchy did not know how to handle the circumstances well and the conflict ended with the '54 shutdown. When I was a boy I remember reading an article in the daily newspaper: "The gentlemen and monsignors of the bountiful table." That was the first attack. The mutual confrontation continued from thereon out, and many innocent lives were taken. The nationalist group within the armed forces did not care about the civilian inhabitants of Plaza de Mayo, and they sent their planes, which had the incredible inscription "Christ Conquers." That disgusts me, it makes me very angry; I am outraged because it uses the name of Christ for a purely political act. It mixed religion, politics, and pure nationalism. Innocent people were killed in cold blood. I do not accept the argument that it was done in defense of the Nation, because you cannot defend the people by killing the people. It is simplistic to say that the Church only supported or only opposed Perón. The relationship was

63. Ivereigh, *The Great Reformer*, 97. Mugica provides his thinking in his book *Peronismo y cristianismo* (Buenos Aires: Merlín, 1973).

much more complex, it came and went: first there was support, later some leaders were in bed with them, and finally there was a confrontation. Rather complex, like Peronism itself.[64]

Bergoglio's harsh criticism referred to the repression of June 11, 1955, when military planes bearing the slogan *Cristo vence* ("Christ conquers") bombed the Plaza de Mayo in Buenos Aires, killing hundreds of union-affiliated protesters. The action was striking not only for its barbarism but also for its mixture of religion, politics, and nationalistic ideology. The bloody Plaza de Mayo episode would remain stamped in the mind of the young Bergoglio. Its memory fueled his critique of political theology, both right- and left-leaning. *Bergoglio has never been a Peronist populist, and he has never professed a Peronist ideology.* Like many Argentine Catholics, he simply saw in Peronism a defense of the interests of the common people and the poor in the face of "liberal" governments concerned only with the affairs of the upper bourgeoisie.

This explains his association with the third way of Peronism, that of the center, when he became, in 1971, a spiritual assistant to some leaders of the "Guardia de Hierro" movement, based at the Jesuit-run Salvador University (USAL).[65] As one of them recalled, "Bergoglio

64. Jorge Mario Bergoglio and Abraham Skorka, *On Heaven and Earth: Pope Francis on Faith, Family, and the Church in the Twenty-First Century*, trans. Alejandro Bermudez and Howard Goodman (New York: Image, 2013), 208–209; orig. *Sobre el cielo y la tierra* (Buenos Aires: Editorial Sudamericana, 2011).

65. "Within the Salvador University, there were three political groupings, each with their own Jesuit chaplain. The conservative one, favorable to the Onganía military dictatorship, seen as a bulwark against communism, was close to Father Alfredo Sáenz; a second, linked to Father Alberto Sily, was the montonero group, which favored armed revolution; while the third group, who looked to Bergoglio and Luzzi, was made up of the *guardianes*: traditional or orthodox Peronist activists and intellectuals preparing the ground for Perón's return. Julio Bárbaro, one of the Guardia's leaders at the USAL who went on to be a Peronist deputy, recalls that Bergoglio and Luzzi were among the few priests who understood the Guardia and supported its commitment to an authentic, nonviolent, pueblo-oriented Peronism" (Ivereigh, *The Great Reformer*, 105).

was completely different from the Third World [MSTM] priests. While they went into politics to make up for what was lacking in their faith, he stayed close to his faith and from there sought to enrich politics. He said what mattered was not ideology but witness."[66] He shared, to be sure, some intellectual interests with the *guardianes*, but remained a shepherd first. "He was a priest who happened to be a Peronist, rather than a Peronist priest."[67]

The Unity of Universal and Particular, Center and Periphery: The Lesson of Amelia Podetti

Among Bergoglio's Peronist contacts of that time, one of particular importance was a thinker of the first order, Amelia Lezcano Podetti (1928–1979). Podetti taught philosophy and the history of modern philosophy at the Salvador University and the National University of La Plata.[68] Bergoglio held her in high esteem. A scholar of Husserl, on whom she had published a book[69] in 1969, Podetti had studied in Paris under the guidance of Jean Wahl, Paul Ricœur, Ferdinand Alquié, and Henri Gouhier. Returning to Argentina, and rejecting the hegemony of positivist scientism and Marxism, she turned her attention to restoring to life a body of thought that had fallen in the cultural tradition of the country as a result of its high-level confrontation with European continental philosophy. In 1975, while serving as National Director of Culture, she created the National Consagración Prize. Podetti was probably the most significant Argentine thinker of the 1970s, and the one who offered the strongest intellectual support to the national Peronist cause and to a "third way" that rejected both individualism and collectivism.

66. Ibid.
67. Ibid.
68. On Amelia Podetti, cf. José Ramiro Podetti, *Advertencia preliminar a A. Podetti: Comentario a la Introducción a la "Fenomenología del Espíritu"* (Buenos Aires: Editorial Biblos, 2007), 15–33; Juan Pedro Denaday, "Amelia Podetti: una trayectoria olvidada de las Cátedras Nacionales," *Agenda de Reflexión* 943, November 4, 2013, http://historiadelperonismo.com/amelia -podetti/.
69. *Husserl: esencias, historia, etnologia* (Buenos Aires: Editorial Estudios, 1969).

The most influential Guardia intellectual in the USAL was Amelia Podetti, whom Bergoglio met in 1970, and who introduced him to left-wing nationalist thinkers like Arturo Jauretche and Raúl Scalabrini Ortiz. She taught the ideas of both at the university and later at the Colegio Máximo, while editing *Hechos y Ideas*, a Peronist political journal that Bergoglio read. Until her premature death in 1979 she was one of a group of thinkers—among them the Uruguayan philosopher Alberto Methol Ferré—who saw the Church as key to the emergence of a new Latin American continental consciousness, *la patria grande*, which would take its place in the modern world and become an important influence on it. This was Bergoglio's intellectual family—a Catholic nationalism that looked to the *pueblo*, rather than to the state, and beyond Argentina to Latin America; and which saw Medellín as the beginning of a journey to the continent becoming a beacon for the Church and the world.[70]

Attentive to the historical and cultural foundations of ideas, Podetti was compared directly with Hegel, especially in her later work. The comparison looks accurate especially in consideration of two of her books, a *Comentario a la Introducción de la Fenomenología del Espíritu*, published in 1978, and *La irrupción de América en la historia*, published posthumously in 1981. In 2007, Bergoglio prepared a preface for a second edition of her Hegelian commentary. He wrote:

> I kept and very much keep in mind her teachings, which made an important contribution to the reflection and self-understanding of the country in a singular moment of its history, the decades of 1960s and 1970s. Her premature death has certainly deprived us of further fruit of her thought, but her university work, her articles, her participation in the fruitful debates that took place in Argentina during those years, were enough to irreversibly establish ideas and lines of research that still have an extraordinary relevance today. Precisely at a time when Latin America needs a renewed self-awareness, capable of fully understanding its condition and its particular needs, in order to produce new and historical answers that are distinctly its own, I think it is extremely opportune that we recover the contributions of our thinkers, our philosophers, as we have done in recent decades with our writers and our poets. Just as the value of

---

70. Ivereigh, *The Great Reformer*, 106.

our literature is appreciated as it rarely has been before—the famous boom of Latin American literature—what is needed is a similar leap in appreciation of our philosophical work.[71]

In Bergoglio's eyes, Professor Podetti's achievement was that she had introduced a way of thinking that opened the Argentine cultural tradition to the outside world without succumbing to the hegemony of its dominant ideas.

> Amelia Podetti encouraged a full and conscious appropriation of classical, medieval, and modern thought, in such a way that our own thought could unfold with a universal, and not only regional, vocation. It would be an arduous task to do philosophy in the contemporary world without regard to Hegel. And Amelia Podetti contributed to a moment of Argentine thought that attempted a dialogue with that of the German philosopher: this included her distinguished teachers, Carlos Astrada and Andrés Mercado Vera, but there were also other important ones. I mean to say that a dialogue is genuine when the questions are authentic, that is to say, ours, not taken up by other cultural contexts; when they arise from a reflection born from within the problems, challenges, concerns, and hopes of a determined community. The great human problems are undoubtedly universal, and in a sense timeless; but in the consciousness of the philosopher they run the risk of evaporating into empty, abstract formulations, if they do not pass through the crucible of hard and pure reality. And reality is always incarnate, particular, concrete. There can be no access to universality without assuming the incarnation integrally.[72]

71. Jorge Mario Bergoglio, preface to Amelia Podetti, *Comentario a la Introducción de la Fenomenología del Espíritu* (Buenos Aires: Editorial Biblos, 2007), 11.

72. Ibid. Carlos Astrada (1894–1970), a student of Scheler, Hartmann, Husserl, and Heidegger, was director of the Institute of Philosophy of the School of Philosophy and Letters at the University of Buenos Aires during the years that Amelia Podetti was a student there (1948–1955). He helped to introduce phenomenology and existentialism to Argentina. Cf. Andrés Mercado Vera, *Carlos Astrada, la revolución existencial* (Buenos Aires: Libros de Hoy, 1953). Mercado Vera (1918–1992) was a student of Astrada and a teacher of Podetti. A professor of philosophy at the University of Buenos Aires, he coauthored *Valoración de la Fenomenología del Espíritu* (Buenos Aires: Devenir, 1964) and many articles on Hegelian thought.

Bergoglio alludes here to a gnoseological concept that he shares with Podetti, the "concrete universal," which we will discuss below. Podetti's historical-philosophical thought, developed through a close engagement with Hegel's, was for him an example of this. Podetti wrote:

> Hegel rightly insists that thinking about the unity of humanity is not contradictory to the multiplicity of people or that the unity of the human species is not contradictory with the multiplicity of cultures, of peoples; that is, of the historical forms in which the human person is incarnate. To think that there is a contradiction between unity and multiplicity, or that there is contradiction between the universality of the species and the particularity of real historical individuals, reflects the traditional logic, the logic of what he calls the understanding. . . . What Hegel wants to say is that in reality there is no contradiction, but rather that it is through a particular type of tension and relationship that is established between the one and the multiple, between the universal and the particular, that the human person is realized in history. Put another way, what Hegel is saying is that the universality of the human person is realized through its historical particularities, and that the unity of the species is realized through multiplicity and variety, through the particular forms in which they are incarnate historically.[73]

The Hegelian model of the synthesis between particular and universal, which is both similar to and different from the Catholic one, demonstrated its limitations by its claim to offer a "universal history."[74] Hegelian history remains, in reality, a "European" history. It represents a narrowing compared to the view that opens up, at the dawn of modernity, with the discovery of the New World.

> There is a moment when European thought seems capable of developing the idea of universality, which comes at the same moment of discovery and conquest. That is to say, for humanism and in the thought of authors like Tomás Moro, or Campanella, or Erasmus,

---

73. Amelia Podetti, *Comentario a la Introducción de la Fenomenología del Espíritu* (Buenos Aires: Editorial Biblos, 2007 ed.), 55–56.

74. On the comparison between the Hegelian model and the Catholic model, cf. Massimo Borghesi, *L'era dello Spirito: Secolarizzazione ed escatologia moderna* (Rome: Studium, 2008), 117–169.

this problem—in some way—appears. It is interesting that in humanist thinking the discovery of America generates what we might call "the rebirth of utopia." Renaissance authors write utopias motivated by the discovery of these new worlds, new cultures. . . . This idea also appears in contemporary Spanish thought on the discovery and conquest. I will only mention the case of Vitoria, a contemporary of Erasmus. Vitoria elaborates the theory of what can be called public international law. This was the first attempt to formulate theoretically this new fact of the universalization of the planet.[75]

This universalist design ends, according to Podetti, with the crisis of the Spanish empire:

But it seems clear that starting from the defeat of the Spanish Empire, which we can call Latin America, an empire that had encompassed the whole world, European thought began to reduce itself again to the European world, and to the European world as already indicated by tradition: that thought, from Descartes to Hegel and still today, moves in the dimensions of the Mediterranean world, in the dimensions of the Roman Empire and its borders, and goes no further. In this sense it is clear that for this body of thought America does not exist as an integral and essential part of the world.[76]

Hegelian universalism remains, despite intentions, a "Western" universalism, different, that is, from the Latin American model that grew in the context of Catholic universalism. Latin America, and Argentina within it, claimed its "inclusion," its being part of the whole. This is why Bergoglio, when he refers to Podetti's book on Hegel, makes reference to the *other* volume, the one on "the eruption of America into history." In the essays collected in that posthumous work, Podetti offered a perceptive historical synthesis between particular and universal. Bergoglio was very aware of this work, to the point of admitting:

The thought of Amelia Podetti, the dean of philosophy at the university, a specialist in Hegel who died young, influenced me. It is

---

75. Podetti, *Comentario*, 51.
76. Ibid.

from her that I received the intuition regarding the "peripheries." She worked a lot on this. One of her brothers continues to publish her writings, her notes. It is by reading Methol Ferré and Podetti that I took something of the dialectic in an anti-Hegelian form, because she was a specialist on Hegel but not Hegelian.[77]

Bergoglio was particularly interested in the topic of the inculturation of the Christian faith in Latin America, which was a focus of Podetti's work.

The peculiar location of America in the world, in space and time, manifests itself in the formation of American culture. It develops and appears in history as a unifying matrix that collects, absorbs, synthesizes, and transforms everything that reaches its territory. It reduces to a complex and richly differentiated unity a wide variety of cultural contributions, even those which are aggressions and attempts to destroy the deep, ultimate, and irreducible core of the *American being*. This unifying virtue is traced in the historical foundations of America, expressed in well characterized profiles. It is here that one observes, as particular facts, on one hand the *mestizadora* will of conquest and colonization, and on the other, the relationship between Christianity and culture, which is established uniquely in America: deeply linked and penetrated to the point that American culture may be the only genuinely Christian culture, that is to say, Christian *from and in* its very beginning. Rightly this vocation for synthesis, this unifying virtue, this attitude to change diverse cultural traditions, particularizes and at the same time universalizes America. There is a vocation of universality within its own cultural particularity.[78]

In this way, Podetti's Hegelian *Comentario* becomes a reflection on the universal destiny of Latin America in the new historical context. As Bergoglio observed, "Precisely for this reason Amelia Podetti begins at that moment to formulate her idea of the irruption of Latin America in history as the fundamental fact of modernity, which initiates the rise of universal history. And while the concept

---

77. Pope Francis, audio recording of January 3, 2017.

78. Amelia Podetti, *La irrupción de América en la historia* (Buenos Aires: Centro de investigaciones Culturales, 1981); Italian trans. in "L'irruzione dell'America nella storia," *Incontri* 7, September–October 1982, 11.

of 'universal history' was used extensively by Hegel, Amelia Podetti's formulation of it is different from his. It is also different from other European visions of History where the fact of 'planetarization,' as she understands it, does not seem to be assumed in all its historical and philosophical significance."[79]

It isn't, because modern "planetarization"—as Zbigniew Brzezinski demonstrates in *Between Two Ages: America's Role in the Technetronic Era*—uses science and technology, which were born in the context of the Christian spiritual horizon of humanity's transcendence of nature, in a Faustian manner.[80] Bergoglio would remember this when, as pontiff, he used Romano Guardini to demonstrate the limits of modern anthropocentrism and technological degeneration. Before the limits of Western universalism, Podetti proposed Latin America as a model: "America is capable of integrating modernity into its own historical and spiritual foundation, because it is capable of conceiving the universality of history and the meaning of the search for unity in the journey of humanity on earth. It seems that America was prepared, from its beginnings and by its history, to carry out an essential mission in this phase of universalization: to propose a path of universalization that is different from that of super-technical societies and capable of incorporating them. Its mission and its destiny is to conceive and to bring about unity."[81]

The "centrality" of Latin America means a displacement of the coordinates, a correction of the envisioned "European" model of the relationship between the center and the periphery. It was for Bergoglio an important correction, which he would later affirm as pope: "It is from her that I received the intuition regarding the 'peripheries.' She worked a lot on this."[82]

This offers a crucial insight. The concept of the "periphery," which has taken a central place in Francis's pontificate, is borrowed not from the pro-Marxist theory of "dependence" that was so much in vogue in the 1970s, but rather from Bergoglio's awareness of the

79. Bergoglio, preface to Podetti, *Comentario*.

80. Zbigniew Brzezinski, *Between Two Ages: America's Role in the Technetronic Era* (New York: Viking Press, 1970).

81. Podetti, *L'irruzione*, 12.

82. Pope Francis, audio recording of January 3, 2017.

change of perspective that arises when one is attentive to what is (seemingly) marginal.[83]

According to Podetti, "The appearance of America in history radically changes not only the view but also the meaning of humanity's journey on earth. The discovery of the 'New World' represents, in reality, the discovery of the world in its totality. It is the discovery of the fact that the world was something completely different from what the people of either side had known until then. Universal history really begins with America."[84] For Bergoglio, the world seen from South America will become the world seen from the peripheries, from the shanty towns, *villas de miseria*, and immense metropolises of Latin America. Such a philosophical transvaluation gives way to the evangelical perspective. In any case, the intuition of the periphery-center relationship will prove to be important.

Podetti's work brought another idea to the attention of the future pope: the relevance of Augustine's *De civitate Dei*. Indeed, one of the chapters in *La irrupción de América en la historia* is titled "Saint Augustine: The Problem of Justice."[85] Its subheadings reveal the particular attention it pays to "the city of God": "Justice and People in the Pagan Tradition (Cicero)"; "Justice in the Christian Vision

---

83. "In the widespread search to identify the deep intellectual background to Pope Francis's words and gestures, some have suggested more or less implicit points of contact between the Bergoglian periphery and theories of dependence. It is an interesting effort, but off target. Bergoglio drew his sense of the center-periphery tension as an analytical instrument that helps explain how things go in the Church and in the world from the Peronist Argentine philosopher Amelia Podetti (1928–79). This Hegel scholar from the Rio Plate school, who taught philosophy at both the state-run University of Buenos Aires and the Jesuit-run University of Salvador and was considered close to the non-Marxist, pro-third-world faction of the Guardia de Hierro, argued that Europe 'saw' in a different way after Ferdinando Magellano's circumnavigation of the earth. Looking at the world from Madrid was not like looking at it from Tierra del Fuego; the view was wider and you could see things that were hidden to those who looked at everything from the 'center' of the empire" (Gianni Valente, "Francesco e il viaggio della Chiesa fuori di se stessa," *Vatican Insider*, May 28, 2016).

84. Podetti, *L'irruzione*, 10.

85. Ibid., 13–20.

(St. Augustine)"; "The People in the Christian Vision (St. Augustine)"; "The Two Cities"; "The Christian and the Century"; "Justice and Universalization"; "Conclusion." The importance of this work was not lost on Bergoglio. In the prologue he provided for Podetti's Hegelian *Comentario*, the cardinal wrote, "Providence would determine that she would offer, as the subject of one of her last courses, in 1978, a Philosophy of History. This course, arguing for the need to undertake our own revision of the history of the West, centered on Saint Augustine and Hegel, gave consideration to the two 'points' of the philosophy of history in the West."[86]

Augustine and Hegel: two poles of theology and political philosophy of the West. While in Hegel the state becomes the kingdom of God on earth, in Augustine the dualism of the two cities, the earthly city and the city of God, prevents any theological-political monism. In her book, Podetti dealt with the "people" but, in the light of Augustine, any "populist" or nationalistic ideology becomes impossible. In Augustine, "there is no confusion of the earthly city with the Roman Empire or with any other state or historical empire, nor of the celestial city with the church. . . . In addition, good or bad people, citizens of one city and another, live in the world and need the goods of the world and the peace of the world; peace is a good proper to the city, both the city of God and the city of man, according to the loves that animate the citizens of those cities."[87]

City of God and Earthly City: The Relevance of Augustine

The confrontation between Augustine and Hegel caught Bergoglio's interest. It allowed him to measure the distance between a theology of politics and the kind of political theology—"*Christo vence*"—that he had always rejected.[88] Christ, he believed, does not conquer with armies, nor through revolution. The victory of Christ is the victory of the cross, and his kingdom is revealed in this world

---

86. Bergoglio, preface to Podetti, *Comentario*.
87. Podetti, *La irrupción*, 16.
88. On the conceptual distinction between "political theology" and "theology of politics," cf. Borghesi, *Critica della teologia politica*, 9–22.

through seeds of light and grace, seeds of justice and works that give life to the *pueblo fiel*.

Bergoglio's rejection of messianic populism led him, in the first years of the new millennium, to rediscover, like Amelia Podetti, the relevance of *De civitate Dei* as a model for a theology *of* politics. It was an interesting rediscovery, because the Augustine of *The City of God* was at that time quite neglected by scholars. Not by all of them, though. In the early months of 1987, the journal *Nexo*, under the leadership of Alberto Methol Ferré, published an article by Pedro Morandé on the vision of *The City of God*. This was followed, in the next issue, by a review by Methol Ferré of the Spanish edition of Erich Przywara's *Augustinus: Die Gestalt als Gefüge*.[89] Beyond these, it is worth noting that the international magazine *30 Giorni*, which includes a Spanish edition, published a series of articles in the 1990s that highlighted the ecclesial and political relevance of Augustine's *De civitate Dei*, based in large part on the scholarly work of Joseph Ratzinger.[90] In this way, the Augustinian "wave" also reached Bergoglio, who, in a 2002 text, "Word and Friendship," contrasted Augustine's thinking with the imperial theology of Eusebius of Caesarea, the bishop and biographer of Constantine. Here Bergoglio took up the hermeneutic line previously laid out by Erich Peterson and Joseph Ratzinger.[91]

> At that time Augustine, a man who had known unbelief and materialism, found the key to giving form to his hope through a profound theology of history, developed in his book *The City of God*. In it, far exceeding the "official theology" of the empire, the saint presents us with a fundamental hermeneutical principle of his thought: the

89. Alberto Methol Ferré, "Erich Przywara. San Agustín. Trayectoria de su genio. Contextura de su espíritu," *Nexo* 12 (1987), 31–32. The review was of the Spanish edition (Madrid: Cristianidad, 1984) of Erich Przywara, *Augustinus: Die Gestalt als Gefuge* (Leipzig: J. Hegner, 1934).

90. Many of these articles were published together as *Il potere e la grazia: Attualità di san'Agostino* (Rome: Trenta Giorni–Nuova Omicron, 1998). Among the Ratzinger texts cited most often in them are *Volk und Haus Gottes in Augustins Lehre von der Kirche* (Munich: Karl Zink Verlag, 1954) and *Die Einheit der Nationen: Eine Vision der Kirchenväter* (Salzburg-Munich: Pustet, 1971).

91. Cf. Borghesi, *Critica della teologia politica*, 65–88.

schema of the "two loves" and the two "cities." In summary, this is his argument. There are two "loves": the *love of self*, which is aggressively individualistic, exploits others for one's own purposes, considers what is common only in reference to its usefulness to oneself, and rebels against God; and *holy love*, which is primarily social, seeks the common good, and follows the commandments of the Lord. Around these "loves" or ends the "two cities" are organized: the "earthly" city and the city "of God." The first is inhabited by the wicked, the other by the "saints." But the interesting thing about Augustinian thought is that these "cities" are not present in history, that is, they cannot be identified in this or that secular reality. The city of God, it is clear, is not the visible church. Indeed, many of those who make up the celestial city reside in pagan Rome, and many of those in the earthly city are members of the Christian church. The "cities" are eschatological entities: only at the Last Judgment will their defined profiles become clear, like the weeds and the wheat after the harvest. Meanwhile, here in history, they remain inextricably intertwined. "Secular" is precisely the historical existence of the two cities. Even though from the eschatological point of view they are separate from each other, in the *saeculum*, in the time of this world, they cannot be clearly distinguished and separated. The dividing line passes . . . through the freedom of human beings, personal and collective.[92]

Then-Cardinal Bergoglio went on to ask:

Why do I repeat these thoughts of a fifth-century bishop? Because they teach us a way of looking at reality. Human history is the ambiguous field in which various projects are in play, none of which are immaculate from the human point of view. But we should recognize that moving through all of them are both the "unclean love" and the "holy love" of which Saint Augustine wrote. Avoiding any Manichaeism or dualism, it is legitimate to try to discern, on one hand, historical events as "signs of the times," seeds of the kingdom, and, on the other hand, those events that—disconnected from the eschatological end—serve to impede the attainment of the highest destiny of humanity.[93]

92. Jorge Mario Bergoglio, "Parola e amicizia" (2002), in Jorge Mario Bergoglio–Pope Francis, *Nei tuoi occhi è la mia parola: Omelie e discorsi di Buenos Aires 1999–2013* (Milan: Rizzoli, 2016), 144–145.
    93. Ibid., 145.

No human project is "immaculate"; this is Augustine's realism. On the other hand, Bergoglio says, his insight of the two "intertwined" cities allows us to overcome the "Manichaeism or dualism" that stands at the center of every political-religious messianism.

Bergoglio returned to Augustine a year later, in 2003, in a talk called "Education Is Choosing Life." Here he refers to the perspective of *De civitate Dei* in order to help clarify the concept of "utopia." For Bergoglio, utopia cannot be reduced to mere imagination; it is a search for new paths on which to move forward and a critique of the present reality. It is a necessary aspect of every nonconformist vision of politics and society. This model, however, this critical visioning of another world, is subject to two serious limitations. The first is "a certain 'mad' quality, proper to its fantastic or imaginary character, which can change it into a mere dream, an impossible desire, if this dimension is accentuated rather than the practical aspects of its construction."[94] The second limitation is that "in its rejection of the present and desire to establish something new, it can fall into an even more ferocious and intransigent *authoritarianism* than that which it wanted to overcome. How many utopian ideals in the history of humankind have not yielded to every kind of injustice, intolerance, persecution, abuse, and dictatorship?"[95]

In light of these two limits of utopia, the value of the Augustinian perspective becomes clear.

> And here we can return to the reading of *The City of God*. Utopia, such as we know it, is a typically modern construction (if indeed it is rooted in millenarian movements that cut across the second half of the Middle Ages). But Saint Augustine, setting out his outline of the "two cities" (the City of God, ruled by love, and the earthly city, by egoism) inextricably juxtaposed in secular history, offers us some keys for pinning down the relation between change and continuity, which is precisely the critical point of utopian thought and the key to all historical creativity. Indeed, *The City of God* is, in the first place, a criticism of the concept that worshiped political power and

---

94. Jorge Mario Bergolio, *Education for Choosing Life: Proposals for Difficult Times*, trans. Deborah Cole (San Francisco: Ignatius Press, 2014), 13; orig. *Educar, Elegir la Vida: Propuestas por tiempos difíciles* (Buenos Aires: Editorial Claretiana, 2005).

95. Ibid., 13–14.

the status quo. And this was not only a question of the pagans; once Christianity was adopted as the religion of Imperial Rome, it began defining an official theology that sustained this political reality as if it were already the kingdom of God consummated upon earth.[96]

Much like Joseph Ratzinger did in his book *The Unity of the Nations*, Bergoglio, too, uses Augustine's theology of history to oppose the political theologies of the right and the left, symbolized, for Ratzinger, by the Christian-imperial theology of Eusebius of Caesarea and the gnostic-subversive theology of Origen.

In 1971, Ratzinger aimed his criticism at the new political theologies of Metz and Moltmann, both influenced by the "utopian" Marxism of Ernst Bloch. In opposition to these, and from a position to the right of them, Ratzinger cited Augustine. "Augustine," he wrote, "did not attempt to work out what a world that had embraced Christianity would look like. His city of God, to be sure, is not a purely ideal community composed entirely of all the people who believe in God, but neither does it have anything to do with an earthly theocracy, with a world that is established along Christian lines; it is, rather, a sacramental-eschatological entity, which lives in this world as a sign of the coming world."[97]

It is this sacramental-eschatological dimension of the church that explains how "in Augustine . . . the newness that Christianity introduced was evident. His doctrine of two states, or cities, aimed neither at a state dominated by the Church nor at a Church domi-

---

96. Ibid., 14. Fr. Antonio Spadaro clearly captures the "Augustinian" soul of Bergoglio when he writes, "Bergoglio in fact fully embraces the Augustinian critique of a religion understood as 'an essential part of the whole symbolic and imaginary construction' that sustains 'society through a sacralized power.' . . . Bergoglio—in this, he is a keen reader of the great Jesuit theologian Erich Przywara, teacher of Hans Urs von Balthasar—postulates the end of the Constantinian era, radically rejecting the idea of the implementation of the kingdom of God on earth, which was the foundation of the Holy Roman Empire and of all similar political and institutional forms" ("La diplomazia di Francesco: La misericordia come processo politico," *La Civiltà Cattolica* 3975 [February 13, 2016]: 215–216, 218).

97. Joseph Ratzinger, *The Unity of the Nations: A Vision of the Church Fathers*, trans. Boniface Ramsey (Washington, DC: Catholic University of America Press, 2015), 113.

nated by the state. Its goal, rather, was—in the midst of the structures of this world, which remained and indeed had to remain what they were—to offer the new power of faith in the unity of men within the body of Christ as an element of transformation whose ultimate form would be shaped by God himself, when history had finally completed its course."[98] And so "the state remained for him, in all its real or apparent Christianization, an earthly state, and the Church remained an alien community that accepted and used the earthly but was not at home in it."[99] Augustinian eschatology remains both revolutionary and law-abiding:

> While in Origen one does not see how this world is supposed to keep going but must simply be ready for the breakthrough of the *eschaton*, Augustine not only counted on the Roman Empire's continuation but even considered the empire so central to the world-age in which he lived that he wished for its renewal. He remained true to eschatological thinking, however, insofar as he viewed the whole world as provisional and consequently did not attempt to give it a Christian constitution; instead he let it remain as it was and allowed it to struggle with its own relative structure. To that extent the Christianity that was now lawful by intention was also revolutionary in the ultimate sense, since it could not be identified with any state but was, rather, a force that relativized everything that was included in the world.[100]

This image of an Augustine who was both law-abiding and revolutionary resonated well with Bergoglio. In a talk he offered in 2000, titled "Well Planted in the Ground, So as Not to Lose the Way to Heaven," the cardinal archbishop of Buenos Aires carefully described his vision of the "kingdom of God." After criticizing overly optimistic or pessimistic visions of a given moment in history, he outlined a positive realism that transcends the optimist-pessimist categories: "The reality of the world today includes many elements that, if oriented rightly, greatly improve the lives of human beings on earth."[101] These include technology, the emancipation of women,

---

98. Ibid., 112–113.
99. Ibid., 114–115.
100. Ibid., 115–116.
101. Jorge Mario Bergoglio, "Bene piantati per terra, per non perdere la rotta verso il cielo" (2000), in Bergoglio-Francis, *Nei tuoi occhi è la mia parola*, 58.

communications, the progress of medical science, and social well-being. "Still we cannot naively ignore the dangers present in the current circumstances: dehumanization, serious social and international conflicts, the exclusion and death of multitudes. . . . The pessimism of the apocalypticists is not without foundation."[102]

This ambiguity, which points to the limits of the modern expectation of progress, challenges us to consider the relationship between eschatology and history. In a clear reference to the brand of liberation theology influenced by Marxism, Bergoglio wrote, "In recent times many Christians had the idea that the presence of the Kingdom could generate, through the historical commitment, a real, concrete anticipation of the new world to come. A better society, more just and more human, that was to seem like a sort of first draft or prelude to what was to come at the end of time. Even more, these Christians believed that their actions could really 'anticipate' the coming of the Kingdom, since the Lord had left in our hands the possibility of completing his work. But things did not go as they had hoped."[103] As a result, "the effort to bring about the utopia was followed by a resignation to accept the internal and external conditions. Striving for what was desirable was reduced to doing what was possible. The promises did not come true. On the contrary, they turned out to be only an illusion. We should ask ourselves whether the current disinterest among young people in politics and for other collective projects is related to this experience of frustration."[104] *Today's disenchantment is the result of a historical process, a backlash against utopias that have failed to fulfill their promises.* "Postmodern individualism and aestheticism, if not pragmatism and a certain contemporary cynicism, are the result of the fall of historical certainties, of the loss of any sense that human action is able to construct something that is objectively and concretely better. Even in the case of some Christians, this takes the form of merely 'living the moment' (even if it were the 'moment' of spiritual experience), waiting passively for the Kingdom to 'fall' from the sky."[105]

102. Ibid.
103. Ibid., 60.
104. Ibid.
105. Ibid., 61.

This Christian pessimism, which implies inertia and disinterest in the fate of the world, has no justification from the point of view of Christian faith and hope.

> But does the postmodern disenchantment—present not only in politics, but also in culture, the arts, and daily life—in fact carry along with it some presage of hope founded on the expectation of the Kingdom? Or, on the contrary, does the idea of the Kingdom that begins among us, the nucleus of the preaching and the ministry of Jesus, and an intimate but not intimistic experience among believers after his Resurrection, still have something to say at this time? Is there, beyond those perhaps too linear identifications, any relationship between the theological message of the Kingdom and the concrete history in which we humans are immersed and for which we are responsible?[106]

This relationship, beyond a linear continuity between history and the fulfillment of the kingdom, Bergoglio says, exists.

> Just as for the vast majority of people, individual fulfillment (the definitive personal encounter with God and transfiguration in the Resurrection) happens through a terrible moment of discontinuity, failure, and destruction—that is, through death—so there is no reason to think that the same sort of process mustn't happen in the case of history as a whole. And here we see the truth of the apocalyptic mentality: this world will pass; there is no final fulfillment without some kind of destruction and loss, although we do not know in advance exactly what kind. But on the other hand, it is not true that there will be no continuity. Just as I know that I myself will be resurrected, so we can say that there will be the same humanity, the same creation, the same history, all transfigured in the fullness of time! Continuity and discontinuity. A mysterious reality of presence-absence, of the "already" fulfillment of promises but "not yet" in a full way.[107]

In his 2000 text, Bergoglio makes clear his embrace of the Pauline-Augustinian model, the paradigm of "already" and "not yet." The

---

106. Ibid., 60.
107. Ibid., 61.

polar tension between awaiting the *parousia* and working in the world is the nature of the Christian's existence in history.

The *Pueblo Fiel* as Theological Source

On one hand, a commitment to work within history for the common good and for the protection of the poor; on the other, an awareness that the kingdom is realized in the world through the designs of God: this is the polar tension that dominates Bergoglio's thought throughout the 1960s and 1970s. For him, there is no resolution of this tension. In the *contradiction* between revolutionary messianism and the anticommunist crusade of men in uniform, antinomian thought sees an endless tragedy. It was a tragedy that divided the very Jesuit order of which Bergoglio is a member. *It is in this division, played out in a specific historical context, that his thought takes shape.* It happened, as Ivereigh points out, in three particular moments.

The first was the reform of the academic program at Colegio Máximo in Buenos Aires that Bergoglio carried out in 1976, during his tenure as rector there.

> He reintroduced the juniorate (the one- or two-year grounding in arts and humanities) and restored the separation of philosophy and theology to replace what he described in his 1990 letter to Don Bruno as "the mélange of philosophy and theology called 'curriculum' in which they began by studying Hegel [sic]." Bergoglio's new juniorate was a chance to root students in Jesuit and Argentine traditions, rather than foreign models. The studies included not just the European classics but also courses in Argentine literature—from *El Gaucho Martín Fierro* to Borges. History was revisionist, restoring the Catholic, Hispanic, and early-Jesuit elements in Argentina's past that were ignored or scorned in liberal history. Bergoglio wanted the Jesuits to value popular religious traditions alongside high culture, to know about gauchos and caudillos as well as railways and telegraphs.[108]

Bergoglio's reform sought to restore a place of dignity to the country's own historical-cultural background, which had become

---

108. Ivereigh, *The Great Reformer*, 140.

somewhat lost in the shadows of the sociology that—fueled by the modernizing, Americanizing, and Marxist currents—had established a certain dominance. He also rejected the confusion between theology and philosophy, the natural and the supernatural, which, as we have seen, was the basis of Gutiérrez's new liberation theology. Finally, he reacted against the hegemony of Hegel and the Hegelianism that was common to philosophical studies in the 1970s. It was a hegemony that logically concluded in Marxism.

The attention Bergoglio's program gave to "popular religious tradition" was not a matter of folklore or archaizing inclinations. It was strongly influenced by the *teología del pueblo* that was the most significant contribution of the Rio de la Plata School to liberation theology. Following this theology, the second point of the Bergoglio reform called for the students at the Máximo to go to into the neighborhoods to play with the children, to teach the catechism, and to understand better the problems faced by the families there. "The concrete service of the poor in weekend missions in the local neighborhoods would connect the Jesuit students to the *santo pueblo fiel de Dios* and keep them rooted in reality."[109] Immersion into this reality reflected the missionary vision that called for the unity of theory and praxis, formulated in Christian rather than Marxist terms. It was marked by the preferential option for the poor that had been embraced by the Latin American church at the Medellín Conference of 1968.

To these two points of reform, Bergoglio added a third: a return to the sources of the spirituality of Ignatius of Loyola, the founder of the Jesuits. During his own theological studies at the Colegio Máximo, between 1967 and 1970, Bergoglio had become close to his philosophy professor, Father Miguel Ángel Fiorito, an advocate of the restoration of the original method of doing the *Spiritual Exercises*. For the young student that lesson had a special value. It brought out Bergoglio's interior, "mystical" side, a side that reacted to the anthropological and naturalistic reduction of Christian commitment in the world as it was articulated by the new political theologies. The *primerea* of the grace of the Spirit over works and rules, of which he would speak as pope, has its premise in the

109. Ibid., 141.

conviction that the Christian is more active the more he becomes passive with respect to the presence and action of God.

The purpose of the three qualifying points of the Bergoglio reform was therefore evident. It was a response to the sociological and praxist drift that was transforming both the Jesuit order and the church, dragging them into a lethal conflict within a divided society. The reform sought to recenter the faith upon the Gospel while at the same time avoiding the spiritualistic flight from the world by a church that was too submissive to the wishes of the government and the military. The three points had, as a premise, two qualifying factors. The first was the concept of the "faithful people"; the second was the theory of the four principles—which at the time appeared to be three—of reality.

Regarding the first, Bergoglio, as we have noted, was indebted to the *teología del pueblo* that, in Argentina, included theologians and thinkers like Lucio Gera, Rafael Tello, Justino O'Farrell, Gerardo Farrel, Fernando Boasso, and Juan Carlos Scannone.[110] Among these, Lucio Gera (1924–2012) played a leading role.[111] Scannone,

110. On the theology of the people and Pope Francis, cf. Juan Carlos Scannone, "Papa Francesco e la teologia del popolo," *Civiltà Cattolica* 3930 (March 15, 2014): 571–590; Scannone, *La teología del pueblo: Raíces teológicas del papa Francisco* (Maliaño: Editorial Sal Terrae, 2017); Rafael Luciani, *Pope Francis and the Theology of the People*, trans. Phillip Berryman (Maryknoll: Orbis Books, 2017); Carlos Maria Galli, ed., *El pueblo de Dios, el pueblo y los pueblos: El papa Francisco y la teología argentina*, a conference presented at the Istituto di Studi Politici S. Pio V, Rome, January 26–27, 2017, http://www.americalatina.va/content/americalatina/es/articulos/el-pueblo-de-dios--el-pueblo-y-los-pueblos--el-papa-francisco-y-.html.

111. Lucio Gera (1924–2012), after studying at Bonn, became professor of dogmatic theology at Universidad Católica Argentina in Buenos Aires. A member of the editorial board of the journal *Teología*, he was a *peritus* at the Second Vatican Council, theological *peritus* at Medellín, editor of the Argentine episcopate's San Miguel Declaration, and finally a *peritus* at Puebla. On his thought, cf. Lucio Gera, *La teología argentina del pueblo* (Santiago de Chile: Centro Teólogico Manuel Larrain, 2015); Gera, *Chiesa, teologia e liberazione in America Latina* (Bologna: EDB, 2015). The volume offers translations of two articles: "Pueblo, religión del pueblo y iglesia" and "La iglesia frente a la situación de dependencia." The afterword by Scannone summarizes his article "Lucio Gera: un teologo 'dal' popolo," *La Civiltà Cattolica* 3954

a Jesuit, has characterized the genesis of the Argentine theology of the people in this way:

> After returning home from the Second Vatican Council, the Argentine episcopate created, in 1966, COEPAL (the Bishops' Commission on Pastoral Ministry), with the aim of creating a national pastoral plan. It included bishops, theologians, pastoral leaders, men and women religious (including Gera and Tello, mentioned above), diocesan priests, and professors of the Buenos Aires faculty of theology; it also included Justino O'Farrell (formerly from the Congregation of Don Orione), Gerardo Farrel (specialist in the social doctrine of the Church), the Jesuit Fernando Boasso (from the Center for Research and Social Action), and others. This commission became the ground from which the theology of the people germinated. Its influence was clear, as already noted, in the Argentine episcopate's San Miguel Declaration (1969), which applied to the church in that country the principles and conclusions of the Medellín Conference, especially document VI on pastoral care of the people. Though COEPAL ceased to exist in early 1973, some of its members continued to meet as a group for theological reflection under the leadership of Father Gera. He worked as an expert at Medellín and Puebla; his theology was more oral than written, though some of his important writings were collected, and many of his comments were recorded and later transcribed. Later I participated in these meetings, together with Gera, Farrel, Boasso, the vicar of Buenos Aires at the time, Msgr. Joaquín Sucunza, Alberto Methol Ferré, who came from Uruguay, and others.[112]

We can say, then, that the occasion that led to the development of the theology of the people was the establishment of COEPAL by the Argentine bishops, and its first document was the San Miguel Declaration.

(2015): 539–550. For an exhaustive study on his thought, cf. R. Ferrara and C. M. Galli, eds., *Presente y futuro de la teología en Argentina: Homenaje a Lucio Gera* (Buenos Aires: Paulinas–Facultad de Teología, 1997). The collected works of Lucio Gera are found at: Virginia Azcuy, Carlos Galli, Marcelo González, and José Caamaño, eds., *Escritos teológicos-pastorales de Lucio Gera*, 2 vols. (Buenos Aires: Ágape–Facultad de Teología, 2006–2007).

112. Scannone, "Papa Francesco e la teologia del popolo," 572.

One part of the document, written by Father Lucio Gera, was the genesis of a peculiarly Argentine version of post-Medellín theology that strongly influenced Bergoglio and other Jesuits around him. While it called for justice, deplored oppression and exploitation, and stood up for the rights of workers, the document rejected Marxism as "alien not only to Christianity, but also to the spirit of our people." This was certainly not a conservative, pre-conciliar view. But nor did it frame *el pueblo* in sociological or Marxist terms, as liberation theology was then doing. The San Miguel declaration saw the people as active agents of their own history; startlingly, it asserted that "the activity of the Church should not only be oriented toward the people but also primarily derive *from* the people." The vision of San Miguel was of a Church with a clear option for the poor, but understood as radical identification with the ordinary people as subjects of their own history, rather than as a "class" engaged in a social struggle with other classes. Bergoglio shared that San Miguel vision.[113]

The theology of the people was not a "conservative" alternative to liberation theology, but a liberation theology without Marxism. As Scannone would recall:

In 1982 there were four currents of Latin American liberation theology. Among these was the theology of the people, a name introduced pejoratively by Juan Luis Segundo, but then adopted by Sebastian Politi, one of its proponents. Gutiérrez described it as "a current with its own characteristics within liberation theology," and Roberto Oliveros, recognizing it as a version of liberation theology, defined it disparagingly as a "populist theology." Such descriptions were later accepted by liberation theologians such as João Batista Libânio, and by its critics, such as Methol Ferré and Msgr. Antonio Quarracino, in the presentation of the [Congregation for the Doctrine of the Faith's] Instruction *Libertatis nuntius*.[114]

In his article, Scannone referred to a 1982 article by Methol Ferré that distinguished between two currents of liberation theology. Methol wrote:

113. Ivereigh, *The Great Reformer*, 95–96.
114. Scannone, "Papa Francesco e la teologia del popolo," 576–577.

It was the Peruvian Gustavo Gutiérrez who introduced the term "liberation theology." He is also the principal architect of the union between theology and Marxism. But there is another important version of liberation theology, intensely opposed to the theology of secularization. It is linked to the rise in Argentina of a vast national and popular movement that would culminate with the return of Perón. There, starting from Medellín, pastoral care of the people deepened and the redemption of popular religiosity began, putting it in a close relationship with the problem of liberation. Lucio Gera is the most typical expression of it. These two tendencies of liberation theology represented, in their interpretations, a growing opposition and came to have a wide range of expressions and intermediate positions in Latin America.[115]

In fact, Gutiérrez's revised 1988 edition of *Liberation Theology* included an entirely reworked section on "Faith and Social Conflict" that explicitly acknowledged the author's appreciation of the theology of the people. In the new introduction, titled "Expanding the View," Gutiérrez admitted that in the seventeen years that had passed since the publication of the first edition, his understanding of the poor and their world had changed considerably. "For myself," he wrote, "this has been the most important (and even crushing) experience of these past years. The world of the poor is a universe

---

115. Alberto Methol Ferré, "Da Rio de Janeiro a Puebla: 25 anni di storia," *Incontri: Testimonianze dall'America Latina* 4, January–February 1982, 22. Cf. also "La Chiesa, popolo fra i popoli," in Alberto Methol Ferré, *Il risorgimento cattolico latinoamericano*, Italian trans. P. Di Pauli and C. Perfetti (Bologna: CSEO, 1983), 157–158. In his introduction to this volume, which is a collection of previously published articles translated into Italian, Methol, referring to his 1976 article, "Quadro storico della religiosità popolare" (pp. 166–190 in the book), wrote, "The recovery of 'popular religiosity' began in 1969 with Rio de la Plata, especially thanks to the Argentine theologian Lucio Gera. On one occasion, Segundo Galilee—one of the propellers of the iconoclast wave of the 1960s—told me that he believed that the first rehabilitation of the people's religion against secularist attacks had been formulated in my article on historical periods. The recovery of popular religiosity led the church inexorably toward the problem of Latin American culture, overcoming the usual exclusively socioeconomic approaches, which ignored and left behind the ethos and the history of our peoples" (16).

in which the socio-economic aspect is basic but not all-inclusive. In the final analysis, poverty means death: lack of food and housing, the inability to attend properly to health and education needs, the exploitation of workers. . . . At the same time, it is important to realize that being poor is a way of living, thinking, loving, praying, believing, and hoping."[116]

Gutiérrez's acknowledgment of this second dimension is the new one. "The economic dimension itself will take on a new character once we see things from the cultural point of view; the converse will also certainly be true."[117] This perspective allows him to recognize the value of the religious dimension of the culture of a people, which he had previously neglected and, in thinking marked by the Enlightenment, judged to be a sort of premodern residue. It is a dimension that involves prayer, an intense aspect of the lives of many among the poor.

> Christian life is commitment in the form of an acceptance of the gift of the reign of God. It is also, and necessarily, prayer. There is no life of faith that does not have its contemplative dimension. The Latin Americans who are struggling for justice are also persons who believe and hope. They are oppressed persons, but also Christians who, like Mary in her Magnificat, remember their obligations of thankfulness and of surrender to God in prayer.
>
> This outlook is characteristic of the faith of our Latin Americans. They cultivate a form of prayer that the modern mind is likely to regard as primitive if not downright superstitious. . . . Deeply rooted as it is in this popular devotion, while also drawing nourishment from the wellspring of protest against oppression and the demand for freedom, the prayer life of the Christian communities that are engaged in the process of liberation possesses great creativity and depth. Those who have claimed from time to time that Latin America has been losing the spirit of prayer have shown only that they themselves are remote from the everyday life of the poor and committed sectors of our peoples.[118]

116. Gutiérrez, *A Theology of Liberation*, rev. ed., xxi.
117. Ibid., xxv.
118. Ibid., xxxi.

It was a new conclusion that overturned the previously pro-Marxist theoretical stance of the original liberation theology and put it more in tune with the Argentine *teología del pueblo*: "What we see here is an authentic spirituality—that is, a way of being Christian. It is from this rich experience of the following of Jesus that liberation theology emerges; the following constitutes the practice—at once commitment and prayer—on which liberation theology reflects."[119] This, noting "the necessary and fruitful links between orthopraxis and orthodoxy,"[120] now openly recognizes the primacy of faith over works: "The ultimate norms of judgment come from the revealed truth that we accept by faith and not from praxis itself."[121]

The preface to the 1988 edition of *Liberation Theology* outlined the conditions for an encounter with the *teología del pueblo*. Gutiérrez now recognized the importance of popular belief, prayer, and dialogue with Latin American culture in its concrete expressions, and he turned away from Marxism's primacy of praxis and revolutionary (counter)violence. This shift by Gutiérrez is important. It confirmed that the theology of the people was rightly understood as a form of liberation theology and that popular devotion, freed from "devotionalism" and the prejudices of an Enlightenment point of view, is a legitimate *locus theologicus*, proof of a distinctly Latin-American enculturation of faith.[122] In his opening speech to the Provincial Congregation of the Argentine Jesuits on February 18, 1974, Bergoglio observed:

119. Ibid., xxxii.
120. Ibid., xxxiv.
121. Ibid.
122. Francis writes in his apostolic exhortation *Evangelii Gaudium*: "Underlying popular piety, as a fruit of the inculturated Gospel, is an active evangelizing power which we must not underestimate: to do so would be to fail to recognize the work of the Holy Spirit. Instead, we are called to promote and strengthen it, in order to deepen the never-ending process of inculturation. Expressions of popular piety have much to teach us; for those who are capable of reading them, they are a locus theologicus which demands our attention, especially at a time when we are looking to the new evangelization" (n. 126). On "the evangelizing power of popular piety," cf. nn. 122–126 of the document.

What is more significant, however, is the recognition of the reserve of religiosity that the *faithful people* possess, which we Argentine Jesuits are coming to understand. I would like to express what this reality, the *faithful people*, means to me personally. By *faithful people* I mean simply the people who make up the faithful, the ones with whom we have so much contact in our priestly ministry and religious witness. It is clear that now, among us, "people" has become an ambiguous term because of the ideological assumptions with which this reality is discussed and perceived. Here, however, I repeat, I mean to refer simply to the *faithful people*. When I was studying theology, when, like you, I reviewed Denzinger and the treatises to prepare my thesis, I was very struck by a formula of the Christian tradition: the *faithful people* are infallible "*in credendo*," in belief. From this I have drawn my own personal formula, which is not very precise but it helps me a lot: when you want to know *what* Mother Church believes, turn to the Magisterium, since it has the role of teaching it in an infallible way; but when you want to know *how* the church believes, turn to the *faithful people*. The Magisterium will teach you who Mary is, but our *faithful people* will teach you how to love Mary. Our people have a soul, and when we speak of a people's soul, we also speak of a hermeneutic, a way of seeing reality, a knowledge. In our Argentine people I see a strong awareness of their own dignity. It is a historical understanding the personality of which is not derived from an economic system (for example, the Argentine people could not be recognized through the "abstract" categories of bourgeoisie and proletariat), but which was developed through a series of milestones. It is not the fruit of a "theory" but of a life that is Christian in its roots.[123]

This acknowledgment by Bergoglio is important. It shows how the category of the *pueblo fiel* is distinctly separate from both the *populist ideologies* and the Marxist system, which is fixed to the

123. Jorge Mario Bergoglio, "Una istituzione che vive il suo carisma: Discorso di apertura della Congregazione provincial" (San Miguel, Buenos Aires, February 18, 1974), in Jorge Mario Bergoglio, *Pastorale sociale*, ed. Marco Gallo, Italian trans. A. Taroni (Milan: Jaca Book, 2015), 236–237. On the people as "infallible *in credendo*," cf. also Jorge Mario Bergoglio, "La gioia dell'evangelizzazione" (2005), in Bergoglio-Francis, *Nei tuoi occhi è la mia parola*, 330. See also Pope Francis, apostolic exhortation *Evangelii Gaudium* 119, https://w2.vatican.va/content/francesco/en/apost_exhortations/documents/papa-francesco_esortazione-ap_20131124_evangelii-gaudium.html.

"abstract" categories of the bourgeoisie and the proletariat. The concept of the believing people refers for him to the *historical* ways that faith animates life, reality, culture. It points to the *how* of the incarnation. It is not a question of academic sociology but of the historical, lived terrain that nourishes the faith of the church. It is *the place of a hermeneutic of symbols*: "If it is true that we recognize ourselves in our symbols, our people are a fertile nursery for such recognition. *Our people who are faithful* to the teaching—the people who baptize their children, who love Mary, who are not ashamed of the cross and who are able to see in it the wood that becomes a staff of shepherding and accompaniment and the tree that bears fruits of eternity."[124] The institutional church does more than give to the people; it also receives from the people. For this reason—Bergoglio would later say as pope, recalling the lesson of Lucio Gera—"it is only when we start from the affective connaturality that love supplies that we can appreciate the theological life present in the piety of the Christian people, especially in that of the poor."[125]

The theme of popular piety passes through that of spirituality and becomes theological. The Christian faith of the people is a theological source, a hermeneutical *locus* of lived, enculturated faith. *Popular spirituality is culture, an organic web that links together all aspects of existence.* As the Puebla Document affirmed, "The Catholic wisdom of the common people is capable of fashioning a vital synthesis. It creatively combines the divine and the human, Christ and Mary, spirit and body, communion and institution, person and community, faith and homeland, intelligence and emotion. This wisdom is a Christian humanism that radically affirms the dignity of every person as a child of God, establishes a basic fraternity, teaches people how to encounter nature and understand work, and provides reasons for joy and humor even in the midst of a very hard life."[126] Commenting on this passage, Bergoglio wrote,

124. Jorge Mario Bergoglio, "Fede e giustizia nell'apostolato dei gesuiti" (1976), in Bergoglio, *Pastorale sociale*, 249.

125. Pope Francis, *Evangelii Gaudium*, n. 125.

126. "Final Document," Third General Conference of the Latin American Episcopate, in John Eagleson and Philip Scharper, eds., *Puebla and Beyond* (Maryknoll: Orbis Books, 1979), 185, n. 448.

The tensions mentioned by Puebla—the divine and the human, spirit and body, communion and institution, faith and country, intelligence and affection—are universal. The *vital* synthesis, the creative union of these tensions, inexpressible in words because it would require all of them, in short, this symbolic and living nucleus—which for our people translates into "proper names" like Guadalupe and Luján, into pilgrim faith, into gestures of blessing and solidarity, into offerings and into songs and dances . . . —this heart with which and thanks to which our people love and believe, is the theological place with which the preacher must be vitally connected.[127]

The heart of the people is the vital synthesis of the tensions of life embraced by the Spirit, a theological locus. No theory, no doctrinism, has the right to ignore this heart. "For this reason," Bergoglio said in 1974,

> our most authentic projects of liberation must favor *unity* over conflict; the enemy divides in order to reign. At stake is the project of a nation and not the establishment of a *class*. . . . This *faithful people* does not separate its Christian faith from its historical expressions, nor mix them up in a revolutionary messianism. This people believes in resurrection and in life; it baptizes its children and buries its dead. Our people pray, and what do they ask for? They ask for health, work, bread, family harmony; and for the nation, they ask for peace. Some will think there is nothing revolutionary about that. But a people that asks for peace knows perfectly well that peace is the fruit of justice.[128]

Here Bergoglio expressed, in passing, one of his four theoretical principles: *unity is superior to conflict*. He did so in the context of the need to safeguard the unity of a people against those who instigate division. The *teología del pueblo* maintained the fundamental values of liberation theology—the preferential option for the poor and the struggle for justice—while rejecting its violent aspect, bor-

127. Bergoglio, "La gioia dell'evangelizzazione," 333.
128. Bergoglio, "Una istituzione che vive il suo carisma," 237–238.

rowed from Marxist doctrine.[129] In fact, thanks to the Rio de la Plata school, whose conclusions were adopted by Pope Paul VI in *Evangelii Nuntiandi* (1975) and, through it, appeared in the Final Document of the Puebla Conference (1979), the theme of popular piety fully became a part of Latin American theology: "From this perspective we can consider popular piety as one of the few expressions, without discarding others, of the Latin American cultural synthesis that runs through all of its eras and which, at the same time, covers all its dimensions: work, production, places of settlement, lifestyles, language and artistic expression, political organization, daily life. And precisely in its role as repository of cultural identity, it has confronted the intentions of modernity aimed at subordinating particular cultures to the demands of reason."[130]

129. "The theology of the people does not neglect the social conflicts that Latin America experiences, even if in its interpretation of 'people' it favors unity beyond the conflict (priorities later repeatedly affirmed by Bergoglio). Thus, although not by assuming the class struggle as the 'determining hermeneutical principle' for understanding society and history, it nonetheless confers a historical place to the conflict—even of class, conceiving it from the prior unity of the people. Thus institutional and structural injustice is understood as betrayal of the people by a part of the people themselves, which becomes anti-people" (Scannone, "Papa Francesco e la teologia del popolo," 574–575).

130. Jorge Mario Bergoglio, "Cultura e religiosità popolare" (2008), in Bergoglio-Francis, *Nei tuoi occhi è la mia parola*, 584. Cf. also Bergoglio's preface to Enrique Ciro Bianchi, *Introduzione alla teologia del popolo*, 13–22.

A Philosophy of Polarity

The Society of Jesus as Synthesis of Oppositions

We have seen how Bergoglio, as a young provincial of the Argentine Jesuits, formulated the *first* of the fundamental principles of his thought: *unity is superior to conflict*. It was conceived in the context of the violent dialectical opposition that divided both the church and society in Argentina in the 1970s. This was not a facile effort to find a "middle ground" between the two opposing sides. Rather, it attempted to offer a different point of view, one that, without ignoring tensions and problems, avoided the fragmentation of the people's unity. In a 1974 text, Bergoglio referred to "fruitless clashes with the hierarchy, destructive conflicts between 'wings' (for example, between the 'progressive' and the 'reactionary') within the Church . . . in essence, all those things in which we 'absolutize' what is secondary, which we seat on a 'great throne of fire and smoke,' giving, in the end, more importance to the parts than to the whole."[1]

We see here a reference to a *second* principle that took shape for Bergoglio: *the whole is superior to the parts*. This arose as a critical response to the tragedy of his time. He concluded that the only way for the Christian follower of Ignatius to escape the polarization of the present moment in history was to accept the "ever greater God" and the plan of God that is always greater than any of our own

1. Jorge Mario Bergoglio, "Una istituzione che vive il suo carisma: Discorso di apertura della Congregazione provincial" (San Miguel, Buenos Aires, February 18, 1974), in Jorge Mario Bergoglio, *Pastorale sociale*, ed. Marco Gallo, Italian trans. A. Taroni (Milan: Jaca Book, 2015), 234.

"projects."[2] This perspective points to *the principle of unity*, which aims not to eliminate contrasts but rather refuses to absolutize them. Bergoglio wrote, "Unity is not achieved through a spiritualist 'abstractionism' (that is, the temptation to build unity by avoiding real conflict), nor through a 'functionalist' methodology (which pretends to seek unity through means divorced from their ends), nor through a 'pseudo-opening of horizons' that would pretend to minimize our problems, as if the universality (*'versus in unum,'* as this very important word for both the Society and the church implies) could be achieved through a 'Rotary-like' internationalism."[3]

For Bergoglio, there were temptations to be overcome: "a sometimes 'ethicistic' position; a propensity toward 'elitism'; a fascination for 'abstract' ideologies that, despite our wishes, do not coincide with reality."[4] He called for a decisive "return to reality," to the category of the possible, against the fascination of revolutionary ideology and the attempt by "elitist" avant-gardes to change the world. And here we find the seed of another principle: *reality is superior to ideas.*

At the same time, Bergoglio did not theorize a unity without conflict, an authoritarian unity imposed from above, like that demanded by military-led governments. Unity is, as we have seen, always the result of a tension that can only be resolved by a synthesis that transcends conflict and finds resolution between its poles. Through his consideration of his own historical circumstances, Bergoglio proceeded, *for the first time,* to articulate the principles that, from this point on, would constitute the core of his thinking: "The fundamental *criteria* for carrying out these processes and that must inspire our work are: unity is superior to conflict; the whole is superior to the parts; time is superior to space. Only in this way can we also achieve a *unity of action.*"[5]

At this point, there are three principles. A fourth—"reality is superior to ideas"—would be added in 1980 (though, as noted

---

2. In one note on this point (p. 235, n. 1), Bergoglio cited Erich Przywara, *Teologúmeno español* (Madrid: Ediciones Cristianidad, 1962), 115–150.

3. Bergoglio, "Una istituzione che vive il suo carisma," 235.

4. Ibid., 236.

5. Ibid., 238.

above, it is present already in Bergoglio's critique of revolutionary abstraction that puts the idea, the ideology, before reality).

For Bergoglio, the relevance of these principles is illustrated by a document of significance in the history of Argentina. On December 20, 1834, the powerful governor of the province of Buenos Aires, Juan Manuel de Rosas, wrote a letter to a caudillo of the La Rioja province, Facundo Quiroga, on the organization of the Argentine nation, from the hacienda of Figueroa in San Antonio de Areco.[6] Bergoglio's reading of the letter, which arises from his strong interest in history, confirmed for him that the principles were useful for solving the problems of the moment. The doctrine of principles— which Bergoglio recognized in de Rosas's letter—assumes its relevance as a response to the polarization of Argentina in the 1970s.

The first two—"unity is superior to conflict" and "the whole is superior to the parts"—are criteria of *synthesis* and are intended to foster social and political peace. "This is why our most authentic efforts at liberation must favor *unity* over conflict; the enemy divides in order to reign. At stake is the project of a nation and not the establishment of a *class*."[7] The third principle—"time is superior to space"—indicates the method for arriving at synthesis, that is, the importance accorded to processes over the desire for domination that calls for the occupation of spaces. The fourth principle, at this point only present potentially—"reality is superior to ideas"—was intended to oppose the abstractness of ideologies and, subsequently, to oppose gnosis in general. As Bergoglio said in 1976, after the assassination of three priests and two seminarians in Buenos Aires: "We are divided because our commitment to people has been replaced by a commitment to systems and ideologies. We have forgotten the meaning of people, concrete people with all their historical experiences and clear aspirations. We must not listen to the call of

6. Cf. Juan Carlos Scannone, "Papa Francesco e la teologia del popolo," *Civiltà Cattolica* 3930 (March 15, 2014): 582. The letter is found in Enrique Barba, *Correspondencia entre Rosas, Quiroga y López* (Buenos Aires: Hyspamérica, 1984), 94ff. An English translation of key excepts is found in Gabriela Nouzeilles and Graciela Montaldo, eds., *The Argentina Reader: Politics, Culture, and Society* (Durham: Duke University Press, 2002), "The Caudillo's Order," trans. Patricia Owen Steiner, 75–79.

7. Bergoglio, "Una istituzione che vive il suo carisma," 237.

systematic ideologies that manipulate people based on their interests. The human person, who is the origin, subject, and goal of every institution, has been absorbed and manipulated by them."[8]

The four principles, therefore, have a synthetic and realistic value. For Bergoglio, they must guide the action of the church and of the Society of Jesus. *Their relevance becomes clear when, in 1976, Bergoglio reconsiders them in the context of an oppositional, antinomian conception of reality.* The young provincial became convinced that the Society of Jesus could serve as a catalyst for a synthesis of the opposites that then divided Argentina and Latin America. In a 1976 text on "Faith and Justice in the Apostolate of Jesuits," Bergoglio wrote, "The Ignatian vision is the possibility of harmonizing opposites, of inviting to a common table concepts that seem irreconcilable, because it brings them to a higher plane where they can find their synthesis."[9] Such synthesis was the fruit of the Ignatian conception of historical memory: "In the end, when St. Ignatius mentions memory, *a conception of unity* is in play. It is therefore possible to synthesize in unity the diversity of the times. This is what happened in our land: the Jesuits came to you with a great history, sixteen centuries of church, and with a very clear position regarding the religious problematic that was debated at the time in Europe, and they made a synthesis with the era of our natives. That synthesis was history."[10] This synthesis was the encounter of Spaniards and the natives of the Americas, an encounter whose history includes lights and shadows, but one that that Bergoglio intends to affirm despite the strong indigenist ideology of the 1970s.

> The subsequent history of the Jesuits will then be marked by a unity capable of shaping the synthesis of opposites. Unity through reduction is relatively easy but not lasting. More difficult is to forge a unity that does not annul differences or reduce conflict. It is the search for this latter unity that marks the Society's work of evangelization. It

8. Jorge Mario Bergoglio, "Testimonianza di sangue," in Bergoglio, *Pastorale sociale*, 243.

9. Jorge Mario Bergoglio, "Fede e giustizia nell'apostolato dei gesuiti," in Bergoglio, *Pastorale sociale*, 246.

10. Ibid.

chose the Indian, a viable project of justice, without forgetting the instruction of the Spaniards and the Creoles of the cities. It brought to these lands the Spanish predilection for baroque art, but with the Americans—who, according to Carpentier, were already baroque even in their geography—produced an art that, while clearly bearing Spanish origins, displayed at the same time an American originality. Responding to the Enlightenment, which gave birth to the pseudo-unity of Europe based on a kind of reason that was blind to transcendence, the Society transmitted the Gospel without rationalism or ingenuity, but with a solid intellectual foundation harmonized with fidelity to revelation and the magisterium of the church. If, on the one hand, it avoided subjectivist mysticism, on the other it knew how to nourish the people with a simple devotion, not at all lacking in affective elements. Nor did it fear, in guiding consciences, to be judged laxist and casuist, succeeding in synthesizing the traditional morality of the body of the church with concrete existence. It is this fidelity to a charism of discernment that the Jansenist rigidity has never been able to understand.[11]

This passage illustrates Bergoglio's thought. It demonstrates his vision of the Society of Jesus as an encounter, a dialogue, and a synthesis among peoples. It highlights the difference between the abstract universalism of Enlightenment reason and the concrete universalism of Catholicism that takes real people, including the dimension of the heart, into account. It notes the relevance of the seventeenth-century controversy between the moral reflection of the Jesuits, always attentive to the concrete, and the rigid and inhuman one of the disciples of Jansen. At the center lies the idea of *"a unity that does not annul differences or reduce conflict."*[12] It is a unity in tension that recognizes the value of *polarity*, rejecting resolution through *contradiction*. Although Bergoglio's doctrine of polarity is not yet theoretically formulated, it is already essentially present. *Unity that does not destroy diversity* is already a dialectical concept that, unlike Hegel's, concludes in a synthesis not reached simply through reason but through a higher principle provided by God who is "ever greater." Such a synthesis always represents an

11. Ibid., 246–247.
12. Ibid., 246. Emphasis mine.

encounter between grace and nature, God and the human person, otherness and freedom. The discovery, in the 1960s, of dialectical tension as the soul of Ignatius's *Exercises* now assumes all its value in relation to the commitment of the Christian in the world. The Christian is called to be a source of unity in the divisions of history, to bring to the tragedies of a given time the presence of the "ever greater" God.

Catholic universality is polyphonic. It is capable of integrating differences without annulling them, because it is based on transcendence. This is a rejection of Hegel's immanent universality, despite its intention to distance itself from the abstractionism of the Enlightenment, to resolve-dissolve the reality of the "particular."[13] The Society of Jesus, in an intellectual confrontation with modern Idealism, is called to carry out a historical synthesis between past and future, between immanence and transcendence: "Remembrance of the past and having the courage to open new spaces to God are united solidly in the Society, knowing that domes can never be raised if solid foundations are not built first. In other words, the goal of drawing together all things in Christ—that is to say, in the universality of the church—cannot be accomplished in the absence of a transcendence that paradoxically recognizes the topography of the various immanences called to be drawn together and transcended."[14]

The universal-particular, the "concrete," arises from the transcendence that integrates and unifies the immanent pluriformity of multiples. It represents an antinomy that the Jesuits live as *tension between Catholic universality and particular inculturation.* As Bergoglio said in 1980, "Both of these realities guarantee that we stand firmly on the frontier, which is typical of us Jesuits. Universality gives us horizons that go beyond the limits of localism; inculturation forces us to take seriously the 'space' that has been entrusted to us. These realities constitute an antinomy. A province that has a 'localist' mindset has already begun to die because it lives far from the border. A province that lives universality without seeking any kind of inculturation confuses Jesuit universalism with an abstract

---

13. Cf. Massimo Borghesi, *L'era dello Spirito: Secolarizzazione ed escatologia moderna* (Rome: Studium, 2008), 73–113.

14. Bergoglio, "Fede e giustizia nell'apostolato dei gesuiti," 247.

spiritualism."[15] *Here Bergoglio offers us the map to understanding the genesis of one of his polar pairs, globalization and localization.* It is an antinomy that the Jesuit conscience knows well.

Bergoglio reaffirmed this antinomian and dialectical vision of the presence of the Christian in the world in his opening address of the provincial congregation of 1978. Here the leader of the Jesuits in Argentina suggested that "*an indication* that we are well grounded in the Lord is that we are able to *maintain the antinomies* that constitute *being Jesuit,* and that classically are summarized in the formula 'contemplative in action.' "[16] To clarify the formula, Bergoglio offers four manifestations of what it means to be "men of synthesis."[17]

The first is "an attitude of *availability* and, at the same time, of *apostolic constancy.* . . . The inculturation that the Society of Jesus requires of us calls for an interior agility capable of recognizing the constants and the variables, together with a great austerity of contemplation that keeps us from confusing what is solid with what is yielding. In simpler terms, living this antinomy in a salvific manner is discipline; it is Ignatian indifference; it is allowing ourselves to be guided by the Lord."[18]

The second is found in the tension between the unity and apostolic dispersion. "Space is another reality in which the Jesuit's ability to support antinomies is demonstrated. On one hand, he is a member of a body, of a *communitas*; but it is a community *ad dispersionem.* This antinomy is maintained by attaining not just any unity, but the unity 'of hearts,' like that of soldiers fighting together in the trenches of the kingdom."[19]

The third antinomy is that which exists between memory of the past and courage to face the future. Coming into play here is one's

15. Jorge Mario Bergoglio, "Criteri di azione apostolica," *Boletín de Espiritualidad de la Compañia de Jesús,* January 1980, in Bergoglio, *Pastorale sociale,* 61, n. 15.

16. Jorge Mario Bergoglio, "Discorso di apertura alla Congregazione provincial," in Bergoglio, *Pastorale sociale,* 252.

17. Ibid.

18. Ibid., 252–253.

19. Ibid., 253.

relationship with time, which challenges both those who want to reduce history to a "restoration shop" and those who want to see it as a "laboratory of utopias": "Neither one nor the other: neither traditionalists nor utopianists."[20] In order to transcend this (false) opposition, Bergoglio says, the Jesuit must

> resort to the "classic," which is very different from the easy recourse to what is "traditional," to the empty traditionalism that is concerned only with maintaining peace . . . but which is actually the peace like one finds at a tomb. By "classics," we refer to those powerful moments of experience and religious and cultural reflection that make history because, in some way, they touch the irreversible events of the journey of a people, of the church, of the Christian. It is a matter of always having before our eyes the fundamental nucleus that constitutes and identifies us (see Heb 10:32ff; 13:7ff), in order to be able to fulfill, without deviating from our identity, the steps that concrete and current historical situations demand from us. We are inspired by the "classics" to bring forward these two apparently antinomian attitudes that reflect our way of being: *remembering the past and having the courage to open new spaces to God.* The "classics" have provided the strength to find synthesis in moments of conflict. These are not easy "compromises" or cheap "irenicism." These are the syntheses that, without denying the contrary elements that cannot be simply combined in such crises, find resolution at a higher level, through a mysterious journey of understanding and of fidelity to what is perennial in history. For this reason, the "classic" possesses this double virtue of being faithful to history and of inspiring new paths to be undertaken.[21]

20. Ibid.

21. Ibid., 255. The reference to the "classics" as a bridge between memory and future explains the reform of the juniorate undertaken by Bergoglio at the Colegio Máximo, according to which the students would study, in addition to the European classics, those of Argentine literature also, from El gaucho Martin Fierro to Borges. On the authors preferred by Bergoglio, cf. Pope Francis with Antonio Spadaro, *My Door Is Always Open: A Conversation on Faith, Hope, and the Church in a Time of Change,* trans. Shaun Whiteside (London: Bloomsbury, 2013), 111–115. As a young man, Bergoglio was professor of literature and psychology at the Institute of the Immaculate Conception in Santa Fe, Argentina, in 1964 and 1965. On his teaching at that time, cf. the recollections of his former students in Jorge Milia, *Maestro Francesco: Gli allievi del Papa ricordano il loro professore* (Milan: Mondadori, 2014).

Finally, the last antinomy is that between piety and apostolic zeal.

Thus we see evidence from both 1974 and 1978 that the young provincial's guiding idea of the Society of Jesus was that of a *coincidentia oppositorum*. In the dramatic awareness that political-social conflicts and ideologies tend to create impassable walls, profound hatreds, and victims, Bergoglio fought for the unity of the church and the unity of the people. He did so starting from the *Catholic* conviction that sees the synthesis of oppositions as an ideal goal. This is, as we have already mentioned, not a Hegelian synthesis. In Hegel the particular is only apparently "conserved" in the universal. In Catholicism the concrete universal calls for *the care for the particular*, the awareness that the smallest is, in the kingdom of God, the greatest. "*Non coerceri a maximo, contineri tamen a minimo, divinum est.*" This synthetic capacity is not Idealism nor the ideologies that have proceeded from it, sacrificing the finite, the limited, the contingent. Authentic totality, opposed to totalitarianism, does no violence to anyone. It insists that we must "*not ignore the limits* [of reality], which is precisely the aggression of idealism. This is also the problem of laboratory or action groups that aim at an operativity based on limits. It is the problem of every 'idealism,' the temptation of which will always be to project the ideal schema upon reality, whatever it may be, ignoring the limits of that reality. Also at the ascetic level the danger of ignoring the limits either by excess (requiring in an absolutist manner), or by defect (by yielding, by not applying the brakes that should be applied) may arise."[22]

---

22. Jorge Mario Bergoglio, "Condurre nelle grandi e nelle piccole circostanze," *Boletín de Espiritualidad* 73, October 1981, 266. On the pedagogical level, "if a limit is ignored, the possibility of continuing to make progress is ignored, the process is ignored. For those who guide, and at any stage of such guidance (even in the objectification of a problem), being wise means moving between the expression of affection and knowing how to set correction limits. The limit that is placed must never be closed in itself, absolutized; rather, it must always show an openness to the horizon of affection and love, which will ultimately be the good spirit to move. Even when the limits are painful, it is necessary to make sure that those who are limited feel—at least implicitly and 'in hope'—the announcement of something greater than an obstacle to their conduct, and which at the moment cannot by understood. Warmth and affection have precisely the task of providing this horizon" (267).

These ideas are explored further in a 1980 paper, "Criteria of Apostolic Action," in which Bergoglio notes several "antinomies" of being a Jesuit, summarized in the formula "to be a contemplative . . . in action."[23] He wrote, "We must avoid the 'disjunctive propositions' that seek only to cancel out each other, because they lead to no solution. Rather, we must resort to creative 'alternatives' that are expressed in a language of antinomies and tensions that we could define as 'dialectic.' "[24] In a footnote, Bergoglio referred to a speech by Fr. Pedro Arrupe, the superior general of the Jesuits, who, "in his closing speech to the last Congregation of Procurators in Rome, refers to these antinomies and 'dialectical tensions.' "[25] The citation of Arrupe clearly offered an important support of Bergoglio's dialectical method.[26]

Bergoglio spoke of "entering the divine *dynamis* of antinomies and dialectical tensions"[27] in order to correct a particular "disjunctive" vision: that of opposing faith with the promotion of justice. In this "pedagogy of antinomies," Bergoglio referred back to a 1976 text of his own, "Faith and Justice in the Apostolate of the Jesuits." And he said that the binomial demanded, in order to be accomplished, a set of three steps: first, to humble oneself and enter into

23. Bergoglio, "Criteri di azione apostolica," 46.

24. Ibid., 50.

25. Ibid., n. 4.

26. The "Working Document on Inculturation" that accompanied Pedro Arrupe's "Letter on Inculturation, to the Whole Society" made reference to this method in points 49 and 50: "But even by overcoming these difficulties of conception, inculturation is a process so rich in aspects and thus draws directly and vitally the evangelization and the man who is Christianized, which inevitably must arise dialectical tensions, apparent aporias and alternatives, whose extremes can and must be reconciled in a serene and constructive balance. For example, between the universal and immutable and the contingent; between the desire to preserve one's identity (both in the Church and in cultures) and the need for purification; between unity and pluralism; between centralism of authority and the principle of subsidiarity; between enlightened paternalism and equality of rights; between audacity/urgency and prudence" (http://www.sufueddu.org/fueddus/inculturazione/0708/04_2_arrupe _inculturazione_oss_.pdf).

27. Bergoglio, "Criteri di azione apostolica," 53.

direct contact with those in need; second, to carry out concrete works of mercy; and third, to become more aware of poverty in society and to reform unjust structures. This succession of steps was a process, but not one that moved uniformly in a single direction. "This is not a linear process," Bergoglio said. "Its dynamic is dialectical. That is to say, one must always return to direct contact, then to the new sensibility, to the new awareness, and so on. Precisely because it is a path inspired by the *magis,* it has its own dialectical rules that, as we have noted above, are never disjunctive, always antinomian."[28]

Here the difference between the forms of the Bergoglian dialetic and the Hegelian becomes clear. Unlike Hegel and his ascending dialectic, *which never returns,* Bergoglio's dialectic lives by antinomies. This means that it is "circular," that its third moment—a deepening social awareness and the reform of structures—implies a return to the first stage: direct contact, *real and not merely theoretical,* with people and in particular with the poor. Here we see his "Thomist" side expressed in the unavoidable tension between essence and existence, form and matter, ideal and real, soul and body. In the specific context, a justice (or a faith) that disregards a real relationship with one's neighbor is a doctrinal approach that degenerates into idealism. *At the beginning is the relationship,* a reality to which one must continually return in order not to become lost. This Judeo-Christian proposition—which we find, in the work of Martin Buber, at the beginning of twentieth-century dialogic thought—is the essential foundation of the antinomian dialectic. It is a dialectic that rejects the idea of an either/or between faith and social commitment that marked the agitated Catholic conscience (on the right as well as on the left) of the 1970s and 1980s.

Our temptations can take on many forms, but all of them are reduced to three—and in fact, even more fundamentally, to just one: that of establishing a dichotomy that forces us to opt for a false reductionism. This is suggested by Paul VI's *Evangelii Nuntiandi,* the *Magna Carta* of evangelization for our time, which cites a series of dichotomies in which we are often expected to choose one over the other:

28. Ibid., 54.

between Christ and the church (n. 16), between explicit and implicit announcement (nn. 21–22), between the Gospel and human development (nn. 31–34), between personal conversion and structural change (n. 36), between gradual change and rapid change (n. 76), and so on. All these supposed dichotomies divide what God has united; "the spirit of Evil," as St. Peter Faber said, is "a spirit of division and not of unity."[29]

Jesuits and Dialectical Thought: Przywara, de Lubac, Fessard

Beginning in the mid-1970s, the thought of Jorge Mario Bergoglio assumed a dialectical form. It was a markedly antinomian dialectic, different from the Hegelian dialectic based on *contradiction* and the ideal *Aufhebung* of contrasts. It owes much to reflection within the Society of Jesus. The root of the polar tension reflects the spirituality and theology of Ignatius, a dynamic thought that places great trust in reconciliation, the work of the "ever greater God." Bergoglio's synthetic thought is a metathought; it identifies a point of resolution of oppositions that is, in fact, a transcendent point, a "mystical" point that operates in the world through the church. Here his thinking falls within a specific line of Catholic thought of the nineteenth and twentieth centuries.[30] Its initiator is Johann Adam Möhler, the brilliant thinker of the Tübingen school, greatest ecclesiologist of the nineteenth century, and author of *Die Einheit in der Kirche* (1825) and *Symbolik* (1832), the latter of which, "even at the beginning of the twentieth century, . . . remained one of the books studied by every German student of theology."[31]

29. Jorge Mario Bergoglio–Pope Francis, *Nel cuore di ogni padre: Alle radici della mia spiritualità* (Milan: Rizzoli, 2016), 290, n. 1.

30. Cf. Massimo Borghesi, *Romano Guardini: Dialettica e antropologia* (Rome: Studium, 2004), 237–298.

31. Zoltán Alszeghy, introduction to the Italian edition of Johann Adam Möhler, *Simbolik* (Cologne: J. Hegner, 1958), Italian trans. *Simbolica* (Milan: Jaca Book, 1984), 24. On the theology of Möhler, cf. J. R. Geiselmann, *Die theologische Anthropologie Johann Adam Möhlers: Ihr geschichtlicher Wandel* (Freiburg: Herder, 1955); Hervé Savon, *Johann Adam Möhler* (Paris: Éditions Fleurus, 1965).

In *Die Einheit in der Kirche* ["On the Unity of the Church"], Möhler explored the thinking of the fathers on the church and used, in an original way, the dialectical method in a sort of distance comparison with Hegel. At the center was the idea of the church as *coincidentia oppositorum,* with the fundamental distinction between "contrariety" (*Gegensatz*) and "contradiction" (*Widerspruch*). The dialectical paradigm is expressed even in the structure of the book: it first considers the church as "unity" (chapters 1 and 2), then moves on to "multiplicity without unity," that is, to heresies (chapter 3), and finally to "unity in multiplicity" (chapter 4). This outline—unity, division, reconciliation—recalls Hegel, even if the internal rhythm of Möhler's thought is closer to Schelling. The basic idea is the notion of the church as an organic unity of positions that, outside its context, become irreducibly contradictory among themselves.

In one important section (part one, chapter 4, section 46) added to the end of the work, Möhler clarified the presuppositions of his thought, dwelling on "the true nature of opposites, within the ecclesial context."[32] In the church, he wrote, "all oppositions, *under the true and sincere dominion of Christianity*, must subsist in unity; in it they must be able to carry out their vitality without any hindrance. And to speak more generally of opposites, the realistic conception of Christianity must be merged with the idealistic one, and true mysticism (both contemplative and practical) must stand next to Christian speculation with its various orientations."[33] This tension is the sign of the truth of the church, since "true life exists only in the real union of opposites."[34] Heresy, on the other hand, is always the absolutization of a single part, breaking the vital bond of a polar tension. "The true opposite, in fact, can only exist in relationship with another opposite that subsists with it, and with which it mixes and unites: opposites demand unity. What has the nature of being opposite within the Church, remains isolated outside it; it is no longer, therefore, a true opposite."[35] It is by now in "contradiction"

---

32. Johann Adam Möhler, *Die Einheit in der Kirche, oder das Princip des Katholicismus* (Tübingen: Laupp Verlag, 1925).

33. Ibid., 195.

34. Ibid., 196.

35. Ibid.

(*Widerspruch*) with the totality of ecclesial life. Möhler will also make use of the dialectical approach in his magnum opus, *Symbolik* ["Symbolism"], in which he corrects many of the weaknesses, deriving from the Romantic culture, present in *Die Einheit in der Kirche*. In *Symbolik*, too, the image of the church as *coincidentia oppositorum* remains central.

We find the same concept in the work of another major Catholic thinker, the Italian-German Romano Guardini, whose thought, as we shall see, will take on a fundamental importance in Bergoglio's intellectual journey. In one of his final works, *The Church of the Lord* (1965), Guardini wrote:

> Long preoccupation with the composition of living things had taught me that everything human is arranged in typical structures and can be determined by these. As long as one does not from the outset limit the Church—historically, sociologically or in some other way—this is not possible here. Of course we find in her all types of human life, but she is not confined to or identical with any one of them. Again and again the danger has threatened that some type would grow too luxuriantly and would dominate her. The history of the heresies delineates these processes one after another. But they were unable to overpower the Church in her essential nature. Sometimes they narrowed or impoverished her, but anyone who knows her true history knows that her essential nature always remained complete and unified. That means that there is something in her that is above all structures and their contraries. Adolf [von] Harnack expressed this by speaking of the *coincidentia oppositorum* in the Church, though he thought of this as a mixture of contradictions. Actually there is something living in the Church which, like the energy that holds together the component parts of the atom, overcomes the tension between the structures and combines them into a whole in a way which, according to all sociological theories, is impossible on an earthly basis.[36]

Ecclesial unity makes possible a *complexio oppositorum* that transcends the sphere of immanence. As in Bergoglio, so in Guardini

---

36. Romano Guardini, *The Church of the Lord: On the Nature and Mission of the Church*, trans. Stella Lange (Chicago: Henry Regnery, 1966), 4–5. Orig. *Die Kirche des Herrn: Meditationen über Wesen und Auftrag der Kirche* (Würzburg: Werkbund, 1965).

the point of synthesis is a transcendent point. However, it is not a unity that erases contrasts in an empty uniformity. The ecclesial form transcends opposites while maintaining their physiognomy. It is inserted into the fluctuating dynamics of time in which

> the intellectual and spiritual current of a period always flows in a particular direction. Harmonious syntheses are achieved only in brief periods of transition between two different epochs, for example when an age whose outlook is extremely objective and in which the social sense is powerfully developed is yielding to an epoch of individualism. Soon, however, one tendency predominates, and moreover, that which is opposite to the former. The Catholic attitude does not preclude the emphasis being laid on one aspect, otherwise it would be condemned to a monotonous uniformity and would deprive man of history. It demands only that the other aspect shall not be rejected, and coherence with the whole preserved. That is to say, a particular aspect brought into prominence by the historical situation is emphasized, but is at the same time brought into a vital and organic relationship with the whole. A door is left open to the particular disposition of the historical present, but it is attached to the whole, which always in a sense transcends history.[37]

From Möhler to Guardini, one can follow a golden thread that leads up to Bergoglio.[38] It sees Catholic thought as a synthesis of opposing polarities, overcoming the contradictory forms into which the poles, if isolated and left to themselves, tend to degenerate. The form of this thought has its center in an antinomian dialectic. It finds particularly fertile ground in the context that formed Bergoglio, that of the Jesuits. At least three authors, among others, serve

37. Romano Guardini, *The Church and the Catholic and The Spirit of the Liturgy* (New York: Sheed and Ward, 1935), 57; orig. *Vom Sinn der Kirche* (Mainz: Matthias Grünewald Verlag, 1922).

38. Interesting in this context is Carlos Maria Galli's article "La 'complexio oppositorum' entre la Iglesia y el mundo: Ensayo de eclesiología especulativa a partir de la paradoja de los opuestos," in *Moral, verdad y vida, en la tradición de santo Tomás de Aquino* (Tucumán: Editorial Unsta, 2008), 135–178. Galli, who knows Bergoglio well, is dean of the faculty of theology of Buenos Aires, teaches at the Pontifical Catholic University of Argentina, and is president of the Argentine Society of Theology.

as especially clear examples of this, and all three are important to Bergoglio: Erich Przywara, Henri de Lubac, and Gaston Fessard.

In the Germany of the 1920s and 1930s, Erich Przywara, the teacher of Hans Urs von Balthasar, was, with Romano Guardini, the Catholic philosopher of polarity. Przywara wrote in 1923: "What we need is a philosophy . . . of polarity that is very different from both the philosophy of restless reversal and that of a static mediety: a philosophy of dynamic polarity. Not subject *or* object, becoming *or* being, person *or* form; not even a static conciliation accomplished once and then considered complete. No: a philosophy of fluctuating movement back and forth between poles, a philosophy of a never-resolved tension between the two poles, a philosophy of a dynamic 'unity of the opposites' (*Spannungseinheit*)."[39]

Bergoglio was familiar with his fellow Jesuit Przywara; on several occasions he cites the Spanish editions of the German philosopher's work, including *Teologúmeno español*[40] and *Criterios católicos*.[41]

---

39. Erich Przywara, "Gottgeheimnis der Welt," in Przywara, *Religionsphilosophische Schriften*, vol. 2 (Einsiedeln: Johannes Verlag, 1962), 215. On the thought of Przywara, cf. Hans Urs von Balthasar, introduction to Erich Przywara, *Sein Schrifttum 1912–1962*, ed. Leo Zimny (Einsiedeln: Johannes Verlag, 1963), 5–18; Vittorio Mathieu, *Erich Przywara nella filosofia d'oggi: introduzione a E. Przywara, L'uomo: Antropologia tipologica* (Milan: Fratelli Fabbri, 1968), 3–28; Paolo Molteni, *Al di là degli estremi: Introduzione al pensiero di Erich Przywara* (Milan: Ares, 1996); Thomas O'Meara, *Erich Przywara, SJ: His Theology and His World* (Notre Dame, IN: University of Notre Dame Press, 2002); Paolo Cevasco, "Vita e opere di Erich Przywara," afterword to Przywara, *Agostino informa l'Occidente* (Milan: Jaca Book, 2007), 129–159; Fabrizio Mandreoli and José Luis Narvaja, Introduzione a Przywara, *L'idea d'Europa: La "crisi" di ogni politica "cristiana"* (Trapani: Il Pozzo di Giacobbe, 2013), 5–63; Claudio Avogadri, *Erich Przywara: Sull'uomo, sul mondo e su Dio* (Assisi: Cittadella Editrice, 2016).

40. Madrid: Ediciones Cristianidad, 1962. Cited in Bergoglio, "Una istituzione che vive il suo carisma," 235, n. 1.

41. San Sebastián: Ediciones Dinor, 1962. Cited in Jorge Mario Bergoglio, "Significato e importanza della formazione accademica (2009)," in Jorge Mario Bergoglio–Pope Francis, *Nei tuoi occhi è la mia parola: Omelie e discorsi di Buenos Aires 1999–2013* (Milan: Rizzoli, 2016), 688; Bergoglio, "La formazione del sacerdote oggi: dimensione intellettuale, comunitaria, apostolica e spirituale (2010)," in Bergoglio-Francis, *Nei tuoi occhi è la mia parola*, 759.

These references were given in 2009 and 2010. But as pope, too, Bergoglio has continued to mention Przywara. In his May 2016 interview with *La Croix*, he said, "As Erich Przywara, the great master of Romano Guardini and Hans Urs von Balthasar, teaches us, Christianity's contribution to a culture is that of Christ in the washing of the feet. In other words, service and the gift of life. It must not become a colonial enterprise."[42] And in the same month, the pope referred explicitly to one of Przywara's works in his speech for the conferral of the Charlemagne Prize: "Erich Przywara, in his splendid work *Idee Europa* [*The Idea of Europe*], challenges us to think of the city as a place where various instances and levels coexist."[43] He refers here to a 1956 book by Przywara.[44] In one case, he suggested an anti-Constantinian model for Christianity in our day; in another he made reference to the " '*Discretio*' against 'syncretism'; as E. Przywara says: where the *syn-* of *syncretism* is the confusion of incompatible and irreconcilable elements," while "the *dis-* of *discretion* brings separation and clarity."[45]

Nevertheless, it would be saying too much to claim that Przywara's polar philosophy played a primary role in forming the dialectical thought of Bergoglio. Of course, that doesn't mean that Przywara did not have an influence, albeit indirect. In 1987, Alberto Methol Ferré, whose work Bergoglio studied attentively, described a current of German Catholic Romanticism characterized by "dialectical, dynamic thought, antithesis and polarization," found in works such as those by Adam Müller, Friedrich Schlegel, and Joseph Görres.[46] Methol Ferré observed, "Dialectical thought is not very

42. Guillaume Goubert and Sébastien Maillard, "Interview Pope Francis," *La Croix*, May 17, 2016, https://www.la-croix.com/Religion/Pape/INTER VIEW-Pope-Francis-2016-05-17-1200760633.

43. Pope Francis, "Conferral of the Charlemagne Prize," May 6, 2016, http:// w2.vatican.va/content/francesco/en/speeches/2016/may/documents/papa -francesco_20160506_premio-carlo-magno.html.

44. Erich Przywara, *Idee Europa* (Nuremberg: Glok und Lutz, 1956).

45. Bergoglio–Pope Francis, "Significato e importanza della formazione accademica," 688.

46. Alberto Methol Ferré, "Iglesia y Pensar social totalizzante," in *Socialismo y socialismos en America Latina* (Bogotá: CELAM, 1987), 220.

strong in the modern expressions of Catholic philosophy, so it is not surprising that those in the church who have wished to recover it, such as Guardini and, to a far greater extent, Erich Przywara, take up threads of it in the work of Adam Müller."[47] In 1987, the year after Bergoglio's stay in Germany to work on his doctoral thesis on Guardini, Methol had identified a German Catholic tendency characterized by a dialectical, polar thought. In the same year, in the June issue of the journal *Nexo*, he explicitly returned to one of these thinkers: Erich Przywara. He did this by reviewing Przywara's "magnificent book" *Augustinus: Die Gestalt als Gefüge*, which had recently been recently translated into Spanish.[48] In his presentation of Augustine, Przywara to a certain extent presents his own thought, and Methol Ferré's review constitutes, in turn, a presentation of his own thought. For Przywara, quoted by Methol, "by virtue of his antithetical style, Augustine is the father of antagonistic positions. By exaggerating them, he suppresses that calm optimism, that greater tone of contented worldliness, which Heraclitus, Aristotle, and Hegel himself met in his 'calming theology.' The style of Augustine seems to tend toward an antithetical beauty, but does not proclaim the peaceful conciliation of opposites. It is the antithetical posture of the 'restless heart' of the contingent creature."[49] According to Methol, Przywara's approach to Augustine, based on the polar tension of a restless heart, relaunches Augustine into the very heart of modernity: "But it is not possible to remain historically in the 'ancient' Augustine. It is necessary to cross with him the philosophies of modern history, in critical and reciprocal purification. For this the perspectives of theologians like Balthasar and Przywara are indispensable."[50]

Through his review of Przywara's book, Methol Ferré introduced the German philosopher to Argentina; he also introduced, indirectly,

---

47. Ibid.

48. Alberto Methol Ferré, "Erich Przywara, *San Agustín: Trayectoria de su genio, Contextura de su espíritu*," 30–32. (Original publ. Dresden: Jakob-Hegner-Verlag, 1934.)

49. Ibid., 30.

50. Methol Ferré, "Erich Przywara, *San Agustín: Trayectoria de su genio, Contextura de su espíritu*," 31.

dialectical thought. It is unlikely that the review would have been missed by young Bergoglio's attentive eye.

In addition to the German Jesuit there was, however, another Jesuit, a Frenchman, who was certainly close to Bergoglio's heart: Henri de Lubac. The great theologian has certainly been a point of reference for his thought. Ivereigh has written that "his lodestars have been two French theologians, Yves Congar and Henri de Lubac,"[51] while to Fr. Spadaro Francis admitted that "the two contemporary French thinkers he prefers are Henri de Lubac and Michel de Certeau."[52] In his 1938 work *Catholicism,* de Lubac pointed out the difference that exists in Christianity between the *social* value of dogma and *personal* salvation:

51. Austen Ivereigh, *The Great Reformer: Francis and the Making of a Radical Pope* (New York: Henry Holt, 2014), xv.

52. Pope Francis with Spadaro, *My Door Is Always Open*, 9. Francis has referred explicitly to de Lubac's thoughts on "worldliness of the spirit," offered on the final pages of his 1953 work *Méditation sur l'Église*: "The greatest temptation to the Church which we constitute—the most subversive, the ever-recurrent, reappearing insidiously when all the rest are overcome, and even strengthened by those victories—is what Abbot Vonier called the temptation to 'worldliness of the mind . . . the practical relinquishing of other-worldliness, so that moral and even spiritual standards should be based not on the glory of the Lord, but on what is the profit of man; an entirely anthropocentric outlook would be exactly what we mean by worldliness. Even if men were filled with every spiritual perfection, but if such perfections were not referred to God (suppose this hypothesis to be possible) it would be unredeemed worldliness.' If this worldliness of the spirit were to invade the Church and set to work to corrupt her by attacking her very principle, it would be something infinitely more disastrous than any worldliness of the purely moral order—even worse than the hideous leprosy which at certain moments in history inflicts so cruel a disfigurement on the Bride; when religion seems to set up the scandalous 'in the very sanctuary itself—represented by a debauchee pope, hiding the face of Christ behind jewels, rouge, and beauty spots.' None of us is wholly immune from this sort of evil. A crafty humanism which is the enemy of the living God (and in secret equally the enemy of man) can find its way into our hearts by a thousand and one paths; our original *curvitas* is never put straight for good and all. The 'sin against the Holy Ghost' is always possible. But none of us is the Church herself, and none of our treacheries can deliver over to the devil that city which is watched over by God" (Henri de Lubac, *The Splendor of the Church*, trans. Michael Mason [San Francisco: Ignatius Press, 1986], 378).

Such an antinomy should not surprise us. This is not the only case in which revelation presents us with two assertions which seem at first unconnected or even contradictory. God creates the world for his own glory, *propter seipsum*, and yet out of pure goodness; man is capable of action and free, and yet he can do nothing without grace, and grace works in him "both to will and to perform"; the vision of God is a free gift, and yet the desire of it is at the very root of every soul; the redemption is a work of pure mercy, and yet the rights of justice are no less respected. And so on. The whole of dogma is thus but a series of paradoxes. . . . Thus the antinomy which we have mentioned obliges us to consider the relations between distinction and unity the better to understand the agreement between the personal and the universal. The dogmatic "paradox" makes us notice the natural paradox, for the former is a higher intensified statement of the latter. The paradox is this: that the distinction between the different parts of a being stands out the more clearly as the union of these parts is closer.[53]

The relationship between community and person, universal and individual, is understood starting from a "polar" model that ties together *unity* and *distinction*:

Unity is in no way confusion, any more than distinction is separation. For does not distinction imply a certain connection, and by one of the most living bonds, that of mutual attraction? True union does not tend to dissolve into one another the beings that it brings together, but to bring them into completion by means of one another. The Whole, therefore, is "not the antipodes, but the very pole of Personality." "Distinguish in order to unite," it has been said, and the advice is excellent, but on the ontological plane the complementary formula, unite in order to distinguish, is just as inevitable.[54]

---

53. Henri de Lubac, *Catholicism: Christ and the Common Destiny of Man*, trans. Lancelot C. Sheppard and Elizabeth Englund, OCD (San Francisco: Ignatius Press, 1988), 327–328; Orig. *Catholicisme: Les aspects sociaux du dogme* (Paris: Éditions du Cerf, 1938).

54. Ibid., 303. De Lubac refers to the title of the work by Jacques Maritain, *Distinguer pour unir ou Les degrés du savoir* (Paris: Desclée de Brouwer, 1932). The internal quotation is from Teilhard de Chardin, SJ, Extract 50.

The same concept is present in Bergoglio's thought. De Lubac makes it the cornerstone of his reflection in *The Church: Paradox and Mystery*. Here returns the definition of Möhler and Guardini for whom the church "is a *complexio oppositorum*," a mystical unity in which "the resounding clash of the *opposita* hides the unity of the *complexio*."[55] The church is the paradoxical unity of that which is, on the immanent level, inexorably divided.

> Multiple or multiform, she is nonetheless *one*, of a most active and demanding unity. She is a people, the great anonymous crowd and still—there is no other word—the most personal of beings. Catholic, that is, universal, she wishes her members to be open to everything and yet she herself is never fully open but when she is withdrawn into the intimacy of her interior life and in the silence of adoration. She is humble and she is majestic. She professes a capacity to absorb every culture, to raise up their highest values; at the same time we see her claim for her own the homes and hearts of the poor, the undistinguished, the simple and destitute masses. Not for an instant does she cease—and her immortality assures continuity—to contemplate him who is at once crucified and resurrected, the man of sorrows and lord of glory, vanquished by, but savior of, the world. He is her bloodied spouse and her triumphant master.[56]

In this way, with the mystery of the church "our minds are confronted with a paradox of a kind that can only be expressed in a series of antithetical, or if you prefer, dialectical sentences."[57] Among these, de Lubac points out three fundamental ones: "the Church is of God (*de Trinitate*) and she is of men (*ex hominibus*); she is visible and invisible; she is of this earth and this time, and she is eschatological and eternal."[58] The third pair regards the relationship between the church and the kingdom of God:

---

55. Henri de Lubac, *The Church: Paradox and Mystery*, trans. James R. Dunne (Staten Island: Alba House, 1969), 2; orig. *Paradoxe et Mystère de l'Église* (Paris: Aubier-Montaigne, 1967).

56. Ibid., 3.

57. Ibid., 23.

58. Ibid.

It is as impossible simply to identify the two (however that might be done), as it is to dissociate them. It has been remarked that on this question St. Augustine seems to oscillate "between two extremes": in some passages, it is said, he speaks of the Church as being, in practice, identical with the kingdom of God (as in *The City of God*, bk 20, ch. 9); in other passages, (as in the Treatise on Holy Virginity, ch. 24) he treats such an opinion as an absurd presumption. This problem has been extended to the full area of Christian tradition so that it has seemed possible to declare that "this uncertainty has never been dissipated in Roman Catholic theology."

In reality, going to the heart of the matter, neither uncertainty nor contradiction is involved. Moreover, a careful re-reading in their contexts of the two passages from St. Augustine shows them to be in complete accord. It is simply a case of two contrasted aspects, both inherent in the mystery of the Church. Here, too, we meet a dialectical pair whose mutual extremes must be safeguarded.[59]

The proximity to Johann Adam Möhler's thinking is clear. De Lubac knew this thought through the work of his Jesuit confrère Pierre Chaillet, professor in the scholasticate of Fourvière near Lyon, who had edited, in the late 1930s, the volume *L'Église est une: Hommage à Moehler*.[60] The text collected essays by Sertillanges, Adam, Goyau, Bardy, Bihlmeyer, Ranft, Geiselmann, Loesch, de Montcheuil, Congar, Tyszkiewicz, Vierneisel, Pribilla, and Jungmann. Also dedicated to Möhler, de Lubac noted in *Catholicism*, was Chaillet's 1937 essay, "L'Esprit du Christianisme et du Catholicisme."[61] In his memoirs de Lubac recalled how

> Father Chaillet had deepened his love of the Church and of her divine charity by placing himself in the school of the Fathers of the first centuries and by frequent reading of the great Catholic theologians of Tübingen. He had undertaken a thesis on Drey, the principal ini-

59. Ibid., 28–29. The quotation about "this uncertainty" is a citation from W. A. Visser't Hooft, *Le renouveau de l'Eglise* (Geneva: Labor et Fides, 1956), 35–37. De Lubac also cites chap. 3, sec. 3, "La dialectique chrétienne," of his book *L'Écriture dans la Tradition* (Paris: Aubier, 1966).

60. Pierre Chaillet et al., *L'Église est une: Hommage à Moehler* (Paris: Bloud et Gay, 1939).

61. De Lubac, *Catholicism*, 321, n. 45.

tiator of that celebrated School, as well as a translation of his works. He had, in the intrepidity of his faith, achieved this tour de force: the publication of an important collective work, in both Germany and France, as an attestation in the face of nazi paganism and the rifts threatening Catholic unity: *L'Eglise est une: Hommage à Moehler* [The Church is one: Homage to Möhler]. It seems to be have been forgotten today.[62]

De Lubac, however, had not forgotten Chaillet, who was the direct inspiration of his 1939 article, "Möhler et sa doctrine sur l'Église."[63]

Möhler, Guardini, Przywara, and de Lubac all shared a vision of Catholicism as a *coincidentia oppositorum*—not in the Hegelian way, but in the awareness that the synthesis of opposites transcends the strength of reason, rooted in the mystery of God. The latter two thinkers, Przywara and de Lubac, are Jesuits. To these we must add a third member of the Ignatian school who was very close to de Lubac: Gaston Fessard. Bergoglio rarely cites him but, as we have seen, his influence is decisive. The pope did make reference to him in his interview with Andrea Tornielli on mercy: "There is a beautiful essay by a great scholar of spirituality, Father Gaston Fessard,

62. Henri de Lubac, *At the Service of the Church: Henri de Lubac Reflects on the Circumstances that Occasioned His Writings*, trans. Anne Elizabeth Englund (San Francisco: Communio Books–Ignatius Press, 1993), 142; orig. *Culture et Vérité* (Paris: Namur, 1989). "Even Fathers Congar and Chenu, who speak of a Möhlerian revival in their recent works, are silent with respect to Father Chaillet, who was the principal architect of it" (142, n. 7). This is a singular omission, given that "the Unam Sanctam series, directed by Yves Congar, included in 1938, as its second volume (though it should have been the first)—with an introduction by the Jesuit Pierre Chaillet—the French translation of Möhler's *Die Einheit in der Kirche*" (Giacinta Spinosa, *Le scuole di Le Saulchoir e Lyon-Fourviere: Teologia cattolica e rinnovamento storiografico* [Rome: Vecchiarelli Editore, 2012], 93).

63. Henri de Lubac, "Möhler et sa doctrine sur l'Église," *Bulletin de l'Union apostolique*, September–October 1939. In the same volume of memoirs, de Lubac recalls, referring to Pierre Chaillet, that "in the years before the war, a shared enthusiasm for the Möhlerian vision of the church, and an ardent love for Catholic unity and the Catholic tradition had closely united us" (*Memoria intorno alle mie opere*, 93). On Pierre Chaillet, cf. Renée Bédarida, *Pierre Chaillet: Témoin de la résistance spirituelle* (Paris: Fayard, 1988).

on the subject of shame, in his book *The Dialectic of the 'Spiritual Exercises' of Saint Ignatius.*"[64] Francis refers here to the second volume of the work.[65] In this book, Fessard's analysis of shame, often called by the Spanish word *vergüenza*, occupies a central place. Xavier Tilliette observed,

> It is with his extensive, ingenious, and subtle analysis of *vergüenza* that Father Fessard has cast a spell and that pulls the rest of the volume in its wake. . . . Besides, *vergüenza*, raised by Fessard to the dignity of concept, is much more than a study of vocabulary; it is the connective thread of a new reading of the *Exercises* and also serves as a touchstone of the Rules for orthodoxy. The notion is so ductile, so fertile in suggestions that Father Fessard is naturally inclined to extrapolate from religious modesty to "instinctive modesty," and from there to sexual relations and family relations, one of his particular interests.[66]

The theme of *vergüenza* was important but, to be sure, did not exhaust Bergoglio's interest in Fessard. The qualifying point—and the controversial point that had resulted in the harshest criticisms by neo-scholastics against Fessard—was precisely the *dialectic* of the Ignatian *Exercises*. As de Lubac recounts, "On more than one occasion he was reproached as if for some defect because of what they called his 'Hegelianism.' The attacks were revived in 1960, when his masterly work *De l'actualité historique* appeared. Confronted with the clearsightedness and rigor of his analyses, it is staggering to note the blindness of those who fought against him: 'Thomism' covered everything, and the bugbear of 'Hegelianism' was enough to dissuade them from studying a work that constitutes perhaps the most competent and most radical criticism of Hegel as

64. Pope Francis, *The Name of God Is Mercy: A Conversation with Andrea Tornielli*, trans. Oonagh Stransky (New York: Random House, 2016), 10; orig. *Il nome di Dio è Misericordia: una conversazione con Andrea Tornielli* (Vatican City–Milan: Libreria Editrice Vaticana–Edizioni Piemme, 2016).

65. Gaston Fessard, *La Dialectique des 'Exercices Spirituels' de Saint Ignace de Loyola*, vol. 2 (Paris: Aubier, 1966).

66. Xavier Tilliette, "Le Père Gaston Fessard et les Exercices," *Gregorianum* 72, no. 2 (1991): 320.

well as the soundest synthesis of Catholic understanding produced in France during the course of this century."[67]

De Lubac refers here to the two dense volumes of *De l'actualité historique*.[68] In the first, Fessard used the Hegelian servant/master dialectic to delineate the opposition between Marxism and National Socialism, Marx and Nietzsche. Augusto Del Noce praised the work, saying Fessard "wrote the most remarkable things, a true philosophical introduction to the topic."[69] In the second part of the first volume, Fessard also introduced another dialectic, that of Gentile/Jew, the same used in the first part of the second volume to criticize the progressism of Marxist Christians in France. The Fessardian rethinking of the dialectic was not subordinate to the Hegelian one. It used Hegel in order to transcend him. As the Catholic philosopher Louis Lavelle wrote to him, on April 26, 1945, "You use the Hegelian dialectics admirably; but for you it is a method of exposition in which you enter, as always, a very different content. And it is fundamentally St. Thomas who inspires you. The center of your thought is, it seems to me, the role played by death in the relationship of lord and slave, opposed to the role played by love in all relationships that take on an interpersonal form."[70]

In the preface to the Italian translation of *Autorité et bien commun* (Authority and Common Good), a text that would remain unpublished,[71] Fessard made it clear that it was possible to find in his work

67. Henri de Lubac, *At the Service of the Church*, 166. Illuminating, in this regard, is de Lubac's previously unpublished review of Fessard's *Autorité et bien commun* (1945), published in *At the Service of the Church*, 277–281.

68. Paris: Desclée de Brouwer, 1960.

69. Augusto Del Noce, *Il problema dell'ateismo* (Bologna: Il Mulino, 1964 [3rd ed. 1970]), 179, n. 114.

70. Louis Lavelle, Letter to Gaston Fessard (April 26, 1945), in Fessard, "Prefazione alla traduzione italiana di *Autorità e Bene commune*," in G. Chivilò and M. Menon, eds., *Tirannide e filosofia* (Venice: Edizioni Ca' Foscari, 2015), 329.

71. On the events that led to the failure to publish the Italian translation of the text, prepared by Michele Federico Sciacca for the publishing house Morcelliana, cf. Giampiero Chivilò, "La tirannide del principe-schiavo secondo Gaston Fessard," in *Tirannide e filosofia*, 305–315.

the beginning of a comparison between the dialectic of Master and Slave and another dialectic that is exactly the reverse of it. Hegel and Marx have not only used the first, one to explain the phenomenological becoming of the universal individual in search of "absolute knowledge," the other to interpret the social and historical development of human society and nature; they have also discovered the elements of the latter, but without recognizing its importance, or above all its fundamental value as the principle of the natural and historical genesis of man. This dialectic that determines the birth first of the family and, later, of the nation, and that proves capable of overcoming the division of the political and the economic, arising within the relationship of Master and Slave, we have called it, in a further work, a Dialectic of Man and Woman. But on pages 100 and following of *Authority and Common Good*, one can glimpse how one can affirm that only Christianity is enabled to present itself as the ideal of the universal common Good, because it reconciles in itself the truths that liberalism, communism, and Nazism dissociate and pervert.[72]

The form of the dialectic was marked, in this way, by a triple polarity. As von Balthasar wrote, "The human being can only be either a man or a woman; in the same interhuman relationship he can only be either a master or a servant; finally, in his relationship with the redeeming Messiah he can only be either a Jew or a Gentile. In the dynamics of these three pairs of relationships, Gaston Fessard has seen the kernel of a dialectic of history and constantly returned to it in his thinking."[73]

In the tension that distinguishes the three pairs, the first, "natural" one of love between man and woman, has a priority over the political-economic dialectic of master and servant. This insight impressed Bergoglio. Alberto Methol Ferré was marked by it, too, to the point of making it the axis of his understanding of historical processes. Above these two forms of polarity, then, is the third,

---

72. Fessard, "Prefazione alla traduzione italiana di *Autorità e Bene commune*," 326.

73. Hans Urs von Balthasar, *Man in History: A Theological Study* (New York: Sheed and Ward, 1968), 306–307; orig. *Das Ganze im Fragment: Aspekte der Geschichtstheologie* (Einsiedeln: Benziger Verlag, 1963).

between Jews and Gentiles. The church is composed of Jews and Gentiles, but even after Christ, Jews and Gentiles continue to live outside of it. That Israel will not recognize Christ until the last day is a mystery:

> Gaston Fessard, following the ideas of Fr. Huby, has argued strongly against Maritain, Journet, and Féret. He holds that the eschatological interpretation is the only one—and the only traditional one—which is acceptable for the theology of history. The New Covenant is founded in the agonizing, crucifying, and rising above Israel according to the flesh. And if it is true that the man on the cross "has broken down the dividing wall of hostility [between Jews and Gentiles] . . . in his flesh . . . that he might create in himself one new man in place of the two" (Eph 2: 14-15), "then one has only to place this text beside Romans 11 to see that the difference between Gentile and Jew can be removed only on the day that the new man has attained his full measure (Eph 4: 13) and fully and finally unites both peoples in his total Mystical Body."[74]

Like Möhler, Przywara, Guardini, and de Lubac, Fessard, too, saw Christianity as a reconciliation of the opposites that, according to Hegel and Marx, dominate history. The unity of the Christian is a dramatic, agonical unity, projected in the eschatological expectation of a fulfillment that only Christ can achieve. It is the dramatic unity that Bergoglio found in Fessard's interpretation of the *Exercises*, in his dialectical reading of the Ignatian message. Philippe Lécrivain has expressed well that Fessard's merit, in his 1956 work, was to overcome the antithesis between two opposing interpretations that divided the Ignatian heritage: the ascetic and the mystical:

> Long matured—his first intuition in 1923 and his first writing in the early 1930s—this book was immediately received by the specialists with great interest, especially since it supported two interpretations of the *Exercises* that were then opposed: the one, quite common, emphasized the ascetic dimension of the Ignatian book by centering everything on "election"; the other, represented by H. Bremond, an old Jesuit, put forward its mystical dimension, "union with God,"

---

74. Ibid., 149. Here von Balthasar quotes Fessard, *De l'Actualite historique*.

but without attaching much importance to the letter. To put it differently, the importance of G. Fessard's work is to show that these two points of view should be united rather than opposed to one another, and to emphasize the relevance of this conjunction in contemporary culture.[75]

The spirit of the Society, in the Ignatian vision of Fessard, puts itself beyond the opposition between ascetics and mystics. Once again, the Catholic model proved to be the point of synthesis of contrasts. This is no less true because Francis, as pope, opts for a decisive superiority of the mystical pole over the ascetic one. Mysticism is the place of the synthesis of oppositions, not a pole that is antithetical to the active life. From this misunderstanding arises a false polarity, like that between a spiritualism outside of history and an activism in the world. Francis told Fr. Spadaro, "Ignatius is a mystic, not an ascetic. It irritates me when I hear that the Spiritual Exercises are 'Ignatian' only because they are done in silence. In fact, the Exercises can be perfectly Ignatian also in daily life and without the silence. An interpretation of the Spiritual Exercises that emphasizes asceticism, silence and penance is a distorted one that became widespread even in the Society, especially in the Society of Jesus in Spain. I am rather close to the mystical movement, that of Louis Lallement and Jean-Joseph Surin."[76]

Mysticism is the point of union between contemplation and action, between doctrine and practice. This is the point denied by the

75. Philippe Lécrivain, "Les Exercices spirituels d'Ignace de Loyola, un chemin de liberté," *Revue d'étique e de théologie morale* 234, no. 2 (2005): 71–86 at 71. On the thought of Fessard, cf. Giao Nguyen-Hong, *Le Verbe dans l'histoire: La philosophie de l'historicité du Père Gaston Fessard* (Paris: Beauchesne, 1974); Michel Sales, *Gaston Fessard, 1897–1978: genèse d'une pensée* (Brussels: Culture et vérité, 1997); Michèle Aumont, *Philosophie sociopolitique de Gaston Fessard, SJ: "Pax nostra"* (Paris: Éditions du Cerf, 2004); Aumont, *Ignace de Loyola et Gaston Fessard: l'un par l'autre* (Paris: L'Harmattan, 2006); Frédéric Louzeau, *L'anthropologie sociale du Père Gaston Fessard* (Paris: Presses Universitaires de France, 2009); Dominique Serra-Coatanea, *Le défi actuel du Bien commun dans la doctrine sociale de l'Église: Études à partir de l'approche de Gaston Fessard SJ* (Zürich: LIT Verlag, 2016).

76. Pope Francis with Spadaro, *My Door Is Always Open*, 27–28.

dualisms of the 1970s that "Catholic," dialectical thought was called to overcome.[77] For this purpose, Fessard's theological-philosophical commentary on the Ignatian *Exercises* proved to be fundamental.

The Dialectical Thomism of Alberto Methol Ferré

Among the proponents of dialectical thought—of the Catholic rather than the Hegelian type—that we have considered, three were Jesuits: Przywara, de Lubac, and Fessard. The last of these did not have a direct influence on Bergoglio; rather, he took a place in Bergoglio's intellectual journey indirectly, through the impact of a *sui generis* Uruguayan Thomist named Alberto Methol Ferré.

Methol Ferré "was the most original Latin American lay Catholic thinker of the second half of the twentieth century and the dawn of the twenty-first."[78] We have already met him, through our

---

77. Cf. Michel de Certeau, "L'universalisme ignatien: mystique et mission," *Christus* 13 (1966): 173–183.

78. Guzmán Carriquiry Lecour, "Più attuale che mai," preface to Alberto Methol Ferré and Alver Metalli, *Il Papa e il filosofo* (Siena: Cantagalli, 2014), 8. Among the works of Methol Ferré, cf. *La crisis del Uruguay y el Imperio británico* (Buenos Aires: Editorial A. Peña Lillo, 1959); *El Uruguay como problema, geopolítica de la cuenca del Plata* (Montevideo: Editorial Dialogo, 1967); *Puebla: proceso y tensiones* (Buenos Aires: Editorial Documenta, 1979); *La América Latina del siglo XXI* (Buenos Aires: Edhasa, 2006); *Los Estados continentales y el Mercosur* (Buenos Aires: Ed. Instituto Superior Dr. Arturo Jauretche, 2009). For a full list of his publications, see http://www.metholferre .com/obras/libros.php. Many of Methol's articles were published in Italian in the journal *Incontri: Testimonianze dall'America Latina*. These include "Dietro l'ingiustizia e la violenza che sconvolge l'America Centrale: La profonda crisi dell'intellettualità cattolica" (1, June–July 1981, 44–53); "Da Rio de Janeiro a Puebla: venticinque anni di storia" (4, January–February 1982, 8–25); "È un ecumenismo che riduce il cristianesimo ad allegoria del marxismo" (5, March–April 1982, 78–80); "Malvinas, nuova frontiera latinoamericana" (6, May–June 1982, 52–54); "Da *Incontri* a *NEXO*: Al servizio della cultura Latinoamericana" (8, November–December 1982, 6–8). On the person and work of Methol Ferré, cf. J. Restán Martinez, *Alberto Methol Ferré: Su pensamiento en* Nexo (Montevideo: Editorial Dunken, 2010); G. Carriquiry Lecour, "Più attuale che mai," 7–12; Alver Metalli, "Methol Ferré ci ha aiutati a pensare," afterword to *Il Papa e il filosofo*, 213–227; H. Ghiretti, "El joven

consideration of Amelia Podetti, in the group of intellectuals of USAL "who saw the Church as key to the emergence of a new Latin-American continental consciousness, *la patria grande.*"[79] It is precisely in the context of USAL that Bergoglio came to know Methol.

Ivereigh recounts: "Bergoglio first met Methol Ferré in 1978 at a lunch with the USAL rector, Francisco Piñón. These Rio de al Plata theologians and intellectuals—including the current head of the Vatican's Commission for Latin America, the Uruguayan Guzmán Carriquiry—formed a short-lived group called Juan Diego de Guadalupe, which met regularly in Argentina in the run-up to Puebla. Bergoglio, recalls Carriquiry, 'came and went' from these meetings but followed them closely."[80]

Methol Ferré and Bergoglio came to know each other, then, in the context of the preparatory work for the great encounter that assembled the Latin American church in Puebla in 1979. Under the leadership of John Paul II, this conference would constitute a turning point for the ecclesial consciousness of those years. Its concluding document affirmed, following the previous meeting of Medellín in 1968, a preferential option for the poor, but one that was understood as referring primarily to culture and popular devotion. It also rejected any Marxist reading of liberation theology.

> Bergoglio saw Puebla as a huge breakthrough. It now became possible to look at Latin America through its own cultural tradition, preserved above all in the spiritual and religious resources of the ordinary faithful people rather than through the lens of imported or elite ideologies. If these resources were liberated, Bergoglio believed, Latin America could free itself from those ideologies as well as from the economic imperialism of money, both of which held Latin

---

Methol: cristianismo, marxismo e izquierda nacional 'argentina,' " *Contemporanea: Historia y problemas del siglo xx* 7 (2016): 15–44. On the relationship between Methol Ferré and Bergoglio, cf. Alver Metalli, "Jorge Mario Bergoglio e Alberto Methol Ferré: affinità elettive di un papa e di un filosofo del Rio de la Plata," preface to *Il Papa e il filosofo*, 13–29; J. R. Podetti, "Confluencias entre Francisco y Alberto Methol Ferré: Iglesia, evangelización y mundo contemporáneo," http://www.academia.edu/15176879/2013_.

79. Ivereigh, *The Great Reformer*, 106.
80. Ibid., 185.

America back by destroying "the Christian originality of the encounter with Jesus Christ which so many of our people still live out in their simplicity of their faith."

The story of Puebla is partly, then, the story of the rise of the Argentine school of post-Medellín theology. The document's rich passages on the evangelization of culture and popular religiosity were drafted by the pioneer of the *teología del pueblo*, Father Lucio Gera, as well as a Chilean theologian in the same line of thinking, Father Joaquín Allende. At Puebla they took Paul VI's *Evangelii Nuntiandi*—which had itself been influenced by Gera—and applied it to Latin America, citing it ninety-seven times in the concluding document.

Another key contributor to the redaction of the Puebla document was Alberto Methol Ferré, a Uruguayan thinker on the CELAM staff who would have a major influence on Bergoglio's ideas about the historic destiny of the Latin-American Church.[81]

This, then, is "Bergoglio's philosopher": Alberto Methol Ferré, a lay collaborator of CELAM in the period from Puebla (1979) to Santo Domingo (1992), a leading intellectual, an interpreter of historical processes and the journey of the church within them. He was the tireless founder and leader of journals—*Nexo* (1955–1958), *Vispera* (1967–1975), and again *Nexo* (1983–1989)—who assembled the best of the Catholic intelligentsia of Latin America. We know that Bergoglio was a careful reader of *Nexo*.[82] Esteem and intellectual affinity link the two deeply. As Francis himself commented: "I spoke at length with Methol Ferré and I read a lot of the things he wrote. The last thing I read about him was an article, published the Sunday before the conclave in which Pope Ratzinger

---

81. Ibid., 184–185. Berogolio's esteem for Methol was shared by Antonio Quarracino, the archbishop of Buenos Aires and president of CELAM: "Both were committed to CELAM, and to the idea of a transnational Catholic unity for Latin America. And both were admirers of the Uruguayan philosopher Alberto Methol Ferré" (ibid., 220).

82. "I know well how much [Bergoglio] appreciated and admired Methol Ferré. He followed his writings with great interest and profit, above all those published in the journal *Nexo*" (Guzmán Carriquiry Lecour, Letter to Marcos Methol Sastre, March 2013, in Alver Metalli, "Jorge Mario Bergoglio e Alberto Methol Ferré: affinità elettive di un papa e di un filosofo del Rio de la Plata," 20).

was elected, in which he said that the time was not yet ripe for a Latin American pope. It is the last text I read by him. Reading Methol Ferré, unconsciously I took things from him, because I liked reading him."[83]

After Methol's death in 2009, Bergoglio, who had intended to honor him with a Laurea Honoris Causa at the Catholic University of Buenos Aires, remembered him as a "dear lost friend."[84] Sharing Methol's understanding of the meaning of faith in the ecclesial/social/political context of Latin America in the decades of the 1970s through the 1990s, Bergoglio appreciated not only his Catholic geopolitics but also his thought in the proper sense. On May 16, 2009, during a talk on "Latin America in the Twenty-first Century" in Buenos Aires, Cardinal Bergoglio commented, "The subject of Methol Ferré's metaphysics is *real being in itself*, and it is precisely this subject—determined and limited—that opens the doors to the concrete universal."[85] Bergoglio points here to the heart of dialectic thought, between finite and infinite, particular and universal, which is the foundation of Alberto Methol Ferré's thought. It is thought that—like that of Möhler, Guardini, Przywara, de Lubac, and Fessard—is situated in the vein of the polar dialectic, typical of a segment of contemporary Catholic philosophy. It is an intellectual vein in which the church, as a mystical body, is the model of an organic-dialectical position that overcomes and transcends the oppositions of the world. As Methol wrote in 1975:

> It would be superhuman to fully understand the *coincidentia oppositorum* that the church is. Some real dimensions always remain in the shadows or are forgotten. The church has essentially two poles, born of the Spirit of God and of Jesus Christ in the Apostles. It is visible and invisible, in a single, indissoluble breath. Ecclesiologies

83. Pope Francis, audio recording of January 3, 2017.

84. Jorge Mario Bergoglio–Pope Francis, *Noi come cittadini, noi come popolo: Verso un bicentenario in giustizia e solidarietà 2010–2016* (Milan: Jaca Book, 2013), 35. Orig. *Nosotros como ciudadanos, nosotros como pueblo: Hacia un Bicentenario en justicia y solidaridad 2010–2016* (Buenos Aires: Editorial Claretiana, 2011). The passages cited in this book are cited from and translated from the Italian edition.

85. Cit. in Alver Metalli, "Jorge Mario Bergoglio e Alberto Methol Ferré: affinità elettive di un papa e di un filosofo del Rio de la Plata," 22.

tend to emphasize one or the other of the poles: at certain times they lean toward "spiritualization," at other times toward "incarnation." Placing emphasis on a single pole leads to deviation and heresy; if a rectifying, corrective movement is not permitted, it becomes contradictory opposition. One's hold on neither of the two poles can be released, yet it is humanly impossible not to give a certain supremacy to one of them. The balance is always unstable, moving, being restored. If allowed to break, the church cannot "breathe" and then either dissolves into abstract mysticism or gets bogged down in institutional forms. Spirit without institution or institution without Spirit—both are false oppositions that destroy the church. An ever-present risk. Perennial temptations. The ecclesiological movement of this century becomes clear; it is a movement from full visibility to pure anonymity. The visible extremities, without Spirit, harden and freeze history. The invisible extremities move the church away from historical reality, becoming ahistorical idealisms, subjectivisms of "beautiful souls," narcissism in imaginary "authenticities" masquerading as prophetisms beyond the visible, historical church.[86]

What Methol wrote in 1975 displays clear similarities with the young Jesuit provincial Jorge Mario Bergoglio's polar vision of the Society of Jesus as a synthesis of opposites. This does not mean that Methol's work is the source of Bergoglio's "antinomian" thought. The former is not the genesis of the latter, but the influence of one upon the other cannot be excluded. In his recorded comments, Pope Francis acknowledged: "It is by reading Methol Ferré and Podetti that I took something of the dialectic. . . . Of André Marc [an author to whom Methol refers] I read something *en passant* but I don't think it left much trace. Methol spoke of a *hylomorphic* dialectic of an Aristotelian-Thomist kind . . . but I believe the root [for me] is Gaston Fessard."[87]

Francis does not deny, then, having drawn from the dialectical thought of Methol Ferré, even if its Aristotelian-Thomist form is not at the root of his thinking, the source of which is Gaston Fessard. The "consonance" of the perspectives, however, is undeniable and significant. It is as if Methol and Bergoglio participated in a

---

86. Alberto Methol Ferré, "La Chiesa, popolo tra i popoli," in Methol Ferré, *Il risorgimento cattolico latinoamericano*, 148–149.

87. Pope Francis, audio recording of January 3, 2017.

koinè and possess the same cultural and intellectual horizon, to the point of convergence in critical diagnoses and in solutions. This explains the sympathy they share for scholars like Przywara, Guardini, Fessard, and the others, united by the idea of Catholicism as a *coincidentia oppositorum*. It is a line of thought that, in the case of Methol Ferré, passes through the formulation of a "dialectical Thomism" that owes much to the work of two French Jesuits, André Marc and Gaston Fessard. Methol's key text, which contains the first systematic expression of his thought, is the volume *La dialectica hombre-naturaleza* ("The Human Person-Nature Dialectic"), published in 1966.[88] It offers a philosophy of history in which a dialectic of opposites finds a central place.

> Historical reality imposes upon reason opposite maxims that are ultimately reducible to the dialectic of the one and the many, to the comprehensive maintenance of the unity of the multiple, and to the respect of the changing and unrepeatable multiplicity in unity. Universal concept, model, abstraction, and ineffable, evanescent multiform reality of the individual, such the bipolarity. Thus, historical understanding requires the simultaneous and oscillating effort to combine the temporal, chronological, living concatenation, and the logic of social "models." To unify narration and typology, story and concept, this is the delicate and difficult task of historical thinking. This requires both the "*esprit de finesse*" and the "*esprit de géometrie*," not separable, but they are mutually summoned, inseparable in every authentic knowledge, each in its own way according to its formal and material object. History is both a "story" and a logical discourse.[89]

The temptation to avoid this *bipolaridad* between concept-intuition, universal-individual, leads to accentuate one pole at the expense of

---

88. Alberto Methol Ferré, *La dialectica hombre-naturaleza* (Montevideo: IEPAL, 1966). We will cite the electronic version of the volume, available online at http://www.metholferre.com/obras/articulos/capitulos.php?id=37, subdivided by sections: 1—Realidad y comprensión de la historia; 2—La relación hombre-cosa: sus tres estrado y dirección; 3—Las epoca de la historia que culminan en la Sociedad Industrial; 4—Apunte sobre la otra faz de la dialéctica; 5—Algunas precisiones sobre la idea de Sociedad Industrial; 6—Recapitulación y perspectivas.

89. Methol Ferré, *La dialectica hombre-naturaleza*, sec. 1.

the other: the general and the typical against the individual, and vice versa; the qualitative against the quantity, and vice versa. The first temptation, the one that sees the universal against the particular, is represented by the "Hegelian danger, shared by many Marxists." On the other hand there is "the empiricist, nominalist, contingentist danger" that pulverizes the totality in unrelated individuals. Then there is the temptation of "logical positivism," which solves the qualitative in the quantitative, in what is measurable, mathematizable. Unlike these reductionisms, history, for Methol,

> is both logical and new, universal and individual, quantity and quality, law and freedom, in indissoluble unity. The necessary comes to life in the contingent, and the contingent, chance, freedom, is built on need. The concrete logic of history includes in itself, subsumes, statistics, physiognomics, and large categories and qualitative-quantitative structures, as it is a hylomorphic dialectic. History is always hylomorphic, that is to say, an inseparable unity of matter and form, understood in the sense that Thomist thought gives them. There is no form without matter, nor matter without form. Therefore the separatisms between "matter" and "form" in the way of the Platonic dualism and of the later Scheler, which is a pessimistic, inverted version of the Marxist materialist optimism with its dualism of "superstructure" and "infrastructure," a distant and unconscious echo of the Cartesian split between "extensive thing" and "thinking thing." But there is no single matter opposed or determinant of the form alone. On the contrary, the hylomorphic structure of reality prevents similar dualisms from its root, and imposes on us the duty to conjugate, then, the three demands, in order to conjure the deviation in the temptations.[90]

In 1965, then, Methol Ferré found, in Thomas's thought, and particularly in its *hylomorphic* vision of reality based on matter-form tension, what he recognized to be the correct form of dialectic thought. "This," he wrote, "is a field of thought newly opened by Gastón Fessard and André Marc within the tradition of Thomist thinking."[91] Methol Ferré points to the works of André Marc—*Dialectique de l'agir* (1954) and *Méthode et Dialectique* (1956)—"rather than to the Hegelian dialectic," and to the text in which "Thomistic dialectical

90. Ibid.
91. Ibid.

ontology of being [is] magnificently developed," *Dialéctica de la Afirmación* (1964).[92] Of Gaston Fessard's work, he cites *De l'actualité historique* (1960) and *El ser y el espiritu* (Madrid 1963).[93] Of these, *De l'actualité historique* held particular importance for Methol. In it the French Jesuit imposed a sort of confrontation at a distance between St. Paul and Hegel. The triple Pauline dialectic, between servant and master, man and woman, Jew and Greek, became, in Fessard, an eternal dialectic, the peculiar form of historical oppositions. In *La dialectica hombre-naturaleza,* Methol took up the first pair, the Pauline-Hegelian one of master/servant, and brought it back to its ontological foundation given by the matter-form pair. *The historical dialectic of Fessard, therefore, cannot be understood apart from the "hylomorphic" dialectic of André Marc.*

As Fessard wrote in 1975, "Even the times are now ripe for an authentic Thomist philosophy of history. The other non-Thomistic, 'existential' Christian philosophies add little to the question, immersed as they are in the 'intersubjective.' . . . This is the extraordinary value that I find in the theological work of Gaston Fessard which, in my opinion, is the first to elaborate a triple dialectic of man-woman, master-slave, and Jew-pagan, which potentially contains the richest instrument for the analysis and rearrangement of historical events. Some Thomists have rejected his ideas, without understanding them; others, though, like André Marc, assimilate it decisively."[94]

---

92. André Marc, *Dialectique de l'Agir* (Lyon: Vitte, 1954); Marc, "Méthode et Dialectique," in *Aspects de la Dialectique* (Paris: Desclée de Brouwer, 1956), 9–99; Marc, *Dialéctica de la Afirmación* (Madrid: Gredos, 1964). André Marc (1892–1961), a Jesuit and professor of philosophy at the Institut Catholique in Paris (1950–1960), was a Thomist, interested in the questions and problems of modern and contemporary thought. His principal works are *L'idée de l'être chez s. Thomas et dans la Scholastique postérieure* (1933); *Psychologie réflexive* (2 vols., 1949); *Raison philosophique et religion révélée* (1955); *L'être et l'esprit* (1958); and *Raison et conversion chrétienne* (1961).

93. Gaston Fessard, *De l'actualité historique*, vol. 1, *À la recherche d'une méthode*; vol. 2, *Progressisme chrétien et Apostolat ouvrier* (Paris: Desclée de Brouwer, 1960); Fessard, *El ser y el espiritu* (Madrid: Gredos, 1963).

94. Alberto Methol Ferré, "Sviluppi della sociologia latinoamericana," *Vispera* 37, April 1975. Italian trans. in *Il risorgimento cattolico latinoamericano*, 117.

In 1965 the model offered by *De l'actualité historique* had as its aim to clarify the way in which *Sociedad industrial*, the rampant industrial development of the 1960s, impacted the relationship between the human person and nature. Establishing that the *bipolaridad* between the human person and objects is a special aspect of the person-nature relationship, Methol used this relationship to understand that of master/servant.

The man-thing dialectic is that of the master and the slave; that is their reciprocal action. On what is this action based? The action follows and derives from being. Beings act according to their own nature. As the agent or the patient, so its action or passion. The real possibility of the dialectical interaction of the correlative opposites of master and slave has deep roots in the being of man and of things, derives and is founded on the primary structure of physical beings, on its radical "hylomorphic" determination (form is the principle of sameness, immanence, independence; matter is the principle of otherness, exteriority, dependence). The form, being for itself, is lordship; matter, being for another, slavery. The hylomorphic constitution of man and of things founds his actions of lordship and slavery. Man is master as "for himself" and slave as "for another." It is a being "for-yes-for-another." Man, in himself, is the contrariety of being master/being slave with respect to the thing. He is a slave of the thing that needs, can, and wants to dominate the thing. Contrariety not only accidental but essential, for its structure and position of being finite. Of being "com-posed" and submitted to the "opposites." Human finitude is at the foundation of and perennially seeks a cure for its congenital limitations through the ever-greater possession of nature, on which its physical survival and spiritual expression depend. Dialectic of opposites, of possession/deprivation, lordship/dependence, which oscillates between the dramatic exclusion of contradiction and the concord of the peaceful relationship. The man-nature relationship is contained in the primordial dialectic of lordship/dependence and its possible principal modes. We must determine this dialectic, specify it, in its categories of realization. Under what main forms is the biblical mandate to "fill the earth and dominate it" carried out in history? What is its meaning?[95]

---

95. Methol Ferré, *La dialectica hombre-naturaleza*, sec. 2.

The final point in this passage, on the person/nature relationship grasped starting from the primordial dialectic of master/servant, leads to the final question: Under what principal forms is the biblical mandate to fill the earth and dominate it realized in history? The oscillation between the poles, in which humanity can dominate as well as be dominated by things, indicates the problematic context of an open dialectic that does not reject the industrial society but critically evaluates it with regard to the "master" dimension of the human person.

> This double face of the dialectic always provokes a renewed ambiguity between humanization and dehumanization. There is appropriation of the thing by man and of man by the thing. However, there is no equivalence, because if there were, there would be no dialectic: one of the terms of the opposition guides the direction and the sense of the movement. It is the man to the thing, the immanence to the efficiency. However, the transit through the thing can lead to the worst alienations, extrapolations, or reductions. It can drown in the thing. It is a duality, inherent in objectification. It signals both the victory and its danger. But always, the fullness of human action is the passage from slavery to "creative obedience," which is creative freedom with respect to the thing—creative obedience that simultaneously discovers order and introduces the new absolute into cosmogenesis. Therefore, human activity is also constitutively co-creative, an image of and a cooperation in the creative action of God, in the wondrous womb of the evolving creation of the cosmos. But to continue would be to complicate the analysis by entering into human action as poetic, generative of forms.[96]

At the conclusion of his book, Methol writes,

---

96. Ibid., sec. 4. Starting from this lordship over nature, Methol opens to the person/God dialectic. The dialectic cannot be dissolved with death, which would represent the victory of thing-ness: "In effect, without the man-God dialectic, without the resurrection, without the 'new heaven and the new earth,' the man-thing dialectic would once again lead to anti-dialectics, repetition, the stupid ferris wheel of eternal return, in the final domain of the thing, of the alienation, of the pure efficiency, and the cosmos would be annulled in the slavery report of 'everything together,' confused and opaque" (ibid., sec. 6; see also sec. 4).

From the Thomistic dialectic of contrariness (not of contradiction, which is when the dialectic ceases, since one of the terms is excluded) that is constitutive of finite beings, not only in their own structure but in their mutual oppositions, we have formulated the dialectic of master and slave, identifying it with the dialectic of possession/deprivation, immanence and efficiency. Man is master inasmuch as he has possession of himself, immanence, and is a slave inasmuch as he is deprived of himself and efficient for another. This is how we have made the transition from the structure of human action to its opposition and interpenetration with things. Things, in turn, in the light of the same dialectic of contrariety and its ontic structure, have appeared to us as exteriority, efficiency, that is, mainly quantity. On this basic relation, we have understood action upon the thing as dominion, appropriation of the thing, immanentization in the efficiency of the thing, objectivable in increase of available quantity and in the service of man.[97]

In 1965 Methol was an exponent of a historical-dialectical Thomism. Undoubtedly, this is an original position that had not been previously explored in Latin American philosophy. The model corresponds to the need—which Methol felt to be acute in the 1960s—for an encounter between Christian thought and the industrial revolution, dominated by a markedly positivistic ideology. Hence the urgency to get away from a spiritualistic, abstract, and atemporal framework, in order to set up the person/nature relationship in the new historical-social conditions.[98] Beyond its application to the problems of the moment, the fact remains that Methol Ferré constructs, in 1965, a dialectical methodology of the first order. This becomes the golden thread that runs through his sociological analyses and his great frescoes of geopolitics. History, he said in 1975, is governed by a dialectic of opposites that, in their reciprocal tension, tend

97. Ibid., sec. 6.
98. Cf. "Scienza e filosofia in America Latina," *Vispera* 5, February 1970, where Methol writes: "The triple polarity man-nature-God is interpenetrated in our social life and the perennial temptation of the modern Christian is to be reduced to the relationship of man's love with man, without the mediation of nature. Without that is a deep socioeconomic criticism, which means slipping into an abstract humanism" (Methol Ferré, *Il risorgimento cattolico latinoamericano*, 186).

at times towards the radical exclusion of the other, his destruction, her death, which is contradiction, and at other times towards "pure relationship," where those that are opposed deny themselves so as not to be confused and affirm themselves to be one for the other, recognizing each other reciprocally. This double movement of opposites ends finally at either God or nothingness. Contrariness leads to the exhaustion of the possession/privation struggle and ultimately to the end of all opposition, that is, to contradiction, the elimination of the other. The law of the contradictories is the inability to exist at the same time, that is, the end of conflict. Strictly speaking, it is the endpoint of the dialectic, the annihilation or annulment of dialectic. But the dialectic movement, on the other hand, with its incessant transformation of possession/privation, bears a difficult and lacerating character; it can resolve conflict peacefully, in pure correlation, in love at the level of persons. The root of these dialectics, which do not overlap but imply each other, is finiteness, contingency, congenital fragility, and the limitedness of our being, which exposes us to risk, to the struggle of contrariety, to the possession/privation that is the movement of history. The struggle of opposites is thus the very process of reality, on all its levels, behind that double resolution which in the last instance is God or Nothingness.[99]

Dialectical movement is therefore not in one direction. It does not necessarily end in the Hobbesian-Hegelian master/slave dialectic. Another dialectic is possible, that of "friendship," which, according to Gaston Fessard, governs the man/woman relationship. It is the only one able to give meaning to the concept of "nation."

"The genesis of the nation," Methol wrote, "implies a certain supremacy of the 'dialectic of friendship,' that which Fessard calls 'of man and woman,' of the primary recognition of man for man, above the dialectic 'of master and slave,' of the enmity of man with man who is rightly the rupture and corruption of the primary dialectic. In history they are indivisible dialectics, whose correlation configures the whole basis of reality and the interpretation of its processes. The more the dialectic of the master and the slave is radicalized, the more the nation is destroyed."[100]

99. Methol Ferré, "La Chiesa, popolo tra i popoli," 142.
100. Ibid., 161.

The concept of "a people" presupposes *this* dialectic, that of the relationship between man and woman, a model for every overcoming of the master/slave relationship:

> "People" is nation, mother; fatherland, father; filiation, concrete universality of brothers, fraternity beyond the lineage. It is based on the "dialectic of friendship," on the opposition of "pure relationship" as an incessant solution of the opposition of possession-privation: man-woman, spouses, mother, father-children, brother. This is the diversified process of the dialectic of friendship which is the original and constitutive one and which acquires its fullness in the church of Christ, which assumes, confirms, and transfigures the meaning of history. It is an always precarious resolution, because the opposition of possession-privation can turn into "a kind of contradiction," as St. Thomas says. For this the nations need equality, justice, and solidarity recognition, despite all the contradictions.[101]

Fessard's model of the triple dialectic thus allowed Methol to interpret history, realistically, as a *contradiction* between servant and master, and, solidaristically, as a *union* of the many in the spousal bond. The first form was also necessary in order to explain the dual form of nineteenth-century atheism. As Methol said to Metalli: "Gaston Fessard in 1960 described the master/slave dialectic, whereas Nietzsche depicted the world seen from the master's side and Marx viewed the world from the slave's point of view. It was an atheism of masters and an atheism of slaves."[102] Nonetheless, the relational form of the dialectic—man/woman—comes first; it precedes every contradiction: "The unity of opposites either is born from the beginning or we no longer encounter it."[103] It is "Fessard's primary dialectic, where *people* implies spousal relationship, fatherhood, motherhood, sonship, and fraternity. And it seems to us that all the names of the church are united under that of 'the People of God,' even if they help to clarify the difference between Israel and the church. Only the church possesses the archetypal perfection of

---

101. Ibid., 162.
102. Methol Ferré and Metalli, *Il Papa e il filosofo*, 38.
103. Methol Ferré, "La Chiesa, popolo tra i popoli," 164.

that which is a People."[104] Fessard's triple dialectic allows us to explain the historical process. It presupposes "the Thomist dialectic of the opposites that form reality and that, according to our thinking, is much richer than Hegelian or Marxist dialectics."[105]

In this way, *dialectical Thomism* constitutes the philosophical *plafond* of the "amateur Thomist," Methol Ferré.[106] It is a school that, as we have seen, includes André Marc and Gaston Fessard as its authors of reference. To them Methol will add, in 1984, a third source, Tomás Melendo Granados's *Ontología de los Opuestos*,[107] which Methol reviewed in the March 1984 issue of the journal *Nexo*.[108] The brief introduction indicated the point of interest of the Melendo volume.

> The dynamic of opposition marks all that is real. Nothing can be thought, except through the mediation of opposites. Since its beginning, philosophy has been the great effort of legitimate reduction of oppositions to unity. Its ultimate foundation is the effort to unify all possible oppositions. The worst solutions are those that "flatten" opposition, diluting it into false unity. Or those that explode unity, degrading it into disaggregated, purely antinomian opposition. Thus, the education of the intelligence passes by way of understanding opposition. In general, this is called a "dialectical" thinking.[109]

In this context, the work of Melendo Granados had the merit of bringing the attention of Thomism to this philosophy of polarity that was already central to the work of scholars well known to Methol:

> I refer to the Belgian Jesuit philosopher André Marc, and in particular to his great work of ontology *Dialectíca de la Afirmación* (Gredos

---

104. Ibid.

105. Ibid.

106. Juan Carlos Espeche Gil and Alberto Methol Ferré, "Un tomista silvestre e integrador," *Criterio*, http://www.revistacriterio.com.ar/cultura/alberto-methol-ferre-un-tomista-silvestre-e-integrador.

107. Pamplona: Eunsa, 1982.

108. Alberto Methol Ferré and Tomás Melendo Granados, "Ontología de los Opuestos," *Nexo* 2, March 1984, 55–56.

109. Ibid., 55.

has published the Spanish translation). To be sure, the backdrop that Marc has in mind in his reflection on opposition, his main interlocutor, is not Hegel but Hamelin, another of the great dialectical philosophers. André Marc, in a remarkable volume of collected articles (*Aspects de la Dialectique*, Desclée de Brouwer, Paris, 1956), in his magnificent "Methode et Dialectique," unfolds the question also with Hegel as an interlocutor. It is surprising that Melendo does not mention it or include in his bibliography. . . . We mention it here because André Marc seems to us, in the above-mentioned works, to be a capital landmark for the renewal of classical metaphysics.[110]

110. Ibid., 56. Methol recalls his review of Melando Granados's book in yet another review, that of Erich Przywara's book on Augustine, cited above. He writes there, indicating a golden thread that connects Melendo with Przywara: "Here it is useful to recall our commentary on Melendo in *Nexo* 2, on the logic of oppositions, which is impossible to maintain without a 'spirit of antagonisms' like that of Przywara" (Methol Ferré, Erich Przywara, *San Augustin*, 21–32).

.

The Theory of Polar Opposition

Bergoglio and Romano Guardini

Doctoral Thesis on Guardini

The path to a polar philosophy traveled by Jorge Mario Bergoglio, and also by Alberto Methol Ferré, is marked by encounters with a group of authors belonging to the Society of Jesus: Erich Przywara, Gaston Fessard, and André Marc. Among these, the most direct source for Bergoglio is Fessard; indeed, he serves as an important point of reference for both Bergoglio and Methol. They differ only in which of Fessard's works impacted them more deeply. Bergoglio was influenced by *La Dialectique des 'Exercices Spirituels' de Saint Ignace de Loyola*, while Methol preferred *De l'actualité historique*, with its triple dialectic. But this difference only represents variations on a common theme, a model of thought that, in Bergoglio's case, was also influenced by Methol himself.

To these authors Bergoglio added another Jesuit thinker, Romano Guardini (an interest in whom Methol did not share). We can speak of "adding" because *Guardini's influence did not come at the early stages of development of Bergoglio's thought*. In his audio recording, Pope Francis says, "Before 1986, I had read Guardini, yes, but only in spiritual reading. The books *The Lord*, *The Mother of the Lord*, and so forth. My reading took on a different element when I took in hand *Der Gegensatz* [Opposition]."[1] The latter—never

---

1. Pope Francis, audio recording of January 3, 2017.

published in English—is Guardini's 1925 work of philosophical anthropology.

We can say, then, that Bergoglio discovered Guardini the philosopher after his dialectical thinking had already taken shape. In some ways, as we shall see, it served as a confirmation and, at the same time, an enrichment of his thinking. This came in 1986, when Bergoglio traveled from Argentina to Germany to work on his doctoral thesis at the Sankt Georgen Graduate School of Philosophy and Theology in Frankfurt. His topic was the thought of Romano Guardini.

As it happened, Bergoglio's time in Germany lasted just a few months and the thesis was never completed.[2] This has led some to hypothesize that it was never really begun and that, in the end, it left no trace on his thought. The Italian columnist Sandro Magister, for example, called Guardini "a teacher that Bergoglio never had."[3] Magister wrote, "In Pope Francis's *La Civiltà Cattolica* interview, in which he dedicates ample space to authors who have influenced him most, Guardini is not there. But above all there is a profound distance between Bergoglio's vision and that of the great Italian-German theologian in the field of liturgy (where his influence on Joseph Ratzinger was very strong), in the critique of modern society, and in the conception of personal conscience."[4] Here Magister categorically dismissed any Guardini-Bergoglio connection. Guardini is Ratzinger's teacher; he could not possibly be Bergoglio's as well. This thesis is conditioned by several stereotypes—Ratzinger the traditional and careful theologian, Bergoglio so progressive and pragmatic.

But it was soon refuted by the publication of Javier Cámara and Sebastián Pfaffen's biography, *Aquel Francisco*.[5] The book made clear that studying Guardini's thought was not a passing interest during

---

2. Cf. Evangelina Himitian, *Francesco: Il papa della gente* (Milan: Rizzoli, 2013), 91–95. Orig. *Francisco: El papa de la gente* (Buenos Aires: Aquilar, 2013).

3. Sandro Magister, "Guardini, un 'maestro' che Bergoglio non ha mai avuto," *Settimo Cielo* blog, *L'Espresso*, October 21, 2013, http://magister .blogautore.espresso.repubblica.it/2013/10/21/guardini-un-maestro-che -bergoglio-non-ha-mai-avuto/.

4. Ibid.

5. Javier Cámara and Sebastián Pfaffen, *Aquel Francisco* (Cordoba: Editorial Raíz de Dos, 2015); Italian ed. *Gli anni oscuri di Bergoglio: Una storia sorprendente* (Milan: Ancora, 2016). The citations will be from the latter.

Bergoglio's brief stay in Germany, but a significant moment in his intellectual formation, and Magister was compelled to correct his stance.[6] From 1990 to 1992, Bergoglio was "in exile" in Cordoba, seven hundred kilometers from Buenos Aires, relieved of all duties in the Society of Jesus after having served as the order's superior in Argentina.[7] "In Cordoba," Bergoglio later said, "I continued to study to see if I could make progress in drafting the thesis, but this purpose waned. I never defended and published it."[8] However, he adds, "even if I wasn't able to defend my thesis, the study I did helped me a lot for everything that came after. That includes the apostolic exhortation *Evangelii Gaudium* ('The Joy of the Gospel'), given that the whole section on social principles is drawn from the thesis on Guardini."[9]

This statement provided in the Cámara and Pfaffen biography is of fundamental importance in understanding Bergoglio's intellectual connection with Guardini. Contrary to Magister's assertions, it suggests that in Frankfurt, Bergoglio at least began his research; that his work on the thesis was not quickly dropped, having been picked up again later in Cordoba; and that the work has continued to influence his thinking, an influence expressed in at least one significant way, through an important section of an apostolic exhortation—part III of chapter 4—that he promulgated as pope, a section Francis himself characterized as "drawn from the thesis on Guardini."

This latter point shows, beyond any reasonable doubt, that Bergoglio's research in Germany remained a fixed point in his thinking, so much so that it found a place in the papal magisterium itself. Magister came to recognize this as well: "And it is true. In *Evangelii Gaudium*, a passage from Guardini, from his book *The End of the Modern World*, is quoted. And this is found in the section (nn. 217–237) in which Pope Francis describes the four principles that he believes must promote the common good and social peace: 1. Time

---

6. Cf. Sandro Magister, "Padre Jorge e i suoi confratelli: Perché vollero liberarsi di lui," *Settimo Cielo* blog, *l'Espresso*, December 17, 2014, http://magister.blogautore.espresso.repubblica.it/2014/12/17/padre-jorge-e-i-suoi-confratelli-perche-vollero-liberarsi-di-lui/.

7. On Bergoglio's "exile" to Cordoba, cf. Cámara and Pfaffen, *Gli anni oscuri di Bergoglio*, 157–205.

8. Ibid., 184.

9. Ibid., 185.

is greater than space; 2. unity prevails over conflict; 3. realities are more important than ideas; 4. the whole is greater than the part. These principles are continually present in Pope Francis's work, not only in his preaching but also in his way of governing the church."[10]

At the end of 2014, then, Magister corrected his previous judgment, recognizing that *Guardini is a teacher that Bergoglio did have,* not in the classroom, of course, but in the sense of having an impact on his thinking. His research on the never-completed doctoral thesis had a profound impact. This is notably clear in the plans Bergoglio had, prior to his election as pope, for his coming retirement. He openly spoke of his intention to move to the retirement home for clergy on Calle Condarco, in the Flores district of Buenos Aires, and to "finish the doctoral thesis I never completed."[11] Clearly, then, his plans for the thesis were never completely abandoned.

From Francis's comment in the Cámara-Pfaffen biography we can even discern the specific topic of that work: *the system of living polarities developed by Guardini in his 1925 volume* Der Gegensatz. This system, in fact, at least partly explains the conception of the polar pairs that the pope offers as social principles in *Evangelii Gaudium*. In his audio recording, he provides further interesting information about it:

> The topic was Guardini's first book of philosophy, *Der Gegensatz*, "polar opposition," the study that Guardini did on "concrete-living." I worked on that book with the help of Guido Sommavilla's study, which became for me the translator of Guardini and, at the same time, an authentic Guardinian thinker. The title of my thesis was "Polar Opposition as Structure of Daily Thought and of Christian Proclamation." But it was not yet completely worked out. . . . Hanna-Barbara Gerl, an expert on Guardini and director of the Guardini Archive in Munich, had a great influence on me. Gerl had a great influence on my studies.[12]

10. Magister, "Padre Jorge e i suoi confratelli."

11. Austen Ivereigh, *The Great Reformer: Francis and the Making of a Radical Pope* (New York: Henry Holt, 2014), 340.

12. Pope Francis, audio recording of September 3, 2017. The pope refers here to the important text of the Jesuit Guido Sommavilla, *La filosofia di Romano Guardini: introduzione a R. Guardini*, Scritti filosofici, 2 vols. (Milan: Fratelli Fabbri, 1964), vol. I, 3–121. Gerl published numerous articles on Guardini's thought and was the author of the biography *Romano Guardini 1885–1968: Leben und Werk* (Mainz: Matthias Grünewald Verlag, 1985).

Beyond the hypothetical title of the future thesis, also interesting here are the references to Sommavilla and Gerl. The latter's biography of Guardini, published in German in 1985, was not available in Spanish.

But these details from the pope do not explain the role his doctoral work may have had with regard to another Guardinian theme that, as the encyclical *Laudato Si'* makes clear, also influenced Bergoglio: criticism of the technocratic paradigm and the indiscriminate increase of uncontrolled power that Guardini develops in his books *The End of the Modern World* (1950) and *Power and Responsibility* (1951).[13] There is no question that the thought of Romano Guardini and his concept of concrete-living serves as an essential reference point. Bergoglio found in Guardini a "synthetic," "integral" model, a "catholic" paradigm similar to his own, capable of explaining and embracing the principal personal/social/political contrasts that tend to crystallize into dialectical contradictions that fuel dangerous conflicts. As he noted to Antonio Spadaro:

> Opposition opens a path, a way forward. Speaking generally, I have to say that I love oppositions. Romano Guardini helped me with his book *Der Gegensatz*, which was important to me. He spoke of a polar opposition in which the two opposites are not annulled. One pole does not destroy the other. There is no contradiction and no identity. For him, opposition is resolved at a higher level. In such a solution, however, the polar tension remains. The tension remains; it is not cancelled out. The limits are overcome, not negated. Oppositions are helpful. Human life is structured in an oppositional form. And we see this happening now in the church as well. The tensions are not necessarily resolved and ironed out; they are not like contradictions.[14]

13. Romano Guardini, *The End of the Modern World: A Search for Orientation* (Wilmington, DE: ISI Books, 1998); first Eng. ed. New York: Sheed and Ward, 1957; orig. *Das Ende der Neuzeit: Ein Versuch zur Orientierung* (Basel-Würzburg: Hess Verlag–Werkbuch Verlag, 1950). Guardini, *Power and Responsibility: A Course of Action for the New Age*, trans. Elinor C. Briefs (Chicago: Henry Regnery, 1961); orig. *Die Macht: Versuch einer Wegweisung* (Würzburg: Wekbund, 1951).

14. Antonio Spadaro, "Le orme di un pastore: Una conversazione con Pope Francis," introduction to Jorge Mario Bergoglio–Pope Francis, *Nei tuoi occhi è la mia parola: Omelie e discorsi di Buenos Aires 1999–2013* (Milan: Rizzoli, 2016), xix. Bergoglio directed his friend and disciple Diego Fares, currently

Bergoglio's clarification is important. It makes clear *what* the former Jesuit provincial drew from Guardini: the idea of life, both personal and communal, as a necessary polar tension between opposites, as oppositional and not contradictory tension. Opposition is the lifeblood of concrete-living; it brings life and dynamism to its unity. Contradiction, like that between good and evil, demands a decision, a choice: evil is not the counterpart of good, as gnosis would have it; it is its negation. The distinction between opposition (*Gegensatz*) and contradiction (*Widerspruch*) is crucial, because it allows us to think of the Catholic *communio* not as a flat, uniform unity, but as a dynamic, polyform reality, which for that reason does not fear to lose its unity. Ecclesial unity isn't to be understood as a monolithic block in which unity comes down from on high, in a fixed and direct manner. It is not afraid of accommodating different poles and reconciling them in the Spirit who unites everything, as in a musical symphony. This *communio* is realized in a *dialogical* form, in the patient development of interconnections that does not pretend to negate the accents, the variety of approaches that remain. This is the concept of the church that Bergoglio found thoroughly confirmed for him in 1986, by Guardini's philosophical anthropology.

Guardini, for his part, wrote in a letter at the end of 1967, just before his death:

> In the *Frankfurter Allgemeine Zeitung* there was an article by the Vatican correspondent on a recently published book by Prof. Guitton. He summarizes several interviews with Pope Paul VI and shows the spiritual character and intention of the pope: not simply to govern, but to establish a dialogue with those who represent the "other." The essence of this approach is that the other is not seen as an ad-

---

professor of metaphysics at the Universidad del Salvador and the Pontifical Universidad Católica of Buenos Aires, to Guardini's book: "Bergoglio has also opened the intellectual path toward the study of Romano Guardini and Hans Urs von Balthasar, on whose phenomenology of truth Fares wrote his doctoral thesis" (Antonio Spadaro, "L'amicizia è questione di un momento," foreword to Diego Fares, *Pope Francis è come un bambù: Alle radici della cultura dell'incontro* [Milan: Àncora–La Civiltà Cattolica, 2014], 8). Spadaro's statement is indirectly confirmed by Fares: "I am well aware of the admiration that Pope Francis has for Romano Guardini" (ibid., 17).

versary, but as an "opposite," and the two points of view, thesis and antithesis, are brought to unity. Then the author cites the names of personalities who support the same method, and for Germany refers to me. Considering the importance of the idea of dialogue today, you see that the right time has arrived for my book on *opposition*. We have already said this explicitly. The theory of opposites is the theory of confrontation, which does not happen as a struggle against an enemy, but as the synthesis of fruitful tension, that is, as a construction of concrete unity.[15]

Guardini summarized here, in a sort of final testament, the fundamental meaning of his thought. In his presentation of a basic set of living polarities in *Der Gegensatz*, Guardini aimed to overcome the profound contrasts that marked the generation that, emerging from the rubble of World War I, found deep divisions and seemingly unresolvable animosities everywhere. It was an ideal alternative to the friend-enemy dialectic that was expressed, in the late 1920s, in the political theology of Carl Schmitt.[16] To Guardini, the polarities of life, the oppositions, are only such when they are not absolutized, when one does not exclude the "other" but presupposes it. Polarity can never become Manichaeism, the reign of contradictions that refuse conciliation.

Principles and Polarity: Similarities between Bergoglio and Guardini

In his polar "system," Guardini proposed a set of opposites that he identified as the *categorical* (subdivided into two: the *intraempirical* and the *transempirical*) and the *transcendental*.[17] As Bergoglio would later explain:

15. Romano Guardini, Letter to Jacob Laubach, November 21, 1967 (Bayerische Staatsbibliothek, Munich), in Hanna-Barbara Gerl-Falkovitz, introduction to Guardini, *Scritti di metodologia filosofica*, vol. 1 of *Opera omnia di Guardini* (Brescia: Morcelliana, 2007), 22.

16. On the political theology of Carl Schmitt, cf. Borghesi, *Critica della teologia politica*, 165–202.

17. On the Guardinian polar system, cf. Massimo Borghesi, *Romano Guardini: Dialettica e antropologia* (Rome: Studium, 2004), 13–71.

Guardini presents the *polar oppositions* as real and living. One can experience this structurally as fullness-form, act-structure, and individuality-totality tensions. Guardini characterizes these oppositions as *intraempirical* categories. A deeper (I would say reflexive) level of tensions comes in the relationship between a person's experience and interiority. This *transempirical* reality is expressed in the opposites of production-disposition, originality-rule, and interiority-transcendence. Finally, Guardini synthesizes the tensions found in all the others, the *transcendental* polar tensions: unity-multiplicity and similarity-difference. That is to say: one must see these tensions between opposites as *indivise et inconfuse*. It is necessary to maintain their difference and their resemblance, their unity and multiplicity, and this is possible through *measure* and *rhythm*. On a gnoseological level, the fundamental tension is between intuition and concept, a tension that allows us to see the tensions *indivise et inconfuse*.[18]

The Guardinian table of opposites, then, can be summarized in this way:

1) CATEGORICAL OPPOSITES

    a) INTRAEMPIRICAL:
        act-structure (*Akt-Bau*)
        fullness-form (*Fülle-Form*)
        individuality-totality (*Einzelheit-Ganzheit*)

    b) TRANSEMPIRICAL:
        production-provision (*Produktion-Disposition*)
        originality-rule (*Ursprünglichkeit-Regel*)
        immanence-transcendence (*Immanenz-Transzendenz*)

2) TRANSCENDENTAL OPPOSITES

    similarity-difference (*Verwandtschaft-Besonderung*)
    unity-multiplicity (*Einheit-Vielheit*)

18. Jorge Mario Bergoglio, "Necessità di un'antropologia politica: Un problema pastorale," *Stromata*, January–June 1989, in Jorge Mario Bergoglio–Pope Francis, *Pastorale sociale,* ed. Marco Gallo, Italian trans. A. Taroni (Milan: Jaca Book, 2015), 292, n. 5.

According to Guardini, these eight pairs represent the fundamental poles of life, opposites that exist in a constant tension. Their rhythm, between one pole and the other, is interwoven throughout personal and social existence. Grasping them means understanding reality in its complexity, avoiding monisms and reductionisms, respecting the ways they disclose truth, and rejecting integralisms and fundamentalisms.

In this vision, and particularly in the Guardinian dialectic, Bergoglio found an ideal model even if, in detail, not all polar opposites find resolution in his thought. Bergoglio reduces Guardini's eight polar pairs to three, which encompass other versions of the polarity and are connected to four principles. He is particularly concerned with their *social* relevance. Guardini himself anticipated such an application when he wrote:

> According to an individualistic vision, the relationship between the individual and the whole is built on the foundation of the individual; it seems that society is derived from individuals, nothing more than a collection of the individuals who make it up, united by certain goals. But this idea is mistaken, since in its essence society—be it the family or the state—is an original and autonomous reality. But the opposite idea, which tends to consider individuals to be merely functions or products of the community, or however such a collectivist conception might be expressed, is also wrong. In fact, the individual, too, is in itself an original reality.[19]

Liberal individualism and socialist collectivism each dissolve that fundamental polar tension between person and community that, for Guardini and for Bergoglio, finds its resolution in *solidarity*. The social implications of the Guardinian polar model are clear.

In his 2011 text "We as Citizens, We as People," written on the occasion of the bicentenary of Argentina, Bergoglio notes the historical context in which the polar pairs arose: that of a country

---

19. Romano Guardini, *L'opposizione polare: Tentativi per una filosofia del concreto-vivente* (Brescia: Morcelliana, 1997), 178–179. Orig. *Der Gegensatz: Versuche zu einer Philosophie des Lebendig-Konkreten* (Mainz: Matthias Grünewald Verlag, 1925). The citations and translations in this book will be from the Italian edition.

emerging from the ironclad repression of a military dictatorship and, subsequently, from a deep economic recession, both of which generated deep social conflicts. Bergoglio understood the democratic model of society as a translation of the Guardinian polar model. It has as its purpose to establish "the conditions for compromise and the mission to overcome the oppositions that hinder the common good."[20] Political dialogue implies overcoming the particular values and interests of specific groups or parties: "We cannot simplistically divide the country's people into the good and the bad, the just and the corrupt, the patriots and the enemies of the state."[21]

Democracy is compromise, the resolution of polar tensions, *the overcoming of Manichaeism*. Its purpose, starting from the pursuit of the common good, is to remove the distinctions between the elite and the people, wealth and poverty, the contrast between individual and community and, above all, of that between citizens and people: "*Citizens* is a logical category. *The people* is a historical and mythical category. We live in a society and we all understand it and logically explain it. *The people* cannot be explained in only a logical way. It contains a *plus* of meaning that escapes us if we do not resort to other ways of understanding, to other logic and hermeneutics. The challenge of being a citizen includes living and understanding oneself in the two categories of belonging: belonging to *society* and belonging to a *people*."[22] This is why the crucial process is *to become a people*. It is a process of *integration* in which "two types of categorization converge: the logical and the historical-mythical. And we must use them both."[23]

---

20. Jorge Mario Bergoglio–Pope Francis, *Noi come cittadini, noi come popolo: Verso un bicentenario in giustizia e solidarietà 2010–2016* (Milan: Jaca Book, 2013), 29. The nucleus of the text (pp. 61–69), in which the author outlines the four principles and the three bipolar tensions, includes a conference of June 30, 2007, "La sfida di essere cittadino" that also appears in Bergoglio, *Pastorale sociale*, ed. Marco Gallo, Italian trans. A. Taroni (Milan: Jaca Book, 2015), 345–54.

21. Bergoglio, *Noi come cittadini, noi come popolo*, 30.

22. Ibid., 37.

23. Ibid., 45. "But *a people* is not a logical category, nor is it a mystical category, if we understand it in the sense that everything that a people does is good and in the sense that the people are an angelic category. But no! It is a

Like Romano Guardini, for whom the knowledge of concrete-living demands a proper act that is polar, intuitive, and conceptual at the same time, so for Bergoglio social unity can only be grasped starting from a double paradigm that is both rational and super-rational.[24] In this regard, in his address to the participants in a conference sponsored by the Romano Guardini Foundation, Francis made reference to the Guardinian living unity between God and the human person:

> This is Guardini's profound vision. Perhaps it is grounded in his first metaphysical book, *Der Gegensatz*. For Guardini this "living unity" with God consists in the concrete relationships of individuals with the world and with those around them. The individual feels inter-woven within a people, namely, in an "original union of men that by species, country and historical evolution in life and in their des-tinies are a unique whole" (*Il senso della Chiesa*, Morcelliana, Bres-cia, 2007, pp. 21–22). Guardini interprets the concept of "people" by distinguishing it clearly from an Enlightenment rationalism that considers real only what can be grasped through reason (cf. *Il mondo religioso di Dostoevskij*, Morcelliana, Brescia, p. 321) and from what tends to isolate man, tearing him away from vital natural relation-ships. Instead "people" signifies the compendium of what is genuine, profound, essential in man (ibid., p. 12). We are able to recognize in the people, as in a mirror, the "force field of divine action." The people—Guardini continues—"feel this operating in all places and perceive the mystery, the restless presence" (ibid., p. 15). Therefore, I prefer to say—I am certain of it—that "people" is not a logical

---

mythical category, if anything. I repeat: 'mythical.' People is a historical and mythical category. A people emerges from a process, through a commitment to a goal or a common project. History is built by this process of generations succeeding one another in a people. It takes a myth to understand a people. When you explain a people, use logical categories, because you have to explain it: they want this from us, of course. But that is not the way to explain the meaning of belonging to a people. The word *people* has something more that cannot be explained in a logical way. Being part of a people is part of a com-mon identity made up of social and cultural bonds" (Pope Francis, in Antonio Spadaro, "Le orme di un pastore," xxvi).

24. For more on concrete living in Guardini, cf. Borghesi, *Romano Guardini*, 59–71.

category, but a mystical category, for the reason that Guardini offers.[25]

For Bergoglio, this mythical vision of the category of "a people" provides the foundation for an *ethos* that overcomes "the power of traditions (Enlightenment/popular, two that are prominent in the *Argentine* context), stories (liberal/revisionist), controversies (agrarian or industrial), and oppositions (unitary/federalist; regime/revolutionary cause; Peronist/anti-Peronist)."[26] The way indicated here is that of "*a culture of encounter and a shared utopian vision.*"[27] The individual, torn from the solitude in which classical liberalism confines her, is defined starting from a belonging. She is "social person,"[28] the protagonist of a "social friendship,"[29] inclined toward the common good. Bergoglio uses the polar model of citizen/people to describe an ethical-sociological-gnoseological tension. The process of integration is not only social; it is also ethical and cognitive. The concepts of the individual person, the solipsist-individualist, and the mass of humanity represent different visions from the citizen understood as part of a people. The political vocation of the citizen revolves around the common good, the concrete good: "This is not an abstract idea of goodness, a theoretical principle that establishes a vague concept of ethics, an 'ethicism,' but an idea that is developed in the dynamism of the good, *in the very nature of the person* and in the person's *attitudes*. They are two different things. What makes a person a citizen is the unfolding of the dynamism of goodness in view of social friendship."[30] On the contrary, an abstract ethic is the fruit of an abstract knowledge, a knowledge that, by dissociating from the transcendentals—the true,

---

25. Pope Francis, "Address to Participants in the Conference Sponsored by the 'Romano Guardini Stiftung,' " https://w2.vatican.va/content/francesco/en/speeches/2015/november/documents/papa-francesco_20151113_romano-guardini-stiftung.html. [Slightly corrected translation.—Trans.]

26. Jorge Mario Bergoglio, *Noi come cittadini, noi come popolo*, 38.

27. Ibid., 39.

28. Ibid., 45.

29. Ibid., 47.

30. Ibid., 47–48.

the good, and the beautiful—is unable to attain the "concrete," the unity of the real.

It is in the context of this perspective that Bergoglio situates his doctrine of principles and polar pairs. In the 2009 text "We as Citizens, We as People," as well as in *Evangelii Gaudium*, he connects the four principles with three polar pairs.

The first polar pair is that of *fullness* and *limit*.[31] It coincides with Guardini's second pair of intraempirical opposites, *Fülle-Form* (fullness-form). At the same time it also summarizes and takes up the first pair, *Akt-Bau* (act-structure). In fact, in *Evangelii Gaudium*, Bergoglio identifies *fullness* and *limit* with the *time-space* polarity that Guardini associates with the *act-structure* pair.[32] He does it in his own way, interpreting time and space in a social perspective: "A constant tension exists between fullness and limitation. Fullness evokes the desire for complete possession, while limitation is a wall set before us. Broadly speaking, 'time' has to do with fullness as an expression of the horizon which constantly opens before us, while each individual moment has to do with limitation as an expression of enclosure. People live poised between each individual moment and the greater, brighter horizon of the utopian future as the final cause which draws us to itself."[33]

The "moment" becomes here the "conjuncture," a time circumscribed "spatially." It needs a point of transcendence, of time in the full sense, of "utopia" understood not as ideology but as ideal future that transcends the conjuncture of the moment: "Fullness is utopia as perception, that is to say: one must go beyond. A citizen must necessarily live according to utopias for the common good. Utopia as a 'journey toward' or, as the scholastics would say, utopia as 'final cause,' that which attracts you; that at which you must arrive: the common good."[34] For Bergoglio, "*Fullness* is that attraction that

---

31. Cf. ibid., 61–63; Pope Francis, apostolic exhortation *Evangelii Gaudium* 222–225.

32. "And if the experience of life as act is connected with the idea of temporally fluid foundation, the experience of life as structure is connected with the idea of firm space" (Guardini, *L'opposizione polare*, 98).

33. Pope Francis, *Evangelii Gaudium* 222.

34. Bergoglio, *Noi come cittadini, noi come popolo*, 61.

God puts in the heart of each one of us, so that we seek what makes us more free; *limitation*, which is always present together with the fullness that attracts us, instead pushes us back; it is the conjuncture, the crisis to be addressed, the daily task. We must untangle this knot. Fullness and limitation are in tension with one another. Neither of them can be ignored. Neither can be allowed to absorb the other. Living in this continuous tension between fullness and limitation favors the journey of citizens."[35]

This is precisely the definition offered by Guardini of polar opposition. It is not, he said,

> a "synthesis" of two moments into a third. Nor is it a whole, of which the two moments constitute "parts." Still less is it a mixture, in some sort of compromise. It is, rather, an entirely distinct, original relationship of an original phenomenon. Neither pole can be deduced from the other, nor rediscovered starting from the other. . . . Rather, both parts are contemporaneous, thinkable, and possible only thanks to each other. This is opposition: two moments are each in themselves without being able to be deduced, transposed, confused, and yet are inextricably linked to each other; on the contrary, they can be thought of only one in the other and one thanks to the other.[36]

In the same way, according to Bergoglio, "*time* and *moment* travel together. Time toward fullness as an expression of the horizon and moment as an expression of the limit. The citizen must live in tension within the conjuncture of the *moment* read in the light of *time*, of the horizon. He cannot remain imprisoned in either of the two. The citizen is the guardian of this *bipolar* tension."[37] This tension does not indicate, however, a perfect equivalence between the opposites. As for Guardini, for whom the series of "formal" opposites had an ideal priority over that of the "material" opposites, so for Bergoglio, from the social point of view of the common good, one of the poles of the pair is more relevant than the other.[38] This prevalence is sanctioned by the "principles" that modulate the polar

35. Ibid.

36. Guardini, *L'opposizione polare*, 100–101.

37. Bergoglio, *Noi come cittadini, noi come popolo*, 62.

38. Cf. Guardini, *L'opposizione polare*, 163–166.

pairs. In the case of the first polar pair, *fullness* and *limit* (*time* and *moment*), the principles are two. The first states that *time is greater than space.*[39] Time, as a utopian *telos*, means here the place of resolution of conflicts, of patient construction of projects that are not limited to the present but keep in mind the future development of peoples. Bergoglio, in *Evangelii Gaudium*, quotes Guardini on the subject: "The only measure for properly evaluating an age is to ask to what extent it fosters the development and attainment of a full and authentically meaningful human existence, in accordance with the peculiar character and the capacities of that age."[40]

The second principle connected to the fullness/limit pair is "*unity is superior to conflict*."[41] "Conflict cannot be ignored or concealed. It has to be faced. But if we remain trapped in conflict, we lose our perspective, our horizons shrink, and reality itself begins to fall apart. In the midst of conflict, we lose our sense of the profound unity of reality."[42] This requires "acknowledging a principle indispensable to the building of friendship in society: namely, that unity is greater than conflict. Solidarity, in its deepest and most challenging sense, thus becomes a way of constructing history in a life setting where conflicts, tensions, and oppositions can achieve a diversified and life-giving unity. This is not to opt for a kind of syncretism, or for the absorption of one into the other, but rather for a resolution which takes place on a higher plane and preserves what is valid and useful on both sides."[43]

After considering the first pair of opposites, fullness/limit, Bergoglio describes the second polar pair, the tension between *idea* and *reality*: "*Reality* is. *Idea* is elaborated, induced. It is instrumental in

---

39. Cf. Bergoglio, *Noi come cittadini, noi come popolo*, 62–63; Pope Francis, *Evangelii Gaudium* 222–225.

40. Pope Francis, *Evangelii Gaudium* 224. The citation is from Romano Guardini, *The End of the Modern World*.

41. Cf. Bergoglio, *Noi come cittadini, noi come popolo*, 63; Pope Francis, *Evangelii Gaudium* 226–230.

42. Pope Francis, *Evangelii Gaudium* 226.

43. Ibid. 228.

understanding, perceiving, and engaging with reality. Between the two there must be dialogue—a dialogue between reality and the explanation of it that I produce. This represents another *bipolar* tension, which rejects the autonomy of idea and word with respect to reality, for which the idea is dominant (from which are derived idealisms and nominalisms). Nominalisms never synthesize. At most they classify, cite, define, but they do not unite. What unites is reality illuminated by reason, by idea, and by their intuitive perception."[44]

This polar tension, as such, is not among Guardini's categorization of opposites. We can find some similarity with his third pair of transempirical opposites, *Immanenz-Transzendenz*.[45] But this is an analogy, and it is because the entire theoretical system of *Der Gegensatz* prescinds methodologically from the problem of reality. By doing so, though, it ignores the fundamental tension between idealism and realism, idea and reality, which Bergoglio opportunely introduces into "his" table of opposites. This is an important step toward a possible meeting between the polar model and the Thomist tradition that Guido Sommavilla had tried to show, with some difficulty.[46] According to that tradition "a third principle comes into play: realities are greater than ideas. This calls for rejecting the various means of masking reality: angelic forms of purity, dictatorships of relativism, empty rhetoric, objectives that are more ideal than real, brands of ahistorical fundamentalism, ethical systems bereft of kindness, intellectual discourse bereft of wisdom."[47] The third principle opposes all "self-centeredness and gnosticism"[48] and "has to do with incarnation of the word."[49] This "helps us to see that the Church's history is a history of salvation, to be mindful of those saints who inculturated the Gospel in the life of our peoples and to reap the fruits of the Church's rich bimillennial tradition, without pretending to come up with a system of thought detached

44. Bergoglio, *Noi come cittadini, noi come popolo*, 65.
45. Cf. Guardini, *L'opposizione polare*, 126–131.
46. Cf. Sommavilla, *La filosofia di Romano Guardini*, 120–121.
47. Pope Francis, *Evangelii Gaudium* 231.
48. Ibid. 233.
49. Ibid.

from this treasury, as if we wanted to reinvent the Gospel."[50] The genesis of Bergoglio's realism has its roots in the historical, ecclesial incarnation of the Christian event. It is a perspective that contributes to freeing the polar model of *Der Gegensatz* from every possible psychological derivation, from every *Lebensphilosophie*: "Reality is superior to ideas."[51]

The third and final polar tension is the pair *globalization-localization*. It corresponds, in the Guardinian table of categories, to the third pair of intraempirical opposites, *Einzelheit-Ganzheit* (individuality-totality).[52] Bergoglio takes it up and, at the same time, updates it in light of the process of post-1989 globalization and Westernization and the problems that this process entails for the cultures of peoples. It is a theme that is important to Latin America. The solution is found, once again, in a correct polarity:

> To be a citizen, one cannot live either in a globalizing universalism or in a folkloristic or anarchist localism. Neither of the two. Neither the global sphere that cancels nor the isolated partiality. Neither of the two. In the global sphere that cancels, all are equal, each point is equidistant from the center of the sphere. There is no difference between the different points of the sphere. This globalization does not grow. What is the model then? Take refuge in the local and close oneself to the global? No, because we would go to the other extreme of *bipolar* tension.[53]

The tension between localization and globalization is not just about the world. Speaking by video to an international theological conference in 2015, the pope said:

> There is no such thing as an isolated particular Church, one who can call herself alone, as if she presumed to be the mistress and sole interpreter of reality and of the action of the Holy Spirit. No one community has a monopoly on interpretation or inculturation. Just as, on the contrary, there is no universal Church that would turn her

---

50. Ibid.
51. Bergoglio, *Noi come cittadini, noi come popolo*, 66.
52. Cf. Guardini, *L'opposizione polare*, 105–110.
53. Ibid., 67.

back, ignore or take no interest in local situations. Catholicity demands, asks that there be a polarity between the particular and the universal, between the one and the many, between the simple and complex. To annihilate this tension would be to go against the life of the Spirit. Any attempt, any quest, to reduce communication, to break the relationship between Tradition handed down and practical reality would be to endanger the faith of the People of God. To consider either of these two instances as insignificant is to throw ourselves into a labyrinth which will not lead to life for our people. To break this communication will easily lead us to construct an ideology out of our point of view, out of our theology.[54]

Localization and globalization do not exclude one another; they coexist in distinction. The model for this that Bergoglio offers is a geometric image that is dear to him and that appears several times in his writings: the *polyhedron*. "Here our model is not the sphere, which is no greater than its parts, where every point is equidistant from the center, and there are no differences between them."[55] The model is "the polyhedron, which is the full union of all partialities, which in unity maintains the originality of the individual partialities. It is, for example, the union of peoples who, in the universal order, maintain their peculiarity as people; it is the union of persons in a society that seeks the common good. A citizen who retains his personal peculiarity, his personal idea, but is inserted into a community, is not annulled as in the sphere, but maintains the different parts of the polyhedron."[56]

The polyhedral differentiation represents well the idea of *unity in difference*, the single reality with many faces: "The 'whole' of the polyhedron, not the spherical 'whole.' This (the spherical) is not superior to its part; it cancels them."[57] Only the polyhedron maintains

54. Pope Francis, "Video Message to Participants in an International Theological Congress Held at the Pontifical Catholic University of Argentina, Buenos Aires, September 1–2, 2015," https://w2.vatican.va/content/francesco/en/messages/pont-messages/2015/documents/papa-francesco_20150903_videomessaggio-teologia-buenos-aires.html.

55. Pope Francis, *Evangelii Gaudium* 236.

56. Bergoglio, *Noi come cittadini, noi come popolo*, 68.

57. Ibid.

the supremacy of the whole without eliminating the polarity with the parts that make it up.[58] It is the image of the fourth principle, according to which *the whole is superior to the parts.* Was this insight

> born through my study of Romano Guardini? Certainly, yes. There is an opposition that I like as I have studied the problem of globalization in the last ten or fifteen years. The comparison between spherical and polyhedraic globalization. The spherical opposition cancels every tension. The only tension is between the center and the periphery. Only one tension *but* the peripheries do not exist and each point is equal to the other. Instead, polyhedraic globalization is the one that realizes the true tension. Spherical globalization is an illusion, an intellectual, Cartesian tension. But the second, polyhedraic one is a true tension between one reality and another reality. They are two realities that are opposed in tension. The polyhedron [represents] the true globalization, the one that allows humanity to grow, always. It always defends the particularity of the person, or of a people or a culture. It does not cancel; it solves the problem at a higher level.[59]

In "We as Citizens, We as People," Bergoglio offered, then, a summary of his multiyear research on the principles and the polar tension that governs ecclesial-social-political anthropology. His table of principles and poles can be expressed as follows:

A. Polarity: FULLNESS (time)—LIMIT (moment)
   Principles:
   1) Time is superior to space.
   2) Unity is superior to conflict.

---

58. The image of the polyhedron appears in the "Working Document on Inculturation" offered by the Thirty-Third General Congregation of the Jesuits, following the Father General's "Letter on Inculturation, to the Whole Society," signed by Fr. Pedro Arrupe on May 14, 1978. Point 10 of the preliminary section of that document affirms, "Inculturation, as one can see, is polyhedraic. It can take sometimes apparently contradictory expressions, which are nothing less than different aspects of the same Spirit, who wills for all people to hear the Word of God and incorporate it into their lives" (http://www.sufueddu.org /fueddus/inculturazione/0708/04_2_arrupe_inculturazione_oss_.pdf).

59. Pope Francis, audio recording of January 29, 2017.

B) Polarity: IDEA—REALITY
Principle:
3) Reality is superior to ideas.

C) Polarity: GLOBALIZATION—LOCALIZATION
Principle:
4) The whole is superior to the parts.

The complementarity of the principles and polar pairs opens the way to an approach in which the "synthesis" does not extinguish opposition but turns it into "diversified and life-giving unity."[60] *This is a point of the utmost importance,* and it makes it clear how similar Bergoglio's perspective is to Guardini's and how far it is from Hegel's. For Guardini, opposition between poles cannot achieve a lasting synthesis. This opposition is, in fact, the figure of a tension proper to the finite human condition:

> In the context of the finite, one of the parts in an opposition is usually dominant. Now, precisely this predominance opens a path toward the external. A system of living opposites, fixed in a constant equilibrium, ought to die. . . . All the forces within the systemic unity would be balanced by opposing forces and all the tensions stabilized. This unit would be self-sufficient. It would be isolated in itself; it would no longer have any relation of opposition of any kind with the outside. But this is impossible. Self-sufficiency like this implies absolute being. If finite life is structured in such a way as to be self-sufficient to its internal, it should die.[61]

For Guardini, "the relationship of equilibrium is an exceptional situation, possible only as a transition. As a lasting condition it would still constitute a limited case that could only be realized with the end of life, with death."[62]

The Guardinian approach does not contrast with the Bergoglian vision of "synthesis," which avoids the problem of falling into the closure of a perfect immanence by introducing the idea-reality,

60. Pope Francis, *Evangelii gaudium* 228.
61. Guardini, *L'opposizione polare,* 168–169.
62. Ibid., 154.

internal-external polarity that is absent from the psychological universe of *Der Gegensatz*. For Bergoglio, the "breakthrough" toward transcendence is not guaranteed by the imbalance of the poles but rather by *the unavoidable tension between ideal and real*. In this way, "synthesis" is not lethal because it does not dissolve the tension between the opposites into the homogeneity of the sphere, but inserts them into the pluriform perspective of the polyhedron. Bergoglio therefore maintains the same intentionality that moves Guardini toward an "open" thought without precluding, however, the possibility of partial and provisional synthesis that is realized in time.

We find this perspective in an essay written by Bergoglio in 1988—two years after his time in Germany—in which Guardini's influence is clear. Here Bergoglio reflected on Decree IV of the Thirty-second General Congregation of the Society of Jesus, titled "The Service of Faith and Promotion of Justice." Two poles, faith and justice, point to a dialectic between a disembodied spiritualism and a secularized activism that dramatically marked the Latin American church of the 1970s and 1980s.

For Bergoglio, the process of drafting the Decree itself offered a method with normative value. It developed in three moments: the *inspiration* of the Spirit, the *conceptualization* of the suggested change, and the confrontation/dialogue of the inspiration and the concept with *reality*. "This dialogue does not develop in a linear way. Through the mediation of *conceptualization*, one must pay attention to *reality* as well as to the *inspiration*. In this way, the work of conceptualization cannot 'appropriate for itself' either reality or inspiration; if it did, it would 'reduce' them to monolithic totalities. If one wants to progress, the dialogue must have another structure, which comes from its own phenomenology: the dialogic fact is possible as such only if it moves between polar partialities in tension toward unity."[63] The dialogic fact—that is, the synthesis—"moves between polar partialities in tension toward unity." The synthesis, for Bergoglio, is not a point of no return but *a movement toward the unity of a pluriform polarity between inspiration-*

---

63. Jorge Mario Bergoglio, "Servizio della fede e promozione della giustizia," *Stromata*, January–June 1988, in Bergoglio, *Pastorale sociale*, 80.

concept-reality: "I believe that within the variety of a *reality* and a *conceptualization* a series of polarities (which is very different from a contradiction) comes into play. They are oppositions, but not exclusionary, whose solution will never be reached through synthesis, but rather through antinomy, an antinomy that, in its very nucleus, preserves the virtuality of opposing polarities but is resolved elsewhere on a higher level."[64]

What we are describing is a bipolar structure that prevents the poles from constituting themselves as self-exclusive systems. This avoids their "'reduction' to a system of thought that is 'contradictory,' self-excluding, closed in itself, the result of which is always, from the logical point of view, a disjunctive proposition and, in the analysis of reality, slavery to an ideology."[65] In order not to be reduced to ideology, the doctrine, the conceptualization, must be nourished by the inspiration of the Spirit and the relationship with reality. The condition of "proximity," of the *empirical* relationship with the otherness cannot be skipped, sublimated, or idealized. What we are talking about here is a "multiple bipolar tension" that "is the opposite of a 'simple exclusionary contradiction' and also of a 'tension resolved through synthesis.'"[66] The tension cannot be dissolved since the three moments of the process—inspiration, conceptualization, reality—continually return to confront each other. "It is a *conceptualized inspiration* that drives us to act on *reality*. However, these three moments—inspiration, conceptualization, reality—interact in action in such a way that reality itself subsequently acts upon the conceptualization, giving rise to the further manifestation of the first inspiration of the Spirit."[67]

Polar Opposition and the Common Good: *Sineidetic* Thought

We have considered the expression of Bergoglio's polar doctrine in his 2011 text, "We as Citizens, We as People." But it would be a

---

64. Ibid., 80–81.
65. Ibid., 80.
66. Ibid., 83.
67. Ibid.

mistake to think that this brief text alone demonstrates the debt that his thought owes to Romano Guardini and the similarities of the former to the latter. Much more significant in illustrating these connections is the text of a lecture that Bergoglio offered at San Salvador University of Buenos Aires, at a conference to inaugurate the 1989 academic year. The lecture was titled "On the Need for a Political Anthropology."[68] Ivereigh observes, "It was the skeleton of what would have been, had he written it, his doctoral thesis: a sophisticated, if at times to a layman impenetrable, exploration of Guardini and Saint Ignatius. . . . His deep reading of Guardini— especially *Contrast* [*Der Gegensatz*] and *The End of the Modern World*—had clearly paid off: the lecture sought to supplant a Hegelian dialectic of clashing opposites by what he calls 'a mutual interaction of realities.' "[69]

In his lecture, Bergoglio celebrated Argentina's return to democracy and insisted that it called for a renewed understanding of the political dimension of society, in order to avoid the mistakes and illusions of the past. In political life, he said, "the temptation is always to orient oneself to resolving conflict poorly, to 'reduce' any tension to an unstable equilibrium . . . or to cancel it by choosing one of its poles."[70] On the contrary, "to recover the value of politics is to recover a vision of synthesis and of the unity of a community, a vision of the harmonization of interests, of the organization of political rationality to settle conflicts."[71] For this purpose politics must "hierarchize, starting from unity, the tension between collective identity and the dignity of the person."[72] In this way it recovers the "classical and Christian conception of that which—according to Aristotle—'makes the human person better.' The tension, in terms of *bonum*, is between the common good and particular goods, which configures political tension as such."[73]

---

68. Cf. Diego Fares, "L'antropologia politica di Pope Francis," *La Civiltà Cattolica* 3928 (2014): 345–360.

69. Ivereigh, *The Great Reformer*, 202.

70. Bergoglio, "Necessità di un'antropologia politica," 290.

71. Ibid.

72. Ibid., 291.

73. Ibid.

This tension can never be completely dissolved; to think that it can is an illusion of politics as immanent totality. Today, according to Bergoglio, such immanentism is a consequence of the modern loss of roots, of the crisis of an autonomy that, rejecting God, works a sort of *transfer* toward different forms of profane messianisms. In his analysis of these messianisms Bergoglio uses, as a critical tool, the model of polarity offered by Guardini in *Der Gegensatz*. For this purpose the interpreter of reference is Alfonso López Quintás, the Spanish philosopher who played an important role in making Guardini's thought known throughout the Spanish-speaking world.[74] Among these messianisms, Bergoglio refers to—without explicitly naming it—Marxism, with its characteristic "*shift* of ethos from the actions of the person to the structures, in such a way that it would not be the ethos that shapes the structures, but rather the structures would produce the ethos."[75] In this imbalance, the polar tension that is constitutive of the person and society is lost: "This fact is at play in the act-structure tension. The ethos does not support the correct tension between act and structure. . . . Consequently, the ethos moves on the structures, these being naturally more stable and of greater weight. Losing the personal character of the end (the good of persons, God) leaves only the strength of the 'quantity' of the structure."[76]

Here Bergoglio uses the first pair of intraempirical Guardinian opposites, act/structure, to criticize the structuralist model as a "quantitative" one that abolishes the human factor, the proper dimension of action and spiritual being. In structuralism, the act/structure polarity is ignored; the structure is absolutized and the act, the human subjectivity, tends to disappear. The structuralist model implies the end of dialectic; it is adialectic. Likewise, he uses another pair of opposites, intuition/concept, which Guardini addressed in the section dedicated to the gnoseology of concrete-living,

---

74. The works of Alfonso López Quintás cited by Bergoglio are: *Pasión de verdad y dialectica en Romano Guardini, postfazione a R. Guardini, El ocaso de la edad moderna* (Madrid: Guadarrama, 1958), 151–184; López Quintás, *Romano Guardini y la dialectica de lo viviente* (Madrid: Cristianidad, 1966).

75. Bergoglio, "Necessità di un'antropologia politica," 294.

76. Ibid.

to criticize the functionalistic-utilitarian-positivistic paradigm of the political. In this conception, "there is a reduction of ethics and politics to physics. Good and evil do not exist in themselves, but only as a calculation of advantages and disadvantages."[77] Here the concept of law is dissociated from the *image* of justice. Bergoglio observes that "this second manifestation moves in the tension between intuition and concept. The fascination exercised by quantity leads political thinking to lose sight of the end. 'Physical' or technical power is unlimited, appears as the most necessary, as that which determines everything else. The struggle for this power leads to losing sight of values."[78] The intuitive-imaginative dimension is thus sacrificed to an aseptic, value-free rationality.

A "cold" functionalism is not the only nightmarish political form that the technical-positivistic model can take. It can also assume a "warm" appearance: "The technological mentality, together with the search for profane messianism, is a revealing trait of humanity today, which we could also call 'the gnostic person': we possess knowledge but we lack unity and, on the other hand, we are in need of the esoteric, in this case secularized, then profane. In this sense one could say that the temptation of politics is to be gnostic and esoteric, unable to manage the power of technology starting from the interior unity that springs from real ends and from the means used on a human scale."[79] Politics tends here to transcend its own limits, to play meta-human, Promethean roles. This calls into question the "bipolar tension between fullness and limit,"[80] the second pair of intraempirical Guardinian opposites whose tension prevents the human person from falling into either tragic finitism or the Dionysian infinite.[81]

Of the three forms of messianism, Bergoglio did not fear Marxism—which in 1989 was at a nadir of influence—so much as the other two, those characterized by *a gnostic-esoteric politics linked to technology*. Hence the therapeutic use of Guardini's polar

77. Ibid.

78. Ibid., n. 13.

79. Ibid., 295.

80. Ibid.

81. Cf. Borghesi, *Romano Guardini*, esp. chap. 5, "L'epoca moderna tra 'dionisismo della totalità' e 'finitismo tragico,'" 161–195.

philosophy in relation to the temptations of political anthropology in the present time: "In the first place one must seek an anthropology that is free from the cages of the *nominalisms*, trying to 'give the concepts used the maximum interior mobility,' which can only be obtained by conceiving the explication of the concept-reality tension."[82] To political nominalism, Bergoglio opposed the second pair of his polar opposites (concept-reality) assimilated to that of Guardini's gnoseology (concept-intuition), together with the second pair of Guardini's intraempirical opposites (form-fullness) analogous to his first polar pair: "This characteristic is at play in the tension between *concept* and *reality*. One must bear in mind that the concept is in tension with the intuition because thought is not abstract. And reality is at the center of all tensions. Here the form-fullness tension is privileged. Nominalism is not limited to form; it is also rhetoric."[83]

Second, anthropology must not yield to the temptations of casting away its roots, typical of the modern autonomy that oscillates between anarchic individualism and the absolutization of forms, between Dionysian and Apollonian. The second pair of transempirical Guardinian opposites makes it possible to transcend this polarization. "Here there is a tension between the opposites of rule/originality, avoiding falling into coercion (the exaggeration of the rule) and impulsiveness (the exaggeration of originality)."[84]

Third, it is a matter of avoiding the dialectic between return to the past and utopia, between archeology and futurology. To this false polarity, which is also typical of an autonomy without foundation, insecure and subject to sudden reversal, Bergoglio opposes a temporal rereading of the third pair of intraempirical opposites, totality/singularity: "The theme of rootedness can be considered according to the vision of Guardini in López Quintás, *Romano Guardini*, Cristianidad, 1966, pp. 324ff. The question of rootedness avoids escapes into the past (pantheist return) or to the future (utopian evolutionism). What Guardini sees in the categories of whole-

82. Bergoglio, "Necessità di un'antropologia politica," 296. The quoted passage is from López Quintás, *Pasión de verdad y dialectica en Romano Guardini*, 163.

83. Bergoglio, "Necessità di un'antropologia politica," 296, n. 19.

84. Ibid., 297.

part, I place them here among the temporal categories: loss of roots following the return to initial pantheism or an escape to the utopian future. Return-evolution."[85] For Bergoglio,

> Modernity, losing objective points of support, resorts to the "classic" (in the sense of the classical world, the ancient world, therefore not what we give it). As an expression of a cultural *having to be*. In this regard, it is remarkable to note how the coarser objectivist empiricism can—in the chaos of modernity—go hand in hand with Kantian valuative subjectivism and be projected toward the search for points of support—true and proper "cultural shelters"—which is cultural *having to be*. The man of today repeats in some way the temptation of returns. Being divided, separated from itself, he confuses the proper *nostalgia* of the call to transcendence with *regret* for immanent mediations that are also uprooted. A culture without roots and unity cannot hold; and rootedness and unity cannot be given by regrets for pantheism (we think of the return of the desperate Hölderlin to the conceptions of Giordano Bruno), nor by the utopian evolutionism of Hegelian historical eschatology.[86]

The whole/part pair is thus supported by that of immanence/transcendence, the third of the transempirical opposites. Both pairs provide a correction of two erroneous forms of political anthropology: a soft, syncretistic totalitarianism and fundamentalism.

The "conciliatory syncretism is the most veiled form of modern totalitarianism: the totalitarianism of those who reconcile, regardless of the values that transcend it."[87] Fundamentalism arises from a reaction to syncretism, from a search for "purity": "Pure reason, pure science, pure art, pure systems of government, and so forth. This anxiety for purity, which sometimes becomes religious, political, or historical fundamentalism, comes at the cost of the values of the peoples. It isolates the conscience to the point that it leads to true nihilism."[88] Against these extremes moves the "transcendence/immanence and whole/part tension, considering totalitarianism

---

85. Ibid., n. 21.
86. Ibid., 297–298.
87. Ibid., 300.
88. Ibid.

(exaggeration of wholeness) starting from its current syncretic aspect; and considering the closure into oneself (exaggeration of interiority) in its fundamentalist characteristic, which reduces to the pure part all of that which presents itself as a conflict and closed in on itself, which corresponds in no way to interiority."[89]

Compared to the false polarizations, due to the technical and esoteric-gnostic messianisms that we have indicated, "an anthropology that hopes to play a role in overcoming this crisis must be dialectic: strictly personal and at the same time in solidarity with others."[90] This means adopting an adequate *method* of thought.

> I am referring to a style of thought that implies a phenomenological method with a dialectic nuance. In this sense, it is necessary to strip the term "dialectic" of every Hegelian resonance, and to understand it simply as *the expression of a reciprocal interaction of reality*. It is a dynamic dialectic between life and thought in which rhythm is decisive, in which mobility does not distract but rather concentrates and intensifies attention. It could be called *sineidetic thought*, in which the particulars must be considered as a function of the whole. In this way of thinking, *unity* and *rhythm* are essential. The *rhythm* comes from the application of the phenomenological method; unity is a "transcendental" being of the oppositions of dynamic and living being. This method requires of the mind a *sineidetic tension* necessary to see the parts in relation to the whole and the whole in relation to the parts, with the awareness that in every vital whole (and the social-political reality is a vital whole), it is impossible to separate the parts from the whole and vice versa, for the simple reason that it is not possible to understand a part without grasping at the same time the whole to which it is connected, nor is it possible to fully understand the whole without grasping its individual parts. It is an operation of bringing together, in tension—a sineidetic way of thinking.[91]

89. Ibid., 299, n. 26.

90. Ibid., 300. Bergoglio cites López Quintás, *Pasión de verdad y dialectica en Romano Guardini*, 171.

91. Bergoglio, "Necessità di un'antropologia politica," 302. On the meaning of "sineidetic thought," Bergoglio refers to A. López Quintás, *Pasión de verdad y dialectica en Romano Guardini*, 165. On the category of "rhythm" in the oscillation of opposites, cf. Guardini, *L'opposizione polare*, 160–162. The etymology of the adjective "sineidetic" suggests that which unites ("sin") ideas ("eidetic").

Here Bergoglio follows the fourth chapter of *Der Gegensatz,* on "the gnoseological problem of the concrete," nearly to the letter. In it Guardini indicated the point of resolution in the contrast that divides formal knowledge and intuition: a simultaneous act of conceptual and intuitive knowledge: "We therefore call it *vision (Anschauung).* It would not be a synthesis of two elements, just as the concrete is not a synthesis of opposites, but an act of concrete-living knowledge, which is accomplished in the greatest tension that can exist between the two poles of life."[92] In a similar way, Bergoglio writes in his 1989 text that "the analytic-objectivist method, borrowed from the natural sciences, failed when it was applied to the sciences of the spirit. Faced with the political problem, it is then crucial to overcome rationalism, but not as a veneration of romantic romanticism, nor as a presumed affective knowledge of reality, but recognizing the full value of the intellect: the ability to reason and also to intuit, that is to say, the capacity for the *vision (Anschauung)* of things."[93] It is this "vision" that allows one to face the dimension of the "concrete," that is, of the real, both personal and social.[94]

> This thought allows man to elevate himself and keep himself at the height of his being, since he adopts as the sphere of intellectual life not so much "the objectivity" or "the subjectivity" of being, but *super-objective* being. The analytical individualistic thought failed to correctly address the social problem, which remains crushed by

92. Ibid., 207.

93. Jorge Mario Bergoglio, "Necessità di un'antropologia politica," 303.

94. "Where one speaks of a gaze that contemplates the organic universality, which keeps in tension the irreducibility of the whole (avoiding the absolutist dogmatism that wants to dominate Being through structures) and the individual value of particular structures (avoiding a schematic universalism that uproots man by depriving him of the regional flavor of individual perspectives). This organic universality is also opposed to relativistic skepticism that breaks the link between concrete structures and the whole. This way of looking starts from what is dynamic (act) in the nucleus of the individual spirit that looks at the Whole, and at the living truth that is revealed not through concepts, but through symbols. The gaze at the whole identifies a particular point of view that continues to guide the whole, but starting from a certain aspect (this tension is 'structure'), and so the whole is made limitedly thinkable" (ibid., 304, n. 39).

the fragmentation of social positivism. Social being is found within the *collective*, which does not mean a "gregarious whole," a *unitas accumulationis* (as the scholastics would say), but an *organic whole*; which is why it is not opposed to the individual, but rather integrates it. *Objective* and *personal* are not opposite terms, since the objective-subjective duality is ontologically incomplete or even confused. The realm of *super-objective* being is, in the sense of reality, strictly "objective." Consequently, if a reality is alive, and therefore organic, it can be at the same time *collective, objective, and personal.*[95]

The result is a solidarity formed in freedom, in which immanence is rooted in a real transcendence and the unity of a people finds its actuality in *desiring God.*[96]

From this point of view and with this sineidetic way of thinking, one can propose a political anthropology in which people form and develop political attitudes rooted in *solidarity*: a term that expresses a dialectical value that unites the *collective* (an element of strength that is essential today) and the *individual* (the individuality of the person, expressed in ethical attitudes of responsibility and loyalty and in an ontological openness of transcendence toward others and toward God). In this sense, *solidarity* is a way of living in time; it is a living environment in which conflicts, tensions, and oppositions reach the pluriform unity that generates life.[97]

---

95. Ibid., 303. On the notion of "super-objective being," Bergoglio (in n. 37) refers to the inobjective being (*ungeständliche Sein*) of which A. López Quintás speaks in *Pasión de verdad y dialectica en Romano Guardini*, 165, n. 2.

96. Cf. Bergoglio, "Necessità di un'antropologia politica," 304.

97. Ibid. "From the point of view of the theory of opposites we must tend toward the most decisive solidarity. This means that individual and group, insofar as they are in a relationship of opposition, cannot derive from one another. Each has its original essence, in its own right; but neither can be without the other; rather it is from the beginning co-present in the other. From the beginning, the whole is present in the individual. . . . An isolated individual, ordered only to itself, does not exist. The 'person,' if we can thus define the authentic core of human individuality, is at the same time autonomy and relation to totality" (Guardini, *L'opposizione polare*, 179). In Bergoglio's use of the category of "solidarity" one can recognize the influence not only of Guardini but also, in all likelihood, the social teaching of Pope John Paul II and the experience of the Polish trade union *Solidarnosc*: "In order to achieve

Power, Nature, Technology: Guardini in *Laudato Si'*

Each of the three writings that we have considered—"On the Necessity of a Political Anthropology" (1989), "We as Citizens, We as People" (2011), and *Evangelii Gaudium* (2013)—manifests Bergoglio's "agonic" vision of social life: "To be citizens means being assembled for a choice, called to a struggle, this struggle of belonging to a society and to a people; to stop being a mass of people in order to be a person, a society, a people. This presupposes a struggle. In the correct resolution of these bipolar tensions there is struggle. There is an agonic construction."[98] In this way, Guardini's *Der Gegensatz* is applied to a social framework that aims at the resolution of contrasts, not their dialectical stiffening: "We cannot admit that a *dual society* is consolidated. . . . We must recover the fundamental mission of the state, which is to ensure justice and a just social order in order to guarantee everyone his or her share of common goods, respecting the principles of subsidiarity and solidarity."[99]

Subsidiarity and solidarity, citizen and people, freedom and equity, are moments of a polar process, an "agonic" process whose model owes much to Guardini's thought. This is not merely an intellectual paradigm, a "technique" with which to settle conflicts; it is something more profound. What we are considering is a "style," a mode of being. Bergoglio is a "calm chaos,"[100] a living synthesis of opposites. As a Jesuit, he values Ignatius's "epitaph," offered as a

---

social justice in the various parts of the world, in the various countries, and in the relationships between them, there is a need for ever new movements of solidarity of the workers and with the workers. This solidarity must be present whenever it is called for by the social degrading of the subject of work, by exploitation of the workers, and by the growing areas of poverty and even hunger. The Church is firmly committed to this cause, for she considers it her mission, her service, a proof of her fidelity to Christ, so that she can truly be the 'Church of the poor' " (John Paul II, encyclical letter *Laborem exercens* 8, http://w2.vatican.va/content/john-paul-ii/en/encyclicals/documents/hf_jp-ii_enc_14091981_laborem-exercens.html).

98. Bergoglio, *Noi come cittadini, noi come popolo*, 69.

99. Ibid., 82–83.

100. Pope Francis with Spadaro, *My Door Is Always Open*, 11.

motto in Hölderlin's *Hyperion*: *Non coerceri maximo, contineri tamen a minimum, divinum est* ("not to be limited by the biggest things, and to be preoccupied with the smallest things—this is divine").[101] The particular assumes its meaning in the horizon of the universal, while the universal is perceived as real only starting from the particular. It is the tension between space and time, between localization and globalization. In his 2013 interview with Fr. Spadaro, the polar tensions indicated by Francis do not seem to be limited to three. They seem to expand to others found in the Guardinian framework of opposites. Among these are the third pair of transempirical opposites, *immanence* and *transcendence* (*Immanenz/ Transzendenz*). This applies to the family, society, the state, and the church. Each "structure" must have a transempirical point, a point of rupture, that makes it possible to break the tendency to immanence and to the closure that qualifies all social bodies, including the church.[102] This is also true of the Jesuits, the pope's own religious order. Francis has said:

101. Ibid., 21, 38–39.

102. "It is rationalistic fiction to think, for example, that the state must first and foremost seek the 'good of citizens.' In reality it behaves like an organism that is built using the cell as a constructive element. It seeks to realize an image it carries within itself, to acquire a form, to develop a character, to carry out an activity, to accomplish its own teleology: all this does not mean pursuing an 'end' that is external to it, not even that of well-being of the citizens, but rather simply existing, realizing itself, living. (The same that can be said of a family, and indeed, even of a friendship.) Only by considering this autonomous consistency of the collective sphere can one perceive the strange indifference with which these structures (state, family, etc.) often ignore specifically the good of the components that constitute them and with which they strongly contradict the theory that they exist in view of this good. From this point of view, they are seeking 'the good of the individual' only out of concern for their own total life; it is the same reason, for example, that the body seeks the good of one of its parts or of a single cell. And this tendency is so strong that an education and moral formation, indeed a rupture, is necessary to overcome the egoism of the superordinate entity, equipped in this regard with a natural blindness. And it seems that here only religion, and only the supernatural, can form the human soul to be attentive to the rights of God over those 'of Caesar' " (Guardini, *L'opposizione polare*, 177–178).

The Society of Jesus is an institution in tension, always fundamentally in tension. A Jesuit is a person who is not centered in himself. The Society itself also looks to a center outside itself; its center is Christ and his Church. So if the Society centers itself in Christ and the Church, it has two fundamental points of reference for its balance and for being able to live on the margins, on the frontier. If it looks too much in upon itself, it puts itself at the center as a very solid, very well "armed" structure, but then it runs the risk of feeling safe and self-sufficient.

The Society must always have before itself the *Deus semper maior*, the always-greater God. . . . This tension takes us out of ourselves continuously.[103]

Here Christ is Guardini's transempirical point, the vanishing point that prevents withdrawal, closure, and bureaucratic crystallization. These correspond to a "systematic," completed, repetitive way of thinking. As we have seen already in Guardini, the knowledge of the living-concrete can be modulated only in a polar tension between concept and intuition, between rational and superrational. This is what Guardini called "vision" (*Anschauung*).[104] Bergoglio said,

When you express too much, you run the risk of being misunderstood. The Society of Jesus can be described only in narrative form. Only in narrative form do you discern, not in a philosophical or theological explanation, which allows you rather to discuss. The style of the Society is not shaped by discussion, but by discernment, which of course presupposes discussion as part of the process. The mystical dimension of discernment never defines its edges and does not complete the thought. The Jesuit must be a person whose thought is incomplete, in the sense of open-ended thinking.[105]

Once again we are sent back to Guardini and to his idea of opposites, which represents "not a closed system, but an opening of the eyes and an interior orientation to living being."[106] Living

---

103. Pope Francis with Spadaro, *My Door Is Always Open*, 23.
104. Cf. Guardini, *L'opposizione polare*, 206–207.
105. Pope Francis with Spadaro, *My Door Is Always Open*, 24.
106. Guardini, *L'opposizione polare*, 238.

thought, both rational and intuitive at the same time, is "open." In this way, as is evident, the idea of polarity guides the entire Bergoglian system of thought. It is not limited to the social context. Bipolar references appear throughout the Spadaro interview: contemplation/action,[107] people/hierarchy,[108] strength/gentleness,[109] primacy/synodality,[110] masculine/feminine,[111] past/present.[112] To these must be added the basic bipolarity between theology and pastoral care. As Francis stated in his video message for the Pontifical Catholic University of Argentina:

> Not infrequently a kind of opposition is constructed between theology and pastoral care, as though they were two opposing, separate realities, which have nothing to do with one another. Not infrequently we identify doctrine with the conservative, the retrograde; and, on the contrary, we think that pastoral care is an adaptation, a reduction, an accommodation, as if they had nothing to do with one another. Thus, we create a false opposition between the so-called "pastorally-minded" and the "academics," those on the side of the people and those on the side of doctrine. We create a false opposition between theology and pastoral care; between the believer's reflection and the believer's life; life, then, has no space for reflection and reflection finds no space in life. The great fathers of the church, Irenaeus, Augustine, Basil, Ambrose, to name a few, were great theologians because they were great pastors.
>
> One of the main contributions of the Second Vatican Council was precisely seeking a way to overcome this divorce between theology and pastoral care, between faith and life. I dare say that the Council has revolutionized to some extent the status of theology—the believer's way of doing and thinking.[113]

107. Pope Francis with Spadaro, *My Door Is Always Open*, 25.
108. Ibid.
109. Ibid., 27.
110. Ibid., 61.
111. Ibid., 62–63.
112. Ibid., 64.
113. Pope Francis, "Video Message to Participants in an International Theological Congress Held at the Pontifical Catholic University of Argentina" (Buenos Aires, September 1–2, 2015), https://w2.vatican.va/content/francesco /en/messages/pont-messages/2015/documents/papa-francesco_20150903 _videomessaggio-teologia-buenos-aires.html.

This passage describes the meaning and direction of an *agonic-organic reflection* that has at its center polar tensions, unresolvable poles that nevertheless require synthesis from time to time. Bergoglio's "dialogical thinking" does not represent, from this point of view, an irenic solution; it is, rather, the result of an ontological conception. *It is the ontology of polarity that requires a dialogue aimed toward a synthetic horizon that must prevent the "contradictory" outcome of the poles.* The picture is that of a "catholic" thought that understands both the church and life as a *complexio oppositorum*, an agonic struggle to overcome conflicts, to prevent polarities from being resolved, manicheistically, into contradictions.

In light of this, it becomes clear that Guardini represents a key point of reference for Jorge Mario Bergoglio, not only for the systematic of living oppositions offered in *Der Gegensatz* but also for the lucid analysis of the polar tension between nature and technology that guided Guardini's thought after the Second World War. In both *The End of the Modern World* and *Power and Responsibility*, the Italian-German author offered a picture of the degradation and exploitation of nature by industrialization and technology not unlike the work of Martin Heidegger. He did not, however, indulge in archaic utopias but realistically posed the question of power capable of dominating the accomplishments brought about by technical progress. *The ability to have power over one's power is the fundamental anthropological question of our time.*[114] It is a problem complicated by the fact that the modern era demonstrates, in its "autonomy," an inability to maintain the values that come from its Christian heritage. The parasitic use of those values, cut off from the roots of faith, is, as Nietzsche's work makes clear, impossible. It is this horizon that makes the relationship between humanity and its own power and technology problematic today.

In his lecture "On the Necessity of a Political Anthropology," Bergoglio observed that the sort of faith in progress that was typical of the Enlightenment is held today by no one. As Guardini highlighted in *The End of the Modern Word*, the three *absoluta* have failed: Nature, Subject, Culture. It is a fact that "*the three elements typical of Modernity (nature that subsists in itself, the autonomous*

---

114. Cf. Borghesi, *Romano Guardini*, 197–236.

subject-personality, and the creative culture that considers itself
capable of establishing its own norms) have lost their referential
validity."[115] The consequence, Bergoglio said (citing López Quintás's
text on Romano Guardini), was that "humanity today feels absurdly
free, with a freedom that, in large part, is *abandonment.* . . . Over-
looked is the fact that creation can generate pride and this causes
an imbalance between the power that one has over things and the
power one has over power."[116] There is a disproportion between
technical power and the ethical maturity of those who would use
it. For this reason, "in the characterization of an anthropology that
does not become a return to ignorance, the question of control of
power is present in the wholeness-form tension, which avoids chaos
and formalism. The challenge of anthropology is to shape and limit
the unlimited fullness of the technology of power. The correct characterization of tensions helps, and is already in itself dominion and
limit that leads to such a crazy force of the culture of modernity."[117]
Bergoglio quoted Guardini directly here: "The wildernesses of nature have long been under the control of man; nature as it exists
round and about us obeys its master. Nature now, however, has
emerged once again into history from within the very depths of
culture itself. Nature is rising up in that very form which subdued
the wilderness—in the form of power itself. All the abysses of pri-
meval ages yawn before man, all the wild choking growth of the
long-dead forests press forward from this second wilderness, all the
monsters of the desert wastes, all the horrors of darkness are once
more upon man. He stands again before chaos."[118]

It is therefore necessary to control this new chaos produced by
humanity. In a 2003 conference titled "*Duc in Altum*: The Social
Thought of John Paul II," Bergoglio addressed the idea of work in
Pope John Paul's teaching:

115. Bergoglio, "Necessità di un'antropologia politica," 293.

116. Ibid. The citation is from López Quintás, *Pasión de verdad y dialectica*
en Romano Guardini, 171.

117. Bergoglio, "Necessità di un'antropologia politica," 298, n. 24.

118. Guardini, *The End of the Modern World*, 91–92. The citation is in
Bergoglio, "Necessità di un'antropologia politica," 298.

The pope reaffirms this concept in light of the very essence of humanity, the essence from which springs the mission of "dominating the earth," and which involves the free choice to be a collaborator of humanity's Creator. We hear echoes here of the prophecy of Romano Guardini, who in his book *The End of the Modern Age* (1950) identified the fundamental reason for the paradigm shift that was coming to dominate our modern world. Guardini saw as a characteristic feature of our modern civilization the fact that power was increasingly turning into something anonymous. And from there, as from a root, all the dangers and injustices we suffer today are born. And the antidote that he proposed was that humanity, each one of us in solidarity, become responsible for power. It is precisely here that John Paul II's vision fits human work as *the place* where the person freely chooses to use power as a service and in collaboration with God's own creative work for the good of all.[119]

This Guardinian understanding of the relationship between technology and power in the "postmodern" era took a central place once again for Bergoglio when, as pope, he wrote his encyclical letter *Laudato Si'*. Noting the process of the uncontrolled exploitation of resources and of sources of water and the degradation of the environment in the disastrous slums of the South American metropolises, the document takes up again Guardini's basic categories. Guardini is the encyclical's most frequently quoted modern thinker. After observing that humanity has never "had such power over itself, yet nothing ensures that it will be used wisely, particularly when we consider how it is currently being used,"[120] the pope quotes Guardini directly. He continues with a paragraph that cites several more passages of Guardini:

> There is a tendency to believe that every increase in power means "an increase of 'progress' itself," an advance in "security, usefulness,

---

119. Jorge Mario Bergoglio, "'Duc in altum': il pensiero sociale di Giovanni Paolo II," in Bergoglio-Francis, *Nei tuoi occhi è la mia parola* (Milan: Rizzoli, 2016), 229.

120. Pope Francis, encyclical letter *Laudato Si'* 104, http://w2.vatican.va /content/francesco/en/encyclicals/documents/papa-francesco_20150524 _enciclica-laudato-si.html.

welfare and vigour; . . . an assimilation of new values into the stream of culture," as if reality, goodness and truth automatically flow from technological and economic power as such. The fact is that "contemporary man has not been trained to use power well," because our immense technological development has not been accompanied by a development in human responsibility, values and conscience. Each age tends to have only a meagre awareness of its own limitations. It is possible that we do not grasp the gravity of the challenges now before us. "The risk is growing day by day that man will not use his power as he should"; in effect, "power is never considered in terms of the responsibility of choice which is inherent in freedom" since its "only norms are taken from alleged necessity, from either utility or security."[121]

For Pope Francis, the crux of the matter is "the globalization of the technocratic paradigm,"[122] which implies an integral reduction, in the economy and politics, of nature to technical power, the elimination of the subject-nature polarity. The encyclical continues:

This subject makes every effort to establish the scientific and experimental method, which in itself is already a technique of possession, mastery and transformation. It is as if the subject were to find itself in the presence of something formless, completely open to manipulation. Men and women have constantly intervened in nature, but for a long time this meant being in tune with and respecting the possibilities offered by the things themselves. It was a matter of receiving what nature itself allowed, as if from its own hand. Now, by contrast, we are the ones to lay our hands on things, attempting to extract everything possible from them while frequently ignoring or forgetting the reality in front of us. Human beings and material objects no longer extend a friendly hand to one another; the relationship has become confrontational.[123]

The man/nature polarity enters into crisis and gives way to the simple negation of nature. The encyclical goes on, citing Guardini

121. Pope Francis, *Laudato Si'* 105. The citations are from Guardini, *The End of the Modern World*, 82–83.
122. This is the title of sec. II of chap. 3.
123. Pope Francis, *Laudato Si'* 106.

again: "Technology tends to absorb everything into its ironclad logic, and those who are surrounded with technology 'know full well that it moves forward in the final analysis neither for profit nor for the well-being of the human race,' that 'in the most radical sense of the term power is its motive—a lordship over all.' As a result, 'man seizes hold of the naked elements of both nature and human nature.' "[124] This ideal of domination, complete and total, is much different from the premodern one that was founded on the inseparable relationship with the natural reality. "*The new dominion,*" Guardini wrote, "*calls into question whether things really are founded on an essence. It resorts to the fundamental elements and constructs the forms, as it wants them to be for it. Its fundamental image is not the king who protects the essence*—the ancient concept of the 'shepherd of the people'—*but the dictator who defines the essence.* This is a good description of Bolshevism and existentialism."[125] The new dominion is the result of the Promethean myth that marks the modern era. Francis writes in *Laudato Si'*, "Modern anthropocentrism has paradoxically ended up prizing technical thought over reality, since"—and here he quotes Guardini yet another time—" 'the technological mind sees nature as an insensate order, as a cold body of facts, as a mere "given," as an object of utility, as raw material to be hammered into useful shape; it views the cosmos similarly as a mere "space" into which objects can be thrown with complete indifference.' "[126]

The solution lies in returning to reality and ridding ourselves of the anthropocentric *excess*: "Modernity has been marked by an excessive anthropocentrism which today, under another guise, continues to stand in the way of shared understanding and of any effort to strengthen social bonds. The time has come to pay renewed

124. Ibid., n. 108. The Guardini citation is from *The End of the Modern World*, 56.

125. Romano Guardini, *Die Situation des Menschen* (Munich: Akademie-vorträge, 1953); Italian trans. "La situazione dell'uomo," in Guardini, *Natura, Cultura, Cristianesimo: Saggi filosofici* (Brescia: Morcelliana, 1983), 203, emphasis mine.

126. Pope Francis, *Laudato Si'* 115. The Guardini citation is from *The End of the Modern World*, 55.

attention to reality and the limits it imposes. . . . Often, what was handed on was a Promethean vision of mastery over the world, which gave the impression that the protection of nature was something that only the faint-hearted cared about. Instead, our 'dominion' over the universe should be understood more properly in the sense of responsible stewardship."[127]

The remedy is an adequate anthropology and not, as certain currents of a radical ecological ideology suggest, in its negation: "A misguided anthropocentrism need not necessarily yield to 'biocentrism,' for that would entail adding yet another imbalance, failing to solve present problems and adding new ones."[128]

Biocentrism, like unilateral anthropocentrism, interrupts the humanity-nature polar relationship. This is why "[w]e need to develop a new synthesis capable of overcoming the false arguments of recent centuries."[129] In this regard, the encyclical *Laudato Si'* seems to represent a "new synthesis" project that Francis offers *in the light of the Guardinian model of polarities*. Promethean anthropocentrism and biocentrism dissolve the constitutive link between the I and the world. They forget that "everything is connected,"[130] that "everything is interrelated"[131]—and not according to the vision of a pantheist One-All matrix, but starting from the personal, fundamental, and paradigmatic relationship between the I and the you.

If the present ecological crisis is one small sign of the ethical, cultural and spiritual crisis of modernity, we cannot presume to heal our relationship with nature and the environment without healing all fundamental human relationships. . . . Our openness to others, each of whom is a "thou" capable of knowing, loving and entering into dialogue, remains the source of our nobility as human persons. A correct relationship with the created world demands that we not weaken this social dimension of openness to others, much less the transcendent dimension of our openness to the "Thou" of God. Our relationship with the environment can never be isolated from our

127. Pope Francis, *Laudato Si'* 116.
128. Ibid. 118.
129. Ibid. 121.
130. Ibid. 117.
131. Ibid. 120.

relationship with others and with God. Otherwise, it would be nothing more than romantic individualism dressed up in ecological garb, locking us into a stifling immanence.[132]

It is clear, then, that *Laudato Si'* offers—along with *Evangelii Gaudium*—further proof of the important place that Romano Guardini's polar-relational anthropology holds in the thought of Jorge Mario Bergoglio/Pope Francis. The whole system of Bergoglio's thought is dominated by the overarching idea of the polarity of life. This is its conceptual core, the hermeneutical key that fuels a "catholic" system of thought. Romano Guardini is indeed one of Bergoglio's teachers.

132. Ibid. 119.

Church and Modernity

Methol Ferré and the Catholic Risorgimento *in Latin America*

Vatican II as the Overcoming of the Reformation and the Enlightenment

We have already considered the importance of Alberto Methol Ferré for Bergoglio. The journals he led—*Nexo*, *Vispera*, and then *Nexo* again—profoundly influenced Catholic intellectuals throughout Latin America. In their pages, Methol developed his vision of an "ecclesial geopolitics" dominated by the church and Latin America,[1] as two poles in tension, united and distinct at the same time. As he wrote in 1975, he wished to provide "a reflection that runs between two poles, Latin America and the church, in order to define the current 'configurations' that both have taken. It is a compelling problem, because we are Latin Americans engaged in the church and Christians engaged in Latin America. But one pole cannot intersect with the other pole and its conflicts without bringing its own along with it. We are engaged in the conflicts of the two poles, the ecclesial and the secular, which interpenetrate. We cannot

---

1. On "ecclesial geopolitics," see Alberto Methol Ferré, "Prologo per Europei," foreword to Methol Ferré, *Il risorgimento cattolico latinoamericano*, trans. P. Di Pauli and C. Perfetti (Bologna: CSEO, 1983), 12.

be engaged in one without also being engaged in the other."[2] It is impossible to separate the poles, he said, because both have the same starting point: the people. He wrote:

> [The church is] a universal people "within" peoples. It is a universal people, because it is the people of God, living in the midst of every nation, encountering all manner of opposition, until the final day of history. Without a home of its own, it is the most fragile of peoples and also the strongest, because it resides in the power of the love of Christ, of God. The mystery of the church is founded on the omnipotence of the crucified God who assumed our weakness in order to redeem us, without a homeland of its own on the earth, but residing within peoples and states, submissive to them, sharing their vicissitudes and traditions, and yet with a consistent, ecclesial tradition of its own, because the church is itself a people. The church assumes the traditions of the peoples that make it up and nourishes itself with them, but at the same time it develops a tradition of its own, different from that of all the peoples of the world, and penetrates them from "outside" to constitute itself "inside" and change the ecclesial "outside" to the "inside" of the people of the world.[3]

In this inside-outside-inside dialectic, the relationships between the church and the world are played out, taking three different forms: secularization, reaction, and inculturation. Exploring these three positions in order to identify the most fitting mode for an encounter of faith with Latin American modernity is the guiding aim of Methol Ferré's work from the 1970s through the 1990s.

For him, the theology of secularization—which was in vogue in the 1970s, thanks to the work of scholars like Gogarten, Bonhoeffer, Robinson, and Cox—found its starting point in the supremacy of the modern world. "Optimistically speaking, the modern world appears as a monolith. It is the 'illuminated' version of the modern world. Taking up the themes of the Enlightenment, it shares the same criticisms of the church that the Enlightenment offered. There can be nothing 'beyond,' nothing 'supernatural': the task of Chris-

---

2. Methol Ferré, "La Chiesa, popolo fra i popoli," in *Il risorgimento cattolico latinoamericano*, 139.
    3. Ibid., 146–147.

tians is only to build the secular world, without distinguishing themselves from the secular world."[4] According to this stance,

> there is no place in the world for anything that is specifically Chris-
> tian, because it would be "objectification," "Christianity," and so
> forth. Religious contaminations of the faith. Whatever is visibly Chris-
> tian is impure; only the profane may be visible. An obsession with
> "purity" that marks the return of the sectarian spirit in the church.
> For the secularizers, a Christian people could only be a "people of
> angels in an earthly world." The process of spiritualization reaches
> its ultimate limit: only faith remains, naked, pure love as a Kantian
> transcendental, without a church, without objective content. Here
> appears an irreconcilable contradiction between secularization and
> the People of God, the visible, historical subject incarnate in history,
> in this or that concrete setting. The logic of secularizers is to make
> the visibility of the church, of the People of God, disappear.[5]

For Methol Ferré, this position, with its uncritical acceptance of
the "Enlightenment" version of modernity, is simply a mirror image
of its antithesis: the reactionary position that opposes everything
modern, conceived, again, in Enlightenment terms. Set against one
another's conclusions, progressives and reactionaries share the same
vision of modernity. The reactionary and progressive positions are
reciprocally subordinate; they share the same flawed model of
modernity.

> The theologies of secularization are an inversion of the approach to
> the modern world that had previously been dominant in the church.
> This approach was largely derived from the "romantic political the-
> ology" (De Bonald, Donoso Cortés, Haller, for example) of the early
> nineteenth century that saw the Enlightenment as an enemy and that
> rejected modernity as a whole, based on a mythical and idealized
> memory of the Middle Ages. It was a reaction of the old, rural world
> against the emerging bourgeoisie. Forever mourning the passing of
> the Middle Ages, modernity can only be viewed as a pure deviation.
> Modernity's antimedieval stance, in this view, can only be understood
> as anti-Christian.

4. Ibid., 154.
5. Ibid.

This is a grave misunderstanding! There are no archetypes, no Christian eras that should be seen as a "model." There is only Christ. But the simplification of the "antimodern" survived in the church until the Second Vatican Council. Then the theology of secularization carried out a reverse, compensatory simplification: all modernity is good and all of medieval Christianity bad. Christianity is anti-Christian contamination; secularizing modernity is Christian maturity.[6]

In this way two positions, because of the one-sidedness of each, collide, giving rise to an antithetical dialectic that divides the church from within. Drawing on the work of Jacques Maritain, Methol could not accept the medievalist ideology—the "return to the Middle Ages"—driven by the neoscholastic movement of the early twentieth century, which was, thanks to the influence of Spain, widespread in Latin American Catholic circles.[7] Nor, however, could he share the optimism of the new, postconciliar theologies. He saw the theology of secularization of the 1970s as a reaction to a frozen, closed church, unable to confront the modern world constructively. What was needed was a "critical" approach, able to distinguish between the positive and the negative aspects of modernity. *It is here that we find the originality of Methol's dialectical Thomism, compared to the scholastic Thomism that was being taught at the Catholic universities of Latin America.* The latter is the heir of the "'defensive' era of the Catholic Church that, in general, lasted until the Second Vatican Council. One cannot resist without adapting oneself to some degree. To resist is like a desperate self-defense; it leads to withdrawal into oneself, into a fortress. Resisting means an inability to generate models, and only to survive in the face of existing models determined by others. To resist means to become dependent, because the fight takes place on terrain chosen by others, imposed by others. The Catholic Church of the eighteenth century up to today can therefore clearly be recognized as a 'dependent society.' "[8] This is

6. Ibid., 155.

7. Cf. Alberto Methol Ferré, "Maritain: un tomista avventuriero e mal tradotto," *Incontri* 8, November–December 1982, 43–48.

8. Methol Ferré, "La Chiesa latinoamericana nella dinamica mondiale" (1973), in Methol Ferré, *Il risorgimento cattolico latinoamericano*, 131.

confirmed by its strenuous resistance and its inability to do anything other than resist, by the way it sets its eyes more on the past than the future, because those who resist look to the ages to which they are oriented. This is the origin of the Catholic "medievalism" that emerged at the beginning of the nineteenth century. But by grasping onto the memory of an era that possessed the dynamism to generate decisive models for itself, and "copying" this era, the church made itself incapable of generating models for its own time. One cannot respond adequately to current situations by nostalgically recalling answers that were effective in other situations and at other times. Indeed, this approach is precisely the best way to make oneself unable to respond effectively to one's own times, and it is precisely the opposite of what medieval Catholics did to generate models. In times of defeat, memory is certainly a support. But the truest and most effective support is the hope and audacity of the project rather than the repetition of what has been and of what, having already been, can never be again.[9]

The approach of the traditionalists is really a surrender to the opposition while standing in opposition to it. Methol wrote, "The reinterpretation of the origin of modernity by the Enlightenment imposed its model. The traditionalist, defensive, dependent integralism accepted the assumptions of the Enlightenment, and in doing so it made the modern age, begun by Descartes, the enemy, seeing it as pure decadence. . . . The integralist is a Catholic who has been conquered by the Enlightenment, who surrenders; the modernist is the same, but is open about it. One freezes, the other dissolves."[10]

Methol effectively grasps the *forma mentis* of both conservative and progressive Catholicism. The failure of both is their failure to rise to a true dialectical thought, capable of integrating opposition: "The church, lacking the energy to offer an opposition that assimilates and overcomes, limited itself simply to 'opposing.' Its main goal was to oppose in the trenches, to repel the opponent. And

9. Ibid., 131–132.

10. Methol Ferré, "Il risorgimento cattolico latinoamericano" (1981), in Methol Ferré, *Il risorgimento cattolico latinoamericano*, 260. On the traditionalist Catholic position that moves "in the shadow of De Bonald," see "Sviluppi della sociologia latinoamericana," *Vispera* 37 (April 1975).

undoubtedly the church carried out a full-blown rejection. If all I do is fight, I am limited to the field of the dominant models; it is precisely these that ultimately condition me."[11] The dialectic in the life of the church oscillates between two forms of dependence: "The risk of resistance is sclerotization, stiffening, and degeneration; the risk of adaptation to another is simply being absorbed by the other. This is what is happening to us today, at various levels. There is so much 'serving' others, without reference to the church or to Christ. These two interdependent moments end either in integralism or in secularization. Both are paths of death, if one does not manage to transcend them by assuming and taking into oneself the other and generating new cultural models."[12]

This assumption/transcendence requires a way of thinking that is critical and dialectical at the same time, an ability to free the core of truth from the ideologies in which it is inscribed.

> To assume and orient a real historical process obviously requires the *conditio sine qua non* of knowing the other, of deeply penetrating the logic of current models, of entering them in order actually to overcome them, in order to respond to reality in a true manner. If I am simply a resister, if I say, "Hegel and Marx are atheists," and this is enough for me and I lock myself in, this is not a journey. Theologians of the last century were clearly aware of the atheism of Hegel and Marx and denounced them. But it was not enough. It was necessary to penetrate deeply into their motivations, to discover the new problems that they generated. And this was not done. And so today a couple of generations of Catholics are trying in vain to assimilate and understand Hegel and Marx. It will happen that many will die of indigestion, because it is not possible to "consume" Hegel and Marx with impunity, and the task of "overcoming" them is difficult.[13]

According to Methol,

> In order to transcend something, I have to incorporate it in some way within myself, by which I mean the church. This is what the

11. Methol Ferré, "La Chiesa latinoamericana nella dinamica mondiale," 132.
12. Ibid.
13. Ibid., 133.

Christians did with Hellenic-Roman culture. This happened in the Middle Ages, when "Averroism" was the strongest intellectual energy and Thomas Aquinas creatively absorbed it. One only overcomes what is digested well, because the other is always a very heavy food and eating it greedily risks an ulcer. It is not a matter of "devouring" it in order to destroy it, but to save it, according to that singular dialectic of death and resurrection in which we are immersed.[14]

This dialectic, Methol said, was actualized in the life of the church with the Second Vatican Council. In his interview with Alver Metalli, Methol commented:

With the Council the church transcends both the Protestant Reformation and secular Enlightenment. It overcomes them, by taking into itself what is best in both of them. We can also say this: it creates a new Reformation and a new Enlightenment. The Reformation and the Enlightenment were at the time the two big, unresolved issues, on which the accounts had never really been closed. With the Council, they both finally recede into the past. They lose substance and their reason for being and realize the best of themselves in the Catholic intimacy of the church. The church, assimilating them, repeals them as adversaries and takes within itself their constructive power.[15]

14. Ibid. "No, nobody needs an enemy. But a mission—the church essentially *is* mission—can be dynamic when it is able to understand the enemy; more precisely, when it acquires the understanding of the 'best' of the enemy it faces. . . . In this sense the enemy is 'outside,' but it is also 'within.' One can see in the enemy a friend who must be redeemed and saved. We need to make the enemy a friend, to find the friend that is in the enemy, knowing that the enemy is already part of us anyway. . . . The originality of Christ is not only love of neighbor, but peculiarly love of one's enemy. The friend-enemy dialectic in Christian terms cannot be resolved by annihilating the enemy, but by recovering the enemy as a friend. In the worldly order, this is not so; the enemy is liquidated. Either the State eliminates the enemy or it is eliminated by the enemy. In the church things are radically different, and when the church has failed to behave as if they are—as in certain moments of the Inquisition and even more so in the religious wars—history has rightly reproached her" (Alberto Methol Ferré and Alver Metalli, *Il Papa e il filosofo* [Siena: Cantagalli, 2014], 54–56).

15. Ibid., 95.

Assimilation is a form of a dialectical overcoming that separates the truth from error:

> In order to respond to the challenges it faced—in order to "update"— the church had to assume into itself the whole of modernity, against which it had spent the entire period of the dissolution of medieval and baroque Christianity defending itself. The fundamental traits of modernity were called Protestant Reformation and secular Enlightenment. The church had given answers to both, but these answers had been limited and somewhat insufficient, in the sense that they had refuted and rejected the unacceptable elements of the Reformation and the Enlightenment, but they had not sufficiently distinguished their truth from their error. An error is powerful precisely because of the truth that it contains; it can therefore be effectively confronted only by understanding the central truth that it bears. . . . In my opinion the Second Vatican Council overcomes modernity for the first time by understanding what was right about the Reformation and what was right about the Enlightenment.[16]

In the case of the Reformation, this truth concerns "the affirmation of the People of God and of the laity as a priestly people. In a sense, the Reformation was a great protest of the laity against clericalism."[17] In the case of the Enlightenment, the truth consists in the fact that "the Council, contrary to the claims of the figures of the late Enlightenment, shows that faith does not disavow the autonomy of the secular, and that it brings new reasons for human development. Heaven fertilizes the Earth, wisely pushes it toward its integral development, elevates it, purifies it. The Council affirms the autonomy of knowledge of nature and history."[18] This twofold overcoming of the Enlightenment and the Reformation not only reconciles the church with the authentic core of what is modern but also places it in a "postmodern" horizon.

> The Second Vatican Council, for the first time, establishes the church in true postmodernity. The postmodernity of which people often

---

16. Ibid., 95–96.
17. Ibid., 96.
18. Ibid., 99. Similar considerations in Methol Ferré, "Evangelizzazione e cultura" (1980), in *Il risorgimento cattolico latinoamericano*, 195–196.

speak is not really that; it is mere decomposition of modernity, not a *post*-modernity. We are the only postmodernity because we have assumed the best of modernity. We have also discarded traditionalism, though not of course tradition. We do not have to defend ourselves against everything. The pope can ask for forgiveness from Luther in peace, absolutely in peace. One only asks for forgiveness when one is really at peace. This points to the worldwide significance of the Second Vatican Council, with its two wings, *Lumen Gentium* and *Gaudium et Spes*, in its two transcendences, in the new epoch that the church places at the level of historical actuality, at the moment that the secular religions have entered in agony the collapse of the secular myth embodied by the USSR: messianic atheism.[19]

From Medellín to Puebla: The Latin American Catholic *Risorgimento*

The approach outlined here, in which we see Catholicism close its accounts with modernity, constitutes, for the church of Latin America, a *new beginning*, a historic opportunity: "Twenty or thirty years ago," Methol wrote in his 1981 essay "Il risorgimento cattolico latinoamericano,"

> no one would have dared to foresee the current dynamics of the church in Latin America. . . . But now everything has changed, almost suddenly. What no one could have thought to be feasible, or even possible, is happening: what was thought to be a residue of the past appears as a tendency projecting toward the future. What was static, reactionary, or simply resigned now rises, dynamic and creative, in the heart of the Latin American peoples. The first signs of this emerged with Medellín and then became clear with Puebla. In fact, we need to take a closer look, to try to understand and trace the lines of this historic surprise: the Latin American Catholic rebirth.[20]

---

19. Methol Ferré, "Grandes orientaciones pastorales de Pablo VI para América Latina," in *Pablo VI y America Latina: Jornadas de estudio (Buenos Aires 10–11 ottobre 2000)* (Rome: Istituto Paolo VI–Studium, 2002), 28.

20. Alberto Methol Ferré, *Il risorgimento cattolico latinoamericano*, trans. P. Di Pauli and C. Perfetti (Bologna: CSEO-Incontri, 1983), 208.

To Methol, the General Conference of the Latin American bishops held in Medellín in 1968 and, above all, the following one held in Puebla in 1979 represent a turning point, the awakening of the Latin American church from hibernation, from a closed clerical horizon aimed at the past.[21] Puebla "establishes a platform that makes possible dialogue, discussion, and development in the relationship between the church and modern culture."[22] It represents, in Latin America, the mature assimilation of the Council, an overcoming of both Catholic traditionalism and the theology of secularization that, in the postconciliar period, arose from an uncritical acceptance of the Enlightenment model. In reality, the authentic "modernity" of the Catholic Church "calls into question the very idea of 'modernity' that has thus far prevailed."[23] From an idea of modernity that excludes the church, we reach a moment in which modernity itself is called into question. This is a development that Methol called "the second postconciliar wave":

> *Evangelii Nuntiandi* and Puebla are part of a second, more substantial postconciliar wave. Integralism's leap toward the Enlightenment assumed that the Council's "*aggiornamento*" was simply an adaptation to the "modern." It meant considering the modern "from outside." The first wave sought only the "modernization" of the church, only a path that was opposite to that of integralism. There was no other way. Perhaps this passage to the Enlightenment was an indispensable moment of denial necessary to break with integralism and, therefore, with the Enlightenment itself. The second postconciliar wave is to understand that it is not a matter of modernizing but of seeing more deeply in oneself (through the other) what makes it possible to redeem the modernity of the church from within. The modern, brought to the depth of itself, reunites the church. Vatican II, the new Pentecost of the church after the Reformation and the Enlightenment, takes up and transcends them both—through the two conciliar poles of *Lumen Gentium* and *Gaudium et Spes*—be-

21. On the significance of the Puebla Conference, cf. Methol Ferré, "Evangelizzazione e cultura," 191–206; Methol Ferré, "Da Rio de Janeiro a Puebla: venticinque anni di storia" (4, January–February 1982, 8–25).

22. Methol Ferré, *Il risorgimento cattolico latinoamericano*, 210.

23. Ibid., 209.

cause it rediscovers within itself the legitimate demands of the Protestant reform and the legitimate secularity of the Enlightenment. This rediscovery is not a mutilation, but a strengthening. It is not a break with Trent and the Catholic Counter-Reformation—which would fall into Protestantism and Enlightenment—but to recover the values of Trent and the Reformation, that is, of the Baroque. To recover the Baroque means recovering Catholic modernity, which allows a deep dialogue with Protestantism and the Enlightenment, not from the outside, but from within.[24]

Methol, in other words, offered an absolutely original interpretation of the relationship between the church and modernity, a reading that was without precedent in Latin America. He pointed to a way that he believed would

enable the church authentically to overcome the Baroque as incomplete modernity: so incomplete as to give way to the Protestant Enlightenment hegemony that today has exhausted its possibilities. It is an end of possibilities that can only be fruitful by going beyond modernity's supposed rejection of Protestantism and Enlightenment, and rediscovering the Catholic capacity at the foundation of modernity. This new historical movement that unleashes Vatican II begins to settle into the collective ecclesial conscience, in my opinion, with Puebla, a fact that implies the carrying out to the end the ecclesial and Latin American historical revision in order really to understand the needs and potentialities of the current Catholic risorgimento. This risorgimento breaks the vicious circle of integralism and Enlightenment; it means having to reinterpret modernity.[25]

Here Methol applied to the Latin American church the category of risorgimento as a step beyond the revolution-reaction dialectic that he drew from his discovery of the philosophical work of the Italian thinker Augusto Del Noce.[26] Thanks to it the possibility of

24. Ibid., 261.
25. Ibid., 261–262.
26. Cf. Augusto Del Noce, "Rivoluzione risorgimento tradizione," *L'Europa* 4, no. 17 (October 15, 1972): 129–141 (in F. Mercadante, A. Tarantino, and B. Casadei., eds., *Rivoluzione risorgimento tradizione* [Milan: Giuffré Editore, 1993], 427–443). Among the contributors to the journal *Incontri: Testimonianze*

the church's encounter with its present moment in history opened up. It was the possibility of a new beginning through which the Latin American church could now, for the first time, become a "source" church.

Methol wrote as early as 1973,

> I believe that Latin America is passing through a privileged moment of its history. I believe it because it is the moment in which its freedom and its capacity for historical protagonism are played out. In these decades to come, growth or death. And in Latin America, the church. Why is the role of Catholics in Latin America so important? Because Latin America is the great Christian area of the Third World; it is the area that is "more dependent" upon Catholicism in its origins, and, at the same time, has immense material and cultural resources that place it as a "singular mediation" between the modern dominant worlds and the Third World. What the church will do in Latin America will have great repercussions throughout the Third World. It will be the greatest advent, the most decisive contribution, of the church in the Third World. Moreover, Latin America, being in a certain sense less distant from modernity than the rest of the Third World, will have a profound effect on the destiny of the church of Europe, the United States, and the European socialist bloc. Latin America and its church have a great opportunity and I believe that ours is to some extent also an opportunity for the church throughout the world.[27]

After 1979, the year of Puebla, this hope seems to have become a certainty. With Puebla the Latin American church emerged from the progressivism/reactionism dialectic and, in a critical dialogue with the modern, began to offer a valid paradigm for the universal church. As Methol wrote in 1983:

> A genuine Latin American Catholic risorgimento is vital for the global church. The church is more deeply rooted in the peoples of

---

dall'America Latina who would utilize the category of "risorgimento" was Del Noce's Italian student, Rocco Buttiglione, in "Tra conservazione e rivoluzione: Il risorgimento ispanoamericano," *Incontri* 6, May–June 1982, 12–15. Issue no. 8 of that year (November–December 1982) included a dossier titled "Si può parlare di risorgimento per l'America Latina?" ["Can One Speak of a Latin American Risorgimento?"] (pp. 12–41).

27. Methol Ferré, "La Chiesa latinoamericana nella dinamica mondiale," 137.

Latin America than in those of any other in the Third World. Europe—and its old Latin Christianity—are indelibly a part of our origins, our history. We are not Europe, but yes, perhaps we are among the most European in the Third World, not in spite of our identity and cultural originality, but by virtue of it. We are already half of the Catholic believers on earth. And all of this allows us to presume the importance of the Latin American church for evangelization, on the threshold of the third millennium. A Latin American Catholic risorgimento concerns not only us, but the whole church. It has repercussions on the global path of history, which is now universal in all its parts. It affects us all, though in different ways. Only by means of its universality can a Latin American originality take hold. Anything that arises today without a vocation to universality, even if it offers a well-defined historical concreteness, lacks interest and practicability. The power of an originality lies in its capacity to live and to shape the universal.[28]

It was the lesson of Amelia Podetti, which Methol made his own—the same lesson offered by the journal *Incontri*, whose issue 7 of 1982 provided an Italian translation of the opening pages of *La irrupción de América en la historia*.

For Methol the rise of the Latin American church to a "universal" role indicated a shift in the relationship between "center" and "periphery." He said, "In the history of the church there exists also a particular dynamic of 'centers' (spiritual, intellectual, artistic) and 'peripheries.' The centers (such as Alexandria and Antioch in antiquity, or the Franco-German churches at the time of the Second Vatican Council) radiate and thus guide the rest of the church, in turn generating new centers in the periphery that will replace the old ones. This is a dialectic full of tensions that shows a singular 'ecclesial geopolitics' of renewal, because ecclesial centers and peripheries always have their concreteness in historical 'space-time.' "[29]

In this dialectic, the Second Vatican Council appears as "the last great Council generated mainly by Western Europe."[30] With the pontificate of John Paul II, Eastern Europe entered the scene, and with Puebla, Latin America did the same. At Puebla, "the two most crucial

28. Methol Ferré, "Prologo per Europei," 11–12.
29. Ibid., 12.
30. Ibid.

ecclesial frontiers of our time—the Polish and the Latin American—
encountered one another. One is located in the sphere of the North
American empire, the other in that of the Soviet empire. A gigantic
historical shift. Two frontiers; not new, well-defined centers. We live
in a moment of transition, still unclear, as if in a shadow, waiting.
There are no centers, only frontiers, which are not simply peripheries."[31]
They are "peripheries" destined to become "centers."

Starting from the early 1970s, Methol's "universalistic" gaze
captured the novelty, the "historical actuality" of the Latin American
church. In the 1975 essay "The Church, a People in the Midst of
the Peoples," the Uruguayan thinker takes up the distinction of the
Brazilian Jesuit Henrique de Lima Vaz between "source church"
and "reflected church": "Lima Vaz distinguishes between 'reflected
church' and 'source church.' The 'reflected' churches are those that
are more determined by other churches than by themselves. The
'source' churches are those that find the energies of renewal more
in themselves. It is an opposition that has many levels. To some
extent, all churches are both source and reflected, but one of these
characteristics always prevails in each of them."[32] In the manner
of Romano Guardini's polar dialectic, the rhythm of polarity always
predicts a momentary prevalence of one pole over another. A pole
that carries itself and, together, its counterpart, is singular and universal at the same time. The new stamp of the Latin American
church lay in its being "popular"—something that the European
church no longer was—and, at the same time, "modern." The dynamic of Vatican II, mediated through Medellín and Puebla, had
allowed the Latin American church to transcend the opposition
between "popular religion" and "modern reason" that lies at the
center of the paradigm of secularization. In this way it could propose
itself as "current," it could become "source," while the European
church became increasingly "reflected":

> In the fourteenth century, the "source" churches were those of Spain,
> Italy, and France. In the twentieth century, they were above all France,
> Belgium, and Germany. The Second Vatican Council was largely a

31. Ibid., 12–13.
32. Methol Ferré, "La Chiesa, popolo fra i popoli," 155.

Franco-German project. But this is now the last European Council. We are at the sunset of Europe as the singular protagonist center of the church. The Catholic Church, now globalized, begins to feel the presence of other local churches that previously were "reflected." While the "embers" of Western Europe are still hot, others try to light their matches. Time will tell. It would seem that in Latin America we are experiencing the transition from "reflected" to "source." The thing is still very recent. Medellín is the first clear example of this new movement.[33]

Medellín was the somewhat ambiguous beginning, and Puebla was the point of maturity:

> Puebla, I think, takes to a higher level the concerns of the great national and "culturalist" Latin American generation of the 1930s and 1960s. Medellín has two sides: on the one hand it reflects those years that gave birth to the secularizing liberation theologies that privilege Marxist analysis; on the other hand, the foundations are laid for the recovery of Latin American popular religiosity, and we begin to see the historical rediscovery of national and popular Latin American culture, thanks to a theological approach that understands that culture to be all-encompassing. This latter side, with its links to the Latin American generation of the 1920s and 1930s, is where Puebla's novelty lies.[34]

Of the generation since then—that of José Rodó, Manuel Ugarte, José Vasconcelos, Tristán de Athayde, Pedro Henríquez Ureña— Methol was preoccupied with identifying a common source of nourishment and with connecting it with Puebla—a national/Catholic/

---

33. Ibid., 155–156. The perspective of Methol Ferré differed from the radical sectors of liberation theology that rejected the Western Christian model understood as an ideological-imperialistic model. The fact that the church began to be multipolar and that its vital center dislocated itself differently from the past did not imply the rejection of the European paradigm as a synthesis between Christianity and culture. In this, Methol did not differ from Lima Vaz, for whom the European model of integration between culture and faith had an exemplary value (cf. Henrique de Lima Vaz, "Quale 'cristianesimo per il popolo,'" *Incontri* 7, September–October 1982, 7–9).

34. Methol Ferré, "Il risorgimento cattolico latinoamericano," 254.

liberal/popular golden thread. For him, Puebla was the final result of an interrupted process that was able to come back to life thanks to the Second Vatican Council, the event that freed Catholicism from the antimodern complex: "What does Puebla say about Latin American history? How is it related to modernity? Puebla formulates its historical perspective with great clarity and coherence. Knowing the meaning of Puebla, it is no exaggeration to say that it represents the current historical self-awareness of the Latin American church."[35] In his 1981 text "Il risorgimento cattolico latinoamericano," Methol Ferré analyzes this "historical self-consciousness" in light of the Final Document of the Puebla gathering. This self-consciousness, centered on the encounter between church and peoples, is articulated in three moments.

The first stage, in the sixteenth century, is marked by an evangelization that, despite many shadows, manifests the light of "the *mestizo* countenance of Mary of Guadalupe, who appeared at the start of the evangelization process."[36] The result was a "people's Catholicism,"[37] imbued with values that perdured into the present. It was a Catholicism that found its cultural expression in the Baroque, the last great creative moment of modern Catholicism.

The second stage of the relationship between the church and Latin America came about through the crisis of the nineteenth and the first half of the twentieth centuries. It saw a church on the defensive, suffering the impact of urban-industrial civilization and the attacks of liberalism and Marxism. Here a rupture developed between elites and the people, between tradition and progress. Despite the acknowledgment of this contrast between the church and secularist modernity, "Puebla never expresses itself in an anti-modern

---

35. Ibid., 210.

36. Third General Conference of the Latin American Episcopate (Puebla, 1979), Final Document §446, in John Eagleson and Philip Scharper, eds., *Puebla and Beyond* (Maryknoll: Orbis Books, 1979), 185; cited in Methol Ferré, "Il risorgimento cattolico latinoamericano," 212.

37. Third General Conference of the Latin American Episcopate, Final Document §444; cited in Methol Ferré, "Il risorgimento cattolico latinoamericano," 212.

language, while still adhering to an anti-enlightenment stance. Implicitly, it differentiates between modernity and Enlightenment."[38]

According to Methol, the third stage began with the Second Vatican Council and its reception by the Conferences of Medellín and Puebla. As the Puebla Document states: "Since Medellín in particular, the Church, clearly aware of its mission and loyally open to dialogue, has been scrutinizing the signs of the times and is generously disposed to evangelize in order to contribute to the construction of a new society that is more fraternal and just; such a society is a crying need of our peoples. Thus the mutual forces of tradition and progress, which once seemed to be antagonistic in Latin America, are now joining each other and seeking a new, distinctive synthesis that will bring together the possibilities of the future and the energies derived from our common roots."[39]

Commenting on this passage, Methol wrote, "Puebla thus begins to characterize the new era: it is the end of the past antinomy; it is a dynamic unity of tradition and progress that now poses a completely different problem. We start again on new bases."[40] This new beginning implies moving beyond the theologies of secularization and, at the same time, beyond the contrast between popular religiosity and modernity, that is, the modernism/traditionalism pair. In Latin America, "the sociology of modernization is what prepared the way, in the Latin American Catholic environment, for the theology of secularization in the middle of the 1960s."[41] Harvey Cox's 1965 work *The Secular City* incorporated the law of the three stages from the founder of positivistic sociology Auguste Comte:[42] "A sociology of modernization and a theology of secularization are the head and tail of the same coin."[43] This link continued in the union

---

38. Methol Ferré, "Il risorgimento cattolico latinoamericano," 215.

39. Third General Conference of the Latin American Episcopate, Final Document §12; cited in Methol Ferré, "Il risorgimento cattolico latinoamericano," 215.

40. Methol Ferré, "Il risorgimento cattolico latinoamericano," 215.

41. Ibid., 232.

42. Harvey Cox, *The Secular City: Secularization and Urbanization in Theological Perspective* (New York: Macmillan, 1965).

43. Methol Ferré, "Il risorgimento cattolico latinoamericano," 232.

between modern theology and Marxism that marked the history of the 1970s:

> In the Catholic environment, the symbols of this period are Camillo Torres and Gustavo Gutiérrez. Most of the "Christians for socialism" (Marxism) shared the sociology of modernization and became radicalized. Nothing more logical. The essential perspective of "modernity," and therefore its relationship with the Church and the Latin American peoples, is the same. The acceptance of modernity expressed by the Enlightenment and its followers, from Althusser to Gramsci, manifests itself with the greatest clarity in Gustavo Gutiérrez. It is the second phase of the modernizing secularization that arose from the Enlightenment and is typical of the 1970s, but that has rejected its own first phase, because it is "dependent."[44]

Liberation theology, influenced by Marxism, developed a critique of the sociology of modernization and its reformism based on "desarrollism" and the model of progress centered on capitalist industrial development. On the other hand, it failed to demonstrate any critical stance with regard to the paradigm of modernization that underpins North American sociology:

> Gustavo Gutiérrez's liberation theology, which is a "neomarxism," welcomed into itself the perspectives of "modernity" typical of the Enlightenment, and was therefore critical of the Church but not of the modernizing ideologies. It was critical of the church but not critical of the interpretation of the modernization that it accepted. Being semi-Marxist itself, it limited itself to gathering this interpretation dogmatically from semi-Marxists. This meant being incapable of a critical thinking that reaches the bottom of the principles. In this sense liberation theology remains an eclecticism, a Christian-Marxist juxtaposition that criticizes what is Christian but not what is Marxist.[45]

This second phase of intraecclesial secularization paid particular attention to people and their faith, just as did the positivistic soci-

---

44. Ibid., 234.
45. Ibid., 249.

ology of the 1960s. It is the same limit that Gutiérrez came to recognize in the 1988 edition of his *A Theology of Liberation*. Methol wrote:

> Thus the largest iconoclastic wave ever known in the Latin American church developed during the immediate postconciliar period. A sort of "enlightened despotism"—all for the people, but without the people—over the Latin American Catholic people, seen, in its baroque symbolism, as religious but without faith. From the viewpoint of the Enlightenment, the Baroque was superstition. By means of the European catechetical institutes, exemplified by the influential one led by Fr. Liege that adopted the Protestant opposition between "religion" and "faith," modernizing sociology and the theology of secularization joined forces with the most active Christian militancy. The contradiction between elites and Catholic masses reached paroxysm.[46]

This position, which was destined to assert itself after Medellín, would not, however, be the only one. Another perspective, that of the *theology of the people* carried out by the Rio de la Plata school of which we have spoken, attempted to articulate the demands of the people. Together with these, we must also note the development of the so-called National Professors of Sociology (Cátedras Nacionales de Sociología), of which an illustrious exponent was Amelia Podetti in Buenos Aires.[47]

---

46. Ibid., 233.

47. "The Argentine political context of the times of the COEPAL [the late 1960s and early 1970s] included the military dictatorship of Onganía, the proscription of Peronism since 1955, the repression of the Peronist labor movement, the emergence of future guerrilla groups, and a new phenomenon: the fact that not a few intellectuals, teachers, and progressive university students supported the Peronism of that day as a popular form of resistance to the military and the social protest movement. This had not occurred during the Perón presidencies. As a result, the so-called National Professors of Sociology (Cátedras Nacionales de Sociología) was born at the University of Buenos Aires, with the participation of figures such as O'Farrell. He was the link between the National Professors and COEPAL because he belonged to both. This explains how both the National Professors and COEPAL, by distancing themselves from both liberalism and Marxism, found the basis for their philosophy in Latin American and Argentine history (real and written) and were

The crisis of the sociology of modernization also produced, however, another outlet that was manifested mainly in Argentina, in the so-called "National Professors". . . . The path of the Latin American generation of the 1930s, so much criticized by the "scientifics," was taken up at other levels. It was returned to history. The result of this journey was a more intense critique of the identification of Enlightenment and modernity. This current of liberation theology had as its center—contrary to Gutiérrez—a critique of the Enlightenment understood to include both Marxism and capitalism. Its political path was more a Latin American national socialism than a purely class-oriented Marxist socialism. The journal *Vispera* was the point of union of these two aspects. . . . Liberation theology, with its tendency to dialogue with Marxism, had predictably greater cosmopolitan resonance, greater metropolitan influence. But the national and popular tendency that took up the question of Latin American culture and rediscovered the roots of popular religiosity, while not achieving the same resonance, entered the heart of Puebla, while the other remained outside.[48]

Puebla marks, therefore, the legitimation of the "theology of the people" and of the "historical-cultural" approach represented by the National Professors. It thus became possible to overcome the antinomy between popular religiosity and modernity: "The fact is that up to now the Enlightenment has imposed its values; it is identified with Modernity. This identity of Enlightenment and Modernity has concretely conditioned the whole second ecclesial historical stage. However, our thesis maintains that this identity does not exist; that the Enlightenment is only a variant of Modernity and does not entirely understand it, not even its best part. This is what makes possible the unity between Baroque and Modernity."[49]

---

enabled to employ distinctive categories such as "people," "antipeople," "peoples" in contrast to "empires," "popular culture," and "popular religiosity" (Juan Carlos Scannone, "Pope Francis and the Theology of the People," *Theological Studies* 77, no. 1 [2016]: 118–135, at 120).

48. Methol Ferré, "Il risorgimento cattolico latinoamericano," 234.

49. Ibid., 215–216. In terms that are different in form but identical in substance, Lucio Gera wrote, "Gathering the religious—and also the anthropological—spirit of the Baroque, and on the other hand the developed self-consciousness of modern man, the church, in its mediating role, tends to overcome both stages, that of the

Catholicism and Modernity: The Lesson of Augusto Del Noce

In his 1981 article "The Latin American Catholic Risorgimento," Methol Ferré described a second modernity, rooted not in Enlightenment principles, but in baroque ones: "Questioning modernization is not integralism. The integralist does not question modernity, but sees it from the same perspective as the Enlightenment—just unfavorably."[50] What the integralist does not understand, along with his Enlightenment adversary, is *the connection between the baroque and modernity*. "Baroque, due to its desire for continuity, possesses in its originality two faces: one medieval, the other modern. This is why, in misunderstanding it, they reduce it to 'medieval.' But with Baroque, modernity is born. Without this we cannot understand either Latin America or Puebla."[51]

Puebla, the splendid city of Mexican Baroque, thus represents the encounter of popular religion and the modern world that is so crucial for the Latin American church. It is a union that goes beyond the reaction-secularization dichotomy. This union, which is a subject throughout Alberto Methol Ferré's work, finds its philosophical legitimation in the work of the thinker Augusto Del Noce (1910–1989), one of the most illustrious Italian Catholic intellectuals of the second half of twentieth century.[52] In a prologue to his 1983 book *Il risorgimento cattolico latinoamericano*—a collection of previously published articles—Methol wrote, with reference to the final essay, which gave the title to the entire volume: "I feel that my thought reaches its principles here."[53] He added: "I would like to note once again that in this last work Augusto Del Noce had a great influence on me with his ideas of modernity and risorgimento."[54]

---

old Baroque and that of Enlightenment modernity, orienting itself toward the configuration of a new synthesis and a new civilization" (Lucio Gera, "L'identità religiosa dell'America latina," *Incontri* 7, September–October 1982, 29).

50. Methol Ferré, "Il risorgimento cattolico latinoamericano," 248.

51. Ibid.

52. Cf. Massimo Borghesi, *Augusto Del Noce: La legittimazione critica del moderno* (Genoa-Milan: Marietti, 2011).

53. Methol Ferré, "Prologo per Europei," 16.

54. Ibid., 17.

He acknowledges, in other words, an essential debt in some essential aspects of his thinking to Del Noce.

How did Methol became familiar with the philosophy of Del Noce, who was then relatively unknown outside the borders of his own country? In his 1983 introduction, Methol concluded by offering thanks to two people, Francesco Ricci and Guzmán Carriquiry. Ricci was a farsighted priest from Forlì, a traveling companion in the educational adventure of Don Luigi Giussani, editor at Edizioni CSEO, a sort of *trait d'union* between the Christianity of Eastern Europe and that of Latin America, which had published the text. Carriquiry was an intellectual disciple of Methol who introduced him to the thought of Augusto Del Noce. Methol met Del Noce in 1982, thanks to Carriquiry.

> He met him personally in 1982. The background goes back to the Third General Conference of the Latin American episcopate. In the beautiful city of Puebla, discussion among the participants was the order of the day. At one point during the work, [Methol] asked a dear friend, Dr. Guzmán Carriquiry, one of his countrymen for many years in Rome, in the Vatican, which Italian Catholic philosopher was worthy of consideration. The answer was Del Noce. Shortly after returning to Italy, Dr. Carriquiry sent him *Il suicidio della rivoluzione*.[55] The rigorously supported anticipation of the suicide of the revolutions was enough to ignite the interest of Methol Ferré. It was an interest seconded by destiny. "At one point" [Methol] recalled years later, "I visited the house of a priest, a Uruguayan biblicist who had recently returned from Italy. Looking in his library, my eye fell on *Il problema dell'ateismo*."[56] He asked his host to borrow the book. "It generated in me a real intellectual shock. For a month I read it continuously, night and day, underlining it on every page." Methol Ferré wrote a letter to Del Noce and sent it to his friend Carriquiry with the request that he pass it along to him.[57]

55. Augusto Del Noce, *Il suicidio della rivoluzione* (Milan: Rusconi, 1978).

56. Augusto Del Noce, *Il problema dell'ateismo* (Bologna: il Mulino, 1964).

57. Alver Metalli, "Methol Ferré ci ha aiutati a pensare," epilogue to Methol Ferré and Metalli, *Il Papa e il filosofo*, 225–226.

The letter initiated an exchange of communications between the two men, two letters each written between 1980 and 1982. In the first, dated October 31, 1980, Methol writes:

Bogotà, 31 October 1980
Prof. Augusto Del Noce

Of my highest consideration:
I have the great satisfaction of writing to you directly, because my friend Guzmán Carriquiry was kind enough to provide me with your address. You are already aware of the intellectual and spiritual impact that reading your book *El problema del ateismo* had upon me this past February-March. You cannot imagine how it moved me. It has providentially shed light on a problem that has haunted me intensely in recent years. It is as if one suddenly felt that he had been saved from years of uncertain reflection and searching, and finds he has reached everything he needed in the essentials. A surprisingly dense work, which I am far from having exhausted and which keeps offering new and fruitful angles. The text that I have at this time must be unreadable by anyone other than me, because it is full of underlining.

The greatest difficulty was in grasping the question of "ontologism." I have not lived the Italian intellectual climate. A translation of Carabellese in the Esprit Collection attracted my attention many years ago. And you prompted me to retrieve from my library, very sparse in Italian, a work by Filiasi Carcano, *Problemática de la filosofia moderna*. Only at that point, thanks to you, did I understand Filiasi, and thanks to Filiasi, you, regarding ontologism. Imagine that I did not know anything beyond some general introductory text about Gioberti, which seems to be the key to continuity [with the moderns before Rev. Francese, that is, Descartes, Pascal, Malebranche, and Vico]. In truth, I think it is certain that Bordas Demoulin, Tocqueville, Buchez, and Gratry knew Gioberti, and vice versa (except with Gratry, subsequently). On Gioberti I only have the work of the French Palhories, and the Introduction to philosophy. Nothing else. With such weak foundations, there were a number of assumptions in his thinking that had escaped me. I would very much like you to guide me on the contemporary Italian ontological literature that you consider valuable.

The most decisive historical category for me has been that of "Risorgimento," and I have already applied it in a paper on religion and culture in Latin America. When it is finished, I will send you copies.

Needless to say, I am in eager expectation of a promise from Guzman to send me your articles and books. I only have[58]

I apologize for writing to you on a typewriter and for being such a bad typist, but it seemed better because my handwriting is not clear enough in Spanish. I believe the typed letter will facilitate understanding.

I greet you with my deepest gratitude and admiration, although I am not very fond of the epistolary genre, I would very much like this to be the beginning of a dialogue, which for me will surely be very fruitful.

Cordially in our Lord Jesus Christ
Alberto Methol Ferré

[Note: My main objective is the publication of *El problema del ateísmo*, but maybe an earlier work on a more urgent and more widely circulated subject, such as *El suicidio de la revolución*, is necessary. This would open the way for the other, main, work, which is very voluminous and expensive to publish, so it is convenient to prepare the ground for its reception.
My address in Montevideo, Uruguay is Brecha 557][59]

Methol's letter documents the positive shock he experienced in reading *Il problema dell'ateismo*, Del Noce's dense 1964 book that dismantled the Hegelian framework of modern philosophy starting from the idea of a double modernity: a secular-rationalistic one and an ontologistic one that culminated in the liberal Catholicism of Antonio Rosmini. Del Noce's work succeeds in overcoming not only the secular vision of modernity but also the neo-Thomist one, dominated by the antimodern reaction. In the letter, Methol raises a question about this ontological tradition, viewed with suspicion

58. Missing page.
59. Alberto Methol Ferré to Augusto Del Noce (October 31, 1980). Unpublished letter, the archives of the Fondazione Centro Studi Augusto Del Noce in Savigliano. The part in brackets was added in handwriting to the typewritten text.

by the "amateur Thomist" that he was. The dilemma was resolved for him after he read the posthumous work of another Thomist, an author of reference for both Methol and for Del Noce: Étienne Gilson's *L'athéisme difficile*.[60] As he said in his interview with Metalli:

> I have always considered myself an amateur Thomist, outside the academy or any seminary. For me the epicenter of everything lies in the ontological argument: the intelligence of man is linked to the splendor of the idea of God. In Gilson's last book on atheism, I read with enormous satisfaction and surprise a note on atheism in which the author wields precisely the ontological argument, which for a Thomist was considered an exoticism. But this relationship has allowed me to understand and join Del Noce in his recapitulation of modernity, not as a line made up of successive steps that lead the church, against its will, from premodern to postmodern, but of parts that have crossed modernity modernly. This means not only that we are fathers of modernity, but that we have coparticipated in its definition . . . —along with the Catholic Descartes—without being antimodern to the bitter end, but against certain tendencies of modernity. The classical antimodernists were the traditionalists of the nineteenth century. It is a species that has become extinct with Vatican II.[61]

And so Del Noce opened Methol's eyes to previously unknown terrain: the "modern" strand of post-Cartesian Augustinianism that culminated in Rosmini. It was the missing link, crucial for properly understanding the relationship between Catholicism and modernity

---

60. Étienne Gilson, *L'athéisme difficile* (Paris: Vrin, 1979). In issue no. 1 (September 1983) of *Nexo*, Methol reviewed two books, one by Raúl Echaurí on Gilson, *El pensamiento de Etienne Gilson* (Pamplona: Eunsa, 1980), and one by Gilson himself, *El ser y los filósofos* (Pamplona: Eunsa, 1980). These make clear the importance of Del Noce's article, "La riscoperta del tomismo in Etienne Gilson e il suo significato presente," in Francesco Carlomagno, ed., *Studi di filosofia in onore di Gustavo Bontadini* (Milan: Vita e Pensiero, 1975), 454–474. On the relationship between Del Noce and Gilson, cf. Massimo Borghesi, introduction to *Caro collega ed amico: Lettere di Étienne Gilson ad Augusto del Noce (1964–1969)* (Siena: Cantagalli, 2008), 5–57.

61. Methol Ferré and Metalli, *Il Papa e il filosofo*, 154.

in a nonextrinsic but essential way and crucial to carrying out a nonreactionary revaluation of the Baroque. Methol was able further to develop this perspective by reading Del Noce's other great historiographical work, *Riforma cattolica e filosofia moderna, vol. i: Cartesio* (*Catholic Reform and Modern Philosophy*, vol. 1: *Descartes*). It was another decisive experience, as we find documented in a January 5, 1981, letter to Del Noce.

Montevideo, January 5, 1981
Prof. Augusto del Noce

My dear friend,

I have received your thoughtful letter and also your book *Riforma Cattolica e filosofia modern: Cartesio*. I thank you from my heart for your generosity and attention. This gives me the opportunity to write again, requesting your counsel on some points.

Philosophy may be my primary intellectual love, but here in Latin America (and in particular in Uruguay) there is a quite impoverished and dependent climate in this respect. We lack our own philosophical tradition. We are children of a Spain that stopped at Suárez and Juan de Santo Tomás, or at the premodern. Though it was decisive in the first configuration of the Catholic Reformation. That is the original stamp of Latin America. Trent is our cultural subsoil. Perhaps Guzmán Carriquiry can share with you an article of mine on science and philosophy in Latin America, which, while I would not fully subscribe to everything in it today, reflects my interest in the relationship between Latin America and modernity. This is the dominant thrust of my current interests. But you can understand that this first phase of modernity (Descartes, Malebranche, Pascal, Vico) is absent from our Latin American origins.

This means that it is, while necessary and vital for a proper understanding of Latin America and the church, more culturally distant from us, and more difficult to access in direct and deep study. On this point, Europeans are irreplaceable. Hence, while not considering it more important, but more directly related to Latin America, the period that follows the French Revolution, the nineteenth century, is the one that most catches my interest. But of course, it represents the first phase of modernity.

Your work, I think, provides me with the bases from which I can think about that second, modern, post–French Revolution phase, which is already the contemporary problematic.

My main angle is from the philosophy of history. A critique of Gutiérrez, a Latin American theologian of liberation, maintained the urgency of returning to Augustine and Vico at the height of our time. The truth is that I see it only in Vico, but I do not know him well. In our environment he is unknown and his bibliography inaccessible. Here I request your advice. I have seen in your work the notice about a third volume about Vico. Is your work about to come out? Have you published studies on Vico?

For my part, I do not have time for a study of Vico. But I do need to address it as well as possible, since he is the father of the philosophy of modern history, and he is therefore a necessary starting point. What basic and minimum bibliography would you recommend about Vico? Books and articles. I am reading your *Cartesio*, and I admire how each page overflows with riches. Here is a very short, very superficial observation. You assert that religious Cartesianism is an Augustinianism without a theology of history. Where do you place Bossuet then? Of course, his *Discourses* and his *Politics* should be read together (with his ecclesiology as well). And it seems that reflection in contrast with Vico was necessary. Perhaps Bossuet is what brings an end, the "old regime," that contaminates the reactionary Catholic thinking of the nineteenth century prior to the "democratic" recovery of Suarez and Thomas, with which Vico, at least, is not incompatible. I was struck by the absence of any mention of Bossuet in your work. I do not know what it could mean or what possible consequences there would be. I believe that the frames of reference of post–French Revolution, catholic, historical thought have been first Bossuet and then Vico. Anyway, it seems that your work on the Catholic Reformation and modern thought requires the consideration of Bossuet, although Vico is much more fertile and fundamental, because the consideration of "history," its understanding, at least for me, is today much more urgent than that of "nature" (which has become "historical").

The same advice that I request with regard to Vico, I extend to Gioberti and Rosmini. Again the basic and minimum. Here in Montevideo there is an Italian bookstore, and with a little patience with the wait, one can ask for anything.

In our environment, Italian thought is a great unknown. Before, only Croce came here from across the ocean. More recently, postwar, Sciacca came, and I heard some of his lectures in Montevideo. But he did not interest me very much. And no one else. But, by a singular conjunction of readings and glimpses (particularly through your work) I am now keenly interested in Italian thought. Among the

Thomists, Bontadini struck me. It seems that the Italian "repetition" of Hegel, with Gentile, has put Italian thought in a dynamic of modern historical understanding superior to the current French and German, which seem to have no exits. Perhaps the Italian drama is that intellectual vigor in the practical quagmire of a small country that is unable to work through its own thinking: only through the mediation of a "European," and not only Italian, vision and action. But it is necessary to unify in a single intellectual process the national philosophical traditions, making them "European."

Maybe Italy is better placed in this respect than France and Germany, which are too "national." Italy, on the other hand, has enough of its own tradition to become "European," in contrast to Spain, which is philosophically much poorer and for now has nothing more to translate. European translator, not creator. To us, in Latin America, the "west" (continental Europe and the Anglo-Saxon world) comes to us chaotically.

As you see, not only has your thinking impacted me, but there is an extension beyond the "Italian question" that it has made possible. Well, I think it helps to powerfully illuminate Latin America. I have used your category of *risorgimento* in a recent study, which I will send you as soon as CELAM publishes it.

Your perspective of modernity I see not only as the most appropriate, but also as possessing unpredictable developments and consequences. I feel that this is where the achievement of Vatican II has been set into action philosophically. I mean the achievement that has been accomplished "already" and "not yet" by Vatican II. Again, you have my appreciation and my intellectual admiration.

Cordially
Alberto Methol Ferré

Note: I appreciate your endorsement in relation to *El Suicido de la Revolucion*. We will write to the editor as soon as we are economically ready to launch the publication, which we hope will be soon.[62]

Between the end of 1980 and the beginning of 1981, Methol, after having received the Del Noce book on Descartes, engaged in

---

62. Methol Ferré to Del Noce (January 5, 1981). Unpublished letter, Fondazione Centro Studi Augusto del Noce, Savigliano.

a careful reading of a text that, inspired by the masterly interpretation of Jean Laporte, radically dismantled the secular reading of the secular and rationalist Descartes. Del Noce argued that the "Cartesian ambiguity" placed Descartes at the origins of both the rationalist and the Catholic veins of modernity. This revolutionized the entire picture of modern philosophy. As Methol wrote in issue 12 of *Nexo* in 1987, "The vision of the antagonistic movement of philosophical modernity leads us today to propose its rereading with the great work of Del Noce, *Reforma católica y el Pensamiento moderno*."[63] This meant a reassessment of Augustine within modernity: "Necessary with it are the philosophies of modern history, in reciprocal critique and purification. For this, the perspectives of theologians like Balthasar and Przywara are indispensable."[64]

The discovery of "another" Descartes, of the importance of Vico, and so forth, all converged toward the category of risorgimento that Methol used fruitfully in his 1981 article "The Latin American Catholic Risorgimento." The first letter from Del Noce received by Methol refers to this article. Dated May 16, 1982, the contents reflect the recent Falkland-Malvinas war between England and Argentina.

00197 ROME Viale Parioli 76
May 16

Dear Methol Ferré,
    I read on <u>Saturday</u> your truly splendid article on the meaning of the conflict between Argentina and England for Latin America. It has cemented unity in such a profound sense that it had never had before; and the unity of Latin America also means its detachment from the West, which is today as never before "the land of the sunset." This conflict could have been the sign for continental Europe to shake the English yoke that has been weighing on it for centuries; one could say since it ceased to be a Europe united by Catholicism. Solidarity between Europe and the Latin American continent is the only possibility for Europe to affirm itself as a moral reality. Or, at least, this

63. Methol Ferré, "Erich Przywara, *San Agustín: Trayctoria de su genio, Contextura de su espíritu*," 31. (Original publ. Dresden: Jakob-Hegner-Verlag, 1934.)
    64. Ibid.

ought to have been particularly felt by the countries of Latin Europe. So far it has not been so: not on the part of the Italian people, of which the majority sides with Argentina, but also from that of politicians. And so a unique opportunity will be lost. God at least wants Italy not to participate in the renewal of sanctions against Argentina. The topic is discussed these days and, unfortunately, I'm rather pessimistic.

I read your article *El Resurgimiento catolico latino-americano* several times with the most lively agreement. Excellent, among other things, is the criticism that addresses the concept of modernity as it is formulated by the sociologist Germani, whose work is also, unfortunately, appearing in Italy today.

With the most lively friendship. I greet you

Augusto Del Noce[65]

Another letter followed a month later, the content of which was again the English-Argentine war and also, this time, the pastoral visit that Pope John Paul II had made to England from May 28 to June 2, 1982.

Viale Parioli 76
00197 ROME
Rome, June 16

Dear Methol Ferré,
I am writing to you in a very sad moment, sadder still for you, back in your land. The spectacle that the West and Europe are offering is truly adequate to the contagion that has morally destroyed them in the postwar decades; and truly we must speak of a last stage of the bourgeoisie in which it has definitively separated itself from "virtue."

The horror inspired by an England that attacks at the very moment that the Pope is about to speak (and certainly the attack at that time was unexpected), which obtains a victory mixed with the sacrilege,

---

65. Del Noce to Methol Ferré (May 16, 1982). Unpublished letter, Alberto Methol Ferré archive in the Centro de Documentación y Estudios de Iberoamérica (CEDEI), Universidad de Montevideo (Uruguay). On the war in the Malvines, cf. Alberto Methol Ferré, "Malvinas, nuova frontiera latino-americana," *Incontri* 6, May–June 1982, 52–54.

is difficult to describe. But even this victory would not have been possible without the decisive support of the United States. And it was true that there is not a Europe! Instead, what has effectively developed in recent decades is a Europe with a North American hegemony (which has corrupted European minds and hearts in a manner that has never before been achieved), and a second-degree power; and it is Europe that assists indifferently, not only in the injustice against Argentina, but in the genocide of Palestinians carried out by the Israelis.

Not even the situation of the church gives me any enthusiasm. Going against the current is extremely difficult. The teachers of the theology of secularization continue in their work as agents of the marginalization of Catholic culture and customs. The pope's intentions are certainly very righteous, but the hearing that he receives among his own Catholic people seems to me very poor. It is sufficient, I believe, that we continue in this state of despair. I'm recalling at this moment your writing on human rights [?] that I read with the most lively interest. Warmest and most affectionate greetings from your Augusto Del Noce.[66]

The exchange of letters stops here, but it certainly does not mark an end of the relationship between the two. Del Noce and Methol were both speakers at the First International Colloquium on Christian Thought, which was on the topic of "Karol Wojtyła: Philosopher, Theologian, Poet," an event organized by ISTRA (Istituti di studi per la transizione) and held in Rome, September 23–25, 1983. It is certain that Methol drew from Del Noce the categories that allowed him to overcome the gap between Catholicism and modernity, not only from the political point of view as happens in Maritain but also from the philosophical point of view. These are the categories that allow him to read Puebla as the true beginning of the Latin American risorgimento:

Starting from Puebla the deepening of Vatican II begins in terms of Latin American history, a fact that requires a revision of great am-

---

66. Del Noce to Methol Ferré (June 16, 1982). Unpublished letter, Alberto Methol Ferré archive in the Centro de Documentación y Estudios de Iberoamérica (CEDEI), Universidad de Montevideo (Uruguay).

plitude, universal, which allows us to reencounter also the Latin American national generation of the twenties and thirties, the criticism and the assumption of modernity through Waldo Frank, Northrop, and Sorokin, but above all Victor Frankl and Augusto Del Noce, that is to rediscover the potentialities of American and ecclesial Baroque, in order to generate the future. Vatican II begins to communicate to us its "virtuality," the breath of its Spirit. We are not at all in the phase of "restoration," but rather of "risorgimento."[67]

Beyond either the restoration of the right-wing clerical regimes or revolution, a third possibility opens up. Here Methol moves on the same wavelength that leads Jorge Mario Bergoglio to conceive, in 1974, the Society of Jesus as a superior synthesis of opposites:

The risorgimento is the breaking of the vicious circle of integralism and Enlightenment that implies the need to reinterpret modernity. This modernity, to be broken and recreated, implies that its current pattern of interpretation, of which Hegel is the most perfect formulation, is put in crisis. An entire generation, from Marx to Weber, refers itself to this supreme spiritual representative of modernity. It is a modernity that distances itself from the Catholic Church because it understands itself as a historical process irreversibly directed toward immanence, secularization, demythologization, the elimination of the supernatural, the death of God. It is a modernity understood as a process of the immanentization of transcendent Christian needs, which leads into contemporary atheism and nihilism, taking forms that are in various ways tragic, indifferent, political. It was this idea of modernity that prompted the harsh reaction of the *Syllabus* in 1864, with its anathema to the proposal that "the Pontiff can reconcile and agree with progress, with liberalism and modern civilization," a syllabus that was derided by many as the last gasp of defiance uttered by the dying papacy against the modern world. Today, however, we witness the failure of that idea-force.[68]

He gives credit for having deconstructed the Hegelian framework, to which the *Syllabus* subjects itself even in its opposition, to Augusto Del Noce.

67. Methol Ferré, "Il risorgimento cattolico latinoamericano," 263.
68. Ibid., 262.

Del Noce, with *Il problema dell'ateismo*, triggers the intellectual destruction of the concept of modernization as a transition from a society unified by a transcendent religion to one unified by an immanentist conception of life. Del Noce is a philosopher through the history of philosophy, so as to be able to be the point of rupture of the Hegelian scheme of modernity that imbues all post-Hegelian thought, which overcomes it by integrating it into a wider and more comprehensive historical vision. Perhaps for Del Noce this step was possible because in Italy the historicist idealism of Gentile and the Marxism of Gramsci, extreme points of Hegelian philosophy, were expressed with extraordinary intensity. Precisely through these extremes, Del Noce has waived it. Performing the last rites upon this version of modernity, Del Noce recovers a more complex and true modernity, a new starting point.[69]

The thought of Del Noce, like the Puebla Conference, constitutes *a new starting point* for Methol. It allows that synthesis between baroque and modern liberties that Puebla suggested without, however, being able to thematize:

For Del Noce the problematic of the concept of "modern philosophy" (presupposed in the concept of "the modern world") is inseparable from the revision of the concept of the Catholic Reformation (Trent). "The idea of the process toward immanence in modern philosophy correlates with the idea of the spiritual sterility of the Counter-Reformation." Del Noce's work is completed with *Riforma Cattolica e filosofia moderna*, whose first masterful volume focuses on Descartes, the indisputable initiator of modern philosophy as such. It is there that he perceives the problematic origin of modernity, its essential conflictual bifurcation that will give rise to the two modern traditions, the "Catholic" and the "immanentist." The former was born from the Baroque, with its classic apex in Descartes, Malebranche, Pascal, and Vico. Its first wave was the configuration of Trent, the reaffirmation of the radical freedom of humanity, a mirror of God's own freedom, expressed in the extraordinary "Thomist Carmelite" (Báñez, Saint Teresa, Saint John of the Cross), "Jesuit" (Molina, Suárez) tension: the first Baroque that fostered the birth of Latin America. In this way is provoked the Frankl–Del Noce short

69. Ibid.

circuit, the second surpassing the first, possible today through the recovery of the popular religiosity of the Latin American substratum, of the Baroque of our people, of our poor, which Puebla realizes through his claims.[70]

In that extraordinary intellectual forge that was the thought of Methol Ferré, the encounter with Del Noce had a decisive place. The Delnocian revaluation of the Baroque age, *qua* modern, allows the reevaluation of the Latin American religious tradition, freeing it from that hypothesis of reaction that exposes it to the blackmail of secularization.

> In this line of "Catholic modernity" of which Del Noce spoke, one finds Tocqueville, Bordas Demoulin, Buchez, Gratry, Cournot, Blondel, and all that ultimately culminates in Vatican II. That "risorgimento" perhaps failed because its needs could only be satisfied by Vatican II. Semantically, risorgimento is the opposite of restoration. Risorgimento is a new development of eternal values, their purification; it demands renewal and historical creations.[71]

In Methol's rethinking of the nature of Latin America, Del Noce is the key to understanding the encounter between Christianity and modernity.

> While in vulgar opinion modernity unfolds against the church, Del Noce shows that the founder of modern thought is a Catholic, Descartes. It will not concede a different paternity and does not allow itself to be appropriated by others. There is an *empiricist* modern tradition, and a *pantheistic* modern tradition, which then becomes materialism, but there is also a *Catholic* modern tradition. While the history of philosophy written by contemporaries ignores any Catholic thinking on modernity and classifies it as premodern, with Del Noce it is legitimate to conclude that the church is not only at the origin of modernity, but has never completely lost a modern dimension, even when it gave birth to an antimodernist reaction before the persecution of the French Revolution—which, it is worth repeating,

70. Ibid., 262–263.
71. Ibid., 265.

had among its other effects the reinforcement of traditionalism. Del Noce must be credited with introducing reflection on the third modern current, the Catholic one; from within this line he realized the most accurate philosophical interpretation of our time: the suicide of the Revolution and the rise of libertine atheism in contemporary society. Therefore it is anti-historical to conceive of overcoming modernity outside of modernity.[72]

Libertine Atheism and the Critique of the Opulent Society

Methol's study of and attention to the thought of Del Noce did not stop in the early 1980s.[73] Del Noce's thinking is useful not only for considering the past—the new vision of modernity—but also for the present, marked by the "suicide of the Revolution" and by the "rise of libertine atheism." These are phenomena that Del Noce had foreseen before 1989, the year of the fall of the Berlin Wall, before the full realization of the era of globalization. With the disappearance of Soviet communism, the historical scenario changed, and for the church the figure of the "enemy" changed. This required

72. Methol Ferré and Metalli, *Il Papa e il filosofo*, 153. According to Rodrigo Guerra López, this anti-Manichean reading of the relationship between the church and modernity also exerts its influence, through Methol Ferré, on Bergoglio: "That is to say, for Pope Francis modernity is not an enemy to be vanquished, but a territory to be won. This I think he learns to a large extent, at a conceptual level, from Methol. And Methol learned it from Augusto Del Noce who, unlike Cornelio Fabro and Etienne Gilson, judges that modernity is not a relentless, more or less deterministic path toward decadence, towards immanentism, but that there are multiple paths. . . . In the case of Francis, it is fundamental, because it is evident that he lives under the premise of having an elementary sympathy with all people, with all positions, with all ideas. Not because all ideas are equally valid or true, but because he always manages to discern the point of encounter, the possibility of building a bridge, the place where there is a possibility of communion" (J. Antúnez and P. Maillet, "La modernidad no es un enemigo a vencer, sino un territorio a conquistar," interview with Rodrigo Guerra López, *Humanitas* 84 [2017]: 31).

73. In 1984, Methol published a review of Del Noce's *Il cattolico comunista* (Milan: Rusconi, 1981), in *Nexo* 4 (1984): 48–49: "Augusto Del Noce, *Il Católico Comunista*."

a historical consciousness that was adequate to the challenge of the moment:

> Certainly. Without historical consciousness there is something fragile about a "mission." Only a good awareness of the characteristics of the enemy—the main one—determines the character of an era, and in the character of an era there is an ecclesial response to this concrete enemy. Another enemy emerges and another: there are in history a successive multiplicity of primary enemies. History cannot be understood without the presence of evil and its opposite, love, which is superior to the former. There is nothing more intelligent than love. Failure to understand what the main enemy is at a given moment in history is not a lack of cunning but a lack of love. Intelligence and love, in the last instance, are inseparable.[74]

It is love that, according to Methol, allows us to overcome the friend/enemy dialectic through "the recovery of the enemy as a friend."[75] It is the second form of Fessard's dialectic, that of love between man and woman, which demonstrates its superiority over the former, the one marked by the master/servant relationship. With this, the *dia-bolical* attitude becomes *dia-logical*.

What, then, is the new adversary after the decline of communism? *Libertine atheism.* "The paradoxical thing is that the death of God is the destruction of messianic atheism itself. In fact, atheism has radically changed its shape. It is no longer messianic, but libertine. It is not revolutionary in the social sense, but an accomplice of the status quo. It has no interest in justice, but in whatever allows us to cultivate a radical hedonism."[76]

For Methol, the description of this turning point, from messianic to libertine atheism, is provided by three American political scientists and the Italian philosopher Augusto Del Noce: "Those who attempt a complete vision of the post-1989 contemporary problematic are three Americans: Fukuyama in 1992, Brzezinski in 1993, and Huntington in 1995. It is interesting to note: a trio of intellectuals from the United States, while at the end of World War II the

74. Methol Ferré and Metalli, *Il Papa e il filosofo*, 55–56.
75. Ibid., 56.
76. Ibid., 53.

movement toward a globalizing synthesis had a predominantly European character, with Pitirin Sorokin, Arnold Toynbee, Karl Jaspers, and the French René Grousset."[77] Of the three political scientists, "Zbigniew Brzezinski is the one who best describes what is emerging. This scholar characterizes the consumption society of the capitalist world as the cornucopia of infinite desires."[78] For Brzezinski,

> The notion of a "permissive cornucopia" involves essentially a society in which the progressive decline of the centrality of moral criteria is matched by heightened preoccupation with material and sensual self-gratification. Unlike coercive utopia, permissive cornucopia does not envisage a timeless state of societal bliss for the redeemed but focuses largely on the immediate satisfaction of individual desires, in a setting in which individual and collective hedonism becomes the dominant motive for behavior. . . . "Greed is good"—the battle cry of the American yuppies of the late 1980s—is a fitting motto for permissive cornucopia.[79]

With the image of "permissive cornucopia," Brzezinski basically points to the same reality to which Del Noce refers with the concept of "opulent society" in his 1963 essay "Appunti sull'irreligione occidentale," published in *Il problema dell'ateismo*.[80] He describes the advent of a new atheism, one that is not messianic but agnostic. It is an empiricist atheism that marks the victory of Comte over Marx. This is why, according to Methol,

---

77. Ibid., 39. The works on globalization by the three American intellectuals are: Francis Fukuyama, *The End of History and the Last Man* (New York: The Free Press, 1992); Zbigniew K. Brzezinski, *Out of Control: Global Turmoil on the Eve of the 21st Century* (New York: Collier Books, 1993); Samuel Huntington, *The Clash of Civilizations and the Remaking of World Order* (New York: Simon and Schuster, 1996).

78. Methol Ferré and Metalli, *Il Papa e il filosofo*, 52.

79. Brzezinski, *Out of Control*, 65.

80. Del Noce, *Il problema dell'ateismo*, 293–333. On Del Noce's notion of the "opulent society," cf. Massimo Borghesi, *Augusto Del Noce: La legittimazione critica del moderno*, 269–309.

Brzezinski and Del Noce travel different paths and arrive at the same conclusion. Contemporary atheism is different from the previous one, which sought the elimination of religion and was organized to achieve this objective. Apparently it does not produce an ordered institutionality for this purpose, but a widespread presence that impregnates the whole of society with a minimum of established social forms. The fact is that in a valueless world, the only value that remains is strength. Where everything has an identical value, only one value prevails: power. Libertine agnosticism becomes the principal accomplice of established power.[81]

Libertine atheism may seem to be rebellious and anticonformist, but in reality it is an essential aspect of the neocapitalism of the 1980s and 1990s: "Messianic atheism wished to root out any Judeo-Christian contamination from the world; libertine atheism does not carry this legacy, or has it to a minimum. Messianic atheism set out to change the world; the libertine version is ordered to power."[82]

Through Del Noce and Brzezinski, the ecclesial geopolitics of Methol Ferré embraced the new historical world, capturing the spirit of post-1989 globalization. In order to understand the new adversary of faith, a universal historical vision was required. In a March 2004 letter, Methol wrote:

Montevideo, March 10, 2004
Dear Massimo Borghesi:

Greetings! It is a great joy to greet you and thank you for your attention, with the articles you have sent me (and years ago with a study by a friend of yours, Maria Teresa Tosetto, about Erich Przywara. What has become of her?).

All of them were valuable to me, but the one that most captured my attention was "Cristianismo y cultura"—along with the interview on the Common Good–. I am passionate about this beginning of the twenty-first century, which urgently needs to be clarified to the maximum, in order to attend pastorally to the People of God in globalization. I think a reflection by you would be very good, <u>a book in which</u>

81. Methol Ferré and Metalli, *Il Papa e il filosofo*, 54.
82. Ibid., 158.

you summarize your global historical perspectives from the European Union (and obviously from the Catholic Church). In the post-1989 period, two or three significant books appeared, all North American, of worldwide scope (Fukuyama, Huntington, Brzezinski). Unlike those from post–World War I and II, which were all European works, now there was no European. It becomes more necessary than ever. Excuse me, but I think that you are one of the most capable and able to carry it out. So that you understand me: a synthetic, universal work, a bit in the model of Brzezinski's Out of Control (1993), which is, on the other hand, I think, convergent with you and Del Noce, without knowing them. Today I feel a great ecclesial paralysis (at least in Latin America) that, thank God, is ready to mobilize for a Latin American Episcopal Conference. Synthetic Catholic works, with regional and world perspectives, become indispensable at this time, and more so at the time of a pontificate's end. A global reading of the new signs of the times is urgent. And without . . . [illegible] I think you can be one of those authors. You can be simple, synoptic and comprehensive. Use your gifts!

A warm embrace, and thank you!
Cordially
Methol[83]

83. Methol Ferré to Massimo Borghesi (March 10, 2004). Methol refers here to the thesis of Maria Teresa Tosetto, *L'antropologia di Erich Przywara* (University of Turin, aa 1983/84), which I had sent him, knowing he was curious about Przywara, and to my writings: "Cristianismo y cultura," in *Secularización y nihilism: Cristianismo y cultura contemporanea* (Madrid: Encuentro, 2007), 117–142; "Il bene comune non si può frantumare," interview in *Tracce*, February 2004, pp. 29–32. We met personally in 1992, in Lima, on the occasion of the Fourth World Congress of Christian Philosophy. It was a relationship that then became rich in exchanges thanks to a mutual friend, Alver Metalli, editor from 1981 to 1982 of the journal *Incontri: Testimonies from Latin America* and, since 1983, first director of the international magazine *30 Giorni*. Metalli currently conducts the blog *Terre d'America: News & Analisi dall'America Latina* (http://www.terredamerica.com/) with the related edition in Spanish, *Tierras de America*. He shares the experience of Fr. Pepe di Paola in the "misery village" known as La Carcova, in the suburbs of Buenos Aires; di Paola was one of the *villeros* priests supported by Bergoglio (see Elisabetta Piqué, *Pope Francis: Life and Revolution: A Biography of Jorge Bergoglio* [Chicago: Loyola, 2014], chap. 11, "The Slums of Christ," 143–154).

The church must bring itself to the center of history. Its missionary dimension requires it. Otherwise it lags behind, fighting enemies that no longer exist, ghosts of the past, and so makes itself an ally of the real adversaries of the moment. Here Methol sees an important connection between Nietzsche and Comte.

> Today, *de facto*, Nietzsche is tied more to postmodernism, to Sade and to the opulent society, than Marx is. But while the atheism of Nietzsche, the tragic atheism of the will to power, ended its quest to be consequential by simply becoming unlivable, its postmodern progeny was content with a pile of toys. The libertinism of consumer societies—a nihilism of consumers—could never be more than a pseudo-alternative, since it is inherently parasitic, unconstructive by definition. Positivist agnosticism remained the only constructive alternative on offer. The real victory, in short, was that of Comte over Marx. This positivist, scientific agnosticism, which oscillates between the previous parasitic nihilism and a vaguely deist humanitarian religiosity, ecumenical in its eclecticism, makes itself a "universal" alternative in the middle and upper classes of the dominant industrial societies. It is an indistinct religiosity that corresponded to the dominant practical materialism, as a protection against the threat of nihilism and the emptiness of the Myth of Revolution.[84]

The opulent society, the globalized world, arises from the alliance of Comte and Sade, positivism and libertinism: "In this sense libertine atheism is allied with a conservative power, parasitic to the status quo that it tends to confirm. Augusto Del Noce already mentioned it a quarter of a century ago, when he argued that the society of consumption and technology digested Marxism by emptying it of its messianic content. In this way he saw Marxism resolve itself— as a paradox—in a support for the construction of a technological and opulent society. A sort of heterogenesis of ends."[85]

The "suicide of the revolution" generates the opulent society: "Messianic atheism and libertine atheism are two antithetical poles; they repel each other and attract each other."[86] They give rise to a

84. Methol Ferré and Metalli, *Il Papa e il filosofo*, 38.
85. Ibid., 150.
86. Ibid., 151.

polarity not grasped by Brzezinski, who stops at the simple opposition between Marxism and bourgeois libertinism.

Augusto del Noce went further. He showed the other face of the crisis outlined by Brzezinski: that the decadence of messianic atheism—at the moment it achieves its end—is converted into a coercive utopia and continues as an opulent society, vulgar materialism. Marx thought the natural ideology of the bourgeoisie was vulgar materialism; Del Noce recognizes that the crisis of Marxism generates two branches: a revolutionary and messianic dialectical materialism on one hand and the vulgar materialism of the victorious society, which elevates irreligiosity to its highest level, on the other. Del Noce's observations about atheism in postmodernity provided a systematic and philosophical foundation to the almost exclusively political approach of Brzezinski, who recognized that the moment of liberal democracy's victory is also the moment that the foundation that supports human rights begins to erode.[87]

The superiority of Del Noce over Brzezinski rests, therefore, in his "dialectical" understanding of contemporary history, in the Vichian category of a "heterogenesis of ends" that offers an explanation for both the realization/dissolution of Marxism *and* the genesis of the opulent society. The thought of Del Noce, then, is fully capable of interpreting the present moment of history, a moment that sees the triumph of Sade, Comte, and Nietzsche over Marx, of a mix of libertinism, nihilism, and technocratic positivism over political messianism. Interesting, from this point of view, is the judgment that Methol offers—in his interview with Metalli—of the pontificates of John Paul II and Benedict XVI. He believed John Paul II's relevance receded after 1989, while Benedict's would be placed in the heart of the present moment:

Ratzinger grew up in contact with two forms of totalitarianism: the messianic type symbolized by Marx, and the will-to-power type symbolized by Nietzsche. One can say that he is the son of a people that took to their extreme consequences both the communist messianism derived from Chamberlain and the racist messianism derived

87. Ibid., 151–152.

from Nietzsche. The latter represents one of the terminal conclusions of that modernity that was to witness the agony of Christianity, and of Christian variations (as Nietzsche considered them) like the French Revolution and socialism. Nietzsche's atheism had its acute expression in Ratzinger's Nazi Germany, in the same way that messianic atheism had a historical realization in Wojtyła's Poland.[88]

This leads to the conviction that

> Pope Benedict is in a position to understand fully the sad destiny of modernity, more than his predecessor was at the moment he became Pope. John Paul II was the son of a country that suffered under modernity, without generating it. Ratzinger belongs to the place and time that experienced the deepest crisis of modernity; he is free to gather up the supposedly premodern tradition previously repudiated by the originators of modernity and to offer a reevaluation of it. Wojtyła knew close-up a Catho-communist Christianity, in which believers and nonbelievers coexisted in a relationship of coexistence and struggle, while Ratzinger saw the manifestations of the greatest crisis of modernity, the final thoughts that were summarized in Germanic culture, from the Reformation onward, passing by way of Hegel, Marx, and Nietzsche.[89]

These are two perspectives that have also affected the Latin American church's way of engaging with the present: "From the beginning of his pontificate, John Paul II met Mexican Catholicism, a brother of Polish Catholicism, both of which were marked by great traditional vigor; Benedict met the decomposition of modernity with its ugliness. He is a man who—like Habermas—spent his youth nurturing the dramatic and compulsive effort of the postwar

88. Ibid., 205–206.

89. Ibid., 206. "In the lucid vision of Pope Benedict, epochal dogmatism is relativism, which tends to try to expunge the need for truth from the expectations of humanity. I am convinced that this is the great doorway to libertine atheism, the Siamese twin of the dominant ethical relativism, even in Latin America. In the current globalized world such a fate is very serious for our poor and dependent countries; the worst subversion of the preferential option for the poor and the demands of sacrifice and friendship of one's neighbor that it implies" (ibid., 163–165).

German intellectual tradition to recover rationality as a basic mental attitude. This is why I say that in Ratzinger's thought novelty and tradition are deeply intertwined."[90] It is a precious synthesis for Latin America, which leads one to think that "with Ratzinger a new Catholic modernity can unfold, as a development of the modernity that had its most all-encompassing manifestation in the Second Vatican Council."[91]

Thanks to Brzezinski and Del Noce, Methol comes, then, to identify clearly the adversary of faith in the era of globalization. He does not intend, however, to place the church in a mere dialectical clash with the new adversary. The opposition of faith cannot be left determined by the enemy; it transcends the friend/enemy dialectic, redeeming the adversary's point of view: "The truth of libertine atheism is the perception that enjoyment is a purpose deeply woven into existence, that life itself is made for satisfaction. Without this existential basis no one could endure life's suffering, except under terrible extremes of duress. Put another way, the deep core of libertine atheism is the hidden necessity of beauty. Life itself is enjoyment: the prostitute, the madman, the libertine, and the murderer each live for what is beautiful in the very act of living."[92]

This truth, however, is perverted by libertine atheism "because it separates beauty from truth and from goodness (from justice); it destroys the unity of beauty, truth, and goodness. In doing so, it perverts beauty."[93] Atheism breaks the unity of the transcendentals, a unity that, as we have seen, has an essential value for Bergoglio: "Beauty maintains an original link with truth and goodness; it is inseparable from them both. When it is torn off, it decays into an aestheticism for intellectuals or gives rise to a vitalism that pursues pleasure at all costs. In both cases it becomes, in the end, an accomplice of injustice."[94]

Faced with this phenomenon, this dimension that takes on a global scope on the momentum of an economy that is based on desire, how

90. Ibid., 206.
91. Ibid., 207.
92. Ibid., 155–156.
93. Ibid., 156.
94. Ibid., 157.

should the church respond? For Methol Ferré, "Historically the church is the only subject on the contemporary world stage that can face libertine atheism. I do not say that this is true always and everywhere, but a survey of our time convinces me that it is true today. It seems to me that only the church is truly postmodern. The fact is that redeeming the core of the truth of libertine atheism is, in the end, not humanly possible. It cannot be done with an argumentative procedure nor a dialectical one, and still less by imposing prohibitions, sounding alarms, or dictating abstract rules."[95]

This is because "libertine atheism is not an ideology; it is a practice. A practice can only be opposed by another practice; a self-conscious practice, to be sure, and therefore intellectually equipped. It is at the level of experience, or morality, that one must engage with libertine atheism."[96] For Methol, the model to keep in mind is Francis of Assisi: "St. Francis is one of the most extraordinary examples of beauty captured and reflected in a historical human figure. In St. Francis the power of the beauty of being shines. Calvin does not overcome libertine atheism, because he simply denies it, rejects it, evades what moves it at its core. Protestant asceticism, even when generous, cannot respond to you. Catholicism, however, can. The greatest beauty is love. And love is the perfect unity of truth, goodness, and beauty. It is an incessant attraction that is incessantly threatened by its opposite. Life is like this."[97]

Only the "attraction," the "Christian attractiveness" of a Christianity lived as a visible expression of the unity of the transcendentals—the beautiful, the good, and the true—can assume the ideal of beauty, distorted by libertine hedonism, and bring it back to truth. In this testimony, Methol identified the path of Christianity in the contemporary world, a way fully embraced by the sensibility and the thinking of Jorge Mario Bergoglio.

95. Ibid., 159.
96. Ibid., 159–160.
97. Ibid., 158–159.

A World without Bonds

The Primacy of the Economy in the Era of Globalization

Globalization and the Latin American *Patria Grande*: Methol Ferré and Bergoglio

Methol Ferré's diagnosis of the opulent society and libertine atheism, informed by Del Noce and Brzezinski, was shared in full by Bergoglio, who became auxiliary bishop of Buenos Aires in 1992. He also shared Methol's great dream—that of a Latin American *patria grande* that embraced the popular Christian tradition and, by doing so, equipped itself to respond in its own way to the globalization of the 1980s and 1990s. Austen Ivereigh writes, "Methol Ferré and the Gera group of Catholic intellectuals foresaw the Latin-American Church as the catalyst of a common Latin-American destiny—*la patria grande*—in a global future marked by continent-states. After the failures of both the North Atlantic model of economic growth and Cuban-style socialism, they were convinced that the stage now belonged to the People of God. During the 1980s, Methol Ferré's journal *Nexo* was the wellspring of these ideas, and Bergoglio, an assiduous reader of the journal, drank deeply from its insights."[1]

---

1. Austen Ivereigh, *The Great Reformer: Francis and the Making of a Radical Pope* (New York: Henry Holt, 2014), 234.

The two ideas—criticism of the technocratic-hedonist model and construction of Latin American unity on the foundation of a Christianity of the people—are connected. On both converged Jorge Mario Bergoglio.[2] Ivereigh explains:

> In the mid- to late 1990s, Bergoglio grew close to an intellectual mentor he had first met back in the late 1970s: Alberto Methol Ferré, a Uruguayan lay Catholic intellectual who worked in the theology commission of CELAM and had been a major influence on the Puebla document.
>
> Methol Ferré was arguably the most significant and original Latin-American Catholic intellectual of the late twentieth century. A writer, historian, journalist, theologian, and auto-didact—he described himself as a "wild Thomist, without either seminary or academy"—he was converted to Catholicism by the writings of G. K. Chesterton while working in the port authority of Montevideo. Follower of Étienne Gilson and Perón, his two passions were the Church and Latin-American continental integration, which came together in his work for CELAM over twenty years, between 1972 and 1992. He and Bergoglio were natural bedfellows: believers in the national and popular tradition of Peronism, fired by Medellín but opposed to the revolutionary Marxism that followed, and deeply committed to continental unity.[3]

Bergoglio grew progressively closer to Methol Ferré in the years following Puebla, especially as they were both concluding a twenty-year collaboration with CELAM in 1992, the year of the fourth General Conference of the Latin American church in Santo Domingo. Methol returned to Montevideo, in Uruguay, where he resumed his academic activity and courses for diplomats at the Ministry of Foreign Affairs' Istituto Artigas. But he continued to meet Bergoglio,

---

2. The ideal of the *patria grande* was shared by the former president of Uruguay, José Alberto Mujica: "For this reason, Methol Ferré was my friend. I think in a Metholian key, and the pope does, too. Methol was a heterodox character with a phenomenal freedom of thought, a kind of tremendous intellectual audacity, something difficult to find in the climate of contemporary intellectual dogmatism" ("Orizzonte Mujica," interview by Alver Metalli, in *Terre d'America*, March 14, 2017).

3. Ivereigh, *The Great Reformer*, 234.

who became a cardinal in 2001. According to Alver Metalli, "In his frequent visits to Buenos Aires, he often visited the second-floor apartment at Viale Rivadavia 415. The visits lasted well beyond their scheduled periods, which were ignored by both of them. This writer was more than once a witness to the seriousness of those visits, the pleasure Bergoglio derived from them, and the satisfaction with which Methol Ferré left the cardinal's house."[4]

From these visits and meetings, a friendship grew that went beyond the mere sharing of ideas and projects. In 2011, Bergoglio spoke of his "dear, late friend, Alberto Methol Ferré."[5] The great intellectual had found in the cardinal an admirer capable of grasping the depth of his vision and the passion of his feeling. Together they shared an understanding of the post-1989 world, which was dominated by a profound individualism. Methol, Bergoglio would later write,

> said that it was a libertine, hedonistic, consumerist individualism, without an ethical or moral horizon. According to him, it was a new challenge for society and for the church in Latin America. This asocial and amoral individualism often infects the behavior of sectors or fragments of our society, which do not recognize themselves in the context of a broader horizon, as parts of a whole. *This is why, faced with current sociopolitical challenges, we must make the effort to recover the individual, personal dimension—which is very important and very relevant in our tradition of thought—and make it interact with the social, collective, and structural dimensions of community life.*[6]

Again in 2011, Bergoglio repeated the same judgment in the preface he prepared for Guzmán Carriquiry Lecour's book, *Il Bicentenario dell'Indipendenza dei Paesi latino-americani: Ieri e oggi*. He wrote there that

---

4. Alver Metalli, *Jorge Mario Bergoglio e Alberto Methol Ferré: affinità elettive di un Papa e di un filosofo del Rio de la Plata*, 21.

5. Jorge Mario Bergoglio–Pope Francis, *Noi come cittadini, noi come popolo: Verso un bicentenario in giustizia e solidarietà 2010–2016* (Milan: Jaca Book, 2013), 35.

6. Ibid., 35–36.

the quotation by Methol Ferré which [Carriquiry] offers on page 113 is quite opportune, where this brilliant thinker of the Rio de la Plata mentions the historical decay of the ideologies on which were constructed the various hermeneutics of the independence of the Latin American nations: after the obvious limits of liberal arguments, there were many interpretations inspired by messianic atheisms and their "salvationist" utopias (which had their ideological grounding in Marxism and produced in the real socialism the historical realization of the first officially atheistic states of history), and today they are inspired by that current of nihilist hedonism in which the crises of ideological beliefs converge. Today hedonist atheism, together with its neo-gnostic "furnishings of the soul," have become a dominant culture with a global reach; they are the atmosphere of the time in which we live. This is the new "opium of the people."[7]

The cardinal continued:

We are witnessing in our time this kind of ideological hermeneutics which, curiously, end up leading to a "single thought" founded on the divorce between *intelligentia* and *ratio*. Knowledge is fundamentally historical. *Ratio* is instrumental to intelligence, but when it becomes independent, it seeks support in ideology or social sciences as autonomous pillars. The "single thought," in addition to being socially and politically totalitarian, has gnostic structures: it is not human, it reproposes the different forms of absolutist rationalism with which the nihilistic hedonism described by Methol Ferré is expressed. A "nebulized," diffused theism, without an historical incarnation, becomes dominant.[8]

Thus, according to Bergoglio, "we see arising in our time the most varied ideologies reduced, in the last analysis, to a theistic gnosticism that, in ecclesial terms, we can define as 'a God without

---

7. Jorge Mario Bergoglio, prologue to Guzmán Carriquiry Lecour, *Il Bicentenario dell'indipendenza dei paesi latino-americani: Ieri e oggi* (Soveria Mannelli: Rubbettino, 2013), vi. The previous edition (2011) did not include Bergoglio's prologue.
8. Ibid., vi–vii.

a church, a church without Christ, a Christ without people.' If we use this hermeneutics, we produce a true disincarnation of history."[9]

The alternative to this abstract universalism is the *patria*, a concept distinct from both "country" and "nation."

> The country is the geographical space, and the nation is the institutional scaffolding. The *patria*, on the other hand, is what we have received from our parents and what we must pass on to our children. A country can be mutilated. A nation can transform itself (we have many examples after the First and the Second World Wars). But the *patria* either maintains its constitutive essence or it dies. *Patria* refers to heritage, to what has been received and which we must return, developed but not damaged. *Patria* alludes to fatherhood and filiation. It evokes that tragic and hopeful scene of Aeneas carrying his father on his shoulders on the evening of Troy's destruction. Yes, *patria* calls for nourishment of what we have received, not sealing it up in a vacuum but passing it on essentially intact but grown along the path of history. *Patria* necessarily implies a tension between memory of the past, commitment to the present, and the utopia that compels us toward the future. And this tension is concrete; it does not undergo strange interventions, and it mustn't, in the marasmus of the present reality, be confused with memory or utopia, generating infertile ideological wastes.[10]

In his 2013 preface to Carriquiry Lecour's book, Bergoglio described the *patria* as a point of resistance to ideology and to a geography deprived of its own history. In fact, the *patria* is a "home." It is, for a people, more than "a place to be," but a landscape that is, above all, historical, existential. Bergoglio wrote:

> Perhaps we could understand this dimension in the context of the big city, thinking of the neighborhood as a place of rootedness and daily life. Although the expansion of cities and the acceleration of the rhythms of life have largely reduced the gravitational centrality the neighborhood once had, even in the whirl of fragmentation many of its elements remain. In fact, the neighborhood, as a common space,

9. Ibid., vii.
10. Ibid., viii–ix.

implies a variety of colors, flavors, images, memories, and sounds that refer to the interweaving of everyday life that are, because it is small and almost invisible, essential. The people of the neighborhood, the colors of the soccer team jerseys, the central square with its transformations and the games, loves, and friendships that play out there, the crossroads and meeting places, the memory of ancestors, the sounds of the street, the music and the lights that illuminate the block, that certain corner—all of this is very much about the feeling of identity. Personal and shared identity, or, more accurately, personal to the extent that it's shared. Will it be the functional transformation of all spaces, according to the logic of wild and mercantile growth, which will condemn to death the dimension of rootedness? Will we soon inhabit only virtual or virtualized spaces, through screens and highways? Or will we, rather, find new ways to plant symbols around us, to give meaning to space, to *dwell*?[11]

For the cardinal, the rootedness of dwelling was essential: "There can be no social bond without this daily, almost microscopic dimension: being together among neighbors, coming into contact at different times of day, worrying about the things that concern everyone, helping each other in small, everyday things."[12] Proximity is the condition of being-in-relationship. For this reason, *to be a people means to dwell together in a common place*. For Bergoglio, in accord with antinomian thought, this never means being closed, polemically, to what is "outside." There is bad localism just as there is bad globalization. Reflecting the polar dialectic between universality and localization, the notion of *patria* does not carry for him a nationalistic, exclusive connotation. The *patria* must, in the globalized world, open itself to a broader horizon, and Argentina must look to the Latin American *patria grande*.

This was the ideal of Methol Ferré. This is what Bergoglio wrote in the preface to another work by Carriquiry Lecour, *Una apuesta por América Latina*, in 2005. Here, after underlining the "collapse of the totalitarian empire of 'real socialism,' " he observed that

11. "Siamo un popolo con vocazione di grandezza" (2006), in Jorge Mario Bergoglio–Pope Francis, *Nei tuoi occhi è la mia parola: Omelie discorsi di Buenos Aires 1999–2013*, 434.
    12. Ibid., 435.

"shortly afterward, the reborn neoliberal recipe book for a triumphant capitalism, fueled by the utopias of the self-regulating market, also demonstrated all its contradictions and limitations."[13] Faced with the process of homogenization shaped by an arrogant and limitless capitalism, Bergoglio pointed toward

> the path of integration toward the establishment of a South American Union and the Latin American *patria grande*. Alone, separated, we amount to very little and we will not go anywhere. This would be a dead end that would condemn us to marginalization, poverty, and dependence upon the great world powers. "It is a great responsibility," Pope John Paul II said in his inaugural address of the Fourth General Conference of the Latin American Episcopate in Santo Domingo, on October 12, 1992, "to foster the process of integration initiated by these peoples definitively united in the journey of history by the same geography, Christian faith, language, and culture." To follow this path, as a Catholic and emerging region of the "extreme West," and in order to become a sort of "middle class" among the nations in the world order, Latin America can and must face the needs and the challenges of globalization and the new scenarios of a dramatic global coexistence, always starting from the interests and ideals that are proper to it.[14]

This is a perspective that Pope Francis would reaffirm in 2016, in a letter marking the bicentennial of Argentina's independence. He wrote:

> We are celebrating the 200-year journey of a Country [*una Patria*] that, in its desire and yearning for brotherhood, projects itself beyond the confines of the country: toward the Great Homeland [*la Patria Grande*], of which St Martin and St Bolivar dreamt. This reality unites us in a family of broad horizons and loyalty of brothers. Today in our celebration let us also pray for the Great Homeland [*esa Patria*

---

13. Jorge Mario Bergoglio, prologue to Guzman Carriquiry Lecour, *Una apuesta por América Latina* (Buenos Aires: Editorial Sudamericana, 2005), available at http://www.terredamerica.com/2013/04/28/lamerica-latina-del-cardinal-Bergoglio-tra-imperialismo-della-globalizzazione-e-progressismo-adolescenziale/.

14. Ibid.

Grande]: that the Lord protect her, make her strong, more a sister, and defend her from every form of colonialization.[15]

Bergoglio did not call for an escape from or direct opposition to the globalized world, both of which would be unrealistic goals. Rather, he called for a rethinking of the dominant form of globalization. In 2005 he wrote:

> It is amazing to realize how the solidity of the culture of the American peoples is fundamentally threatened and weakened by two weak currents of thought. We can call one of them the imperialist conception of globalization. One might imagine it as a perfect, clean sphere; all peoples come together in a uniformity that eliminates any tension between diversities. Benson foresaw this in his famous novel *The Lord of the World*. This globalization constitutes the most dangerous totalitarianism of postmodernity. True globalization is not a sphere, but a polyhedron; every facet (the idiosyncrasies of peoples) retains its identity and particularity, but they are united in a harmonious tension in search of the common good.
>
> The other current that looms menacingly is what, in family parlance, we can call "adolescent progressivism," a kind of enthusiasm for progress that is exhausted in mediation, aborting the possibility of a sensible and fundamental development in close relationship with the roots of peoples. This "adolescent progressivism" fuels the cultural colonialism of the empires and is closely related to a conception of the State largely as a militant secularism. These two attitudes are anti-people, anti-national, and anti-Latin American pitfalls.[16]

Bergoglio's judgement, as expressed in these prefaces to the two volumes of Methol Ferré's intellectual disciple Guzmán Carriquiry, matched perfectly that of the Uruguayan thinker. The critique of libertine atheism, after 1989, and the dream of the Latin American *patria grande*, are united for Methol in a single design. They are the

---

15. Letter of His Holiness Pope Francis for the Bicentennial of Independence of the Argentine Republic, https://w2.vatican.va/content/francesco/en/letters/2016/documents/papa-francesco_20160708_indipendenza-argentina.html. [Passages in brackets from the official Spanish version.—Trans.]

16. Bergoglio, prologue to Carriquiry Lecour, *Una apuesta por América*.

two sides, critical and constructive, of a perspective that sees Latin America and popular Catholicism joined not in a traditionalist direction, but aimed together toward the future. It was the union between the baroque and modernity that the dialectical Ferré hoped for following the historiographical revolution of Del Noce. The *patria grande* was, however, not a new dream. Already in 1968 Methol Ferré had written, "At the apogee of European imperialism and the appearance of the American version, a new moment began that was common to all of Latin America. It was the awakening of its intellectual and student elites to the ideal of the 'Patria Grande,' with Rodó, Rubén Darío, and many others. It was the great movement of Latin American university reform of 1918. Some Catholics played an important role: the Argentine socialist Manuel Ugarte was a tireless advocate of the Patria Grande; the Mexican José Vasconcelos opposed 'Bolivarismo' and 'Monroismo' and started the first, original philosophy of Latin American Catholicism."[17]

Methol always considered himself an intellectual offspring of that generation, "which one might say initiated the transition from a nationalist vision to a Latin American one."[18] The great Mexican intellectual José Vasconcelos, the Uruguayan José Rodó, the Argentinian Manuel Ugarte, the Venezuelan Blanco Fombona, the Peruvian García Calderón, the Mexican Carlos Pereira—each of them "understand that in order to survive, Latin America must achieve something similar to what is being carried out by the United States of America."[19] To this end, even though they were not all Catholic, they recognized the value of Latin American Catholic faith and culture in supporting the integration of different nations. "They introduce the idea of the 'Patria Grande' as opposed to the small, individual countries whose inexorable destiny is to shrink more and more."[20] According to Methol,

---

17. Alberto Methol Ferré, "I periodi storici della Chiesa latinoamericana," *Vispera* 6 (1968), Italian trans. in Methol Ferré, *Il risorgimento cattolico latino-americano*, trans. P. Di Pauli and C. Perfetti (Bologna: CSEO-Incontri, 1983), 40.

18. Methol Ferré and Metalli, *Il Papa e il filosofo* (Siena: Cantagalli, 2014), 71.

19. Ibid.

20. Ibid., 123.

The project of integration, to be viable, needs two equal partners; only in this way can real unity come about. In the Argentine-Brazilian alliance, we have, on one hand, the most important Spanish-speaking country and, on the other, the only Portuguese-speaking country on the continent. Argentina, much more than Brazil, needs not only a good strategy in its relationship with its main partner, but also a wise and realistic tactic of unity with the other eight Spanish-speaking countries. It is the only way for Argentina to be able to represent a power equivalent to that of Brazil. Without real equality it would be difficult to build a lasting integration. The countries of South America must be aware that their destiny is linked to the equality of Argentine-Brazilian power.[21]

Methol Ferré's vision of "utopia" demonstrated that he had his feet firmly planted on the ground. The plan for integration was realistic, founded on a polar dialectic in which the weight of the Spanish pole was equal to the Portuguese one. Otherwise, integration involved the necessary hegemony of one party over the other.[22] The results of such an integration would include, first, the possibility of avoiding the North American economic and cultural hegemony and, second, the new importance that the church would have in the world. "Carriquiry, in his study of contemporary Latin America, establishes a link between Catholic culture and a convincing and nonextrinsic integration. Statistical observation alone shows that most of the Catholic people on the planet are concentrated in Latin America."[23]

The hopes of the 1970s and 1980s for a Latin American Catholic risorgimento find here, in the idea of the *patria grande*, their political implications. Latin America could never enter fully into world history, as Amelia Podetti wanted, as a collection of small states, condemned

---

21. Ibid., 123–124.

22. In Carriquiry, the bipolar framework of Methol (Brazil on one side; Argentina + Spanish-language nations on the other) become tripolar: Brazil/Argentina/Mexico. Cf. G. Carriquiry Lecour, *Una apuesta por América Latina*, 59; and *Il Bicentenario dell'indipendenza dei paesi latino-americani*, 109–110. Methol, for his part, excluded Mexico because of NAFTA, the 1994 free trade agreement between the United States, Canada, and Mexico. Cf. Methol Ferré and Metalli, *Il Papa e il filosofo*, 126, 130.

23. Ibid., 131.

to subordination and irrelevance; it had to become a confederation capable of playing a role in the era of globalization.

Pope Benedict XVI's *Caritas in Veritate*

The ideal of the *patria grande* shared by Methol Ferré and Bergoglio came from afar. It was shared by the entire Latin American church. We find it in the final document of the Third General Conference of the Latin American Episcopate at Puebla (1979). Here, after emphasizing that the church "sees with satisfaction the aspirations of humanity towards integration and a universal communion," the bishops asserted:

> But the Church, as one would expect, calls into question any "universality" that is synonymous with uniformity or levelling, that fails to respect different cultures by weakening them, absorbing them, or annihilating them. With even greater reason the Church refuses to accept universality when it is used as a tool to unify humanity by inculcating the unjust, offensive supremacy and domination of some peoples or social strata over other peoples and social strata.
>
> The Church of Latin America has resolved to put fresh vigor into its work of evangelizing the culture of our peoples and the various ethnic groups. It wants to see the faith of the Gospel blossom and be restored to fresh life. And with this as the basis of communion, it wants to see it burgeon into forms of just integration on all levels— national, continental Latin American *[una grande patria latinoamericana]*, and universal. This will enable our peoples to develop their own culture in such a way that they can assimilate the findings of science and technology in their own proper way.[24]

The same position was reiterated by the Fifth General Conference of the Latin American Episcopate held in Aparecida, Brazil, from May 13 to 31, 2007.[25] But while Aparecida seems to repeat Puebla,

24. Third General Conference of the Latin American Episcopate, Final Document §§427–428.

25. On the "patria grande," cf. Fifth General Conference of the Latin American Episcopate (Aparecida, 2007), Concluding Document §§525–526. Available at http://www.celam.org/aparecida/Ingles.pdf.

in reality, because the world picture had changed profoundly between 1979 and 2007, the same words took on a different meaning. In 1979, uniform and homogenous "universalism" meant, for Latin America, North American commercial imperialism with its consumptionist ideals and its individualistic vision of life. By 2007, long after the fall of communism, that ideal had become universal and no longer found any obstacles in its path. The era of globalization had overwhelmed states, nations, parties, trade unions, associations, popular ethos, common values, and customs. It had acted as a great leveler in which the only recognized "value" is money, albeit in the intangible and ethereal form of financial transactions. The new universality was not the "concrete universal" desired by Bergoglio and Methol Ferré. It was not the polyhedron; it was the sphere that homogenizes without retaining differences.

The answer, for Aparecida, lay not in the return to a satisfied existence as small countries, localisms, and provincialisms, but in a different version of globalization. Following the third pair of opposites, this is a *multipolar globalization.* As Francis said in a 2014 speech to the Council of Europe:

> The history of Europe might lead us to think somewhat naïvely of the continent as *bipolar,* or at most *tripolar* (as in the ancient conception of Rome-Byzantium-Moscow), and thus to interpret the present and to look to the future on the basis of this schema, which is a simplification born of pretentions to power.
>
> But this is not the case today, and we can legitimately speak of a "multipolar" Europe. Its tensions—whether constructive or divisive—are situated between multiple cultural, religious, and political poles. Europe today confronts the challenge of "globalizing," but in a creative way, this multipolarity. Nor are cultures necessarily identified with individual countries: some countries have a variety of cultures and some cultures are expressed in a variety of countries. The same holds true for political, religious, and social aggregations.
>
> Creatively globalizing multipolarity, and I wish to stress this creativity, calls for striving to create a constructive harmony, one free of those pretentions to power which, while appearing from a pragmatic standpoint to make things easier, end up destroying the cultural and religious distinctiveness of peoples.
>
> To speak of European multipolarity is to speak of peoples which are born, grow, and look to the future. The task of globalizing Eu-

rope's multipolarity cannot be conceived by appealing to the image of a sphere—in which all is equal and ordered, but proves reductive inasmuch as every point is equidistant from the center—but rather, by the image of a *polyhedron*, in which the harmonic unity of the whole preserves the particularity of each of the parts. Today Europe is multipolar in its relationships and its intentions; it is impossible to imagine or to build Europe without fully taking into account this *multipolar* reality.[26]

It is a model that, as we have seen, Bergoglio has put to good use, beginning with his doctrine of polar opposition. Whether it is to manage the tensions within the Society of Jesus, within the church, between the *patria grande* and its various small nations, or between Europe and its nations, the point is the same: the proper balance between the whole and the parts, between the universal and the particular. The law of polarity allows for peace and justice, guaranteeing the common good—a common good that globalization promises but does not realize. Its technological/economic unidimensionality does not recognize the pluriformity that only political action can guarantee. Hence the grave threat to the democratic model posed by the economic processes of globalization that only consider the political factor to be an obstacle to the markets. Addressing the European Parliament, Francis said:

> The proper configuration of the European Union must always be respected, based as it is on the principles of solidarity and subsidiarity, so that mutual assistance can prevail and progress can be made on the basis of mutual trust.
>
> Ladies and Gentlemen, Members of the European Parliament, within this dynamic of unity and particularity, yours is the responsibility of keeping democracy alive, democracy for the peoples of Europe. It is no secret that a conception of unity seen as uniformity strikes at the vitality of the democratic system, weakening the rich, fruitful and constructive interplay of organizations and political parties. This leads to the risk of living in a world of ideas, of mere words, of images, of sophistry . . . and to end up confusing the reality of

26. Pope Francis, "Address to the Council of Europe," November 25, 2014, https://w2.vatican.va/content/francesco/en/speeches/2014/november /documents/papa-francesco_20141125_strasburgo-consiglio-europa.html.

democracy with a new political nominalism. Keeping democracy alive in Europe requires avoiding the many globalizing tendencies to dilute reality: namely, angelic forms of purity, dictatorships of relativism, brands of ahistorical fundamentalism, ethical systems lacking kindness, and intellectual discourse bereft of wisdom.

Keeping democracies alive is a challenge in the present historic moment. The true strength of our democracies—understood as expressions of the political will of the people—must not be allowed to collapse under the pressure of multinational interests which are not universal, which weaken them and turn them into uniform systems of economic power at the service of unseen empires.[27]

The "polyhedron" coincides here with the defense of democracy, the universal-particular, the *vox populi* not crushed by "nonuniversal" multinationals. It is certainly a perspective that is opposed not to globalization itself, but to its present form. Bergoglio would later make this clear, as pope, with his apostolic exhortation *Evangelii Gaudium*. Before him, Pope Benedict XVI took a stand in the face of globalization with his 2009 encyclical *Caritas in Veritate*. If in *Centesimus annus* (1991) John Paul II marked the end of communism and tried to outline the challenges for the church in that new era, then *Caritas in Veritate* is in some way the document that takes account of the new economic unification of the world. In doing so, it makes clear that not everything about the new processes of economic development are negative; there is an overall improvement of global well-being, the raising of some parts of the world population from poverty, a global advance of communication systems, and so forth. And yet, deep shadows remain. "As society becomes ever more globalized," Benedict wrote, "it makes us neighbors but does not make us family. Reason, by itself, is capable of grasping the equality between people and of giving stability to their civic coexistence, but it cannot establish kinship."[28]

27. Pope Francis, "Address to the European Parliament," November 25, 2014, https://w2.vatican.va/content/francesco/en/speeches/2014/november/documents/papa-francesco_20141125_strasburgo-parlamento-europeo.html.

28. Pope Benedict XVI, encyclical letter *Caritas in Veritate* (2009) 19, http://w2.vatican.va/content/benedict-xvi/en/encyclicals/documents/hf_ben-xvi_enc_20090629_caritas-in-veritate.html. [Vatican English translation revised to eliminate three (!) instances of sexist language in a single sentence.—Trans.]

Acknowledging that global economic development has brought progress to many countries, Benedict notes:

> Yet it must be acknowledged that this same economic growth has been and continues to be weighed down by *malfunctions and dramatic problems*, highlighted even further by the current crisis. . . . The technical forces in play, the global interrelations, the damaging effects on the real economy of badly managed and largely speculative financial dealing, large-scale migration of peoples, often provoked by some particular circumstance and then given insufficient attention, the unregulated exploitation of the earth's resources: all this leads us today to reflect on the measures that would be necessary to provide a solution to problems . . . of decisive impact upon the present and future good of humanity.[29]

The encyclical cited new evidence that the line of demarcation between rich countries and poor ones was not as clear as in the past: "*The world's wealth is growing in absolute terms, but inequalities are on the increase.* In rich countries, new sectors of society are succumbing to poverty and new forms of poverty are emerging. In poorer areas some groups enjoy a sort of 'superdevelopment' of a wasteful and consumerist kind which forms an unacceptable contrast with the ongoing situations of dehumanizing deprivation. 'The scandal of glaring inequalities' continues."[30]

Benedict XVI thus offered a "critical" perspective, positive and negative, of globalization. His approach was not notably strong, but it was enough to prompt the skepticism of some noted North American scholars, including Michael Novak and George Weigel.[31] In reality, the main criticism that Benedict XVI offered on globalization was about the global primacy of the economy, calling for a restoration of control and vitality to individual nations through the *logic of subsidiarity* played out on a global scale. *Caritas in Veritate*,

29. Ibid. 21.

30. Ibid. 22. (The internal quotation is a citation of Pope Paul VI's encyclical *Populorum Progressio* 9.)

31. Cf. Andrea Tornielli and Giacomo Galeazzi, *This Economy Kills: Pope Francis on Capitalism and Social Justice*, trans. Demetrio S. Yocum (Collegeville, MN: Liturgical Press, 2015), chap. 7, "American Theocon Criticism . . . of Benedict XVI?," 81–87.

promulgated on the occasion of the fortieth anniversary of Paul VI's *Populorum Progressio* (March 26, 1967), served to update the latter document.

Compared to Paul's encyclical, which presumes that the state still set the priorities of its economy and that this was mostly carried out within national borders, Benedict notes, "In our own day, the State finds itself having to address the limitations to its sovereignty imposed by the new context of international trade and finance, which is characterized by increasing mobility both of financial capital and means of production, material and immaterial."[32] *Caritas in Veritate* calls into question this decreasing ability of a state to control its own economy: "Today, as we take to heart the lessons of the current economic crisis, which sees the State's public authorities directly involved in correcting errors and malfunctions, it seems more realistic to *re-evaluate their role* and their powers, which need to be prudently reviewed and remodelled so as to enable them, perhaps through new forms of engagement, to address the challenges of today's world."[33] Faced with an internationalization of financial markets that limits the effectiveness of government actions and the role of local economies, the encyclical states, "The integrated economy of the present day does not make the role of States redundant, but rather it commits governments to greater collaboration with one another. Both wisdom and prudence suggest not being too precipitous in declaring the demise of the State. In terms of the resolution of the current crisis, the State's role seems destined to grow, as it regains many of its competences."[34]

Caritas in Veritate, then, offers *a significant reevaluation of the role of the State*. Globalization, with the delocalization and deregulation of labor, causes a conspicuous reduction of social safety nets.[35] This poses a grave threat to the rights of workers and to the

32. Benedict XVI, *Caritas in Veritate* 24.

33. Ibid.

34. Ibid. 41.

35. "From the social point of view, systems of protection and welfare, already present in many countries in Paul VI's day, are finding it hard and could find it even harder in the future to pursue their goals of true social justice in today's profoundly changed environment. The global market has stimulated first and

forms of solidarity implemented in the traditional expressions of the welfare state.

Faced with this process, the encyclical restates John Paul II's recognition, in *Centesimus Annus*, of "the need for a system with three subjects: the market, the State and civil society."[36] Benedict writes, "*Economic life* undoubtedly requires *contracts*, in order to regulate relations of exchange between goods of equivalent value. But it also needs *just laws* and *forms of redistribution* governed by politics, and what is more, it needs works redolent of the *spirit of gift*. The economy in the global era seems to privilege the former logic, that of contractual exchange, but directly or indirectly it also demonstrates its need for the other two: political logic, and the logic of the unconditional gift."[37] The latter refers not only to the vast and generous world of volunteerism. "Space also needs to be created within the market for economic activity carried out by subjects who freely choose to act according to principles other than those of pure profit, without sacrificing the production of economic value in the process."[38] Here *Caritas in Veritate* introduces the important theme of "gratuitousness," which corresponds to the spirit of "solidarity" that is continually eroded by the processes of secularization.

> In the global era, economic activity cannot prescind from gratuitousness, which fosters and disseminates solidarity and responsibility for

---

foremost, on the part of rich countries, a search for areas in which to outsource production at low cost with a view to reducing the prices of many goods, increasing purchasing power and thus accelerating the rate of development in terms of greater availability of consumer goods for the domestic market. Consequently, the market has prompted new forms of competition between States as they seek to attract foreign businesses to set up production centers, by means of a variety of instruments, including favorable fiscal regimes and deregulation of the labor market. These processes have led to a downsizing of social security systems as the price to be paid for seeking greater competitive advantage in the global market, with consequent grave danger for the rights of workers, for fundamental human rights and for the solidarity associated with the traditional forms of the social State" (25).

36. Ibid. 38.
37. Ibid. 37.
38. Ibid.

justice and the common good among the different economic players. It is clearly a specific and profound form of economic democracy. Solidarity is first and foremost a sense of responsibility on the part of everyone with regard to everyone, and it cannot therefore be merely delegated to the State. While in the past it was possible to argue that justice had to come first and gratuitousness could follow afterwards, as a complement, today it is clear that without gratuitousness, there can be no justice in the first place. What is needed, therefore, is a market that permits the free operation, in conditions of equal opportunity, of enterprises in pursuit of different institutional ends. Alongside profit-oriented private enterprise and the various types of public enterprise, there must be room for commercial entities based on mutualist principles and pursuing social ends to take root and express themselves. It is from their reciprocal encounter in the marketplace that one may expect hybrid forms of commercial behavior to emerge, and hence an attentiveness to ways of *civilizing the economy*.[39]

It is not just a question of a formula for an economy that offers a middle way between the market and the welfare state, but of *a fundamental way through which the processes of socialization are carried out*. In fact, it is not only the market that erodes the social bonds by developing a uniquely competitive system. *Welfare*, too, when it is conceived as the foundation of any practice of solidarity, discourages rather than builds up the sense of personal solidarity:

When both the logic of the market and the logic of the State come to an agreement that each will continue to exercise a monopoly over its respective area of influence, in the long term much is lost: solidarity in relations between citizens, participation and adherence, actions of gratuitousness, all of which stand in contrast with giving in order to acquire (the logic of exchange) and giving through duty (the logic of public obligation, imposed by State law). In order to defeat underdevelopment, action is required not only on improving exchange-based transactions and implanting public welfare structures, but above all on gradually increasing openness, in a world context, to forms of economic activity marked by quotas of gratuitousness and communion. The exclusively binary model of market-plus-State is corrosive of society, while economic forms based on solidarity, which

39. Ibid. 38.

find their natural home in civil society without being restricted to it, build up society.[40]

Benedict calls for models that go beyond the familiar nature of the conventional *nonprofit*.

When we consider the issues involved in the *relationship between business and ethics*, as well as the evolution currently taking place in methods of production, it would appear that the traditionally valid distinction between profit-based companies and non-profit organizations can no longer do full justice to reality, or offer practical direction for the future. In recent decades a broad intermediate area has emerged between the two types of enterprise. It is made up of traditional companies which nonetheless subscribe to social aid agreements in support of underdeveloped countries, charitable foundations associated with individual companies, groups of companies oriented towards social welfare, and the diversified world of the so-called "civil economy" and the "economy of communion." This is not merely a matter of a "third sector," but of a broad new composite reality embracing the private and public spheres, one which does not exclude profit, but instead considers it a means for achieving human and social ends.[41]

It is in this context of recasting the concept of labor in social terms that the encyclical considers the concept of *subsidiarity*. If it has an irreplaceable value in giving shape to the processes of globalization,[42] it is also true that "*the principle of subsidiarity must remain closely linked to the principle of solidarity and vice versa*, since the former without the latter gives way to social privatism, while the latter without the former gives way to paternalist social assistance that is demeaning to those in need."[43] In this way, the encyclical links subsidiarity and solidarity in a single binomial. Their union prompts individuals and societies to commit to and "to establish the common good."[44]

---

40. Ibid. 39.
41. Ibid. 46.
42. Cf. ibid. 57 and 67.
43. Ibid. 58.
44. Ibid. 67.

Evangelii Gaudium's Critique of Inequality

Caritas in Veritate considered the church's social doctrine on subsidiarity in the current historical context. This distinguishes it from Pius XI's *Quadragesimo Anno*, in which the doctrine of subsidiarity stands as a "liberal" bulwark against the overwhelming power of the totalitarian states of the 1930s. Today's adversary in the West is no longer the totalitarian state but the totalitarianism of a globalization without rules that destroys social and ethical bonds, reducing everything to instrumental reason. *Caritas in Veritate* offers constructive criticism of this new adversary, trying to offer alternatives—the economy of the gift—capable of softening the harshest effects of the iron laws of the market economy.

With respect to this approach, the social criticism offered in Pope Francis's 2013 apostolic exhortation *Evangelii Gaudium* is more direct. After the failure of Lehman Brothers in 2008 and the threat of world bankruptcy, the problems of the neocapitalist globalization that had been dominant from the 1980s onward could be ignored. These are not incidental problems, but structural ones. The very model calls for rethinking.[45] Even *Caritas in Veritate* had observed, "Lowering the level of protection accorded to the rights of workers, or abandoning mechanisms of wealth redistribution in order to increase the country's international competitiveness, hinder the achievement of lasting development. Moreover, the human consequences of current tendencies towards a short-term economy—sometimes very short-term—need to be carefully evaluated. This requires *further and deeper reflection on the meaning of the economy and its goals*, as well as a profound and far-sighted revision of the current model of development, so as to correct its dysfunctions and deviations."[46] Benedict XVI had written, "After the collapse of the economic and political systems of the Communist countries of Eastern Europe and the end of the so-called opposing blocs, a complete re-examination of development was needed."[47]

---

45. On Pope Francis's view of globalization, cf. Andrea Riccardi, *La sorpresa di papa Francesco: Crisi e futuro della Chiesa* (Milan: Mondadori, 2013), 119–153.

46. Benedict XVI, *Caritas in Veritate* 32.

47. Ibid. 23.

This reexamination called for by Benedict has never happened. Instead, a single model of development has been imposed like a dogma, and with nothing (such as the Soviet bloc) to stand in its way, it doesn't even need to legitimize itself by even pretending to offer some effort to reduce poverty. Profit and efficiency become absolute values, favored and imposed by the electronic revolution on the one hand and the opening to the Asian markets on the other. The result is a reduction of the workforce, a notable increase in unemployment (especially of young adults), a wide gap between the elite and the rest of the population, the proletarization of the middle class, the growth of large sections of new poverty, and the drastic reduction of social services offered by government. *Evangelii Gaudium* recognizes this process, which elevates Hobbesian-Darwinian anthropology to a paradigm, and it responds with a critique that is direct. The document is a clear "No to an economy of exclusion."[48] Pope Francis writes:

> Just as the commandment "Thou shalt not kill" sets a clear limit in order to safeguard the value of human life, today we also have to say "thou shalt not" to an economy of exclusion and inequality. Such an economy kills. How can it be that it is not a news item when an elderly homeless person dies of exposure, but it is news when the stock market loses two points? This is a case of exclusion. Can we continue to stand by when food is thrown away while people are starving? This is a case of inequality. Today everything comes under the laws of competition and the survival of the fittest, where the powerful feed upon the powerless. As a consequence, masses of people find themselves excluded and marginalized: without work, without possibilities, without any means of escape.
>
> Human beings are themselves considered consumer goods to be used and then discarded. We have created a "throw away" culture which is now spreading. It is no longer simply about exploitation and oppression, but something new. Exclusion ultimately has to do with what it means to be a part of the society in which we live; those excluded are no longer society's underside or its fringes or its

---

48. Pope Francis, apostolic exhortation *Evangelii Gaudium* (2013) 53 (section heading).

disenfranchised—they are no longer even a part of it. The excluded are not the "exploited" but the outcast, the "leftovers."[49]

The content of *Evangelii Gaudium* closely reflects that of the closing document of CELAM's Aparecida conference, which Bergoglio had played a decisive role in writing. "In globalization," the latter document said,

> market forces easily absolutize efficacy and productivity as values regulating all human relations. This peculiar character makes globalization a process that fosters many inequities and injustices. . . . A globalization without solidarity has a negative impact on the poorest groups. It is no longer simply the phenomenon of exploitation and oppression, but something new: social exclusion. What is affected is the very root of belonging to the society in which one lives, because one is no longer on the bottom, on the margins, or powerless, but rather one is living outside. The excluded are not simply "exploited" but "surplus" and "disposable."[50]

As Aparecida makes clear, Francis's severe judgment on the "economy that kills" was not born out of an ideological "Peronist" stance, as some *liberal* criticism of the pope suggests, but from the direct experience of his Argentina, of the grave economic crisis that, between the end of the 1990s and the first years of the following decade, had destabilized the entire society, throwing millions of people into poverty. This was done by the government of Carlos Menem, who was in office for two consecutive terms, from 1989 to 1999. Menem, the first Peronist executive since the time of the General and Isabelita, had

> forged an unexpected bond with the very part of society Argentine that had always been at odds with Peronism: the financial and agro-export sector. Their talented leaders served in Menem's administration, crafting his economic policy and carrying out his reforms,

---

49. Ibid. On the "global inequality" of the modern economy, cf. Pope Francis, encyclical letter *Laudato Si'*, nn. 48–52.

50. Fifth General Conference of the Latin American Episcopate, Concluding Document §§61, 65. Available at http://www.celam.org/aparecida/Ingles.pdf.

persuaded that only a Peronist government had the political legitimacy to deliver the necessary shock therapy to Argentina's bloated and state-dependent economy.

That shock came in the form of a mass sell-off of public-owned enterprises and a so-called convertibility law that replaced the national currency with a new one, the peso, making it convertible to the US dollar at a rate of one to one.[51]

The result was the flow of foreign capital into the country and the elimination of inflation. "However, the government's failure to build a social-security network alongside the free market left the poor unprotected, and statistics showed an alarming increase in poverty and unemployment despite economic stability and growth. The architects of the policy—led by Domingo Cavallo, the economy minister—put their faith in the workings of the markets, confident that investment and growth would eventually trickle down to the poor; but at the end of the Menem decade they were still waiting."[52]

The crisis became clear in 1998 and brought serious consequences. In October 1999, a new government came to power, through a coalition of radicals and dissident Peronists, led by the radical-conservative Fernando de la Rúa, who followed the same neoliberal economic policy that Menem had implemented. Faced with a crisis in December 2001, the new president was forced to abandon the Casa Rosada in Buenos Aires by helicopter, to escape the wrath of an angry crowd. It is this experience and the sight of millions of people on the streets, and not a Peronist ideology, that stands behind the firm criticisms that have earned Francis the opposition of capitalist ideologues.[53]

---

51. Ivereigh, *The Great Reformer*, 218.

52. Ibid.

53. As an illustration of the reaction of the American *liberal*-capitalist right, the judgment of Edward Luttwak serves well: "No one reflects on an objective fact. The ideas of Pope Francis are *typical of a whole class of Argentine intellectuals*, who in the space of a century brought Buenos Aires from the first places among the richest countries in the world—around the twenties of the twentieth century—to about the sixtieth in current ranking for *per capita income*. That is the ideas of those Argentinians deployed against the free market, against modernization, against progress. In part, they are the ideas of

In light of the Argentine lesson and faced with an economic crisis that, after 2008, threatened to overwhelm the world, the pope was clear:

> The need to resolve the structural causes of poverty cannot be delayed, not only for the pragmatic reason of its urgency for the good order of society, but because society needs to be cured of a sickness which is weakening and frustrating it, and which can only lead to new crises. Welfare projects, which meet certain urgent needs, should be considered merely temporary responses. As long as the problems of the poor are not radically resolved by rejecting the absolute autonomy of markets and financial speculation and by attacking the structural causes of inequality, no solution will be found for the world's problems or, for that matter, to any problems. Inequality is the root of social ills.[54]

Francis insists, "We can no longer trust in the unseen forces and the invisible hand of the market. Growth in justice requires more than economic growth, while presupposing such growth: it requires decisions, programs, mechanisms and processes specifically geared to a better distribution of income, the creation of sources of employment and an integral promotion of the poor which goes beyond a simple welfare mentality."[55] The growth of "inequality" requires

---

Peronist culture" ("Edward Luttwak contro Papa Francesco: 'Estremista, le sue idee poco serie. Quelli come lui hanno rovinato l'Argentina,'" *Libero Quotidiano*, September 21, 2015, http://www.liberoquotidiano.it/news /italia/11830155/Edward-Luttwak-contro-Papa-Francesco-.html). Luttwak "forgets" to note that the imposition of a "free market" without corrective measures was the cause of the collapse of the Argentine economy between the end of the 1990s and the early 2000s. With regard to Bergoglio's formation, Luttwak demonstrates profound ignorance, to the point of affirming "that Pope Francis comes from the intellectual circles of Buenos Aires. Those who at the time supported the liberation theology of Father Torres" or "guerrilla warfare to remedy social injustices" ("Luttwak, una feroce verità sul Papa: '. . . da due soldi. Chi era da giovane,'" *Libero Quotidiano*, July 31, 2016, http://www.liberoquotidiano.it/news/personaggi/11936665/luttwakpapa -francesco-marxista-isis.html).

54. Pope Francis, *Evangelii Gaudium* 202.
55. Ibid. 204.

decisions that reject a paradigm based on two fixed points: the technocratic model on one hand and the individualistic-hedonistic-relativistic vision on the other. On this vision, Cardinal Bergoglio was fully in agreement with his friend Methol Ferré. Ivereigh reminds us that after the conclusion of the 1992 Santo Domingo conference, "Methol Ferré left CELAM . . . and moved back to Montevideo, from where he would regularly visit Bergoglio over the River Plate in Buenos Aires. They spent many hours discussing the state of the world, and Latin America's place in it, concerned that the decline of liberation theology and the rise of neoliberalism had undermined the Church's engagement with the poor. Methol Ferré was convinced that the enemies of that engagement were now relativism and consumerism, and that the Latin-American Church needed to recover its option for the poor, asserting the sacrifices needed for true solidarity."[56]

The ethic of solidarity had stood in the way of the spread of the technocratic, functionalistic model that now imposed its hegemony upon the economic disciplines. Pope Francis would later write in his encyclical letter *Laudato Si'*:

> The technocratic paradigm also tends to dominate economic and political life. The economy accepts every advance in technology with a view to profit, without concern for its potentially negative impact on human beings. Finance overwhelms the real economy. The lessons of the global financial crisis have not been assimilated, and we are learning

---

56. Ivereigh, *The Great Reformer*, 236–237. The decline of liberation theology, concurrent with the fall of communism, freed theology from its fascination with Marxism and, at the same time, implied a denial of the relationship between evangelization and human development. The crisis of liberation theology coincided, in Latin America, with the abandonment of Catholic social teaching. As Methol commented to Metalli: "In a certain way, the 'evaporation' of liberation theology has diminished the willingness of the entire Latin American church to take on the condition of the poor with courage. I believe the church is paying the price for being too easily liberated from liberation theology. *Liberation theology should have offered its greatest contribution after the fall of communism*, not burned itself out with Marxism. It is urgent today that we fill the vacuum it left" (Methol Ferré and Metalli, *Il Papa e il filosofo*, 114; italics mine).

all too slowly the lessons of environmental deterioration. Some circles maintain that current economics and technology will solve all environmental problems, and argue, in popular and non-technical terms, that the problems of global hunger and poverty will be resolved simply by market growth. They are less concerned with certain economic theories which today scarcely anybody dares defend, than with their actual operation in the functioning of the economy. They may not affirm such theories with words, but nonetheless support them with their deeds by showing no interest in more balanced levels of production, a better distribution of wealth, concern for the environment and the rights of future generations. Their behavior shows that for them maximizing profits is enough. Yet by itself the market cannot guarantee integral human development and social inclusion.[57]

The technocratic paradigm is the result of the "transition from Marx to Comte," from Marxism to positivism, which occurred in the West after 1989. This transition was lucidly foreseen by Augusto Del Noce in his 1964 book *Il problema dell'ateismo*, the thesis of which was shared by Alberto Methol Ferré and, indirectly, by Jorge Mario Bergoglio. The latter noted in 2014:

To our dismay we see technical and economic questions dominating political debate, to the detriment of genuine concern for human beings. Men and women risk being reduced to mere cogs in a machine that treats them as items of consumption to be exploited, with the result that—as is so tragically apparent—whenever a human life no longer proves useful for that machine, it is discarded with few qualms, as in the case of the sick, of the terminally ill, the elderly who are abandoned and uncared for, and children who are killed in the womb.

This is the great mistake made "when technology is allowed to take over"; the result is "confusion between ends and means." It is the inevitable consequence of a "throwaway culture" and an uncontrolled consumerism. Upholding the dignity of the person means instead acknowledging the value of human life, which is freely given us and hence cannot be an object of trade or commerce.[58]

---

57. Pope Francis, encyclical letter *Laudato Si'* (2015) 109.

58. Pope Francis, "Address to the European Parliament," https://w2.vatican.va/content/francesco/en/speeches/2014/november/documents/papa-francesco_20141125_strasburgo-parlamento-europeo.html#_ftn6. (The two internal quotes are both from Pope Benedict XVI, *Caritas in Veritate*, n. 71.)

The technocratic model that guides today's economy is combined, in this era of globalization, with an *individualistic and relativistic philosophy.* The positivist neo-empiricism that constitutes post-1989 culture is *the meeting point between technocracy and relativism.*

> Hence we should not be surprised to find, in conjunction with the omnipresent technocratic paradigm and the cult of unlimited human power, the rise of a relativism which sees everything as irrelevant unless it serves one's own immediate interests. There is a logic in all this whereby different attitudes can feed on one another, leading to environmental degradation and social decay.
>
> The culture of relativism is the same disorder which drives one person to take advantage of another, to treat others as mere objects, imposing forced labor on them or enslaving them to pay their debts. The same kind of thinking leads to the sexual exploitation of children and abandonment of the elderly who no longer serve our interests. It is also the mindset of those who say: Let us allow the invisible forces of the market to regulate the economy, and consider their impact on society and nature as collateral damage. In the absence of objective truths or sound principles other than the satisfaction of our own desires and immediate needs, what limits can be placed on human trafficking, organized crime, the drug trade, commerce in blood diamonds and the fur of endangered species? Is it not the same relativistic logic which justifies buying the organs of the poor for resale or use in experimentation, or eliminating children because they are not what their parents wanted?[59]

Faced with the double challenge of economic technocracy and ethical relativism, *Evangelii Gaudium* proposes a *primacy of politics*, a politics that returns to considering the "common good" of a people within a nonimmanentist horizon. Today, politics can "transcend" the economy only if it moves within the polar tension between immanence and transcendence. "I am firmly convinced," Francis writes, "that openness to the transcendent can bring about a new political and economic mindset which would help to break down the wall of separation between the economy and the common good of society."[60] Politics must reconcile the economy and the

---

59. Pope Francis, *Laudato Si'* 122–123.
60. Pope Francis, *Evangelii Gaudium* 205.

common good. In an economy dominated by individualism, it must manifest itself as a profound dissonance. Only in this way does social peace, which presupposes not the opposition between the "weak" and the "strong" but their unity, become possible.

Faced with an economy of "inequality" that divides, that tosses away any nonproductive "waste," politics is called to reshape the face of the economy and society, to "tend to fragility, the fragility of individuals and peoples. To tend to this fragility takes strength and tenderness, effort and generosity in the midst of a functionalistic and privatized mindset which inexorably leads to a 'throwaway culture.' To care for individuals and peoples in need means protecting memory and hope; it means taking responsibility for the present with its situations of utter marginalization and anguish, and being capable of bestowing dignity upon it."[61] *Politics, as protection of the weak against the strong, becomes a concern for "fragility."* For Francis, these "fragile" ones must also include unborn children.

> Among the vulnerable for whom the Church wishes to care with particular love and concern are unborn children, the most defenseless and innocent among us. Nowadays efforts are made to deny them their human dignity and to do with them whatever one pleases, taking their lives and passing laws preventing anyone from standing in the way of this. Frequently, as a way of ridiculing the Church's effort to defend their lives, attempts are made to present her position as ideological, obscurantist and conservative. Yet this defense of unborn life is closely linked to the defense of each and every other human right. It involves the conviction that a human being is always sacred and inviolable, in any situation and at every stage of development. Human beings are ends in themselves and never a means of resolving other problems. Once this conviction disappears, so do solid and lasting foundations for the defense of human rights, which would always be subject to the passing whims of the powers that be. . . . This is not something subject to alleged reforms or "modernizations." It is not "progressive" to try to resolve problems by eliminating a human life.[62]

61. "Address to the European Parliament." [Vatican translation corrected.— Trans.]

62. *Evangelii Gaudium* 213, 214.

As a model of this policy, Francis points in *Evangelii Gaudium* to the same guiding criteria that he had cited in his speech to the Jesuits in 1974,[63] and the same he had recalled in his essay on the bicentenary of Argentina in 2011.[64] These are the four principles that govern the polar tensions: time is superior to space, unity prevails over conflict, realities are more important than ideas, the whole is superior to the part.[65] The second and fourth—the fourth in particular—are not to the liking of the *liberal* wing of globalization and of the Catholic right.[66] In reality, in the "polar" vision of Bergoglio they indicate a point of harmonization of contrasts, the condition of a social peace that politics has the task of implementing. This is the principle, central to Christian social doctrine, whereby solidarity among the social classes implies a principle of *fairness* in the distribution of goods. "Solidarity," *Evangelii Gaudium* insists, "is a spontaneous reaction by those who recognize that the social function of property and the universal destination of goods are realities which come before private property. The private ownership of goods is justified by the need to protect and increase them, so

63. Jorge Mario Bergoglio, "Una istituzione che vive il suo carisma: Discorso di apertura della Congregazione provincial" (San Miguel, Buenos Aires, February 18, 1974), in Jorge Mario Bergoglio, *Pastorale sociale*, ed. Marco Gallo, Ital. trans. A. Taroni (Milan: Jaca Book, 2015).

64. Jorge Mario Bergoglio, "Noi come cittadini, noi come popolo."

65. *Evangelii Gaudium* 221–237.

66. "It is not surprising at this point that Francis often repeats one of his dearest mantras: the whole is superior to the parts. It is a way of saying that the *pueblo*, a mythical and divine entity, transcends the individual" (L. Zanatta, *Un papa peronista?*, 245). "The problem is that the principle, as it is formulated, does not express a balance between the whole and the parts; it speaks plainly of the *superiority* of the whole to the parts. And this is in contrast with the social doctrine of the church, which declares, yes, the person as a constitutively social being, but at the same time reaffirms the primacy and irreducibility of the person to the social organism. . . . There is a risk that the fourth postulate, offered without further clarification, can be understood in a Marxist sense and thus justify the subordination of the individual to society" (Giovanni Scalese, "I postulati di Papa Francesco," in Sandro Magister, "I quattro chiodi a cui Bergoglio appende il suo pensiero," *Settimo Cielo* blog, May 19, 2016, http://chiesa.espresso.repubblica.it/articolo/1351301.html).

that they can better serve the common good; for this reason, solidarity must be lived as the decision to restore to the poor what belongs to them."[67] The *Catechism of the Catholic Church* teaches the same thing: "The right to private property, acquired by work or received from others by inheritance or gift, does not do away with the original gift of the earth to the whole of mankind. The universal destination of goods remains primordial, even if the promotion of the common good requires respect for the right to private property and its exercise."[68]

But such details did not prevent disagreements, reservations, and clear opposition to the papal document. Francis's analysis of capitalism in the era of globalization as a model erosive of democracy and welfare could only attract the severe criticism of the liberal right, which did not appreciate such a harsh critique by the pope on the present form of economic power.[69] Thus, many in the United

---

67. *Evangelii Gaudium* 189.

68. *Catechism of the Catholic Church* 2403.

69. For an overview of the criticisms of Francis by the liberal apologists of the economy, see Tornielli and Galeazzi, *This Economy Kills: Pope Francis on Capitalism and Social Justice* (Collegeville, MN: Liturgical Press, 2015); Nello Scavo, *I nemici di Francesco* (Milan: Piemme, 2015), 15–35. For accusations that Bergoglio is a South American populist and Peronist, see, in addition to many articles by Sandro Magister, also Loris Zanatta, *Un papa peronista?*, 240–249; Maurizio Blondet, "Ritratto di Bergoglio come ideologo: Paleo-marxista," in *Blondet & Friends*, November 27, 2016. Also critical of Francis is Flavio Cuniberto, *Madonna povertà: Papa Francesco e la rifondazione del cristianesimo* (Vicenza: Neri Pozza, 2016), which comments, "(Global) poverty is reduced; inequality increases. This apparent paradox, which is constitutive of the late globalized capitalism, seems to completely escape the analysis of the Vatican document, to the point of probably being the main cause of its off-target diagnosis" (41). For Cuniberto, Francis's position represents a pauperistic ideology, the legacy of a third-worldism overcome by history. In reality, the papal position emerges from the lens of the 1970s and fully grasps the modern problem. In the passage quoted earlier, the Pope writes: "It is no longer simply about exploitation and oppression, but something new. Exclusion ultimately has to do with what it means to be a part of the society in which we live; those excluded are no longer society's underside or its fringes or its disenfranchised—they are no longer even a part of it. The excluded are not the 'exploited' but the outcast, the 'leftovers' " (*Evangelii Gaudium* 53). The increase in overall well-being occurs through the increase in inequality

States did not like it.[70] In response to the positive assessments offered by the *Washington Post* and the British labor newspaper *The Guardian*, the American economic-financial journal *Forbes* published a series of articles in a period of just a few days highly critical of *Evangelii Gaudium*.[71] For *Forbes*, the pope's Peronist ancestry, his search for a "third way" between capitalism and socialism, the reminders of liberation theology, and the similarity of his analysis to that of Nobel Laureate Joseph Stiglitz (highly esteemed by Bishop Marcelo Sanchez Sorondo, the Argentine chancellor of the Pontifical Academy for Social Sciences) were all problematic.

---

and social outcasts, young and old, who are rejected by the social system. Cuniberto's critique of the pope, repeated by certain commentators as representing Catholic conservatism, actually derives from a form of esoteric anti-modernism borrowed from Jacob Böhme, in whose work Cuniberto specializes, and from René Guenon. See Cuniberto, *Il cedro e la palma: Esercizi di metafisica* (Milan: Edizioni Medusa, 2009).

70. Paolo Mastrolilli, "'Ipocrita e marxista': L'America del Tea Party contro Papa Francesco," *La Stampa*, December 4, 2013, http://www.lastampa .it/2013/12/04/esteri/ipocrita-e-marxista-lamerica-dei-tea-party-contro-papa -francesco-HoCJ97yPb059xWiFOypaIJ/pagina.html.

71. Tim Worstall, "In Which a Good Catholic Boy Starts Shouting at the Pope," *Forbes*, November 26, 2013, https://www.forbes.com/sites /timworstall/2013/11/26/in-which-a-good-catholic-boy-starts-shouting-at-the -pope/#5d01f4a42bda; Bill Frezza, "Pope Francis Is No Economist," *Forbes*, December 3, 2013, https://www.forbes.com/sites/billfrezza/2013/12/03/pope -francis-is-no-economist/#762389af6998; Louis Woodhill, "Papal Bull: Why Pope Francis Should Be Grateful for Capitalism," *Forbes*, December 4, 2013, https://www.forbes.com/sites/louiswoodhill/2013/12/04/papal-bull-why-pope -francis-should-be-grateful-for-capitalism/#ec5037965ee3; Alejandro Chafuen, "Pope Francis and the Economists," *Forbes*, December 4, 2013, https://www .forbes.com/sites/alejandrochafuen/2013/12/04/pope-francis-and-the -economists-2/#2408179f53de; Chafuen, "Pope Francis: Espousing a Peronist Rather than a Marxist Liberation Theology?," *Forbes*, December 5, 2013, https://www.forbes.com/sites/alejandrochafuen/2013/12/05/pope-francis -espousing-a-peronist-rather-than-a-marxist-liberation-theology/#5ae 791705ce2; Harry Binswanger, "Top Ten Reasons Why Rush Limbaugh Is Right: The Pope's Statement IS Marxist," *Forbes*, December 19, 2013, https:// www.forbes.com/sites/harrybinswanger/2013/12/19/top-ten-reasons-why-rush -limbaugh-is-right-the-popes-statement-is-marxist/#5ff8e02d4413.

Standing out as the crown of all of this criticism is the position of the most illustrious exponent of American Catho-capitalism, Michael Novak, whose 1982 book *The Spirit of Democratic Capitalism* served as a point of convergence between Catholics and Republicans in the great political-religious alliance against world communism promoted in the 1980s by President Reagan. Novak was struck by "how partisan and empirically unfounded" several of the pope's criticisms seemed to him to be. "About six of his swipes," he wrote, "are so highly partisan and biased that they seem outside this pope's normal tranquility and generosity of spirit. Exactly these partisan phrases were naturally leapt upon by media outlets such as Reuters and the *Guardian*. Among these are 'trickle-down theories,' 'invisible hand,' 'idolatry of money,' 'inequality,' and trust in the state 'charged with vigilance for the common good.'"[72] Such talk about the capitalist system was, to Novak, unacceptable: "Ever since Max Weber, Catholic social thought has been blamed for much of the poverty in many Catholic nations. Pope Francis inadvertently adds evidence for Weber's thesis."[73]

Novak's ire was understandable. Having risen to fame as the Catholic Weber, who had offered, in place of Weber's *The Protestant Ethic and the Spirit of Capitalism*, the "Catholic" ethic as the true foundation of "democratic capitalism," he could not countenance a pope who called into question the very system that he had long helped to legitimize and defended from every possible criticism.

One point among many in *Evangelii Gaudium* was particularly unacceptable to Novak: "his careless mention of 'trickle-down theories.'" After all, the *trickle-down theory* stands at the very center of the liberal model of economics. But the pope writes in his letter: "In this context, some people continue to defend trickle-down theories which assume that economic growth, encouraged by a free market, will inevitably succeed in bringing about greater justice and inclusiveness in the world. This opinion, which has never been confirmed by the facts, expresses a crude and naïve trust in the goodness of those

72. Michael Novak, "Agreeing with Pope Francis," *National Review*, December 7, 2013, https://www.nationalreview.com/2013/12/agreeing-pope -francis-michael-novak/.
73. Ibid.

wielding economic power and in the sacralized workings of the prevailing economic system. Meanwhile, the excluded are still waiting. To sustain a lifestyle which excludes others, or to sustain enthusiasm for that selfish ideal, a globalization of indifference has developed."[74]

Novak didn't like this criticism, particularly the suggestion that the capitalist model as a general source of well-being is not confirmed by the facts. Novak's response, stinging given the pope's nationality, is that "in Argentina and other static systems with no upward mobility, this comment might be understandable. In nations with generations of reliable upward mobility, it is not true at all. The upward movement promoted by certain capitalist systems is the experience—not a 'crude and naïve trust'—of a large majority of Americans."[75]

Such a response, revealing the anxiety of the most illustrious Catho-capitalist in the United States, demonstrates how squarely *Evangelii Gaudium* hit its mark. The pope himself, in an interview with Andrea Tornielli for *La Stampa*, chose to respond to the controversial point raised by Novak:

> There is nothing in the Exhortation that cannot be found in the social Doctrine of the Church. I wasn't speaking from a technical point of view, what I was trying to do was to give a picture of what is going on. The only specific quote I used was the one regarding the "trickle-down theories" which assume that economic growth, encouraged by a free market, will inevitably succeed in bringing about greater justice and social inclusiveness in the world. The promise was that when the glass was full, it would overflow, benefitting the poor. But what happens instead, is that when the glass is full, it magically gets bigger. Nothing ever comes out for the poor. This was the only reference to a specific theory. I was not, I repeat, speaking from a technical point of view but according to the Church's social doctrine. This does not mean being a Marxist.[76]

74. *Evangelii Gaudium* 54.

75. Novak, "Agreeing."

76. Pope Francis interview with Andrea Tornielli, "Mai avere paura della tenerezza," *La Stampa*, December 12, 2013, http://www.lastampa.it/2013/12/14/esteri/vatican-insider/en/never-be-afraid-of-tenderness-5BqUfVs9r7W1CJIMuHqNeI/pagina.html.

The final clarification is particularly striking. In the post-1989 context, when global capitalism maintains an unquestioned supremacy and is celebrated as "the end of history" and panacea of all evils, every criticism of it appears crypto-communist. *Evangelii Gaudium* breaks the code of silence and throws a heavy rock into the pool of ideas. Benedict XVI had tried to do the same thing with *Caritas in Veritate*, an encyclical that contained important new ideas and important criticisms. With respect to it, Francis's apostolic exhortation appears more resolute; it takes the bull by the horns and is not afraid of insisting to the world that there are problems, more evident after the financial debacle of 2008, with this economic model that, left to its own devices, risks overwhelming the whole world, and that these are *structural* limits, not incidental ones.

Novak also argues that any potential dehumanizing effects of capitalism can be mitigated, on the margins of the system, by the charitable activity proper to Christianity. But he fails to recognize that charity can translate into politics in order to tackle those "structural" causes that today, according to Pope Francis, undermine the internal and external harmony of peoples and threaten peace. The critique of the capitalist-financial system imposed after 1989 is a critique of an "asocial" system based on exclusion—exclusion of those who are unemployed, young, poor, or invisible; exclusion of ethics and of politics. "How many words prove irksome to this system! It is irksome when the question of ethics is raised, when global solidarity is invoked, when the distribution of goods is mentioned, when reference is made to protecting labor and defending the dignity of the powerless, when allusion is made to a God who demands a commitment to justice."[77]

For Pope Francis the point is clear: "We can no longer trust in the unseen forces and the invisible hand of the market."[78] We need to intervene actively to promote an equality that does not merely mean economic growth. "I am far from proposing an irresponsible populism," writes the pope, "but the economy can no longer turn to remedies that are a new poison, such as attempting to increase profits

---

77. *Evangelii Gaudium* 203.
78. Ibid. 204.

by reducing the work force and thereby adding to the ranks of the excluded."[79] The economic sphere cannot claim absolute autonomy, let alone a priority over politics. A return to the primacy of politics is necessary, but one that it has as its horizon the common social good: "Politics, though often denigrated, remains a lofty vocation and one of the highest forms of charity, inasmuch as it seeks the common good. We need to be convinced that charity 'is the principle not only of micro-relationships (with friends, with family members or within small groups) but also of macro-relationships (social, economic and political ones).' I beg the Lord to grant us more politicians who are genuinely disturbed by the state of society, the people, the lives of the poor!"[80]

One thing is certain: rarely has the social teaching of the church been expressed more forcefully. Striking in this exhortation is Francis's tone, the transition from descriptive analysis to the first person, the pope's direct involvement, the indignation in the face of a world that possesses every possible means to alleviate suffering and the marginalization of millions of human beings but refuses to do it. "The Pope," Francis said, "loves everyone, rich and poor alike, but he is obliged in the name of Christ to remind all that the rich must help, respect and promote the poor."[81] It was a stance that neither *Forbes* nor Michael Novak welcomed.

79. Ibid.
80. Ibid. 205. The internal quotation is from Benedict XVI, *Caritas in Veritate* 2.
81. Ibid. 58.

At the School of Saint Ignatius

Life as Witness

Narrative Thought and *Theologia Crucis*: An Ignatian Tension

The integration model that Methol Ferré and Bergoglio imagined post-1989 is multipolar, with several layers: the individual country, the *patria grande*, the globalized world. Each layer is a pole that is in tension with the other two, each coexisting only if a balance between the parts is maintained. We find the same perspective in Benedict XVI's *Caritas in Veritate*: "In order not to produce a dangerous universal power of a tyrannical nature, *the governance of globalization must be marked by subsidiarity*, articulated into several layers and involving different levels that can work together. Globalization certainly requires authority, insofar as it poses the problem of a global common good that needs to be pursued. This authority, however, must be organized in a subsidiary and stratified way, if it is not to infringe upon freedom and if it is to yield effective results in practice."[1]

The "Catholic" model privileges the universal-particular, the concrete universal that is at the center of the thought of both Methol Ferré and Bergoglio. It offers the Thomistic paradigm as an alternative to Platonizing, abstractly universalizing idealisms, and to particularistic nominalism. The concrete universal is a *tangible* way of thinking in which the imaginative spatio-temporal factor is essential.

---

1. Pope Benedict XVI, encyclical letter *Caritas in Veritate* (2009) 57.

As Francis notes, "According to St. Ignatius, great principles must be embodied in the circumstances of place, time and people."[2] This gives rise to a "concrete" way of thinking that Bergoglio calls, on several occasions, "narrative."[3] He does so particularly when he talks about the Society of Jesus and the protagonists who have woven its history: "The Society of Jesus can be described only in narrative form. Only in narrative form do you discern, not in a philosophical or theological explanation, which allows you rather to discuss."[4] Educated in the Jesuit tradition, Bergoglio knows well the differences between the various "styles" of thought—for example, between a lecture and preaching that can never abstract from the "dialogic" dimension between preacher and people, from the existence of the one who speaks, who is present with his life and his personal feelings in what he says, who is the witness of the truth of the word. For this reason, as Fr. Spadaro writes, "Francis's language is not speculative, but missionary, attentive to the interlocutor as much as to the message, which is uttered not to be 'studied' but to be 'heard,' immediately compelling one who hears it to react. In reality, more than 'communicating,' he creates 'communicative events,' in which the recipient of his message actively participates. In this sense there is a reconfiguration of the language that sets different accents and new priorities."[5]

2. Pope Francis with Antonio Spadaro, *My Door Is Always Open: A Conversation on Faith, Hope, and the Church in a Time of Change*, trans. Shaun Whiteside (London: Bloomsbury, 2013), 21.

3. Misunderstanding Bergoglio's position, Gian Enrico Rusconi writes, "'Narrative theology' means semantic reinvention, emotional expressiveness accompanied by conceptual flexibility, which leads to a language rich in metaphors, as we find in the parables of the gospels" (*La teologia narrativa di papa Francesco* [Rome-Bari: Laterza, 2017], 4). Rusconi suggestions that in Bergoglio, we are faced with a tension between full fidelity to tradition and an imaginative, literary language: "Bergoglio does not intend to completely change the doctrine in its 'fundamentals.' . . . But in fact he re-encodes the traditional doctrine with semantic-rhetorical-metaphorical or 'mythical' codes" (147). In reality, the "narrative" method of Bergoglio has nothing "mythical" about it. On the contrary, it responds to the need to restore our understanding of reality to its dual form of universal-particular, set in time and space.

4. Pope Francis with Spadaro, *My Door Is Always Open*, 24.

5. Antonio Spadaro, *Il disegno di papa Francesco: Il volto futuro della Chiesa* (Bologna: EMI, 2013), 31. On Francis's language, cf. Alessandro Gisotti, "El

It is a conscious choice. Francis's language is not simple because it lacks academic grounding. Its simplicity is a point of arrival that is preceded by the complexity of profound and original thought. It is not theological or philosophical simplicity, but evangelical simplicity. In Francis, the richness and variety of creative language is surprising. Spadaro writes:

> Both his literary formation and the theological formation influence the expressive capacity of the pope. But these elements are led by the factors of his personal sensitivity and missionary dynamism. Bergoglio "inhabits" the words he speaks. Just as he cannot live by himself but needs a community, so in his speech he allows space for those in front of him. It is never pronounced for its beauty, but to create an evangelical relationship. Bergoglio's speech is the daughter of St. Augustine's *sermo humilis*, because it wants to be a "word-home," beautiful, accessible and clear, sweet. For this reason it is always and in any case marked by its orality, by dialogue, even if it is written. The words take on a "body."[6]

In this way Francis's words arrive where, in Christianity, they must arrive: at the heart.[7] As he said in *Evangelii Gaudium*:

> Dialogue is much more than the communication of a truth. It arises from the enjoyment of speaking and it enriches those who express their love for one another through the medium of words. This is an enrichment which does not consist in objects but in persons who share themselves in dialogue. A preaching which would be purely moralistic or doctrinaire, or one which turns into a lecture on biblical exegesis, detracts from this heart-to-heart communication which

---

perfil humano y pastoral del papa Bergoglio," in Jacinto Nuñez Regodon, ed., *Los lenguajes del papa Francisco* (Salamanca: Universidad Pontificia de Salamanca, 2016), 15–32.

6. Spadaro, *Il disegno di papa Francesco*, 31–32.

7. The reconciliation between heart and reason, ignored by the Reformation, is, according to Bergoglio, the foundation of the Ignatian vision. Cf. Jorge Mario Bergoglio–Pope Francis, *Reflexiones espirituales sobra la vita apostolica* (San Miguel [Buenos Aires]: Ediciones Diego de Torres, 1987), partial Italian trans. *Chi sono i gesuiti: Storia della Compagnia di Gesù* (Bologna: EMI, 2014), 24.

takes place in the homily and possesses a quasi-sacramental character: "Faith comes from what is heard, and what is heard comes by the preaching of Christ" (Rom 10:17). In the homily, truth goes hand in hand with beauty and goodness. Far from dealing with abstract truths or cold syllogisms, it communicates the beauty of the images used by the Lord to encourage the practice of good.[8]

This synergy of the transcendentals (the true, the good, the beautiful), which we will consider further below, finds its style in a narration that, beyond formal logic, restores us as living-concrete persons. In a 1977 lecture on the history and presence of the Society of Jesus in Argentina, Bergoglio commented that "like *Don Quixote*," this Society's story "is so simple that children could watch it."[9] This is possible when it is approached "from the narrative point of view, the implications of which bear a symbolic value."[10] *Narrative* thought is *symbolic* thought in which individual people take on universal value. They are the witnesses to the synthesis between the ideal and history, the church and reality, revelation and peoples. Bergoglio proposes a "concrete," symbolic-narrative way of thinking, capable of offering us, in a Guardinian way, the "vision" (*Anschauung*). It aims to make the category of "witness" intelligible. Witness is the universal-concrete, and it is Jesus Christ, the Son who manifests the love of the Father, who represents witness *par excellence*. Witness symbolizes the universal-concrete of a people, the point of synthesis that unifies the opposing poles, the factor that binds beauty and truth, which in libertine atheism separate and contradict each other.

In his speech to the United States Congress, Pope Francis drew the attention of his listeners to "three sons and a daughter of this land, four individuals and four dreams: Lincoln, liberty; Martin Luther King, liberty in plurality and non-exclusion; Dorothy Day, social justice and the rights of persons; and Thomas Merton, the capacity for dialogue and openness to God."[11] These four represen-

---

8. Pope Francis, apostolic exhortation *Evangelii Gaudium* 142.

9. Jorge Mario Bergoglio, "Storia e presenza della Compagnia di Gesù in Argentina" (1977), in Bergoglio-Francis, *Chi sono i gesuiti*, 45.

10. Ibid., 55.

11. Pope Francis, *The Allure of Goodness and Love: Pope Francis in the United States: Complete Texts* (Collegeville, MN: Liturgical Press, 2015), 28.

tatives of the American people are symbols, expressing attempts at "synthesis." The heroes, saints, and martyrs of the Society of Jesus are as well. Bergoglio wrote in 1976:

> I prefer to illustrate the symbols in which the Society has expressed its mission, its vision of reality, its possibilities for action. Symbols that have shaped its men; symbols of ardor and total fidelity, like St. Roque; symbols of patience that establishes a people, like Florián Paucke; symbols of the scientific approach and of the value given to the American novelty, such as Sánchez Labrador and Dobrizhoffer; symbols of an original philosophical thought, such as Domingo Muriel; symbols of fruitful continuity, even after the expulsion of the Society, in the Indians who mourned their absence, in the ideas that founded the patriotic revolutions, and even in the courage of that woman who continued to preach the Exercises and that our people know as Mother Antula.[12]

These men and women are symbols of the Society, of the church, of Christ. They are representatives of others and of an Other. Bergoglio's symbolic, narrative thought is a "representational" thought. Human reality, the reality of peoples, is the cord connecting the particular and the universal, the human and the divine. Reality "represents" something beyond it; it is itself and, at the same time, more than itself. This is reflected in the Ignatian spirituality of Jorge Bergoglio. The Jesuit is a contemplative and, at the same time, a man of action. He is a man of God in the world. He is "representative." At the school of Ignatius, wrote von Balthasar,

> [t]he imitator of the Lord places himself, in total "indifference," at the disposal of his Master's will and command, without ceasing, for all that, to be a spontaneous and free human subject. For himself and for others, he is still only the agent, the representative, of his Lord, like a viceroy, who more perfectly represents the king the more absolutely he places his personal, intellectual, and creative powers at the service of the thought and will of his monarch. He remains a person, but his own person becomes as it were completely transparent to the person

12. Jorge Mario Bergoglio, "Fede e giustizia nell'apostolato dei gesuiti" (1976), in Jorge Mario Bergoglio, *Pastorale sociale*, ed. Marco Gallo, Italian trans. A. Taroni (Milan: Jaca Book, 2015), 247–248.

who sends him. Self-abnegation is no less radical in Ignatius than in Francis or Eckhart, but he avails himself of the Thomist metaphysical doctrines of secondary causality and the *analogia entis*, which is now at least taken seriously. By so doing, Ignatius achieves the inner synthesis of the two major parallel currents of the middle ages—scholasticism and mysticism. Baroque culture, in those aspects which from a Christian point of view are the most positive, builds upon the idea of representation. It underlies not only the apostolate of a man like Francis Xavier and of the entire Jesuit mission, including the experiment in Paraguay, but also the theatre, both secular and sacred, where a man—Calderon!—plays the "role" entrusted to him in the "costume" lent him and consequently makes present, re-presents, a fragment of eternal knowledge. The idea of representation thus brings about a new awareness of the manifestation of divine glory in the world. For now this glory finds a receptacle, in and by which it manifests itself, not, as with Eckhart, Ockam and Luther, a receptacle it has to smash to pieces in order to reveal itself in its uniqueness. No, this is a receptacle in which it can stand out clearly as the real glory of the Lord, the manifestation of absolute sovereignty.[13]

"Representative" thought reflects the glory of God in the world. It reflects it in the manner of the Baroque, that is, *tangibly*. Bergoglio has a *physical* conception of Christian witness that accompanies the dialogical preaching of the Word with a real, empirical proximity. It is a matter of *seeing* and *touching*. He has said, "When I speak to a crowd, I do not see it as a crowd; I try to look at a single person, a particular face. Sometimes it's just impossible because of the distance. It's bad when I'm really far away. Sometimes I try unsuccessfully, but I try. If I'm able, I look at someone there, and something clicks. If I look at one, then maybe others will also feel like they are being seen, not as a crowd, but as individuals, as people. I look at an individual and everyone feels like they are seen."[14]

13. Hans Urs von Balthasar, *The Glory of the Lord*, vol. 5, *The Realm of Metaphysics in the Modern Age*, trans. Oliver Davies et al. (San Francisco: Ignatius Press, 1991), 106–107; orig. *Herrlichkeit: Eine theologische Ästhetik*, III, I: *Im Raum der Metaphysik*, Part II: *Neuzeit* (Einsiedeln: Johannes Verlag, 1965).

14. Jorge Mario Bergoglio–Pope Francis, *Nei tuoi occhi è la mia parola: Omelie e discorsi di Buenos Aires 1999–2013* (Milan: Rizzoli, 2016), vii.

It is a "look" that requires a *touch*. As Francis said to Fr. Spadaro: "There must be contact. We must touch people, caress them. Touch is the most religious sense of the five. To touch children or the sick is good for them. Shake hands, caress . . . Or silently look into their eyes. This too is contact."[15]

Touch is the most religious sense of the five. It is a surprising comment. It is Aristotelian-Christian, and it sweeps away, at the root, all Gnostic idealism and offers insight into the depth to which Bergoglio thinks it is necessary for the incarnation of the Christian in the world—her sharing of reality, her relationship with her neighbors—to go. It also clarifies his mistrust of *mediations* that, stiffening and absolutizing themselves, stand in the way of an *immediate* and direct relationship. This "empiricism," which recalls 1 John 1:1-3, is the evangelical *tone* of Bergoglio. Spadaro writes, "This physical dimension for Pope Francis is not ancillary, a mere question of 'style,' but part of the communication of the powerful message of the Incarnation. The paradigm of this communicative capacity is the parable of the Good Samaritan (Lk 10: 29-35), which he explicitly mentioned during his visit to Saint Francis of Assisi Hospital. The Aparecida Document had just spoken of a 'Samaritan Church.' "[16]

Behind his words, once again, is the spirituality of Ignatius and, in particular, of the *Exercises*. We can see reflected in this spirituality the words of the German Carthusian Ludolph of Saxony's *The Life of Jesus Christ*, which directly inspired Ignatius:

Take it as a general rule that wherever you do not find material for reflection in following a narrative, it suffices to picture in your mind's eye something the Lord Jesus said or did, and simply talk with him so that you might become more familiar with him. For it seems that greater sweetness and more devotion is to be had in this way; in fact, almost all the efficacy of these reflections consists in always and everywhere attentively contemplating the deeds and behavior of Jesus. Picture him among his disciples and in the company of sinners, when he converses and preaches, when he walks and when he sits,

---

15. Ibid., xv.
16. Spadaro, *Il disegno di papa Francesco: Il volto futuro della Chiesa*, 29.

when he sleeps and when he keeps vigil, when he eats and when he serves others, when he heals the sick and when he performs other miracles.[17]

Embracing the call for this "cinematic" perspective that allows the gospel story to become real and actual for the Christian through the imagination, Ignatius wished to develop in Christians a "sensibility" that "must . . . extend from the concreteness of the simple happenings in the Gospel to a point where the Godhead itself becomes concrete by being experienced."[18] We recall how, at the end of the first day of the second week of the *Exercises*, on the incarnation of Christ, he calls upon the retreatant to see in their imagination all persons, to hear what they say, to taste and smell the sweetness of their souls, to touch them, to kiss their clothes and the places where they walk.[19]

Here we are faced with a *mystical empiricism* that explains the style of Bergoglio as pope, seen in his homilies, in his narrative, realistic, direct language. Not only because he understands his listener to be the *pueblo fiel* rather than an academy of scholars, but also because his narrative thought is aimed at actualizing the concrete, at restoring its real dimension as temporally present. One cannot speak of the presence of Christ unless one sees him in the eye of one's imagination, "present," alive, and real, now. For Bergoglio, none of this is theater. It is not decadent baroque. It is *immediatization*. In the audio recording Francis provided, he observes, "For example, in the contemplation of the *Exercises*, St. Ignatius tells the practitioner to imagine the Gospel scene *as if he were*

17. Ludolph of Saxony, *The Life of Jesus Christ: Part One; Volume 1, Chapters 1–40*, trans. Milton T. Walsh (Collegeville, MN: Liturgical Press, 2018), 18–19; cited in Hans Urs von Balthasar, *The Glory of the Lord*, vol. 1, *Seeing the Form*, trans. Erasmo Leiva-Merikakis (San Francisco: Ignatius Press, 1982), 377–378; orig. *Herrlichkeit: Eine theologische Asthetik*, I: Schau der Gestalt (Einsiedeln: Johannes Verlag, 1961).

18. Balthasar, *The Glory of the Lord*, vol. 1, *Seeing the Form*, 376.

19. Ignatius, *The Spiritual Exercises of Saint Ignatius*, trans. Pierre Wolf (Liguori: Liguori Publications, 1997), 35, §§122–125. Cited in Balthasar, *The Glory of the Lord*, vol. 1, *Seeing the Form*, 373–376.

present in it."[20] *Narrative* thought is thought that *requires the iden-tification between the subject and the object.* It is *"tensioned" thought*, a conceived and lived *polarity*. The narrator enters into the scene, becomes a spectator and, at the same time, an actor, participating in what is happening.

This adherence to "reality," called for by the third polar pair—"reality is superior to ideas"—lies in a singular tension with the exercise of separation from the world required, in some way, by the first pair, "time is superior to space." It is a tension between realism (physical and metaphysical) and detachment, which is also typical of Ignatius. In Bergoglio, it is manifested in the form of deep adherence to concrete reality, in the repudiation of ideologies, in the "physical" embrace of the neighbor, of the individual "you"—and, on the other hand, in absolute simplicity, in an indifference to the ways in which a person can become "attached" to the world: wealth, luxury, power. This "polarity" between realism and indifference derives directly from Ignatius, who, although dependent on German-Dutch spirituality, differs from it in the way he understands "indifference." He sees indifference not as a denial of the self or of the material reality of the world, but as absolute availability to the work of God. As von Balthasar writes:

What is absolutely decisive, however, is that, though Ignatius continued the idea of abandonment in all its Christian radicalism, he did not adopt the metaphysical formulation given it by the German mystics, most notably Eckhart. Christian abandonment does not imply, even when conceptualized and lived in an uncompromising way, the ancient hylomorphic model whereby God is form and the creature is matter. The practice of indifference, as understood by Ignatius, does not therefore mean the inevitable annihilation of man's own being and will. That interpretation, which is to be found in varying degrees of strength in spirituality from Eckhart to Fénelon, is the symptom of a latent monothelitism, not to say eastern-style pantheism. No, the true mystery of Christian revelation is this: the perfection of the kingdom of God ("God all in all," "it is no longer I who live, but Christ who lives in me") can be pursued as the universal operation of God in the active co-operation of the creature—in

20. Pope Francis, audio recording of January 29, 2017.

abandonment, surrender, service. This co-operation can no longer remain at the level of indifference in the sense of *merely* letting things happen; no, the particular will of God, which is to be actively grasped and carried out, must also be actively pursued. For the Rhineland mystics, abandonment came in at the end; Ignatius transfers it to the beginning.[21]

According to von Balthasar:

Ignatius lays aside the metaphysical (hylemorphic) shell and concentrates on its theological kernel. This enables the spirituality of the modern era to survive, when Fénelon is discredited, the abrupt end of so-called "mysticism" with more than a banal and enlightened Stoic moralism. The process demonstrated moreover how the fundamental evangelical attitude of receptive contemplation could survive inwardly and authentically, without involving strict monasticism, in an active apostolate in the Church and the world. Models for this had already been provided not only by Francis and Dominic but also by such influential figures as Ramon Lull, Catherine of Siena, Bridget, Angela Merici, and Joan of Arc. In these cases the contemplative act itself was regarded as a work of the greatest fruitfulness, for both world and Church (an idea which continues from the Rhineland mystics through Teresa of Avila to Therese of Lisieux). But that is not all. This fundamental act, this fundamental work, of contemplation could also now be translated without compromising its Christian integrity, into specific deeds in an active apostolate of service to neighbor.[22]

The arc that stretches between contemplation and action has its center in the Ignatian *theologia crucis*. "The First Week of the Exercises involves the purgative and preparatory 'hell of self-knowledge' (*Theologia Germanica*), which strips the sinner as he stands before the cross of Christ, of any consciousness of his own goodness. This enables him, dispossessed of any self-constructed pattern of life, to enter into the imitation of Christ, to which he is introduced in the Second, Third, and Fourth Weeks of the Exercises by means of con-

---

21. Balthasar, *The Glory of the Lord*, vol. 5, *The Realm of Metaphysics in the Modern Age*, 104–105.
22. Ibid., 105–106.

templation of the life of Jesus."[23] Disclosure, *indifference*, comes from contemplation of the mystery of the cross, which precedes *immersion* in the world. Gazing upon the humiliated, pierced Christ, stripped of all majesty, brings purification from every ambition, the necessary condition for one to enter freely into the drama of history. The spirituality of Bergoglio is nourished at the school of Ignatius. Here we find the source of his embrace of the poor, the suffering, the humiliated: the hard wood of the cross. Cross and *realism* are the two poles of an agonic, tensioned way of thinking that deeply and tenderly loves the ephemeral and particular reality of the world but that, at the same time, does not wish to possess it.

A confirmation of this perspective, which holds the crucified Christ at the heart of faith, is offered by the recollections of Jorge Milia, one of Bergoglio's students at the College of the Immaculate Conception in Santa Fe, Argentina, in 1964. On the occasion of Easter, Bergoglio spoke to the young men about the death of a man nailed to a cross:

> He told them about the *flagrum* or *flagellum* with which they flayed the flesh, to prepare it for the crucifixion to come. Bergoglio read to them about the wine mixed with myrrh, about the *patibulum* with which they nailed his hands, about the asphyxia and the spear. . . . "I wanted to read you this sort of medical report to make you aware of what the crucifixion really is. . . . The man nailed to that cross is not a puppet; he is the very son of God. Over time, art has stereotyped this instrument of torture, turned it into an object of costume jewelry. Would you hang the image of a hanged man around your neck? . . . Think about it: it would not have been very different to hang a cross around your neck in the first century. Don't look at it with eyes of today, but with those of that time. Try to think. Reason. Would you hang a guillotine or an electric chair around your neck? Difficult to imagine, isn't it? Then art came. The crosses have become an aesthetic motif. They changed the material. They even made them in gold. They put precious stones in place of nails, they embellished them . . . how preposterous! Today no one even remembers that the real crosses were made of wood, soaked with the urine of the crucified people, and stained with blood and mud. Today everything is beautiful and

23. Ibid., 103.

clean. And in some cases, to make it even cleaner, they took away the Christ, who was bleeding, so dirty, full of snot and drool . . . truly unpresentable. We sell this product and we buy it, made of silver, gold, often from prestigious brands. But this cross that you sell and buy for so much money is real junk, not worth squat. A cross without Christ has no meaning, it is only an instrument of torture, because it is devoid of Mercy, devoid of the Resurrection."[24]

What we see here is not a "pauperistic" approach, but a realistic vision that disdains gold and silver because they are contrary to the reality of what really happened on Golgotha. Gold and silver betray the historical memory of the cruel and inhuman sacrifice of Christ. The description of the young teacher Bergoglio does not intend, in its crudeness, to artfully provoke emotions, in the manner of a baroque speech. Faithful to Ignatius's intentions, he wants to look back on what happened. *Narrative*, imaginative thought is the opposite of fantastical thought. It aims to restore, starting from the senses, a reality that no concept can "represent." Only a "representational" thought can provoke ("call forth"), call for a decision, for a change— not thanks to rhetoric or to any technique of persuasion, but *by keeping our feet grounded in reality*, in order to reactualize the past and make it present today, as it was two thousand years ago. Then the crucifix is no longer a medal to be worn, but the tortured one who stands before the gaze of the world and challenges its power.

The example of the crucified Christ remembered by Milia is significant. He describes with clarity Bergoglio's Ignatian spirituality. This is the *theologia crucis*, which is opposed, not to a *theologia gloriae,* but to triumphalism. At a 1985 conference called "What Are the Jesuits?" Bergoglio took up a quotation from Ignatius's so-called spiritual testament of 1556: "It begins like this: 'Jesus, my love, was crucified.' They are the words of Ignatius of Antioch. It is his great love: Jesus crucified. He wants to wear the royal mantle of Christ crucified which is humiliation."[25] This is a legacy that

24. Jorge Milia, *Maestro Francesco: Gli allievi del Papa ricordano il loro professore* (Milan: Mondadori, 2014), 33–34.

25. Jorge Mario Bergoglio–Pope Francis, "Che cosa sono i gesuiti?," in Bergoglio, *Chi sono i gesuiti: Storia della Compagnia di Gesù* (Bologna: EMI, 2014), 38.

Ignatius shares with St. Francis, whom the Jesuits have often disregarded. A misunderstood realism and opportunistic search for compromise have nullified the legacy. Bergoglio wrote:

> If, as we said, the core of Jesuit identity is found—as St. Ignatius says—in adhering to the cross (through poverty and humiliation), the cross as true *triumph*, then the fundamental sin of the Jesuit will be precisely the caricature of the triumph of the cross: a *triumphalism* that sits at the heart of all his actions; the "myth of success," the search for himself, for his own things, for his own opinion, for the admiration of people, for power. That triumphalism that every form of sin contains (because every sin is, ultimately, a false step, the pretension of anticipating the eschatological triumph). Such a triumphalism deprives the Society of *its best quality*, which St. Ignatius himself gave to it: that of being "*minimal.*" And it deprives the Jesuit of the *greatest honor* he can receive and to which he can aspire: that of being a simple, distinguished soldier.[26]

The Jesuit who trusts in power *as an anticipation of the kingdom* gives glory to the world. He removes the tension between earth and heaven, between humanity and God, which reaches its climax precisely in the hard wood of the cross. He eliminates the polar dialectic by which "the mystery of the cross is the culmination of the whole set of polar tensions."[27] Loyalty to the cross is freedom from power: "In Spain," Bergoglio wrote, "the mysticism of spiritual conquest has a symbol: Saint Teresa the Great. In Spain a real battle broke out to decide who deserves to be the patron of the nation—the apostle James, whom legend held to be the miraculous commander-in-chief against the armies of the Moors, or, once peace was achieved, St. Teresa, the guide in the deep, interior battle. I believe that St. Ignatius understood this twofold Spanish tendency and reached a synthesis: he became the master of the interior battle, but also the commander-in-chief of the great strategies of the kingdom of God."[28]

---

26. Ibid., 41.

27. Jorge Mario Bergoglio, "Servizio della fede e promozione della giustizia," *Stromata*, January–June 1988, in Bergoglio, *Pastorale sociale*, 89.

28. Jorge Mario Bergoglio, "Che cosa sono i gesuiti?," 53.

Ignatius turned the external battle—St. James against the Moors, the *Reconquista*—into an interior battle that embraces, and does not annul, the stage of history. The banner of the cross is the standard held high in the fight against sin. In the *Exercises*, Ignatius concludes his "colloquy on mercy" before the Lord, who is dying for me on the cross, no longer speaking of mercy, but of the *Pietà*:

> In the fifteenth century the Pietà is represented with the figure of the Mother with many children, a theme that Raphael also takes to represent the Eucharist in the church. But in the convulsive sixteenth century, the *Pietà* is the Mother with her tortured and dead son in her arms, trusting in the midst of the torment that there is resurrection. This hope, the culmination of the Ignatian theology of sin (and also of the Jesuit theology of sin), lacks the Lutheran conception of anguish and will always lack it. The Pietà is a qualified expression of the *revolution of affection* with which God has saved humanity.[29]

Michel de Certeau's Biography of Peter Faber

If there is someone who represents for Bergoglio the ideal of Jesuit life, it is Peter Faber (1506–1546). This companion of Ignatius, with whom he shared a room when the two were students at the Sorbonne, is the author of a journal now known as the *Memoriale,* which Bergoglio read assiduously. Faber carried on a profound dialogue with the Protestants, participating in the Colloquy of Worms and the Colloquy of Ratisbon (1540–1541), to the point of being called by Pope Paul III to the Council of Trent as a theologian.[30] In his 2013 interview with Fr. Spadaro, Pope Francis spoke of his ad-

---

29. Ibid., 42–43.

30. On Peter Faber, cf. Georges Guitton, *Le bienheureux Pierre Favre, premier prêtre de la Compagnie de Jésus* (Lyon: Vitte, 1959). On his writings, cf. Michel de Certeau, "Le texte du 'Mémorial' de Favre," in *Revue d'Ascétique et de Mystique* 36 (1960): 343–349; de Certeau, *Introduction à P. Favre, Mémorial* (Paris: Desclée de Brouwer, 1960), 7–95; Antonio Spadaro, ed., *Pietro Favre: Servitore della consolazione* (Milan: Àncora–La Civiltà Cattolica, 2017). An English translation of the *Memoriale* can be found in *The Spiritual Writings of Pierre Favre*, ed. and trans. Edmond C. Murphy and J. Martin E. Palmer (St. Louis: Institute of Jesuit Sources, 1996).

miration for Faber's "dialogue with all, even the most remote and even with his opponents; his simple piety, a certain naïveté perhaps, his being available straight away, his careful interior discernment, the fact that he was a man capable of great and strong decisions but also capable of being so gentle and loving."[31] It seems like a self-portrait of Pope Francis, which, evidently, is a reflection of Faber.

Faber is also dear to Francis for a particular reason: he, like Ignatius, "was a mystic."[32] In his 2016 interview with *La Croix*, the Pope said,

> France is also a land of great saints, great thinkers such as [Jean] Guitton, [Maurice] Blondel, [Emmanuel] Levinas, who was not Catholic, and [Jacques] Maritain. I am also thinking of the depth of its literature. I also appreciate how French culture is impregnated with Jesuit spirituality compared to the more ascetic Spanish current. The French current, which began with Pierre Favre, gave it another flavor, while continuing to emphasize discernment of spirits. There have also been great French spiritual figures such as [Louis] Lallemant, or [Jean-Pierre] de Caussade. And the great French theologians who helped the Society of Jesus so much, namely Henri de Lubac and Michel de Certeau. I really like the last two. Two Jesuits who are creative.[33]

These comments help us understand Bergoglio's preference for the French (rather than Spanish) way of being a Jesuit. It is a "mystical" form, affective and active together, not unilaterally ascetic. Speaking to Spadaro, the Pope said, "There have been periods in the Society in which Jesuits have lived in an environment of closed and rigid thought, more instructive-ascetic than mystical: this distortion of Jesuit life gave birth to the *Epitome Instituti*."[34] As von Balthasar writes:

31. Pope Francis with Spadaro, *My Door Is Always Open*, 27.

32. Ibid., 28.

33. Guillaume Goubert and Sébastien Maillard, "Interview Pope Francis," trans. Stefan Gigacz, *La Croix*, May 17, 2016, https://www.la-croix.com /Religion/Pape/INTERVIEW-Pope-Francis-2016-05-17-1200760633.

34. Pope Francis with Spadaro, *My Door Is Always Open*, 24.

Suspicions and condemnations, in the part of the order's authorities, of the "mystical" tendency gave an impetus to the opposite extreme, which, with relative correctness, emphasized the spontaneity of human action in the analogy of freedom and election, and thereby brought active asceticism to the fore (represented by P. Rodriguez' *Manual of Perfection*); in consequence, unexpectedly but inevitably, Ignatian "indifference" was mistakenly interpreted to mean "achievement" in the Stoic or Buddhist sense. This distortion becomes recognizable in the studied aloofness of its attitude to the world as creation and in the pseudo-ethical superiority that follows from it, where one's fellow human beings are regarded as illusory, irrelevant, perhaps even dangerous, which compromises the authentic Christian idea of the encounter of I and Thou.[35]

Bergoglio's preference for the Society's "mystical" vein explains the privileged place he accords to Faber. Consistent with the polar vision, Faber is a mystic who does not disregard the active life. Contemplation and action are the two essential poles of the Christian life, and Faber provides a perfect example of both. When he was provincial of the Argentine Jesuits, Bergoglio owned an edition of Faber's *Memoriale* edited by Miguel Á. Fiorito and Jaime H. Amadeo. But "an edition that he particularly likes is the one by Michel de Certeau."[36] This text, published by Desclée de Brouwer in 1960, includes a lengthy introduction by de Certeau. This scholar, whom Francis mentions along with de Lubac in his *La Croix* interview, is an anomalous figure in the Jesuit world.[37]

35. Balthasar, *The Glory of the Lord*, vol. 5, *The Realm of Metaphysics in the Modern Age*, 113.

36. Pope Francis with Spadaro, *My Door Is Always Open*, 26–27; https://www.americamagazine.org/faith/2013/09/30/big-heart-open-god-interview-pope-francis.

37. The Jesuit Michel de Certeau (1925–1986) was a member of Jacques Lacan's "École freudienne." He taught in the department of anthropology of Paris Diderot University (also known as Paris 7) and in the theology department of the Institut Catholique. He was also director of studies at l'École des Hautes Études en Sciences Sociales. On his thought, cf. Giuseppe Riggio, *Michel de Certeau* (Brescia: Morcelliana, 2017).

The pope remembers de Certeau and de Lubac together, even though the latter broke off his friendship with the former because of an article by de Certeau, "La rupture instauratrice," published in 1971 in the journal *Esprit*. But the work of de Certeau—a scholar of Surin, Faber, and Jesuit mysticism who served on the editorial board of the journal *Christus*—that most interests the pope came before 1971. It can be presumed that his appreciation largely depends on the 1960 edition of the Faber *Memoriale*. The long introduction, really a book of its own, included a biography of Faber in which Bergoglio could have recognized himself. It provided, in some way, the paradigm of what a Jesuit *ought to be today*.

"Thirty years of preparation and attempts, a few years as an itinerant minister—this was his life."[38] This is de Certeau's lapidary summary of Faber's life. The young Peter—whose contemporaries described him as tall, blond, attractive, and very good—had an artist's sensibility. In him, "the seduction of the 'particular' and the aspiration to the 'universal' gradually find their balance."[39] Raised in a small valley of Savoy, "he remained loyal to the countryside. In harmony with the desires of a peasant, he always understood the grace of good weather and the difficulty of life in the country. He remained attached by predilection to the humble things of religion; it wasn't condescension, but the inclination of his heart: the litanies, the 'children's catechism,' the beautiful ceremonies, the processions held on the Assumption and Corpus Domini. He sought these out, not just for others, but because he liked to pray like that, to enjoy those universal and simple devotions."[40]

Peter Faber had the same feeling that would later lead the School of the Rio de la Plata to embrace the *teologia del pueblo*: "Having become a scholar, an advisor to the great, and even to diplomats, Favre lost nothing of his simplicity or his simple tastes. He never forgot his peasant and provincial origins. . . . This man, whose

---

38. Michel de Certeau, "Un prete riformato: Pierre Favre (1506–1546)," in de Certeau, *Politica e mistica: Questioni di storia religiosa* (Milan: Jaca Book, 1975; orig. *Introduction à P. Favre, Mémorial* [Paris: Desclée de Brouwer, 1960]), 26–27.
    39. Ibid., 27.
    40. Ibid., 30–31.

relationships included the great figures of his time and whose correspondence is full of famous names, prefers more modest people for intimate conversation, and he gives them a privileged place in his *Memoriale*: the vagabond, the peasant farmers, a rude brat, the gruff doorman, and so forth."[41]

This explains his language, which, in the *Memoriale*, remains simple despite the literary and philosophical training he received in Paris for eleven years. "This popular vein runs through the *Memoriale*, despite its Latin-Spanish flavor: unexpected imaginations or creations, frank sensibility, humble wisdom. His diary is rooted in the land, as attested by many rural terms: trees, grapes, branches, fruits, the harvest, and so on, those 'hands' of the worker, the hands of God that create and share good things, the hands of the Spirit that shape, the hands of men, hard-working, tireless, hands that gather the harvest and keep working."[42]

During his studies in Paris he sought *eruditio* and *pietas*, to the point of being happy "finally to see the appearance of the 'masters in the emotional life' (*magistri in affectus*)."[43] Ignatian spirituality meets with Franciscan spirituality in a fruitful exchange. Faber is a mystic, attentive to the authors of the Rhineland. Nonetheless "he felt, even him, the danger of the Enlightenment, the German one. He noted the development of dangerous 'mystical' conceptions that were incompatible with the faith: everything is permitted to the spiritual (nos. 107–108); everything comes from God and therefore asceticism is useless, and is even a sacrilege (no. 174); he who has returned to God has nothing more to fear (no. 202); reward and punishment, merit and demerit are notions that are irreconcilable with divine omnipotence (no. 290)."[44] Personally wary, he wanted to remain faithful to the Catholic tradition and avoid the misunderstandings of the Rhine-Flemish. His apostolate kept him on the move, on foot or the back of a mule: "The missionary's pilgrimages revealed to him the tension that already, more or less openly, opposed Catholic Spain to the Rhineland reached by Protestantism.

41. Ibid., 31.
42. Ibid.
43. Ibid., 42.
44. Ibid., 53.

He also felt this tension within himself: his sympathies were more in agreement with Spain, of which he shared the traditional faith and knew the language, where he had made many friends since the College of Sainte-Barbe; but his apostolic zeal brought him incessantly to the Rhineland, care for which is evident throughout all the letters he wrote from Spain."[45]

In a divided Europe, Faber put himself at the service of reunification: "An agent of conciliation and entrusted with pontifical missions into these enemy countries, he proceeded thoughtfully in a humanly hopeless enterprise, at a time when the unhinging of Christendom marked the birth of modern Europe. His 'universal spirit' put him on the path of ecumenism; he united in his own prayer those who led this divided Europe: the pope, the emperor, the king of France, the sultan, Luther and Calvin. In the secret of the heart, he reconciled the ancient and new capitals of these powerful enemies: Wittenberg, Geneva, Constantinople, Jerusalem, Moscow, Alexandria, and Antioch."[46]

He carried out his work with discretion, empathy, and a generous capacity for friendship. A contemporary remembered that "he had a rare and delicious sweetness of relationships that I have not found in anyone to such degree."[47] This is the same "sweet" Faber mentioned by Pope Francis in his interview with Fr. Spadaro.

In his Worms and Regensburg talks with the Lutherans, he, whose position was close to Contarini's, stood at the center of the combat that divided the extreme wings. He did not want "to argue with Protestants, in a spirit of contradiction, nor exasperate them, nor compromise the fruits that could be hoped for in them."[48] In the face of the unstoppable momentum of the Reformation that was spreading through the Catholic lands, Faber was adamantly convinced that only a spiritual renewal of the church could offer a solution. What was needed was saints. "We need arguments of works and of blood," he wrote. "Words are useless now. . . . The remedy

45. Ibid., 57.
46. Ibid., 59.
47. Ibid., 67.
48. Ibid., 76.

is not in the Colloquies, as has been recognized more than once."[49] Two solutions remained: either the sword or the formation of a Christian elite. Personally he had no doubt: crushing the Protestants was not the answer; what was needed was to bring Catholics to a fervent life of faith and to pray for all.

> I am afflicted to see that the powers and authorities of the earth, the Cherubs and the Seraphim, have no other activity, no other care, no other thought than to extirpate the notorious heretics; so, as I have often said publicly, the two hands of those who build the cities are busy wielding the sword against the enemies. Why then, O good God, do we not build with the other hand? Why is nothing being done for reform—I don't mean the reform of the faith or the reform of the doctrine on works (nothing is missing on this subject), but the reform of the life and condition of all Christians? Why then do we not return, thanks to the teaching of yesterday and today, to the conduct that was in the beginning that of the early Christians and the holy Fathers?[50]

Faber's ideal is "a return to the life of the primitive church."[51] It was the answer to the moral and religious crisis of the profoundly worldly church of the time. It was from such a change of life, from an authentic witness of faith and charity, that the church would start again, since evil does not dwell primarily in the intellect, in ideas, but in the soul: "For Faber, the fracture had its origins beyond the moral or the intellectual; its beginning lay in the heart, and so any reunification could only begin there as well."[52] It was necessary to cure the heart. This was the aim of the Ignatian *Exercises*—to reform the church through personal reform. It is a project that closely resembles that of the young provincial Bergoglio in the Argentine church of the 1970s.

In his *Memoriale*, Faber describes this apostolic life: "The Body of Christ, the life of the church, the small tasks of daily life, the poor and children, everything that Faber turns his attention to in this world also allows him to touch the unfathomable and invisible

49. Ibid.
50. Ibid., 77.
51. Ibid., 78.
52. Ibid., 81.

Activity that also is present under the species of the visible and the particular, in daily fidelity."[53] He notes with precision

> a succession of "new" and "particular" surprises. A succession of surprises, his life is the story of "what happens to him": not only the unexpected missions and meetings that determine it, but even more the inspirations that guide him and the tasks that attract his attention from time to time. The experience of grace is above all that of an event. . . . The passion, which always smolders in Faber and which will become, little by little, a "constant hunger and thirst to serve Christ and to imitate him for the salvation of souls," becomes inflamed at the slightest sign; it is brusquely relieved, through the opportunities that "present themselves," for example, the great personalities of the time or the poor of Mainz.[54]

Thus the life of a person in love with Christ takes on a mystical face. "Here the mystery of God is only grasped through its Action, and this Action in the movement of personal activity, in an activity that is at the same time participation in the divine activity and the revelation of God in what he does. A mysticism of action, one might say."[55]

The masterful biography of Faber offered by de Certeau makes clear why Bergoglio so admires the French Jesuit, and Peter Faber as well. In the portrait that de Certeau paints, it is not difficult to recognize the Christian paradigm to which Bergoglio himself adheres. The love for popular religiosity, the simplicity of language, the affective theology, the sweetness and the fraternal sense of relationships, the absolute faith in the work of grace, the centrality of gestures and witness with respect to intellectual controversies, the passion for the unity of the church and ecumenism, the patience with the divisions, the attention to the poor, the idea that the *Exercises* can contribute to the renewal of the church—all of this demonstrates the profound harmony between Bergoglio and Faber. Peter Faber is the Jesuit, the friend of Ignatius, whom Jorge Mario Bergoglio wants to make present in our own day.

53. Ibid., 99–100.
54. Ibid., 91.
55. Ibid., 102.

Being and the Unity of the Beautiful, the Good, and the True: Bergoglio and Hans Urs von Balthasar

We have seen how Bergoglio's gnoseology of the concrete aims, like Guardini, to overcome "abstract" thinking. "Representative," narrative, sineidetic thought unites image and concept, particular and universal. It goes beyond the modern contrast between rationalism and empiricism that, by dissociating truth from beauty and logic from aesthetics and ethics, makes the category of witness, of one who *tangibly* "represents" the true, impossible. In his effort to restore this rupture, *Bergoglio's ontology* comes to light. It is a classical, Thomist conception of Being as a *unity of the transcendentals*. In a 2007 conference titled "The Challenge of Being a Citizen," Bergoglio said, "Abstract thinking runs the risk of ruminating on abstract or abstracting objects, dazzled by a sterile search for truth and forgetting that the aim of all human reflection is real being as such and, therefore, only one, from which one cannot separate the three fundamental elements of being, which the philosophers define as transcendental: truth, goodness, and beauty. They must be together. Within the citizen there must develop a dynamic of truth, goodness, and beauty. If one element is missing, being breaks down, becomes idealized, becomes an idea; it is not real."[56]

This passage is decisive for understanding the metaphysical horizon of Bergoglio's thought. The *metamorphosis* of Being, its transition to an abstract idea (ideology), depends on its "rupture," on a fissure that separates it from the transcendentals to which it is organically connected. Bergoglio's realism depends on his ontology, on the doctrine of Being as *one* with the transcendentals. The "rupture," separating Being from the true, the good, and the beautiful, is the cause of deviations: formalism, moralism, aestheticism. Every deviation represents a shift, an escape from reality understood as totality, a partialization of Being. Hence the corrective value of the third polar pair—"reality is superior to ideas"—with respect to the

---

56. Jorge Mario Bergoglio, "La sfida di essere cittadino" (2007), in Bergoglio, *Pastorale sociale*, 348. The passage also appears in Jorge Mario Bergoglio–Pope Francis, *Noi come cittadini, noi come popolo: Verso un bicentenario in giustizia e solidarietà 2010–2016* (Milan: Jaca Book, 2013), 49.

nominalisms and ethics that Bergoglio often criticizes. The rupture of the transcendentals has theoretical, social, and even political consequences: "In the metaphysical separation is rooted every deformation of the conception of being a citizen: the common good is reduced to the particular good, and goodness that is not accompanied by truth and beauty ends up turning into a good only for me or for my group, but not a universal good, the common good, the good that I must look for as a citizen. One of the challenges of being a citizen is to reconnect goodness, truth, and beauty, without separating them."[57] The perspective outlined here illuminates the metaphysical premises of Bergoglian sociology, its idea of the relationship between unity and distinction, the conception of the common good as a synthesis of the transcendentals.

The above citation is from a 2007 essay, but it is not the first text in which this thinking emerges. "The true, the beautiful, and the good exist," he wrote in 1999. "The absolute exists."[58] Bergoglio was referring in this instance to the vision that must guide the educational process of young people. In 2002, addressing the topic of information, he wrote that "good, truth, and beauty are inseparable at the moment of communication between us, inseparable in their presence and also in their absence. And when they are absent, good will not be good, truth will not be truth, and beauty will not be beauty."[59] Taken together, statements such as these demonstrate that this concern for the unity of the transcendentals *constitutes the distinctive feature of his recent thought.*

In a 2008 essay, "Insegniamo a non temere la ricerca della verità" (We Teach that There Is Nothing to Fear in Searching for Truth), on the topic of education, the transcendental doctrine becomes central:

---

57. Jorge Mario Bergoglio, "La sfida di essere cittadino," 349 (cf. Bergoglio-Francis, *Noi come cittadini, noi come popolo*, 50).

58. Jorge Mario Bergoglio, "Educare alla cultura dell'incontro" (1999), in Bergoglio-Francis, *Nei tuoi occhi è la mia parola*, 29.

59. Jorge Mario Bergoglio, "Comunicatore, chi è il tuo prossimo?" (2002), in Bergoglio-Francis, *Nei tuoi occhi è la mia parola*, 183.

We must remember that truth cannot be found by herself. Next to her is goodness and beauty. Or, to put it better, the truth is good and beautiful. "A truth that is not entirely good always hides a good that is not true," said an Argentine thinker. I insist on the fact that all three go together and that it's not possible to look for or to find one without the others. This is a very different reality from the self-sufficient "possession of the truth" claimed by fundamentalisms: in those cases the formulas are valid as such, but they lack goodness and beauty, and so end up being imposed on others with aggression and violence, doing damage and conspiring against the life itself. What can we do that our students will seek and find the Truth in Goodness and in Beauty? How do we teach them to reach for the good that brings us knowledge of the truth, knowing that there are truths that call upon the whole person, and not only his intellect? How do we teach them to perceive beauty, to have truly aesthetic experiences, those that mark milestones revealing the meaning of our life? How do we teach them to receive without fear the goodness that expands and to discover love in its gratuitousness?[60]

The answer, he says, cannot be an approach that reduces formation to in-formation, to an encyclopedic accumulation of knowledge totally separated from the student's life: "Just as truth, goodness and beauty go together and our encounter with them will always be insufficient and preliminary, the same thing happens in the educational process: content alone is not enough; it must be assimilated together with assessments and behavior habits, together with the brilliance of certain experiences. In the dialogue of the educative process, the content shines and thus causes or transmits a value and finally creates a lifestyle. Therefore, searching for truth implies a relational harmony between content, habits, evaluations, and perceptions that go beyond the mere accumulation of information."[61]

It implies a harmony that involves, above all, the figure of the teacher, who cannot be reduced to a sterile dispenser of information. If she becomes that, she betrays her vocation as an educator, a demanding vocation that presupposes the involvement of the one who

60. Jorge Mario Bergoglio, "Insegniamo a non temere la ricerca della verità" (2008), in Bergoglio-Francis, *Nei tuoi occhi è la mia parola*, 630.

61. Ibid., 631.

educates with *what* she teaches and *whom* she teaches. The teacher is, in fact, a *witness* to what she says. "This somewhat aesthetic dimension of the transmission of truth—aesthetic and not superficially aestheticistic—transforms the teacher into a living icon of the truth that he teaches. Here beauty and truth converge. Everything becomes interesting, attractive, and finally the bells sound that awaken the healthy 'restlessness' in the hearts of children."[62]

For Bergoglio, "the paradigmatic example of the teacher-witness is Jesus himself."[63] In fact, "in none of Jesus's teaching is the content ever separated from perceptions or judgments and habits. As a good Teacher, Jesus speaks to the whole person and his words are never merely explanatory. He does not come to bring us a new version of the law or an innovative, though brilliant, explanation. No, the absolutely innovative aspect of Jesus's claim is that he himself is the Word, the Logos of the Father, as John attests in the prologue of his gospel. Jesus Christ is the Way, the Truth and the Life."[64] The figure of Christ, of Jesus the teacher of doctrine and of life, becomes here the paradigm of every educator: "Like Jesus, the educator must unite the truth she teaches, whatever the field, with the testimony of her life."[65] In the link between the communication of knowledge and witness, knowledge comes to life, and the truth is enriched with charm and positivity. This is because, first of all, it is such for those who educate: "Only those who show themselves fascinated by beauty can introduce their students to contemplation. Only those who believe in the truth that they teach can ask for true interpretations. Only those who believe in the good . . . can aspire to shape the hearts of those entrusted to them. The encounter with beauty, with the good, and with truth fills a person and produces a certain ecstasy. What fascinates us transports and transforms us. The truth that we encounter—or rather, that comes to meet us—makes us free."[66]

In his 2008 conference, Bergoglio sheds light on the concept of witness by addressing the unity between aesthetics, ethics, and logic

62. Ibid., 632.
63. Ibid.
64. Ibid.
65. Ibid., 634.
66. Ibid., 635–636.

that the doctrine of transcendental Being points to. It is a synthesis that found a paradigm in the life of Peter Faber. Behind this discovery stands an author whose influence is particularly important in Bergoglio's later thought: Hans Urs von Balthasar. An eccentric Jesuit who left the order and a friend of de Lubac, this great Swiss theologian is the author of a monumental, multivolume work that revolutionized twentieth-century theology. In Bergoglio's text "We Teach Students Not to Fear the Search for Truth," von Balthasar is not mentioned. But his presence is clear. Bergoglio writes: "Beauty— I do not mean what is simply attractive, but what in its tangible form gives us a mysterious and therefore marvelous foundation— lends priceless service in this regard. By the splendor of its beauty, truth offers us its logical clarity. The good that appears as beautiful brings with it its own evidence of its having to be carried out. How many abstract rationalisms and extrinsicist morals are resolved here and would open themselves to thinking of reality first as beautiful, and only then as good and true!"[67]

The passage traces closely what von Balthasar writes in the first volume of *The Glory of the Lord*:

> In a world without beauty . . . the good also loses its attractiveness, the self-evidence of why it must be carried out. Man stands before the good and asks himself why *it* must be done and not rather its alternative, evil. For this, too, is a possibility, and even the more exciting one. Why not investigate Satan's depths? In a world that no longer has enough confidence in itself to affirm the beautiful, the proofs of the truth have lost their cogency. In other words, syllogisms may still dutifully clatter away like rotary presses or computers which infallibly spew out an exact number of answers by the minute. But the logic of these answers is itself a mechanism which no longer captivates anyone. The very conclusions are no longer conclusive. And if this is how the transcendentals fare because one of them has been banished, what will happen with Being itself?[68]

The echo of von Balthasar is clear. His theological aesthetics is the source from which Bergoglio, from the late 1990s, drew his

---

67. Ibid., 631.
68. Balthasar, *The Glory of the Lord*, vol. 1, *Seeing the Form*, 19.

thought on the transcendentals.[69] We find confirmation of how influential von Balthasar is for Bergoglio's thinking in an important 2009 text, "Significato e importanza della formazione accademica" (The Meaning and Importance of Academic Formation). In this essay, the future Pope speaks of "existential peripheries."[70] He points to the two poles for the inculturation of the Gospel: immersion in the culture of the *pueblo fiel* and philosophical formation.

> At the same time, in order for the sciences to enrich formation and bring their specific knowledge—which has grown so much and is so specialized nowadays—a solid philosophical formation is necessary that opens one's mind to the mystery of Being and its transcendental properties. *The solid truths of philosophy are an opening to the mystery of Being.* Just as openness to revelation has as its object the mystery of Christ, which opens us to the mystery of the Triune and One God, so in the same way philosophical openness has as its object the mystery of being and of each of its transcendental properties. Therefore, in the philosophical field a formation is necessary that opens those being formed to the transcendental properties of being,

69. And it is clear that von Balthasar was known to Bergoglio well prior to this time. In 1984, Bergoglio included a long comment on von Balthasar's book *The Truth Is Symphonic: Aspects of Christian Pluralism* (San Francisco: Ignatius Press, 1987; orig. *Die Wahrheit ist symphonisch* [Einsiedeln: Johannes Verlag, 1972]) in his article "Sobre pluralism teológico y eclesiología latinoamericana," *Stromata* 40 (1984) (republished with the title "El pluralismo teológico," *Humanitas* 79 [2015]: 458–475). On von Balthasar, cf. 461–466. Bergoglio, as we have already mentioned, had directed Diego Fares to the study of Balthasar: "Bergoglio also opened the intellectual path towards the study of Romano Guardini and Hans Urs von Balthasar, on whose phenomenology of truth Fares wrote his doctoral thesis" (Antonio Spadaro, "L'amicizia è questione di un momento," preface to Diego Fares, *Papa Francesco è come un bambù: Alle radici della cultura dell'incontro*, 8). Fares, for his part, writes, "Hans Urs von Balthasar, one of the favorite authors of Francis, places aesthetics and theological drama before logic" (12). In *Nexo* 14 (1987), Alberto Methol Ferré reviewed (pp. 40–43) *Puntos centrales* (Madrid: Ed. Bac, 1985) of von Balthasar's *Klarstellungen: Zur Prüfung der Geister* (Freiburg im Br.: Herder, 1972).

70. Jorge Mario Bergoglio, "Significato e importanza della formazione accademica" (2009), in Bergoglio-Francis, *Nei tuoi occhi è la mia parola*, 686.

where the true, the good, and the beautiful, in their unity, are always open to the Divine Good, True, and Beautiful.[71]

This is why "it is necessary to look for the transcendent foundation of reality, where the ultimate questions of humanity do not clash against the different categorical systems that are always in struggle with each other, but allow fruitful dialogue with all thoughts authentically seeking truth."[72] As proof of this, Bergoglio points to a passage by von Balthasar, a critic of sociology and theological positivism, in a 1946 article, "On the Tasks of Catholic Philosophy in Our Time."[73] Previously, where he indicated the ability of a solid truth to "open up" a person more to truth and transcendent truth, Bergoglio wrote:

Here we follow von Balthasar, who speaks of the art of "openness" of all human truths to the unity of the truth of the mystery of Christ, showing that all words, finally, are a single Word. He also speaks of the art of the "clarifying transposition" that translates the one Word into many, establishing horizontal relations between the systems of thought and between human truths. This "reduction" of all truths to the mystery of Christ is not at all a reductive and decadent syncretism, but rather a true recapitulating glance that participates in Christ's work of recapitulating all things in himself.[74]

Bergoglio's reading of von Balthasar's text offered him two precious ideas. The first, as he explicitly indicated, regards the inculturation of faith. Speaking of the recapitulation of every human

---

71. Ibid., 686–687.

72. Ibid., 687.

73. Hans Urs von Balthasar, "On the Tasks of Catholic Philosophy in Our Time," trans. Brian McNeil, *Communio* 20 (Spring 1993): 147–187, available at http://www.communio-icr.com/files/1993_Spring-Balthasar_On_the_Tasks _of_Catholic_Philosophy_in_Our_Time.pdf (orig. "Von den Aufgaben der katholischen Philosophie in der Zeit," *Annalen der Philosophischen Gesellschaft der Innerschwies* 3 [1946–1947] 2/3: 1–38).

74. Jorge Mario Bergoglio–Pope Francis, "Significato e importanza della formazione accademica," 971, n. 9.

truth in Christ, von Balthasar speaks of a single word capable of expressing itself in all human words.

For the only task of the disciple of Christ is not to return to the unity with the booty of the whole plurality: he must equally (if not more so) bear the unity out into the whole plurality. The Spirit of Pentecost gives him the fundamental ability to do this, without ever dispensing him from his own endeavor of the most various concepts and forms of thought of humanity, so that he can express in these the message of eternal truth. The commandment to make this proclamation includes the commandment to make oneself comprehensible to every age and to every people. Thus Paul became Greek to the Greeks, not only by quoting Greek poets on the Areopagus but also by introducing his thoughts into Greek forms of thought; while he understands how to be a Jew to the Jews in the letter to the Hebrews, and indeed is not ashamed to present faith in Christ as the true form of Pharisaism (Acts 22:3; 23:6). From an innermost point which is unshakable, he draws the power for a mobility such that the forms of expression are on occasion contrary, but never stand in mutual contradiction. But not even the most contrary statements—for example, about the law—are the result of a syncretistic synthesizing of separated aspects, but are the portrayal of the superabundant richness of a total vision that is ultimately divine, and which therefore transcends even the speaker himself. In the course of Christian history, the spirit from Paul's spirit is seen in every achievement of thought that has succeeded at integrating wholly new images of the world into the *philosophia perennis,* not merely externally, but from within, something that however involves translating the *philosophia perennis* into ever new languages which are living at the precise moment and can be understood.[75]

Here von Balthasar indicates the model of inculturation that is held in tension in the "polar" relationship between unity and multiplicity, the same relationship Bergoglio had described in his 1984 essay, "On Theological Pluralism and Latin American Ecclesiology," also influenced by Balthasar. In the 2009 conference text, Bergoglio brought the idea together with that of the transcendentals. In "On

75. Balthasar, "On the Tasks of Catholic Philosophy in Our Time," 160–161.

the Tasks of Catholic Philosophy in Our Time," Balthasar wrote: "The Alexandrine symbolic thought explicitly calls on the aid of the mobile unity of the transcendentals as organs of this premonitory knowledge, a knowledge that does not separate itself from the possibilities of the good and the beautiful for reasons of methodological neatness, but specifically includes them to strengthen and intensify itself. It understands the mutual presupposition and inclusion of these properties of Being. Where the *agathón* and *kalón* are understood as in the truth itself, and where the *circumincessio* of the transcendentals is taken seriously, wholly new possibilities emerge for the encounter between Christian thought and modern thought."[76]

The metaphysical position that von Balthasar delineates here would later provide the structural framework of his sixteen-volume systematic theology, which is divided into three parts: *The Glory of the Lord*, *Theo-Drama*, and *Theo-Logic*. It is clear that Bergoglio was impressed by the Balthasarian approach, linking the transcendentals to the unity of Being, summarized in the title he chose for his 1984 book, *The Truth Is Symphonic*. The Guardinian polar pair of unity and multiplicity is essential to grasping the distinction/unity between the transcendentals and Being, distinct and inseparable. It is this relationship that supports the notion of witness, which is a "representation" of truth in the forms of beauty and goodness. Deprived of one of the transcendentals, it lapses into a formal, unattractive, moralistic position.

We find the same line of thought in Pope Francis's *Evangelii Gaudium*:

> Every form of catechesis would do well to attend to the "way of beauty" (*via pulchritudinis*). Proclaiming Christ means showing that to believe in and to follow him is not only something right and true, but also something beautiful, capable of filling life with new splendor and profound joy, even in the midst of difficulties. Every expression of true beauty can thus be acknowledged as a path leading to an encounter with the Lord Jesus. This has nothing to do with fostering an aesthetic relativism which would downplay the inseparable bond

76. Ibid., 183.

between truth, goodness and beauty, but rather a renewed esteem for beauty as a means of touching the human heart and enabling the truth and goodness of the Risen Christ to radiate within it. If, as Saint Augustine says, we love only that which is beautiful, the incarnate Son, as the revelation of infinite beauty, is supremely lovable and draws us to himself with bonds of love. So a formation in the *via pulchritudinis* ought to be part of our effort to pass on the faith.[77]

Truth is the splendor of what is true. The Balthasarian lesson is fully acquired.[78]

77. Pope Francis, *Evangelii Gaudium* 167.
78. On the aesthetic implications of Pope Francis's thought, cf. Rodolfo Papa, *Papa Francesco e la missione dell'arte* (Siena: Cantagalli, 2016).

Christianity and the Contemporary World

Mercy and Truth: *Amoris Laetitia* and the Morenita's Gaze

Bergoglio's thought on the aesthetic dimension of truth, which he has developed since the late 1990s in the light of von Balthasar, is closely connected to the idea of witness. The communication of the true and the practice of the good require their joyful manifestation in the beautiful. In Balthasarian terms:

> It is not enough that our truth be orthodox and that our pastoral work be effective. Without the joy of beauty, the truth becomes cold and even merciless and arrogant, as we see in the speeches of many bitter fundamentalists. It would seem that they are chewing *ashes* rather than savoring the glorious sweetness of the truth of Christ, who illuminates all reality with a soft light, taking it every day as it is. Without the joy of beauty, work for the good is transformed into *gloomy* efficiency, as we see happening in the work of many fanatical activists. One would say that they are dedicated to covering reality with statistical sorrow, rather than anointing it with the spiritual oil of joy that transforms hearts, one by one, from within.[1]

1. Jorge Mario Bergoglio, "La verità che più brilla è la verità della Misericordia" (2011), in Jorge Mario Bergoglio–Pope Francis, *Nei tuoi occhi è la mia parola: Omelie e discorsi di Buenos Aires 1999–2013* (Milan: Rizzoli, 2016), 845.

Truth and good require the "third sphere," "the glory which is the beauty of God."[2] Bergoglio uses here the term "glory," which von Balthasar takes as the title of his theological aesthetics. Glory is the *manifestation* of the true and just God. Similarly, witness is the concrete manifestation of the unity of the transcendentals. There is no witness except as a union of the true, the good, and the beautiful. The contents of truth and goodness cannot remain abstract. This is the weakness of those intellectualistic positions that Bergoglio criticizes as doctrinarianism and ethicism. This means that the *essential* truth must be found in the *existential* truth, and the same with regard to the good, because the Thomist distinction between essence and existence indicates a "polar," antinomic tension. In "The Tasks of Catholic Philosophy Today," with which Bergoglio was familiar, the Swiss theologian wrote:

> All that Scholasticism needs to do is to draw the consequences from the real distinction as the fundamental constitutional structure that permeates finite Being for its transcendental properties in order to arrive at the insight that thereby these too, in the properties of truth, goodness, and beauty, cannot in the least remain untouched by the distinction between essence and existence. On the contrary: the tension, the fracture goes right through these transcendental properties. Thus just as one can grasp finite Being only in the tension between essence and existence, and the two poles always explain, illuminate, support, and point to one another, so the truth too—let us mention only this here—will always be held in a tension in which the essential and the existential truth are the poles that demand one another and explain one another.[3]

The unity in polar tension between essence and existence, a figure of human finitude, *crosses* all three of the transcendentals. Each of them runs the risk of stopping at the ideal plane of essences, of not becoming manifest in flesh, in life, in the concrete particular. The unity of the transcendentals implies the polar unity between essence and existence. This double unity, of the real distinction and of the

---

2. Ibid., 844.

3. Hans Urs von Balthasar, "On the Tasks of Catholic Philosophy in Our Time," *Communio* 20 (Spring 1993): 147–187, at 185.

transcendentals, constitutes the form of "witness." It is a key category that allows us to move beyond the dissociation between reason and heart that permeates modernity and is the root of its "anaffectivity." It is a split that is typical of the Reformation, of Calvinism in particular, and also of the Enlightenment. "Calvinism provokes in *the person* a *schism between reason and emotion*. It separates reason from the heart."[4]

A similar dissociation can be associated with the Enlightenment. In a 1988 article, "Proiezione culturale ed evangelizzazione dei martiri rioplatesi" ("Cultural Projection and Evangelization of the Rio de la Plata Martyrs"), Bergoglio speaks of the "projects of the heart" that animated the Jesuits in their encounter with the peoples of the New World, projects that were violently interrupted with the advent of Charles III to the throne of Spain: "The fruitful universality that complements and respects differences was replaced by a metropolitan hegemony that absorbs and dominates. These lands, which were 'provinces' of the Kingdom, became 'colonies.' And there was no room for projects of heart; it was the age of the enlightenment of the mind."[5]

The mind against the heart, the true against the good and the beautiful: rationalism breaks the unity of the transcendentals. On the other hand, "the Ignatian vision is never merely theoretical, but presupposes a dimension of pathos."[6] Concrete thinking is marked by such pathos; it is a thought that bears the impact of being immersed in the flesh, one's own and that of the people to which one belongs. The two dimensions are, for Bergoglio, inseparable. Concrete thought is that which arises in the polar I/you relationship, in the relationship with the other, with the neighbor. It is the thought for which *realities are superior to ideas*. The Christian as a witness

---

4. Jorge Mario Bergoglio, "Che cosa sono i gesuiti?," in Jorge Mario Bergoglio–Pope Francis, *Chi sono i gesuiti: Storia della Compagnia di Gesù* (Bologna: EMI, 2014), 23.

5. Jorge Mario Bergoglio, "Proiezione culturale ed evangelizzazione dei martiri rioplatesi" (1988), in Jorge Mario Bergoglio, *Pastorale sociale*, ed. Marco Gallo, Italian trans. A. Taroni (Milan: Jaca Book, 2015), 106.

6. Jorge Mario Bergoglio, "Servizio della fede e promozione della giustizia," *Stromata*, January–June 1988, in Bergoglio, *Pastorale sociale*, 87.

becomes one who "hides, full of tenderness, in those small gestures, gestures of proximity, where the whole word becomes flesh: flesh that comes close and embraces, hands that touch and blindfold, that grease oil and soothe wounds with wine; meat that approaches and accompanies, that listens; hands that break bread."[7] As Francis says in his conversation with Fr. Spadaro: "The image that comes to my mind is that of the nurse in a hospital who heals our wounds, one at a time. Just like God, who gets involved and meddles in our miseries, He gets close to our wounds and heals them with His hands. And to actually have hands, He became man. It is a personal work of Jesus. A man made sin, a man comes to cure it. Closeness. God doesn't save just because of a decree, a law; he saves us with tenderness, he saves us with caresses, he saves us with his life, for us."[8]

It is to have hands that God became a human person—this is an image that dynamically illustrates Bergoglio's idea of witness as an immersion in reality. Hands indicate the sense of touch—touching, hugging, caressing, working. Christianity appears here as a *physical* fact, incarnation from beginning to end. "What is fundamental for me is the closeness of the Church. The Church is a mother, and mothers don't communicate 'by correspondence.' A mother gives affection, touch, kisses, love. When the Church, busy with a thousand things, neglects closeness, it forgets about it and only communicates in written documents, it's like a mother communicating with her son by letter."[9]

Bergoglio's *Christian empiricism* does not like mediations, the intermediaries that dominate in a bureaucratic church in which people are defined by "roles." A mother "touches, kisses, loves." The maternal image of the church confirms the priority of the *aesthetic*, tangible factor. The "glory" of God shines in the "Samaritan" church, that is, in the form of *mercy*. In the contemporary world,

---

7. Jorge Mario Bergoglio, "Omelia pronunciata durante la messa di chiusura del Congresso nazionale di dottrina sociale della Chiesa," in Bergoglio, *Pastorale sociale*, 151.

8. Pope Francis with Antonio Spadaro, *My Door Is Always Open: A Conversation on Faith, Hope, and the Church in a Time of Change*, trans. Shaun Whiteside (London: Bloomsbury, 2013), 71–72.

9. Ibid., 68–69.

which no longer knows the gratuitousness of true love, divided as it is between anaffectivity and eros, mercy unites beauty and goodness in the communication of truth. *It is this gratuitous love that can respond to the need for beauty, which has been coveted and violated by libertine atheism.* It was the point recalled by Methol Ferré, the essential factor in the comparison between Christianity and the contemporary world: only the witness based on a living experience of faith could respond to libertine atheism, which arises from a need of beauty but then "separates beauty from truth and goodness (from justice); it breaks the unity of beauty, truth and goodness. In doing so, it perverts the beauty."[10]

In the same way, for Bergoglio, too, only mercy, a witness that arises from the heart of God, can awaken a closed-off humanity. The priority of mercy is accompanied by a historical judgment, corresponding to the "signs of the times": "Yes, I believe that this is a time for mercy. The Church is showing her maternal side, her motherly face, to a humanity that is wounded. She does not wait for the wounded to knock on the doors, she looks for them on the streets, she gathers them in, she embraces them, she takes care of them, she makes them feel loved. And so, as I said [in July 2013, during the return trip from Rio de Janeiro], and I am ever more convinced of this, this is a *kairós*, our era is a *kairós* of mercy, an opportune time."[11] Francis points to a way of being Christian in relation to historical time. The priority of mercy does not suggest an irenic character of the faith, an opposition between truth and mercy. *Mercy is not being placed "against" the truth, but as a manifestation of the truth.* It is the typical case of an antinomian, polar, and nondisjunctive truth.

This is a point of the utmost importance and not understood by those who, after the publication of the apostolic exhortation *Amoris Laetitia* in 2016, have repeatedly criticized Francis, accusing him of prioritizing the pastoral dimension over doctrine, of attenuating the objective value of truth in favor of praxis, of breaking with the two-thousand-year-old tradition of the church on marriage and the

---

10. Alberto Methol Ferré and Alver Metalli, *Il Papa e il filosofo* (Siena: Cantagalli, 2014), 156.

11. Pope Francis, *The Name of God Is Mercy: A Conversation with Andrea Tornielli*, trans. Oonagh Stransky (New York: Random House, 2016), 6.

sacraments. Among them we find a group of moral philosophers linked more or less directly to the previous pontificates: Robert Spaemann, Josef Seifert, Stanislaw Grygiel, John Finnis.[12] The accusation refers to footnote 351 of the document's section 305, which suggests that the help the church offers to "those living in 'irregular' situations," such as the divorced and remarried or those cohabiting, "in certain cases . . . can include the help of the sacraments." This is an approach that diverges, in part, from John Paul II's *Familiaris Consortio*, in which the cohabiting or divorced are asked to dissolve their bond or to live "as brother and sister" in order to approach the Eucharist.[13] It diverges only in part, because *Amoris Laetitia* does not remove this expectation; it only suggests the possibility of, under certain conditions, *particular* exceptions. But that was enough, in the eyes of some "moral philosophers," to accuse Francis of *disassociating Truth from Mercy*, of affirming a priority of love and tolerance over doctrine, of sliding toward a pastoral approach whose only outcome is dogmatic relativism. For example, the Vatican affairs journalist Aldo Maria Valli, one of the pope's critics, has written:

> When, as happens at times in *Amoris Laetitia*, there emerges a tendency to put at the center not God and his objective Truth, but humanity with the needs and the conditions to which humans are subjected, human persons are not helped to be more free: they merely

12. Anian Christoph Wimmer, "Full text: Interview with Robert Spaemann on *Amoris Laetitia*," Catholic News Agency, April 29, 2016, https://www.catholicnewsagency.com/news/full-text-interview-with-robert-spaemann-on-amoris-laetitia-10088; Wimmer, "Die Kirche ist nicht grenzenlos belastbar," *Die Tagespost*, June 17, 2016; J. Seifert, "Freuden, Betrübnisse und Hoffnungen: Josef Seifert umfassende Analyse zu Amoris Laetitia," Katholisches.info, August 3, 2016; S. Grygiel, "Il dramma di Papa Francesco: Amoris laetitia svela l'impossibilità di coniugare il discernimento nei casi concreti con il compito della chiesa di predicare la Verità," *Il Foglio*, May 26, 2016; Grygiel, "Verità, non compassione: È questo che i cardinali chiedono al Papa," *Il Foglio*, December 2, 2016; John Finnis and Germain Grisez, "An Open Letter to Pope Francis," *First Things*, September 12, 2016, https://www.firstthings.com/web-exclusives/2016/12/an-open-letter-to-pope-francis.

13. Pope John Paul II, apostolic exhortation *Familiaris Consortio* 84.

pretend to be so. When, as we see at times in *Amoris Laetitia*, it is said that the important thing is not so much the content of the norm, but the way in which a particular situation is experienced in conscience by the individual, we risk leaving a door open to the spread of subjectivism and relativism. We no longer have humans listening to God because they are aware that God is Truth and that this Truth is objectively good, but we have God adapted to human subjectivity. We no longer have the rights of God and the duties of humanity, but the rights of humanity and the duties of God.[14]

In reality, as the philosophers Rocco Buttiglione and Rodrigo Guerra López—two of the most distinguished scholars of the thought and moral doctrine of John Paul II—have demonstrated, there is in *Amoris Laetitia* no yielding to praxism and moral relativism. The doctrine of the indissolubility of marriage is maintained in its absoluteness, without granting anything, for example, to the possibility of a second marriage, as happens in the Orthodox Church. The novelty that *Amoris Laetitia* brings to the traditional doctrine lies in the possibility that in specific and particular cases the confessor priest, evaluating motives, conscience, and the concrete situation of a couple, may, after careful discernment, allow access to the Eucharist. We are not faced here with a collapse into "situation ethics," as the critics claim,[15] but rather, as Buttiglione writes,

14. Aldo Maria Valli, "'Amoris Laetitia,' la legge, la libertà: Risposta al padre Sorge," November 10, 2016, http://www.aldomariavalli.it/2016/11/10/amoris -laetitia-la-legge-la-liberta-risposta-al-padre-sorge/. By the same author, cf. *266: Jorge Mario Bergoglio Franciscus P.P.* (Macerate: Liberilibri, 2016). On Valli's position, see the observations of Luigi Accattoli in "Bergoglio visto prima da sinistra e poi da destra: Lettera ad Aldo Maria Valli," *Il blog di Luigi Accattoli*, http://www.luigiaccattoli.it/blog/collaborazione-a-riviste/bergoglio -visto-prima-da-sinistra-e-poi-da-destra-lettera-ad-aldo-maria-valli/.

15. For a response to the critics, cf. "Conversazione con il cardinal Schönborn sull' 'Amoris laetitia': intervista a cura di A. Spadaro," in *La Civiltà Cattolica* 3986 (2016): 130–152; Cardinal Francesco Coccopalmerio, *Commentary on Chapter Eight of* Amoris Laetitia (Mahwah, NJ: Paulist Press, 2017); Ennio Antonelli and Rocco Buttiglione, *Terapia dell'amore ferito in* Amoris Laetitia (Milan: Edizioni Ares, 2017).

a pastoral choice regarding the discipline of the sacraments that follows a path whose premises were established by John Paul II. . . . At one time the Church excommunicated the divorced and remarried. . . . John Paul II said that the divorced and remarried are not to be excommunicated, recalling that in every sin there are objective factors and subjective factors. There are people who can do the wrong thing, which remains evil, but without being totally responsible. And then Pope Wojtyła provided the opening, inviting the divorced and remarried to enter the church, welcoming them, baptizing their children, reintegrating them into the Christian community. But without readmitting them to communion—this is section 84 of *Familiaris Consortio*—unless they return to their legitimate spouse, separate from their new spouse, or live the second union as brother and sister, that is, refraining from sexual relations.[16]

It is on this last point that Francis's approach introduces a novelty, suggesting the possibility, under certain conditions, of reception of the Eucharist. Buttiglione continues:

But neither the morality nor the doctrine on the indissolubility of marriage has changed. What has changed is the pastoral discipline of the church. Until yesterday, on the sin committed by the divorced and remarried there was a presumption of total guilt. Now for this sin the subjective aspect is also taken into consideration, as is also done for murder, for not paying taxes, for exploiting workers, for all the other sins that we commit. The priest listens to and evaluates the mitigating circumstances. Are these circumstances such as to change the nature of the situation? No. Divorce and the new union remain objectively evil. Are these circumstances such as to change the responsibility of the subject involved? Maybe yes. One must discern.[17]

The accusation that Francis opposes Mercy and Truth is, then, unwarranted and foundationless. To oppose the two stands in con-

---

16. Rocco Buttiglione, "Amoris laetitia fa un passo nella direzione segnata da Wojtyła," interview by *Vatican Insider*, May 30, 2016.

17. Ibid. Cf. "L'approccio antropologico di San Giovanni Paolo II e quello pastorale di Papa Francesco," http://www.lastampa.it/2017/02/03/approccio -di-giovanni-paolo-ii-e-di-francesco-ZsTTMYETfwjOTD3IGhbwvM/pagina .html.

trast with both the theory of polarity and the doctrine of the unity of the transcendentals, two axes on which the thought of Bergoglio rests. In the relationship between Truth and Mercy, two poles are in tension, united and indissociable.[18] The tension is between the universal value of truth and the practice of mercy that is always particular. The two poles are bound together, to the point that no situational morality can relativize the truth, and no abstract doctrinalism can take away the specific form of charity required by the same truth. For this reason *Amoris Laetitia* does not offer "a new set of general rules, canonical in nature and applicable to all cases. What is possible is simply a renewed encouragement to undertake a responsible personal and pastoral discernment of particular cases, one which would recognize that, since 'the degree of responsibility is not equal in all cases,' the consequences or effects of a rule need not necessarily always be the same."[19]

In this regard, the exhortation quotes Thomas Aquinas: "Although there is necessity in the general principles, the more we descend to matters of detail, the more frequently we encounter defects. . . . In matters of action, truth or practical rectitude is not the same for all, as to matters of detail, but only as to the general principles; and where there is the same rectitude in matters of detail, it is not equally known to all. . . . The principle will be found to fail, according as we descend further into detail."[20] Commenting

---

18. Cf. Georges Cottier, Christoph Schönborn, and Jean-Miguel Garrigues, *Verità e Misericordia: Conversazioni con P. Antonio Spadaro* (Milan: Àncora, 2015). On the polarity between pastoral practice and doctrine in Francis, cf. Gilfredo Marengo, *Papa Francesco incontra il "nuovo" mondo: Un saggio di magistero pastorale a 50 anni dal Vaticano II* (Città del Vaticano: Libreria Editrice Vaticana, 2015), 49–116.

19. Pope Francis, apostolic exhortation *Amoris Laetitia* (2016) 300, https://w2.vatican.va/content/dam/francesco/pdf/apost_exhortations/documents/papa-francesco_esortazione-ap_20160319_amoris-laetitia_en.pdf.

20. Ibid. 304. The passage from Thomas is from *Summa Theologiae* I–II, q. 94, art. 4. With regard to the "scholastic" critics of Francis, Guerra López correctly observes: "First of all, there is a faulty interpretation of St. Thomas Aquinas. The Angelic Doctor understood and loved the particular with passion. All the universal categories that he identified, including those of the moral order, diminish in their necessity and increase in their contingency as they

on Thomas, the pope writes, "It is true that general rules set forth a good which can never be disregarded or neglected, but in their formulation they cannot provide absolutely for all particular situations. At the same time, it must be said that, precisely for that reason, what is part of a practical discernment in particular circumstances cannot be elevated to the level of a rule."[21]

Therefore, the gap between universal and particular remains, a gap that cannot be removed by any relativization of the norm. The polar tension is unavoidable. This gap is bridged by a discernment the purpose of which is to keep from closing to anyone the way to God, *by a judgment that unites the universal (canonical law) and the particular case, Truth and Mercy.* This prevents an "abstract" generalization, unable to measure itself against determined reality.

> The divorced who have entered a new union, for example, can find themselves in a variety of situations, which should not be pigeonholed or fit into overly rigid classifications leaving no room for a suitable personal and pastoral discernment. One thing is a second union consolidated over time, with new children, proven fidelity, generous self giving, Christian commitment, a consciousness of its irregularity and of the great difficulty of going back without feeling in conscience that one would fall into new sins. The Church acknowledges situations "where, for serious reasons, such as the children's upbringing, a man and woman cannot satisfy the obligation to separate." There are also

---

become more and more concrete reality. There are many ways that some Thomists have failed to understand this point, but I would like to underline only one: the more or less widespread tendency to interpret reason as a faculty that concerns the universal, neglecting the important contributions of Aquinas to the recognition of the 'ratio particularis' and its role in theoretical and practical knowledge. The path of knowledge begins in the singular, passes through the universal, but returns again to the concrete. Methodologically neglecting this elementary ingredient has produced a sort of ahistoricity in much contemporary Thomist reflection and a difficulty in understanding the level at which the pastoral concern of the church is found and multiple comments, teachings, and judgments that Pope Francis develops in his apostolic exhortation" (Rodrigo Guerra López, "Fedeltà creativa: Dalla riflessione di Karol Wojtyła all'esortazione 'Amoris Laetitia,'" *L'Osservatore Romano,* July 22, 2016, http://www.osservatoreromano.va/it/news/fedelta-creativa).

21. Pope Francis, *Amoris Laetitia* 304.

the cases of those who made every effort to save their first marriage and were unjustly abandoned, or of "those who have entered into a second union for the sake of the children's upbringing, and are sometimes subjectively certain in conscience that their previous and irreparably broken marriage had never been valid." Another thing is a new union arising from a recent divorce, with all the suffering and confusion which this entails for children and entire families, or the case of someone who has consistently failed in his obligations to the family. It must remain clear that this is not the ideal which the Gospel proposes for marriage and the family.[22]

In this way, keeping in mind the particular cases, Truth, minimally attenuated in its value as norm, may appear as Mercy because "mercy does not exclude justice and truth, but first and foremost we have to say that mercy is the fullness of justice and the most radiant manifestation of God's truth. For this reason, we should always consider 'inadequate any theological conception which in the end puts in doubt the omnipotence of God and, especially, his mercy.'"[23]

This confirms the foundation of Bergoglio's thought and magisterium. Christian truth, without any praxist weakening, coincides with the Face of God, that is, with Mercy. A point that, in addition to having a perennial meaning for the faith, coincides with the *kairòs*, that is, with what the present moment in history requires. *On this point, Francis's spiritual perception fully coincides with that of Pope Benedict XVI.* Benedict confirmed this in a 2016 interview with the Jesuit theologian Jacques Servais:

I believe it is a "sign of the times" that the idea of God's mercy is becoming increasingly central and dominant. . . . Pope John Paul II felt this impulse very strongly even though this was not always immediately apparent. But it is certainly no coincidence that his last book, which was published just before his death, talks about God's mercy. . . .

Pope Francis fully shares this line of thought. His pastoral practice finds expression in his continuous references to God's mercy. It is

22. Ibid. 298.
23. Ibid. 311.

mercy that steers us towards God, while justice makes us fearful in his presence. I believe this shows that beneath the veneer of self-confidence and self-righteousness, today's mankind conceals a profound knowledge of its wounds and unworthiness before God. It awaits mercy. It is certainly no coincidence that people today find the parable of the Good Samaritan particularly attractive. And not just because it strongly highlights the social aspect of human existence, nor just because in it the Samaritan, a non-religious man, seems to act according to God's will towards religious representatives, while official religious representatives have become immune, so to speak, to God.

Clearly the people of today like this. But I also find it equally important that deep down, humans expect the Samaritan to come to their rescue that he will bend down and poor oil on their wounds, take care of them and bring them to safety. Essentially, they know they need God's mercy and gentleness. In today's tough and technified world where feelings no longer count for anything, expectations are growing for a redeeming love that is given freely. It seems to me that in divine mercy, the meaning of justifying faith is expressed in a new way. Through God's mercy—which everyone seeks—, it is possible even today to interpret the crux of the doctrine of justification, fully ensuring its relevance.[24]

The words of Benedict XVI serve as an important confirmation of the vision of Pope Francis.[25] They point to a golden thread that

---

24. "Benedict XVI: 'It's mercy that steers us towards God,'" *Vatican Insider*, March 16, 2016, http://www.lastampa.it/2016/03/16/vaticaninsider/eng/the -vatican/benedict-xvi-its-mercy-that-steers-us-towards-god-tK2kdh2mTaRezhy 5HgibEL/pagina.html.

25. Gian Enrico Rusconi acknowledges plainly that in these words "Pope Francis is located and legitimated [by Benedict XVI] in line with his predecessors, and in particular with John Paul II" (*La teologia narrativa di papa Francesco* [Bari: Laterza, 2017], 57). This is a significant recognition by Rusconi, because he constructs his book around the idea of a contradiction in Francis between his clear fidelity to the tradition and the primacy of mercy that would reduce the importance of the divine punishment due in response to original sin. But it is a contradiction that is present in both Francis and Benedict, despite the desire of some Catholics to criticize Francis for it. Also for Rusconi, "Ratzinger does not directly call into question, if not by allusion, original sin as the

unites the last three pontificates. Along with Benedict, Francis insists on mercy as, on the one hand, the essence of Christianity and, on the other, the adequate response to the challenge that the contemporary world brings to faith, the question that it addresses to the church. In our day, with the West marked by nihilism and, in the rest of the world, by regressions to fundamentalism, the path of love—the third way indicated by von Balthasar in his book *Only Love Is Credible,* beyond the cosmological vision of the ancients and the anthropological vision of the moderns—is the right one. There is no other way out of the deep, existential, and metaphysical skepticism that characterizes the present time. Today

> humanity is wounded, deeply wounded. Either it does not know how to cure its wounds or it believes that it's not possible to cure them. And it's not just a question of social ills or people wounded by poverty, social exclusion, or one of the many slaveries of the third millennium. Relativism wounds people too: all things seem equal, all things appear the same. Humanity needs mercy and compassion. Pius XII, more than half a century ago, said that the tragedy of our age was that it had lost its sense of sin, the awareness of sin. Today we add further to the tragedy by considering our illness, our sins, to be incurable, things that cannot be healed or forgiven. We lack the actual concrete experience of mercy. The fragility of our era is this, too: we don't believe that there is a chance for redemption; for a hand to raise you up; for an embrace to save you, forgive you, pick you up, flood you with infinite, patient, indulgent love; to put you back on your feet.[26]

Today's humanity does not believe in this possibility because it exists in a world without communal bonds, a society that is dominated

---

cause of evil, and therefore he eludes (like Bergoglio) the question of why God's mercy would not be manifested immediately to the progenitors. Moreover, Ratzinger goes so far as to criticize the position of Anselm of Canterbury, who with an irreproachable logical process justifies the terrible punishment inflicted on the progenitors as the only adequate response to the offense made to the infinite nature of God. . . . Ratzinger reiterates that Anselm's conceptualization has become incomprehensible for us and therefore invites us to understand 'in a new way the truth that is hidden in his way of expression' " (58–59).

26. Pope Francis, *The Name of God Is Mercy,* 15–16.

by a profound individualism and feels a sense of a radical solitude.[27] For Bergoglio-Francis, loneliness is the cause of the sadness that characterizes the West. As he said in his speech to the European Parliament: "In my view, one of the most common diseases in Europe today is the *loneliness* typical of those who have no connection with others. This is especially true of the elderly, who are often abandoned to their fate, and also in the young who lack clear points of reference and opportunities for the future. It is also seen in the many poor who dwell in our cities and in the disorientation of immigrants who came here seeking a better future."[28] This loneliness is the result of the loosening of bonds, of closeness, of lasting affections. In this "monadic" world there is no longer any father or mother, husband or wife, children or siblings. It is, said Francis, a world of *spiritual orphanhood*.[29]

The pope writes, "The loss of the ties that bind us, so typical of our fragmented and divided culture, increases this sense of orphanhood and, as a result, of great emptiness and loneliness. The lack of physical (and not virtual) contact is cauterizing our hearts (cf. *Laudato Si'* 49) and making us lose the capacity for tenderness and wonder, for pity and compassion. Spiritual orphanhood makes us forget what it means to be children, grandchildren, parents, grandparents, friends and believers. It makes us forget the importance of playing, of singing, of a smile, of rest, of gratitude."[30] Faced with this "orphanhood," with a world without a father or mother, *God can return to being a Father only if the church presents herself as a Mother*. In being "maternal" lies the "merciful" face of the church, the answer to the present emptiness of the world.

This judgment of the pope coincides, almost to the letter, with what Romano Guardini wrote in 1950, in the final pages of *The*

27. Cf. Massimo Borghesi, *Senza legami: Fede e politica nel mondo liquid: Gli anni di Benedetto XVI* (Rome: Studium, 2014).

28. Pope Francis, "Address to the European Parliament," https://w2.vatican .va/content/francesco/en/speeches/2014/november/documents/papa-francesco _20141125_strasburgo-parlamento-europeo.html.

29. Pope Francis, "Homily for Mass on the Solemnity of Mary, the Holy Mother of God," January 1, 2017, https://w2.vatican.va/content/francesco/en /homilies/2017/documents/papa-francesco_20170101_omelia-giornata -mondiale-pace.html.

30. Ibid.

End of the Modern World. Guardini saw, even then, both the decline of the cultural tradition of the church and the crisis of the secularization of Christian values, which were becoming obsolete and fading away. In the face of this general decadence of the church and of culture, Guardini wrote, the only way that remains is a renewal of the faith that will draw forth "the theological significance of dogma" as well as its "practical and existential significance."[31] The formal repetition of the dogma will not be enough; what is needed is its existential declension, the free witness of the truth. Only a responsible and confident Christian personality can revive what is fading. "Loneliness in faith will be terrible. Love will disappear from the face of the public world (Matthew 23:12), but the more precious will that love be which flows from one lonely person to another, involving a courage of the heart born from the immediacy of the love of God as it was made known in Christ. Perhaps man will come to experience this love anew, to taste the sovereignty of its origin, to know its independence of the world, to sense the mystery of its final why? Perhaps love will achieve an intimacy and harmony never known to this day."[32]

Guardini's apocalyptic prophecy does not coincide fully with Francis's thinking. The "Latin American Catholic risorgimento" allows Bergoglio to hope for the *pueblo fiel*, that "people" which, in Europe, had given way to a "solitary" faith. But Guardini's judgment about the unique value of charity and mercy in a world marked by nihilism and solitude is fully shared by the pope. In a world of sin without grace, in a society that no longer has the sense of sin, only the gaze of mercy can restore the sense of *shame* in the face of one's own evil: "Shame is one of the graces that Saint Ignatius asks for during his confession of his sins before Christ crucified."[33] This "shame" can arise only from a "gaze," from being looked at by a gratuitous love that is not closed in the limits of a condemnation,

---

31. Romano Guardini, *The End of the Modern World: A Search for Orientation* (Wilmington, DE: ISI Books, 1998), 106.

32. Ibid., 108–109.

33. Pope Francis, *The Name of God Is Mercy*, 10. Cf. Pope Francis, "Prayer at the Via Crucis at the Colosseum," March 30, 2018, http://w2.vatican.va /content/francesco/en/speeches/2018/march/documents/papa-francesco _20180330_via-crucis.html.

nor does it demand anything. It is a "gaze," like Mary's, that frees us from "orphanhood." "We want to meet her maternal gaze. The gaze that frees us from being orphans; the gaze that reminds us that we are brothers and sisters, that I belong to you, that you belong to me, that we are of the same flesh. The gaze that teaches us that we have to learn how to care for life in the same way and with the same tenderness that she did: by sowing hope, by sowing a sense of belonging and of fraternity."[34]

Francis spoke at length about that gaze in his address to the bishops of Mexico, in the Cathedral of Mexico City in 2016. The verb "to see," in an active and passive form, is the golden thread of this key text in the pastoral magisterium of this pope.[35] It helps shed light on a perspective that he had already developed previously. We see it, for example, in the autobiographical note reported in his conversation with Fr. Antonio Spadaro. After recalling his visits to the Church of San Luigi dei Francesi in Rome, the pope recalled his impressions before Caravaggio's *The Calling of St. Matthew*: "That finger of Jesus, pointing at Matthew. That's me. I feel like him. Like Matthew. . . . It is the gesture of Matthew that strikes me: he holds on to his money as if to say, 'No, not me! No, this money is mine!' Here, this is me, a sinner on whom the Lord has turned his gaze."[36]

Here the gaze of Christ is connected to the awareness of sin that emerges only in relation to mercy, to the encounter with a face that loves. Explaining why he had chosen his episcopal motto "*miserando atque eligendo*," Francis has said: "I like to translate *miserando* with a gerund that doesn't exist: *mercifying*. So 'mercifying and choosing' describes the vision of Jesus, who gives the gift of mercy and chooses, and takes unto himself."[37]

Mercy is learned in a "look," it hangs in a glance, at the face of the other/Other. This *closeness* is the *transcendental* condition through

34. Pope Francis, "Homily for Mass on the Solemnity of Mary, the Holy Mother of God."

35. Pope Francis, "Address to the Bishops of Mexico," February 13, 2016, https://w2.vatican.va/content/francesco/en/speeches/2016/february/documents/papa-francesco_20160213_messico-vescovi.html.

36. Pope Francis with Antonio Spadaro, *My Door Is Always Open*, 18–19.

37. Pope Francis, *The Name of God Is Mercy*, 12.

which Christianity becomes *historical*, capable of communicating. Francis's phenomenology of perception corresponds fully, as in von Balthasar, to Mystery's giving of itself in tangible "form" (*Gestalt*). To understand the faith we must grasp the dynamic by which Jesus, the Word of God, has manifested himself in the world. In his address to the representatives of the Fifth National Convention of the Italian Church, in the Cathedral of Santa Maria del Fiore in Florence in 2015, after observing, "We must not domesticate the power of the face of Christ. His face is the image of his transcendence. It is the *misericordiae vultus*. Let us allow ourselves to be looked at by him," the pope said, "And let us look once again to the features of Jesus' face and to his gestures. We see Jesus who eats and drinks with sinners (Mk 2:16; Mt 11:19); we contemplate him as he converses with the Samaritan woman (Jn 4:7-26); we perceive him as he meets Nicodemus at night (Jn 3:1-21); with fondness we savour the scene where he allows a prostitute to anoint his feet (cf. Lk 7:36-50)."[38]

Here the Pope adopts a "cinematic" perspective. It is important, even for catechesis, to imagine Christ in his *reality*—to see him working, walking the streets, healing the sick, comforting the afflicted, embracing children. Christianity must include, in its perception and its communication, the *optical* element, as well as the *auditory* or the *tactile* elements.

This approach is particularly clear in the address to the bishops of Mexico. Here the gaze that is central is that of Our Lady of Guadalupe, who is so close to the heart of the faith of the Mexican people: "Could the Successor of Peter, called from the far south of Latin America, deprive himself of seeing *la Virgen Morenita*? . . . I know that by looking into the eyes of the Blessed Virgin I am able to follow the gaze of your sons and daughters who, in her, have learned to express themselves."[39] For this reason, Francis said, he had for some time

---

38. Pope Francis, "Meeting with the Participants in the Fifth Convention of the Italian Church," November 10, 2015, https://m.vatican.va/content /francesco/en/speeches/2015/november/documents/papa-francesco_20151110 _firenze-convegno-chiesa-italiana.html. [Minor correction to Vatican translation.—Trans.]

39. Pope Francis, "Address to the Bishops of Mexico."

nourished *a desire to see la Guadalupana* just as St Juan Diego did, and successive generations of children after him. And I have desired, even more, to be captured *by her maternal gaze.* I have reflected greatly *on the mystery of this gaze* and I ask you to receive in these moments what pours forth from my heart, the heart of a Pastor.

Above all, *la Virgen Morenita* teaches us that the only power capable of conquering the hearts of men and women is the tenderness of God. That which delights and attracts, that which humbles and overcomes, that which opens and unleashes, is not the power of instruments or the force of law, but rather the omnipotent weakness of divine love, which is the irresistible force of its gentleness and the irrevocable pledge of its mercy.[40]

The force of this gentleness and mercy must be reflected in "*a gaze that is capable of reflecting the tenderness of God.* I ask you, therefore, to be bishops who have *a pure vision*, a transparent soul, and a joyful face."[41] The gaze of the shepherds must be able to recognize the cry that comes from the people:

> And it is in this very world, as it is, that God asks you to have *a view capable of grasping that plea which cries out from the heart of your people*, a plea which has its own calendar day, the Feast of Crying Out. This cry needs a response: God exists and is close in Jesus Christ. God is the only reality upon which we can build, because "God is the foundational reality, not a God who is merely imagined or hypothetical, but God with a human face" (Benedict XVI, Address to CELAM, 13 May 2007).
>
> *Observing your faces, the Mexican people have the right to witness the signs of those "who have seen the Lord"* (cf. Jn 20:25), of those who have been with God. This is essential.[42]

What is essential today, as in the past, is the vision of those who "have seen the Lord." Christianity is not communicated through techniques or displays of power, but in the simplicity of people who have experienced the work of God in history. "*If our vision does*

---

40. Ibid. Emphases mine.
41. Ibid. Emphases mine. [Vatican translation slightly corrected.—Trans.]
42. Ibid. Emphases mine.

not witness to having seen Jesus, then the words with which we recall him will be rhetorical and empty figures of speech. They may perhaps express the nostalgia of those who cannot forget the Lord, but who have become, at any rate, mere babbling orphans beside a tomb. Finally, they may be words that are incapable of preventing this world of ours from being abandoned and reduced to its own desperate power."[43]

Hence the pope's invitation to the bishops to be close to the people, to the humble ones, to the young: "I think of the need to offer a maternal place of rest to young people. *May your vision be capable of meeting theirs*, loving them and understanding what they search for. . . . *May your vision, always and solely resting upon Christ, be capable of contributing to the unity of the people in your care*; of favouring the reconciliation of its differences and the integration of its diversities."[44] The pope intuits and describes here the essential point from which to regenerate, unite, open to hope. This is not first of all a doctrine or a cultural position. In Florence he had said: "I do not want to design here a '*new humanism*' in the abstract, a certain idea of man, but to present in a simple way some of the traits of Christian humanism which is the humanism of the 'mind of Christ Jesus' (Phil 2:5)."[45] Christian personhood shines not as a new theory but as a new *being* that is ostensibly experienced in the sphere of bodily and spiritual "feeling." Faith without life becomes an ideology, a presumptuous fundamentalism, an elitist puritanism disconnected from history. This is why in Mexico City the pope told the bishops:

> It is necessary for us Pastors to overcome the temptation of aloofness . . . and clericalism, of coldness and indifference, of triumphalism and self-centeredness. Guadalupe teaches us that God is known, and is closer to us, by his countenance and that closeness and humility, that bowing down and drawing close, are more powerful than force.

43. Ibid. Emphasis mine.
44. Ibid. Emphases mine.
45. Pope Francis, "Meeting with the Participants in the Fifth Convention of the Italian Church."

As the wonderful *Guadalupana* tradition teaches us, *la Morenita gathers together those who contemplate her, and reflects the faces of those who find her.* It is essential to learn that there is something unique *in every person who looks to us in their search for God.* We must guard against becoming impervious to such gazes but rather gather them to our hearts and guard them.

Only a Church able to shelter the faces of men and women who knock on her doors will be able to speak to them of God. If we do not know how to decipher their sufferings, if we do not come to understand their needs, then we can offer them nothing. The richness we have flows only when we encounter the smallness of those who beg and this encounter occurs precisely in our hearts, the hearts of Pastors.[46]

In the physical image of the eyes of Our Lady of Guadalupe, one can find those whom she "saw" when the garment of flowers of Juan Diego fell to the ground. The *Guadalupana* is guarded by the faithful people because she, first, has looked at them. Likewise, pastors must not wait for the simple people to look to them, waiting for signs of obsequiousness and respect, but they must look first, embrace the people in their eyes. In the interview with Fr. Spadaro, Francis admitted to being unaccustomed to talking to such large crowds: "I can look at individual persons, one at a time, to come into contact in a personal way with the person I have before me. I am not used to the masses."[47]

The Christian encounter is only possible as a personal relationship, as an I/you relationship. You can see "all" only because you see "someone," and in the end only because we have first been "seen," and not just "looked at," by someone. In Mexico City, it is the gaze of the Madonna of Guadalupe that prompts us to look at her, to see her in the faces of all those who, united in their gaze, become a people.

Only by looking at *la Morenita* can Mexico be understood in its entirety. And so I invite you to appreciate that the mission, which the Church today entrusts to you, demands, and has always done

---

46. Pope Francis, "Address to the Bishops of Mexico." Emphases mine.
47. Pope Francis, *My Door Is Always Open*, 8.

so, a vision embracing the whole. This cannot be realized in an isolated manner, but only in communion.

La Guadalupana has a ribbon around her waist which proclaims her fecundity. She is the Blessed Virgin who already has in her womb the Son awaited by men and women. She is the Mother who already carries the humanity of a newborn world. She is the Bride who prefigures the maternal fruitfulness of Christ's Church. You have been entrusted with the mission of enrobing the Mexican nation with God's fruitfulness. No part of this ribbon can be despised.[48]

Encounter as "Beginning": The New Balance between *Kerygma* and Morality

Beginning in the second half of the 1990s, one can see in Bergoglio's words a greater emphasis on "aesthetic" factors: "seeing," "touching," the gaze, and so forth. It is clear that the theological aesthetics of von Balthasar enriched the Bergoglian *realism*. We have confirmed this directly from him: "Regarding Balthasar, I vividly remember the chapter dedicated to Irenaeus of Lyons in *Clerical Styles*. His position against the two heresies that I always emphasize, Gnosticism and Pelagianism, is brilliant. Irenaeus's critique of Gnosticism is decidedly brilliant. His aesthetic impressed me a lot."[49]

The reference to von Balthasar's chapter on Irenaeus, in the volume of *The Glory of the Lord* called *Clerical Styles*, is of great interest. It is there, in fact, with Irenaeus, the great father of the church who wrote *Adversus Haereses* against the Gnostics, that the great Aesthetics and, according to Balthasar, Christian theology in the proper sense, begins.

The height of the spring betrays the force of the pressure which drives it up, and here the stimulus is not the general enemy, paganism, but a personal one, fully recognized and fully mastered for the first time by Irenaeus, who not only sees through [Justin] to the heart but is also enabled by him to employ his intellectual and existential indignation at such a radical falsifying of the truth in an attempt to capture

48. Pope Francis, "Address to the Bishops of Mexico."
49. Pope Francis, audio recording of January 29, 2017.

and represent the centre of reality. Justin and the Apologists had no such enemy. The ordinary pagan religion was too amorphous. . . . But Gnosis, which, largely with the tools and materials of the Bible, had erected a totally un-Christian structure of the highest intellectual and religious quality and won over many Christians, Gnosis was the opponent Christian thought needed in order to fully find itself. [50]

Before this emptying of the meaning of the incarnation that "gnostic" knowledge produces, Irenaeus "risk[s] the statement that Augustine repeated after him: all heresy can be reduced to the common denominator of the denial that the Word became flesh."[51] On this "flesh," and from it on the role of the senses in "seeing," "hearing," and "touching," von Balthasar's book offers a fully developed gnoseology of the concrete drawn from the school of Irenaeus. Bergoglio, with his Ignatian realism, could not fail to be struck by this remarkable portion of the Balthasarian theological aesthetics.

In addition to Balthasar, another author who, in the same span of years, also caught Bergoglio's attention and engaged his thought in similar ways was Luigi Giussani.[52] Cardinal Bergoglio himself, in presenting the Spanish edition of Giussani's *The Religious Sense* in Buenos Aires in October 1998, confessed: "In presenting Monsignor Luigi Giussani's book *The Religious Sense,* I am not simply carrying out a formal gesture of protocol, nor am I demonstrating merely a scholarly curiosity about a project that focuses on sharing our faith. More than anything, I am offering a dutiful act of gratitude. For many years, the writings of Monsignor Giussani have inspired my reflection."[53] He shared a similar insight almost three years later, in

---

50. Hans Urs von Balthasar, *The Glory of the Lord,* vol. 2: *Clerical Styles,* trans. Andrew Louth, Francis McDonagh, and Brian McNeil (San Franciso: Ignatius Press, 1984), 32. Orig. *Herrlichkeit. Fächer der Stile: Klerikale stile* (Freiburg: Johannes Verlag Einsiedeln, 1962).

51. Ibid., 42.

52. On the thought of Luigi Giussani (1922–2005), cf. Massimo Borghesi, *Luigi Giussani: Conoscenza amorosa ed esperienza del vero: un itinerario moderno* (Bari: Edizioni di Pagina, 2015).

53. Jorge Mario Bergoglio, "La gratitudine di Buenos Aires," *Tracce* 4 (1999): 20. Giussani's text was published originally in Italian: *Il senso religioso* (Milan:

April 2001, on the occasion of the presentation of another volume by Fr. Giussani, *El actrativo de Jesucristo* (The Attractiveness of Jesus Christ), published in Spanish in 2000.[54] At that point, Cardinal Bergoglio said, "I accepted the invitation to present this book by Fr. Giussani for two reasons. The first, more personal reason is the good that this man has done for me, in my life as a priest, in the last ten years through his books and his articles. The second reason is that I am convinced that his thought is profoundly human and reaches the human person's most profound desires."[55] With this second point, Bergoglio was referring to the theme of *The Religious Sense*, the book in which Giussani offered his original religious anthropology, with its conception of humanity marked by the thirst for the infinite.

"I would dare to say," Bergoglio commented, "that it is the most profound and, at the same time, most comprehensible phenomenology of nostalgia as a transcendent fact. There is a phenomenology of nostalgia, the *nóstos algos*, the feeling of being called home, the experience of feeling attracted to what is particularly our own, to what is most in keeping with our being. In Don Giussani's reflections, we see brushstrokes of a real phenomenon of nostalgia."[56]

This line of thought finds its center—in the Bible and in the work of Augustine—in the notion of the *heart*. In the 1998 presentation, Bergoglio noted that the heart is "that set of original needs that every person possesses: the need for love, happiness, truth, and justice. The heart is the core of the inner transcendent, where truth,

---

Rizzoli, 1997). The Spanish edition presented by Bergoglio was *El sentido religioso* (Buenos Aires: Ediciones Encuentro-Sudamericana, 1998). The English edition is *The Religious Sense*, trans. John Zucchi (Montreal: McGill–Queen's University Press, 1997). Besides his presentation of *El sentido religioso*, Bergoglio presented, in Buenos Aires, the Spanish editions of three other Giussani books, *El actrativo de Jesucristo* in 2001, *Porqué la Iglesia* in 2005, and *¿Se puede vivir asì?* in 2008.

54. Luigi Giussani, *El actrativo de Jesucristo* (Madrid: Ediciones Encuentro, 2000); orig. *L'attrattiva Gesù* (Milan: Rizzoli, 1999).

55. Bergoglio in Silvina Premat, "L'attrattiva del cardinale," in *Tracce* 6 (2001): 33.

56. Ibid.

beauty, goodness, and unity give harmony to the whole being."[57] In Giussani's presentation of the Augustinian concept of the *heart* as a complex of the fundamental needs of human nature—the true, the good, and the beautiful—Bergoglio found the "subjective" pole of his conception of Being as a unity of the transcendentals. The heart is the root of the true and, therefore, of the very reason for its inexhaustible search for a total meaning that embraces life and death. The cardinal said,

> Humanity cannot be satisfied with reduced or partial answers, obliging ourselves to censor or to forget some aspect of reality. In fact, we do it: and this is an escape from oneself. We need a total response that understands and saves the whole horizon of our "I" and its existence. Within us we possesses a yearning for infinity, an infinite sadness, a nostalgia—the *nóstos algos* of Odysseus—that is satisfied only with an equally infinite answer. The heart of the human person turns out to be a sign of a Mystery, that is, of something or someone who is an infinite response. Outside the Mystery the desire for happiness, love, and justice never receive an answer that fully satisfies the human heart. Life would be an absurd desire if this answer did not exist. The human heart presents itself not only as a sign, but also as the whole reality. . . . On the other hand, to question oneself before signs is an extremely human capacity, the first we have as men and women: the wonder, the ability to be astonished, as Giussani calls it, to have, in the last instance, the heart of a child. It only knows wonder. Note that moral and cultural degradation begins to arise when this capacity for astonishment weakens, disappears, or dies. Cultural opium tends to cancel, weaken, or kill this capacity for wonder. The principle of any philosophy is amazement. There is a comment by Pope Luciani that says that the tragedy of contemporary Christianity lies in the fact of putting categories and norms in place of awe. Awe comes before the categories. It is what leads me to seek, to open myself. It is what makes the answer possible, which is neither a verbal nor a conceptual answer. Because if amazement opens me as a question, the only answer is *encounter*: and only the encounter satisfies the thirst. Nothing else can.[58]

57. Bergoglio, "La gratitudine di Buenos Aires," 21.
58. Ibid., 22.

In his 1998 presentation Bergoglio drew connections between the heart, reality understood as a sign, astonishment, and encounter. These latter two categories are at the center of Giussani's 1999 book *L'attrattiva Gesù*. "Everything in our life," Bergoglio said, "today as in the time of Jesus, begins with an encounter. An encounter with this man, the carpenter of Nazareth, a man like everyone and at the same time different. The first ones—John, Andrew, Simon—discovered themselves to be seen to their very depths, and a surprise was generated in them, an amazement that immediately made them feel connected to him, that made them feel different."[59] In *L'attrattiva Gesù*, Giussani outlines the form of the Gospel *encounter*. Bergoglio follows him and gives it, immediately, the stamp of mercy: "We cannot understand this dynamic of the encounter that arouses amazement and adherence if it is not made to unleash on it—forgive me the word—the trigger of mercy. Only one who has encountered mercy, who has been caressed by the tenderness of mercy, is right with the Lord. I ask that the theologians present do not report me to the Holy Office or the Inquisition, but I would push the argument a bit farther by saying that the privileged place of the encounter is the caress of the mercy of Jesus Christ toward my sin."[60] Here the cardinal showed that he fully shared Giussani's ontological view: "The ultimate definition of God—the last one!—philosophy could not find; once it has said 'the first cause,' 'the unmoved mover,' 'the supreme being,' or 'the Mystery,' it cannot move any further. Instead, the word *Mercy* is the true name of the mystery, the true name of Being. *Deus caritas est*: this is the definition."[61]

Starting from this unprecedented ontology, it is possible to develop an approach to Christian morality that is also unprecedented:

---

59. Bergoglio in Premat, "L'attrattiva del cardinale," 34.

60. Ibid.

61. Giussani, *L'attrattiva Gesù*, 273. "This is the nature of Being. It is not a metaphysical necessity; rather, we must choose to imitate it. Since we participate in Being, the dynamic of Being is our dynamic. The law is a dynamic, the description of a dynamic. The stable dynamic of the mystery of God is love, charity. The stable dynamic of humanity, made in the image of God, is love, it is mercy" (277).

In the experience of this embrace of mercy—and I continue according to the lines of Giussani's thought—there is a desire to respond, to change, to engage, and a new morality arises. We are faced with the question of ethics, an ethic that arises from the encounter, from this encounter that we have so far described. Christian morality is not the titanic, willful effort of those who decide to be coherent and succeed, a solitary challenge facing the world. No. Christian morality is simply a response. It is the response prompted by a mercy that is surprising, unpredictable, and unfair (I will repeat this adjective). The surprising and unpredictable mercy—unfair by any purely human criteria—of one who knows me, knows my betrayals and still loves me, esteems me, embraces me, calls me back, hopes in me, and waits for me. This is why the Christian conception of morality is a revolution; it is not to never fall, but to always get up again.[62]

Christian morality is the response to an encounter. It is a response to a merciful embrace that goes to the heart of the misery, as the etymology of *mercy*[63] suggests. It is not, in Kantian terms, the outcome of an imperative of autonomous reason. It has nothing stoic about it: "This authentically Christian conception of morality that Giussani offers has nothing to do with the spiritualistic quiet-isms that the shelves of religious stores are full of nowadays. Lies. And even with Pelagianism, so fashionable in its diverse and sophisticated manifestations. Pelagianism, put simply, is rebuilding the tower of Babel. Spiritualistic quietisms are efforts of prayer or of an immanent spirituality that never go out of themselves."[64]

Bergoglio recalls here the two great dangers of the "spiritual worldliness" that mark the church: gnosis and Pelagianism. He addressed gnosis in his prologue to Carriquiry's book, *El bicentenario de la indipendencia de los paises latinoamericanos*. He wrote then, "The 'single thought,' in addition to being socially and politically totalitarian, has Gnostic structures: it is not human, it reproposes the different forms of absolutist rationalism with which are ex-

---

62. Bergoglio in Premat, "L'attrattiva del cardinale," 34.

63. The author refers to the etymology of the word in the Romance languages: *misericordia* in Latin, *misericordia* in both Spanish and Italian, *miséricorde* in French.—Trans.

64. Bergoglio in Premat, "L'attrattiva del cardinale," 34.

pressed the nihilistic hedonism described by Methol Ferré."[65] According to Ivereigh, the perception of this danger arose from a historical judgment: "What held the *pueblo* back was no longer messianic Marxist ideology but what he called a 'theist Gnosticism,' a new, disembodied thinking that in Church terms could be expressed as 'God without Church, a Church without Christ, Christ without a people.' Against this elite 'airspray theism,' Bergoglio set what he called *lo concreto católico*, the 'concrete Catholic thing,' which was at the heart of the history and culture of the Latin-American people."[66]

In *Evangelii Gaudium*, Gnosticism would be associated with Pelagianism as a symptom of the spiritual worldliness of the church:

> This worldliness can be fueled in two deeply interrelated ways. One is the attraction of gnosticism, a purely subjective faith whose only interest is a certain experience or a set of ideas and bits of information which are meant to console and enlighten, but which ultimately keep one imprisoned in his or her own thoughts and feelings. The other is the self-absorbed promethean neopelagianism of those who ultimately trust only in their own powers and feel superior to others because they observe certain rules or remain intransigently faithful to a particular Catholic style from the past. A supposed soundness of doctrine or discipline leads instead to a narcissistic and authoritarian elitism, whereby instead of evangelizing, one analyzes and classifies others, and instead of opening the door to grace, one exhausts his or her energies in inspecting and verifying. In neither case is one really concerned about Jesus Christ or others. These are manifestations of an anthropocentric immanentism.[67]

65. Jorge Mario Bergoglio, prologue to Guzmán Carriquiry Lecour, *Il Bicentenario dell'Indipendenza dei Paesi latino-americani: Ieri e oggi* (Soveria Mannelli: Rubbettino, 2013), vii.

66. Austen Ivereigh, *The Great Reformer: Francis and the Making of a Radical Pope* (New York: Henry Holt, 2014), 310. The triple negation referred to by Bergoglio is also found in Methol Ferré, who said that with secularization, "a bare faith and 'pure love' is accepted as a transcendental Kantian, without a church, without objectification of any kind: a God without a church, a church without Christ, a Christ without people" (Methol Ferré and Metalli, *Il Papa e il filosofo*, 171).

67. Pope Francis, *Evangelii Gaudium* 94.

Both Gnosticism and Pelagianism miss the interconnection of faith with history. The first closes off ecclesial experiences in an immanent self-referentiality, while the second builds bastions of pseudopurity against the impurity of the world. Both disincarnate Christianity. It is the risk of the current time. It is no coincidence that these are the same two dangers that Francis warned against in his address to the church in Italy in 2015:

> *The first is that of the Pelagian.* It spurs the Church not to be humble, disinterested and blessed. It does so through the appearance of something good. Pelagianism leads us to trust in structures, in organizations, in planning that is perfect because it is abstract. Often it also leads us to assume a controlling, harsh and normative manner. Norms give Pelagianism the security of feeling superior, of having a precise bearing. This is where it finds its strength, not in the lightness of the Spirit's breath. Before the evils or problems of the Church it is useless to seek solutions in conservatism and fundamentalism, in the restoration of obsolete practices and forms that even culturally lack the capacity to be meaningful. Christian doctrine is not a closed system, incapable of raising questions, doubts, inquiries, but is living, is able to unsettle, is able to enliven. It has a face that is supple, a body that moves and develops, flesh that is tender: Christian doctrine is called Jesus Christ.[68]

The second deviation is the one denounced by Irenaeus, whom Bergoglio, an attentive reader of von Balthasar and the proponent of a gnoseological and metaphysical *realism*, presents as a current danger: "*A second temptation to defeat is that of gnosticism.* This leads to trusting in logical and clear reasoning, which nonetheless loses the tenderness of a brother's flesh. . . . The difference between Christian transcendence and any form of gnostic spiritualism lies in the mystery of the incarnation. Not putting into practice, not leading the Word into reality, means building on sand, staying within pure idea and decaying into intimisms that bear no fruit, that render its dynamism barren."[69]

---

68. Pope Francis, "Meeting with the Participants in the Fifth Convention of the Italian Church."
69. Ibid.

Both the self-referential and conservative formalism of the Pelagians and the interioristic purism of the Gnostics move away from the historical Christ, from the flesh of Christ in history. They renounce

the realism of the social aspect of the Gospel. For just as some people want a purely spiritual Christ, without flesh and without the cross, they also want their interpersonal relationships provided by sophisticated equipment, by screens and systems which can be turned on and off on command. Meanwhile, the Gospel tells us constantly to run the risk of a face-to-face encounter with others, with their physical presence which challenges us, with their pain and their pleas, with their joy which infects us in our close and continuous interaction. True faith in the incarnate Son of God is inseparable from self-giving, from membership in the community, from service, from reconciliation with others. The Son of God, by becoming flesh, summoned us to the revolution of tenderness.[70]

For Francis,

isolation, which is a version of immanentism, can find expression in a false autonomy which has no place for God. But in the realm of religion it can also take the form of a spiritual consumerism tailored to one's own unhealthy individualism. The return to the sacred and the quest for spirituality which mark our own time are ambiguous phenomena. Today, our challenge is not so much atheism as the need to respond adequately to many people's thirst for God, lest they try to satisfy it with alienating solutions or with a disembodied Jesus who demands nothing of us with regard to others.[71]

Hence the appreciation for popular piety, not for pietism but for the realism dictated by the incarnation:

Genuine forms of popular religiosity are incarnate, since they are born of the incarnation of Christian faith in popular culture. For this reason they entail a personal relationship, not with vague spiritual energies or powers, but with God, with Christ, with Mary, with the saints. These devotions are fleshy, they have a face. They are capable

70. *Evangelii Gaudium* 88.
71. Ibid. 89.

of fostering relationships and not just enabling escapism. In other parts of our society, we see the growing attraction to various forms of a "spirituality of well-being" divorced from any community life, or to a "theology of prosperity" detached from responsibility for our brothers and sisters, or to depersonalized experiences which are nothing more than a form of self-centredness.[72]

Gnosis and Pelagianism, the two dangers constantly recalled by Francis, were the two dangers noted, with a look at the Catholic-religious panorama of the 1980s and 1990s, by the Italian weekly *Il Sabato* and the international monthly *30 Days*, two magazines close to the teaching and the theological perspective of Fr. Luigi Giussani. In one of Francis's audio recordings, he explicitly states, "I read *30 Giorni*."[73] He adds:

> For me in the incarnation is found the weakness and concreteness of the Catholic faith. Pelagianism and Gnosticism are resolved in the incarnation. These heresies deny the weakness of God or the strength of God. Reading Giussani on this has helped me enough. In the drafting of Aparecida these things appear. . . . Certainly I always

72. Ibid. 90.

73. Pope Francis, audio recording of January 29, 2017. Starting in 2002, the monthly *30 Days* published several interviews with Cardinal Bergoglio, articles about him, and also his own contributions: "Il volto idolatra dell'economia speculativa," interview with Gianni Valente, 1 (2002), 29–31; Gianni Valente, "The President and the Cardinal," 6 (2003), 16–17; "The Holy Spirit Defender and Consoler," Homily of Cardinal Jorge Mario Bergoglio, 6 (2006), 49–52; "What I Would Have Said at the Consistory," interview with Sefania Falasca, 11 (2007), 18–21; Gianni Valente, "The Friends of Father Bergoglio," 8 (2008), 22–30; "'They Are Priests Who Pray and Work,'" interview with Gianni Valente, 4 (2009), 23–25; "We Are Not Owners of the Gifts of the Lord," interview with Gianni Valente, 8 (2009), 21–23; Jorge Mario Bergoglio, "'Grant What You Command': The Time of the Church according to Augustine," 10–11 (2009), 38–41; Jorge Mario Bergoglio, "Jesus Will Give Us Strength. Not You but Him in You," 1–2 (2012), 89–92; Jorge Mario Bergoglio, "My Friend Don Giacomo," 5 (2012), 36–39. These are each available online in the *30 Days* archives, at http://www.30giorni.it/index_l3.htm. The first listed above is from the Italian edition, because the online archives of the English edition go back only as far as 2003; the rest are available in English.

liked to go to the incarnation to see the strength of God against the Pelagian—in quotes—"force," and the weakness of God against the Gnostic "force." In the incarnation is found the right relationship. If we read, for example, the Beatitudes or Matthew 25, which is the protocol by which we will be judged, we find this: In the weakness of the incarnation human problems and heresies are resolved. What is the greatest point in which this weakness of the incarnation manifests itself? Ephesus. I believe that Ephesus is the key to understanding the greatest mystery of the incarnation. When the people cry out to the bishops at the entrance to the cathedral, "Holy Mother of God!" it is the moment when the church proclaims Mary to be the mother of God. What does this mean? There is weakness and strength in the incarnation.[74]

Gnosis and Pelagianism constitute two constant risks to the faith. In their genesis they depend so much on a diminishment of awe, on the habit that reduces faith to possession, which brings the loss of the sense of grace, of having been given a gift. In his interview with Tornielli on mercy, Francis made reference to those who even today tie up heavy burdens and lay them on the shoulders of others, saying,

This conduct comes when a person loses the sense of awe for salvation that has been granted to him. When a person feels a little more secure he begins to appropriate faculties which are not his own, but which are the Lord's. The awe seems to fade, and this is the basis for clericalism or for the conduct of people who feel pure. What then prevails is a formal adherence to rules and mental schemes. When awe wears off, we think we can do everything alone, that we are the protagonists. And if that person is a minister of God, he ends up believing that he is separate from the people, that he owns the doctrine, that he owns power, and he closes himself off from God's surprises. "The degradation of awe" is an expression that speaks to me.[75]

Christianity lives by its *attractiveness*,[76] by the surprise of encountering Another who works in one's own life. If the attractiveness,

74. Pope Francis, audio recording of January 29, 2017.
75. Pope Francis, *The Name of God Is Mercy*, 69–70.
76. Pope Francis, *Evangelii Gaudium* 39.

the beauty, the surprise is removed, the heart is extinguished and all that remains is moralism and formalism: "Thanks solely to this encounter—or renewed encounter—with God's love, which blossoms into an enriching friendship, we are liberated from our narrowness and self-absorption."[77] Continuing his reflections on Giussani, Bergoglio states:

> It is about beginning to say You to Christ, to say it to him often. It is impossible to desire it without asking for it. And if one begins to ask for it, then he begins to change. On the other hand, if one asks for it, it is because in the depths of his being he feels attracted, called, seen, awaited. The experience of Augustine: there from the depths of being something attracts me to someone who has first sought me out, who has waiting for me first, it is the almond blossom of the prophets, the first that blooms in spring. It is that quality which God has and which I will permit myself to define with a word of Buenos Aires: God, Jesus Christ in this case, always "firsts" us, anticipates us. When we arrive, he was already waiting for us.
>
> One who encounters Jesus Christ feels the impulse to witness to him or to bear witness to what she has encountered, and this is the Christian vocation: to go and to give witness. You cannot convince anyone. The encounter happens. You can prove that God exists, but through the way of persuasion you can never get someone to meet God. This is pure grace. Pure grace. From the beginning of history until today, grace always "firsts," grace always comes first, then all the rest comes.[78]

In his intellectual dialogue with Fr. Giussani, Bergoglio focused on a series of categories that return frequently to his teaching. It is as if the perspectives of von Balthasar and Giussani came together in the intersection—in the polarity—between visibility and gratuity, flesh and mystery, encounter and attraction. In this intersection lies the response to "linear thought," which, after 1989 and the end of the Marxist provocation, imposed itself, in a subtle and silent way, on a church that became ever more immobile and occupied with itself. To this Bergoglio opposed his conception of *"tensioned* think-

---

77. Ibid. 8.
78. Bergoglio in Premat, "L'attrattiva del cardinale," 35.

ing," a living way of thought, dominated by the unity/diversity of opposites. In an early 2007 letter to the Vatican affairs journalist Lucio Brunelli, who had sent him a review of Don Giacomo Tantardini's book, *Il cuore e la grazia in sant'Agostino: Distinzione e corrispondenza*,[79] Bergoglio wrote:

> In this linear thought there is no place for *delectatio* and *dilectio*, there is no place for amazement. And this is so because linear thought proceeds in the direction contrary to grace. Grace is received, it is pure gift; in linear thought is seen an obligation to give, to possess. It cannot open itself to the gift, it moves only at the level of possession. *Delectatio* and *dilectio* and awe cannot be possessed: they are simply received. . . . The Manichean essence of the Pharisee will not leave open a crack for grace to enter; he is enough in himself, he is self-sufficient, he has a linear thought. The publican, on the other hand, has a tensioned thought that opens him to the gift of grace. He possesses a conscience that is not self-sufficient, but is profoundly mendicant.[80]

Compelled by the Brunelli review, the cardinal went on to write, in turn, the preface to a new volume by Tantardini on Augustine.[81] In it he commented on Augustine's description of the encounter between Jesus and Zacchaeus:

> The most striking image to me of how we become Christians that emerges in this book is the way in which Augustine recounts and comments on the encounter of Jesus with Zacchaeus (pp. 279–281). Zacchaeus is small, and he wants to see the Lord passing by, and he climbs into the sycamore tree. Augustine recounts: "*Et vidit Dominus ipsum Zacchaeum. Visus est, et vidit.*" "And the Lord looked at Zacchaeus. Zacchaeus was seen, and then he saw." It is striking, this triple sight: that of Zacchaeus, then that of Jesus, and then that of

79. Rome: Città Nuova, 2006.

80. Jorge Mario Bergoglio, Letter to Lucio Brunelli, January 30, 2007, in Lucio Brunelli, "L'attrattiva amorosa della grazia: Don Tantardini, Bergoglio e Agostino: Storia di incontri imprevisti e di un pensiero 'tensionante,'" *Terre d'America*, June 26, 2016.

81. Giacomo Tantardini, *Il tempo della Chiesa secondo Agostino* (Rome: Città Nuova, 2010).

Zacchaeus again, after having been seen by the Lord. "He would have seen Jesus pass even if Jesus had not raised his eyes," says Don Giacomo, "but it would not have been an encounter. His minimal curiosity, the reason he climbed up the tree, would have been satisfied, but it would not have been an encounter" (page 281). Here is the point: some believe that faith and salvation come with our effort to see, to seek the Lord. Instead it is the opposite: you are saved when the Lord looks for you, when he looks at you and you allow yourself to look and to seek. The Lord looks for you first. And when you find him, you understand that he was looking for you, he was waiting for you first.

Here is salvation: He loves you *first*. And you let yourself love. Salvation is just this encounter where he works first. If this encounter doesn't happen, we are not saved. We can make speeches on salvation. We can invent reassuring theological systems that transform God into a notary and his gratuitous love into an act according to which he would be forced by his nature. But we would never enter the people of God. Instead, when you look at the Lord and you realize with gratitude that you are seeing him because he is seeing you, all intellectual pretensions go away, that elitism of the spirit that belongs to intellectuals without talent and that is ethics without goodness.[82]

During the period from the end of the 1990s to the beginning of the 2000s, Bergoglio focused on the themes that we find at the center of the final document of the great gathering of the Latin American church in Aparecida in 2007. The basic idea is given by a principle that Bergoglio finds exemplarily expressed by Pope Benedict XVI in his encyclical *Deus Caritas Est*: "Being Christian is not the result of an ethical choice or a lofty idea, but the encounter with an event, a person, which gives life a new horizon and a decisive direction."[83] The statement appears in the introduction to the final document of

82. Jorge Mario Bergoglio, preface to Giacomo Tantardini, *Il tempo della Chiesa secondo Agostino* (Rome: Città Nuova, 2010), 7–8. After Don Tantardini's death on April 19, 2012, Cardinal Bergoglio evoked the image again: "My Friend Don Giacomo," *30 Days* 5 (2012), 36–39.

83. Pope Benedict XVI, encyclical letter *Deus Caritas Est* (2005) 1, http://w2.vatican.va/content/benedict-xvi/en/encyclicals/documents/hf_ben-xvi_enc_20051225_deus-caritas-est.html.

Aparecida.[84] It has a decidedly "Giussanian" flavor. The fact that it is offered by Benedict XVI and then taken up later by Francis in *Evangelii Gaudium* 8 gives it a particular value. It indicates the starting point of faith, in the past and the present, and also represents a historical judgment on *the "moralistic" drift that characterizes Catholicism in the era of globalization.* After the era of the dominance of the left, through the 1970s, characterized by political theologies, revolution, hope, and so forth, we have witnessed, since the 1980s, a kind of reflux, a withdrawal into a protected enclosure. Commitment in the world is limited to the defense of a defined and select set of values that descend from ethics and Christian anthropology and are understood as threatened by the relativistic wave that characterizes the new era. At the same time, less attention is paid to the social question, and the perception of a missionary church, projected beyond its own boundaries into the dimension of the "encounter," is greatly reduced. The process of secularization prompted, in the Christian world, *an ethical reaction.* With this, the vision of Methol Ferré, shared by Bergoglio, of Christian witness lived as an adequate response to libertine atheism was lost. The church *opposes,* but is not able, positively, to *propose,* to affirm a human typology in which the "attraction of Jesus" is stronger than the aesthetic appeal of the opulent society. The church's moralistic drift is rooted in a strategy of resistance, not an era of rebirth. This ethical imbalance, in which the Christian encounter falls into the background, makes it possible to contextualize the correction made by Francis in *Evangelii Gaudium.* It is a matter of highlighting what is *fundamental*: the grace of a proclamation offered by a humanly credible witness.

> The biggest problem is when the message we preach then seems identified with those secondary aspects which, important as they are, do not in and of themselves convey the heart of Christ's message. We need to be realistic and not assume that our audience understands the full background to what we are saying, or is capable of relating what we say to the very heart of the Gospel which gives it meaning, beauty and attractiveness.

84. Fifth General Conference of the Latin American Episcopate, Concluding Document §12; available at http://www.celam.org/aparecida/Ingles.pdf.

Pastoral ministry in a missionary style is not obsessed with the disjointed transmission of a multitude of doctrines to be insistently imposed. When we adopt a pastoral goal and a missionary style which would actually reach everyone without exception or exclusion, the message has to concentrate on the essentials, on what is most beautiful, most grand, most appealing and at the same time most necessary. The message is simplified, while losing none of its depth and truth, and thus becomes all the more forceful and convincing.

All revealed truths derive from the same divine source and are to be believed with the same faith, yet some of them are more important for giving direct expression to the heart of the Gospel. In this basic core, what shines forth is the beauty of the saving love of God made manifest in Jesus Christ who died and rose from the dead. In this sense, the Second Vatican Council explained, "in Catholic doctrine there exists an order or a 'hierarchy' of truths, since they vary in their relation to the foundation of the Christian faith." This holds true as much for the dogmas of faith as for the whole corpus of the Church's teaching, including her moral teaching.[85]

In this hierarchy, according to Thomas Aquinas, the greatest of the virtues is *mercy*: "In itself mercy is the greatest of the virtues, since all the others revolve around it and, more than this, it makes up for their deficiencies. This is particular to the superior virtue, and as such it is proper to God to have mercy, through which his omnipotence is manifested to the greatest degree."[86] From this it is clear that

Christian morality is not a form of stoicism, or self-denial, or merely a practical philosophy or a catalogue of sins and faults. Before all else, the Gospel invites us to respond to the God of love who saves us, to see God in others and to go forth from ourselves to seek the good of others. Under no circumstance can this invitation be obscured! All of the virtues are at the service of this response of love. If this invitation does not radiate forcefully and attractively, the edifice of the Church's moral teaching risks becoming a house of

85. Pope Francis, *Evangelii Gaudium* 34–36. The internal quotation is from Second Vatican Council, Decree on Ecumenism *Unitatis Redintegratio*, n. 11.

86. Thomas Aquinas, *Summa Theologiae*, ii–ii, q. 30, art. 4. Cited in Pope Francis, *Evangelii Gaudium* 37.

cards, and this is our greatest risk. It would mean that it is not the Gospel which is being preached, but certain doctrinal or moral points based on specific ideological options.[87]

The *ethicization* of the Christian message is really its *secularizing* reduction. The true and proper defense, in the public arena, of the values deriving from Christian humanism in the face of dominant relativism does not exhaust the Christian presence in the world. In a secularized, neo-pagan society, the first task of the church is *kerygma*, proclamation. This is why Francis insists in his conversation with Fr. Spadaro,

> We cannot dwell only on issues related to abortion, gay marriage, and use of contraceptive methods. This is not possible. I have not spoken much about these things, and I have been reprimanded for that. But when we speak about these issues, we have to talk about them in context. The position of the Church, for that matter, is known, and I am a son of the Church, and therefore it is not necessary to talk about these issues all the time.
>
> The dogmatic and moral teachings of the Church are not all equivalent. The Church's pastoral ministry cannot be obsessed with the transmission of a disjointed multitude of doctrines to be imposed insistently. Proclamation in a missionary style focuses on the essentials, on the necessary things: this is also what fascinates, and is a more attractive proposition, what makes the heart burn, as it did for the disciples at Emmaus. We have to find a new balance; otherwise the moral edifice of the Church is likely to fall like a house of cards, and risk losing the Gospel's freshness and fragrance. The Gospel's proposal must be simpler, more profound, more radiant. It is from this proposition that the moral consequences then flow.[88]

Aparecida: The Christian Style in the Twenty-first Century

The intuition that Christianity could still have a place in the contemporary world thanks to an "encounter," an evangelical witness similar to that of the Christians of the first centuries, was

---

87. Pope Francis, *Evangelii Gaudium* 39.
88. Pope Francis with Spadaro, *My Door Is Always Open*, 62.

offered by Cardinal Bergoglio, delegated by the great majority of Latin American bishops, in the drafting of the final document of the Fifth General Conference of the Latin American episcopal conference, held in the sanctuary of Aparecida, in Brazil, from May 13 to 31, 2007. Some cardinals—such as Cardinal Óscar Rodríguez Maradiaga and Cardinal Cláudio Hummes—collaborated closely with Bergoglio in this work. Important contributions to the editing were made by Victor Manuel Fernández—the vice-chancellor of the Catholic University of Buenos Aires, to whom Bergoglio entrusted the final revision and reformulation of the document—and by Father Carlos Galli, a disciple of Lucio Gera, who provided his theological expertise. In the initial part of the document, undoubtedly one of its most beautiful, was the hand of Professor Guzmán Carriquiry and Bishop Filippo Santoro, the bishop of Petropolis, Brazil. The parts on missionary discipleship bore the stamp of Bergoglio. The great hope of Methol Ferré on the Latin American church as a "source" church received new life.

> The Church in Latin America had been a "reflection" throughout the colonial and early-national period, but had started to move in the direction of becoming a source in the 1950s, when Pius XII encouraged the creation of CELAM, a regional Church body with a vocation to unify and integrate Latin America. CELAM was the first continent-wide collegial structure in the modern Church, one that enabled Latin-American Catholicism both to express its distinctiveness and to decide on its own pastoral policies. Methol Ferré saw the distinctive theology that came out of the CELAM gathering at Medellín in 1968 as characteristic of a source Church. Marxism had deviated it, but the CELAM gathering at Puebla in 1979 had rescued it. That self-confidence, however, had since evaporated.[89]

After Puebla and, above all, after 1989, many hopes had evaporated, and the Fourth General Conference of Santo Domingo in 1992 was unable to arouse great enthusiasm. The decline of liberation theology coincided with a spiritualistic retrenchment of the church, no longer interested in the fate of the world, and with a

---

89. Ivereigh, *The Great Reformer*, 234–235.

progressive, clericalist centralization. The Puebla event setting, which was concerned with offering an orthodox, non-Marxist version of liberation theology, came to appear important but not decisive in a new context in which nihilism and hedonistic relativism were dissolving every popular and religious reality. As Methol told Metalli in 2006, "Then the collapse of communism happened and Puebla did not bear fruit in the new historical conditions. Puebla was intimately linked to *Evangelii Nuntiandi*, and the papacy has reiterated that *Evangelii Nuntiandi* is the basis of the evangelization of the new millennium. *It is necessary to rethink* Evangelii Nuntiandi *and Puebla within the new conditions of the twenty-first century.*"[90]

Methol was fully aware that popular piety was important and that, however, in the face of the advance of a secularization that dissolved every *materiality* of the Christian Fact, only a missionary dynamic, a dynamic of witness, could restore life to a body that was under mortal threat. The opportunity for the Latin American church to be "source" was dependent on the coming of a missionary season able to engage a post-Christian, globalized world. Hence the appreciation for the new Christian movements "that tend to embrace the whole of the real, the real in its totality, and that demonstrate an understanding of the essence of secularization, that is, of modernity."[91] They "are fully aware that they are dealing with a human person who is not an heir to Christianity. Therefore they direct themselves to the human subject born of the process of secularization, that is to say, a person who does not know Christianity and who cultivates prejudices toward it."[92] This awareness was important, above all, because it did not have the pretense of totalizing the panorama of faith.

In fact, Aparecida achieved a synthesis between the popular faith of the *pueblo fiel* and the need for a new encounter with the secular world by missionary, mature, and prophetic witnesses. The new evangelization does not disregard popular religiosity:

90. Methol Ferré and Metalli, *Il Papa e il filosofo*, 112–113. Emphasis mine.
91. Ibid., 174.
92. Ibid.

We cannot deprecate popular spirituality, or consider it a secondary mode of Christian life, for that would be to forget the primacy of the action of the Spirit and God's free initiative of love. Popular piety contains and expresses a powerful sense of transcendence, a spontaneous ability to find support in God and a true experience of theological love. It is also an expression of supernatural wisdom, because the wisdom of love does not depend directly on the enlightenment of the mind, but on the internal action of grace. That is why we call it popular spirituality, that is, a Christian spirituality which, while it is a personal encounter with the Lord, includes much of the bodily, the perceptible, the symbolic, and people's most concrete needs. It is a spirituality incarnated in the culture of the lowly, which is not thereby less spiritual, but is so in another manner.[93]

Calling to mind that meeting, Bergoglio would later say:

The work of the Conference took place in an environment located under the sanctuary [of Aparecida]. And from there they kept hearing the prayers, the songs of the faithful. In the final document there is a point concerning popular piety. These are beautiful pages. And I believe, I am sure, that they were inspired by this. After those contained in *Evangelii Nuntiandi*, they are the most beautiful things written on popular piety in a document of the church. In fact, I would dare to say that the Aparecida document is the *Evangelii Nuntiandi* of Latin America, it is like *Evangelii Nuntiandi*.[94]

This popular religiosity finds in the Madonna of Guadalupe, in the tender gaze of the *Morenita*, the essential message of the Gospel. Guadalupe, the Mestizo Virgin, is the synthesis of the Latin American peoples, the tangible expression of the inculturation of faith. She is the point of union of the different peoples of South America. "What is lacking is rather the possibility of this diversity converging into a synthesis, which, encompassing the variety of meanings, can project it toward a common historic destiny. Therein lies the incompa-

---

93. Fifth General Conference of the Latin American Episcopate, Concluding Document §263.

94. S. Falasca, "La fedeltà è sempre un cambiamento," interview with Cardinal Bergoglio, in Gianni Valente, *Francesco, un papa dalla fine del mondo* (Milan: EMI, 2013), 36.

rable value of the Marian spirit of our popular religiosity, which under different names, has been able to merge different Latin American histories into a shared history: one that which leads to Christ, Lord of life, in whom the highest dignity of our human vocation is achieved."[95] It is this synthesis that is threatened by "a globalization without solidarity,"[96] whose impetuous wind sweeps away nations, families, all that is "bound," fostering extreme individualism and affecting the less protected sectors. "It is no longer simply the phenomenon of exploitation and oppression," said the bishops at Aparecida, "but something new: social exclusion. What is affected is the very root of belonging to the society in which one lives, because one is no longer on the bottom, on the margins, or powerless, but rather one is living outside. The excluded are not simply 'exploited' but 'surplus' and 'disposable.' "[97]

This passage, taken up almost verbatim in *Evangelii Gaudium*, points to the vision shared by the two documents.[98] On one hand, it positively recognizes that "the risks of reducing the Church to a political actor"[99] have diminished and, on the other hand, rejects the "emphasis on ritualism" and "an individualistic spirituality."[100] The promotion of popular piety is not a ritualist or folkloric escape from the world; it implies a "preferential option for the poor,"[101] the legacy of an authentic theology of liberation. The bishops' reaction to the negative effects of globalization arises not from an ideology but from

95. Fifth General Conference of the Latin American Episcopate, Concluding Document §43.

96. Ibid. 65.

97. Ibid.

98. Cf. Pope Francis, *Evangelii Gaudium* 53. At Aparecida, "speaking first of all as president of the Argentine episcopal conference, Bergoglio said that those who in the past had been defined marginalized or oppressed could today be called sobrantes, the superfluous, because they do not serve the market economy, which does not need them. He linked the concept with that of the culture of the descarte, the culture of waste: we were displaced by the poor, the elderly, the children, the unborn, the migrants as well as gadgets outdated" (Ivereigh, *The Great Reformer*, 342).

99. Fifth General Conference of the Latin American Episcopate, Concluding Document §99.

100. Ibid. 100.

101. Ibid.

a defense of the *pueblo fiel,* from a struggle to preserve those values of solidarity, sacrifice, and dedication that individualistic relativism and libertine atheism mock and dissolve. *This is why the bishops seek to look at the world from the "periphery."* Looking from the "center" is like being inside a bubble that does not allow us to see "outside"; we are part of a "sphere" in which everything is uniform, without even stretch marks. Only from the periphery do we perceive the "polyhedron," the diversity of values and disvalues. Cardinal Bergoglio spoke about this in his homily at a large Mass at the shrine of Aparecida during the Conference. Here he "used another striking metaphor when he spoke . . . of *las periferias existenciales,* the existential margins. Almost every bishop at Aparecida lived in a city whose peripheries were being constantly swelled by the arrival of migrants, and the phrase struck many chords. It suggested not just the slums, but a world of vulnerability and fragility, a place of suffering and longing and poverty, yet also joy and hope—the place where Christ had chosen to reveal himself in contemporary Latin America."[102]

Bergoglio had learned the concept of "periphery" from Amelia Podetti. From her he had received the intuition that the world, seen from its places of "fragility," looked different. This was the direction taken by Aparecida, thanks in part to the influence of Bergoglio, who, as archbishop of Buenos Aires, had "evangelized the city from its margins."[103] In 2009 the cardinal had created a vicariate responsible for pastoral and social work in the shantytowns. The idea did not arise from a pauperistic ideology, *which Bergoglio never had,* but from the perception of a segment of humanity imbued with faith that had something to teach the upper classes of the city. And this was the case even if working in the *villas miseria* meant risking one's life, as was the case for Fr. José Maria Di Paola ("Father Pepe"), coordinator of the vicariate, because of his opposition to drug traffickers.[104] In a 2012 interview, Bergoglio said that two things had struck him about the barrios:

102. Ivereigh, *The Great Reformer,* 298.

103. Ibid., 305.

104. On Fr. Pepe, cf. the book-length interview, José Maria Di Paola, *Dalla fine del mondo: Il mio cammino tra i più poveri* (Rome: Castelvecchi, 2017); Ivereigh, *The Great Reformer,* 307–309. On the experience of the *curas villeros,* cf. Valente, *Francesco, un papa dalla fine del mondo,* 9–21.

First is a great sense of solidarity. You can be pretty pissed at someone, or whatever, but there's a need and immediately solidarity makes
itself felt. It does me good to see solidarity. There's less egotism than
in other parts, there's more solidarity. The second thing is the faith
that is here, faith in the Virgin, faith in the saints, faith in Jesus. . . .
These two things have always struck me: solidarity and faith. Put
them together, and what do you get? The ability to celebrate. It's
great how in these barrios people celebrate, make fiesta—they're
joyful. So you have those two things, faith and solidarity, and when
you put them together you get joy.[105]

Faith, solidarity, joy: it was the trinomial that the individualistic
and sad agnosticism of the era of globalization often dissolved. The
church, patron of the *villeros*, defended those values in the awareness that that tradition was wearing out. As Aparecida asserted:
"Our cultural traditions are no longer handed on from one generation to the next with the same ease as in the past. That even affects
that deepest core of each culture, constituted by religious experience,
which is now likewise difficult to hand on through education and
the beauty of cultural expressions."[106] Hence the answer: "We Christians must start over from Christ."[107] The church was called to rethink its mission in the new circumstances of Latin America and
the world.

What is required is confirming, renewing, and revitalizing the newness of the Gospel rooted in our history, out of a personal and community encounter with Jesus Christ that raises up disciples and
missionaries. That depends not so much on grand programs and
structures, but rather on new men and women who incarnate that
tradition and newness, as disciples of Jesus Christ and missionaries
of his Kingdom, protagonists of new life for a Latin America that
seeks to be rediscovered with the light and power of the Spirit.
    A Catholic faith reduced to mere baggage, to a collection of rules
and prohibitions, to fragmented devotional practices, to selective
and partial adherence to the truths of the faith, to occasional

105. Ivereigh, *The Great Reformer*, 307.
106. Fifth General Conference of the Latin American Episcopate, Concluding Document §39.
107. Ibid. 12, 41.

participation in some sacraments, to the repetition of doctrinal principles, to bland or nervous moralizing that does not convert the life of the baptized would not withstand the trials of time.[108]

And here, in §12, the Aparecida document repeats the teaching of Benedict XVI's *Deus Caritas Est*, that "being Christian is not the result of an ethical choice or a lofty idea, but the encounter with an event, a person, which gives life a new horizon and a decisive direction." The same sentence is repeated in §243. It makes the document's essential point: It is important, but not enough, to defend the faith of the *pueblo fiel*, which is a faith from which all, including clergy, must learn how to believe. It is necessary to move "from a pastoral ministry of mere conservation to a decidedly missionary pastoral ministry,"[109] from a traditional faith to a rebirth of faith. The Latin American Catholic risorgimento is nourished by two lungs: the witness of the faithful people and that of those who, near that people, "start again from Christ." The pages of Aparecida that call for "beginning again" reveal the hand of Bergoglio and closely resemble the particular insights of Fr. Luigi Giussani. It is no coincidence that, after having recognized the concept of *encounter* as the keystone, that of *experience*, which is also typical of Giussani's thought, follows.

This is precisely what all the gospels have preserved, while presenting it differently, as the beginning of Christianity: a faith encounter with the person of Jesus (cf. Jn 1:35-39). The very nature of Christianity therefore consists of recognizing the presence of Jesus Christ and following Him. That was the marvelous experience of those first disciples, who upon encountering Jesus were fascinated and astonished at the exceptional quality of the one speaking to them, especially how he treated them, satisfying the hunger and thirst for life that was in their hearts. The evangelist John has portrayed for us the image of the impact produced by the person of Jesus on the first two disciples who met him, John and Andrew. Everything starts with a question: "What are you looking for?" (Jn 1:38). That question is followed by the invitation to live an experience: "Come and you will

108. Ibid. 11–12.
109. Ibid. 370.

see" (Jn 1:39). This account will remain in history as a unique synthesis of the Christian approach.[110]

Encounter, awe, following, experience, method, the encounter of Jesus with John and Andrew as a paradigmatic model—Aparecida introduces, in sequence, all of the most significant categories of the formational vision of Father Giussani. It is not difficult to imagine the pen of Cardinal Bergoglio behind all of it. Being Christian begins with the gaze, with seeing.

> We look to Jesus, the Master who personally formed his apostles and disciples. Christ gives us the method: "Come and see" (Jn 1:39), "I am the Way, the Truth, and the Life" (Jn 14:6). . . . The formative itinerary of the follower of Jesus sinks its roots down into the dynamic nature of the person and in the personal invitation of Jesus Christ, who calls his own by name, and they follow him because they know his voice. The Lord awakened the deep aspirations of his disciples and drew them to himself, full of astonishment. Following him is fruit of a fascination that responds to the desire for human fulfillment and to the yearning for full life. A disciple is someone who is passionate for Christ, and recognizes him as the master leading and accompanying him.[111]

Being a Christian is to follow a Presence that attracts, that awakens awe, that engages one's deepest aspirations. For this reason, the *kèrygma*, as *Evangelii Gaudium* insists, comes first. Aparecida conveys this with the words of Benedict XVI: "We recall that in the oldest tradition of the Church, the formative itinerary of the Christian 'always had an experiential character. While not neglecting a systematic understanding of the content of the faith, it centered on a vital and convincing encounter with Christ, as proclaimed by authentic witnesses.'"[112] The outcome of this encounter is a process marked by four moments: conversion, discipleship, communion, mission. Among these, communion as a lived community

110. Ibid. 243–244.
111. Ibid. 276–277.
112. Ibid. 290. The internal quote is from Pope Benedict XVI, apostolic exhortation *Sacramentum Caritatis* (2007), n. 64.

takes on a particular educative value. For Aparecida, "We find the paradigmatic model of this community renewal in the early Christian communities (cf. Acts 2:42-47), which were able to keep seeking new ways of evangelizing in accordance with cultures and circumstances."[113] The same idea is taken up again in the document's conclusion: "All of us who are baptized are called to 'begin again from Christ,' to recognize and follow his Presence with the same reality and newness, the same power of feeling, persuasion, and hope produced by his encounter with the first disciples along the banks of the Jordan two thousand years ago, and with the 'Juan Diegos' of the New World."[114]

Like two thousand years ago. Aparecida indicated the "method," the modality for the rebirth of faith today, within a nihilistic and secularized context: returning to Christ, seeing him speak, act, love, as a Presence in our own day. The *pueblo fiel*, the poor, the witnesses, the ecclesial communities become "theological places," places where the face of Christ manifests itself today. It is the face of the humiliated Christ, the Samaritan, the crucified one, the one who surprises and attracts by his mercy, his embrace, his singular humanity. Aparecida valued everything. It was the "baroque" synthesis of tradition and modernity imagined by Methol Ferré, of traditional faith and new proclamation. It corresponded fully to the *coincidentia oppositorum* desired by Bergoglio.

Catholicism is synthesis, like the Madonna of Guadalupe that unites Hispanics and natives. It draws together contrasts in a polar tension between past and present, tradition and progress, memory and future. It does so not by placing itself "above" or merely "in the center," equidistant between poles. The *Morenita* appeared to the Indian Juan Diego, and Jesus was born in Bethlehem rather than Jerusalem: the view of the world is better understood from the peripheries. This means that peace and unity can only be achieved by healing wounds, taking care of frail places, offering shelter to the oppressed. It is the Christian style in the new millennium, a style that repeats that of the early church, immersed in the pagan universe.

113. Ibid. 369.
114. Ibid. 549.

Aparecida was, in fact, Bergoglio's "manifesto." It was "his" Conference, and it bears his stamp from beginning to end.[115] Here the former provincial of the Jesuits, who went on to become the cardinal archbishop of Buenos Aires, anticipated the programmatic outlines of his future pontificate, which will find a natural expression in *Evangelii Gaudium*.[116] There is a whole world behind it. First of all, the belonging and internal events of the Society of Jesus. Then the experience of CELAM, of Medellín, the dramatic era of the 1970s and 1980s, divided between terrorism and fierce military dictatorship. There is Puebla, the transformative friendship with Alberto Methol Ferré, the expectations motivated by the Latin American Catholic risorgimento, the disappointments, the hopes after Aparecida. *Behind that is a system of thought* that Bergoglio has developed since the mid-1970s, a Catholic-dialectical vein nourished by Jesuit authors and, later, by the polar philosophy of Romano Guardini. It is a system of thought that owes much to Gaston Fessard, particularly his *La Dialectique des 'Exercices Spirituels' de Saint Ignace de Loyola*. From the Jesuit, from his Pauline response to Hegel, comes the idea of Christ as a point of resolution for the great contrasts that mark the historical dialectic: those between slaves and free, men and women, Jews and Greeks, contrasts that are resolved on the basis of grace, not of nature. Hence an antinomian dialectic, governed by principles and polar pairs that constitute the

115. Cf. Cardinal Bergoglio's address, of May 2007, to the Aparecida Conference: "Una sola sfida: la crisi della civiltà e della cultura," in Bergoglio-Francis, *Nei tuoi occhi è la mia parola*, 537–547. For account-taking by Bergoglio, following Aparecida, cf. "Cultura e religiosità popolare" (2008), in ibid., 577–603; id., "Tornare alle radici della fede: la missione come proposta e sfida" (2008), in ibid., 615–623; id., "Il messaggio di Aparecida ai presbiteri" (2008), in ibid., 661–670; id., "La missione dei discepoli al servizio della vita piena" (2009), in ibid., 710–715. As pope, Francis offered a summary of Aparecida on July 28, 2013, at the Centro Studi di Sumaré in Rio de Janeiro, with the bishops leading the various departments of CELAM (cf. L. Badilla, "L'eredità di Aparecida dieci anni dopo: La celebre conferenza del 2007 nel santuario brasiliano riletta e riproposta da Bergoglio Papa," *Terre d'America*, May 30, 2017).

116. Cf. Lucio Brunelli, "Segreti di un'elezione: Il ritorno ad Aparecida e il sorprendente filo rosso tra due pontificati," *Terre d'America*, July 17, 2013.

framework of a complex, "polyhedraic" thought that does not surrender to contradictions but seeks, everywhere, points of similarity
that can dissolve antitheses and "diabolical" divisions. It is a system
of thought that is heir of that of Romano Guardini, who, for Francis,
following Paul VI and Benedict XVI, is truly the author of reference
of three popes. Once again, the church is a *complexio oppositorum*,
the only reality on the global scale that proposes itself as a place of
reconciliation at a historical moment in which, faced with the failure
of globalization, the great contrasts and divisions between peoples
are clear.

Index